Reform Capacity and Macroeconomic Performance in the Nordic Countries

Reform Capacity and Macroeconomic Performance in the Nordic Countries

Edited by
Torben M. Andersen, U. Michael Bergman,
and Svend E. Hougaard Jensen

OXFORD
UNIVERSITY PRESS

OXFORD
UNIVERSITY PRESS

Great Clarendon Street, Oxford, OX2 6DP,
United Kingdom

Oxford University Press is a department of the University of Oxford. It furthers the University's objective of excellence in research, scholarship, and education by publishing worldwide. Oxford is a registered trade mark of Oxford University Press in the UK and in certain other countries

First Edition published in 2015

Impression: 1

Published in the United States of America by Oxford University Press
198 Madison Avenue, New York, NY 10016, United States of America

British Library Cataloguing in Publication Data
Data available

Library of Congress Control Number: 2014951694

ISBN 978–0–19–871710–2

Printed and bound by
CPI Group (UK) Ltd, Croydon, CR0 4YY

Contents

List of Figures

List of Tables

List of Contributors

Torben M. Andersen, Department of Economics and Business, University of Aarhus

Fredrik Andersson, Lund School of Economics and Management

Erling Barth, Institute for Social Research, Oslo

Andreas Bergh, Lund University and the Research Institute of Industrial Economics

U. Michael Bergman, Department of Economics, University of Copenhagen

Roberto M. Billi, Sveriges Riksbank

Hilde C. Bjørnland, BI Norwegian Business School and Norges Bank

Niels Blomgren-Hansen, Professor emeritus, Copenhagen Business School

Henrik Braconier, Chief Economist, Swedish Financial Supervisory Authority

Michael Burda, Humboldt University of Berlin

Anders Møller Christensen, Economics, Danmarks Nationalbank

Niels Arne Dam, Economics, Danmarks Nationalbank

Thorvaldur Gylfason, Professor of Economics, University of Iceland

Niels Lynggård Hansen, Economics, Danmarks Nationalbank

Steinar Holden, Department of Economics, University of Oslo

Seppo Honkapohja, Bank of Finland

Michael M. Hutchison, Department of Economics, University of California, Santa Cruz

Svend E. Hougaard Jensen, Department of Economics, Copenhagen Business School

Lars Jonung, Centre for Financial Studies, Department of Economics, School of Economics and Management, Lund University

Sixten Korkman, Aalto University School of Business

Junior Maih, Norges Bank

Karl Ove Moene, Department of Economics, University of Oslo

Søren Bo Nielsen, Department of Economics, Copenhagen Business School

Jesper Rangvid, Copenhagen Business School

Bjørn Tangaa Sillemann, Macro Policy, Danish Economy, Ministry of Economic Affairs and the Interior

Hans Tson Söderström, Stockholm School of Economics

List of Contributors

Peter Birch Sørensen, Department of Economics, University of Copenhagen

Erling Steigum, Department of Economics, BI Norwegian Business School, Oslo

Antti Suvanto, Advisor to the Board, Bank of Finland, Helsinki

Michael Svarer, Department of Economics and Business, University of Aarhus

Øystein Thøgersen, Department of Economics, NHH Norwegian School of Economics, Bergen

1

Macroeconomic Perspectives on the Nordic Economies

Past, Present, and Future

Torben M. Andersen, U. Michael Bergman, and Svend E. Hougaard Jensen

1.1 Introduction

The outbreak of the financial crisis in 2008 has had significant effects on economic activity, unemployment, and public finances for all European countries. However, European economies do not form a homogenous region, and any serious analysis of macroeconomic imbalances in Europe must account for the fact that different economic and political models and circumstances operate across the continent.

Specifically, it is important to distinguish between the southern part of Europe (such as Greece, Italy, Portugal, and Spain) and the northern European economies, including the Nordic countries (Denmark, Finland, Iceland, Norway, and Sweden). By contrast with southern Europe, the Nordic countries are nearly always ranked in the top 10 in any ranking of economic performance, and they have a good record of undertaking fiscal and structural reforms after their own financial and debt crises in the 1980s and 1990s.[1]

Against that background, the experience with structural reforms and fiscal management in the Nordic countries has attracted quite a lot of international attention, from both academic and policy perspectives.[2] However, while the

[1] Iceland may deviate from this pattern. As pointed out by Gylfason (2015), in some ways Iceland resembles Italy, Japan, and Russia more than it resembles its Nordic neighbours or even Ireland.

[2] For example, in a special feature entitled 'The Nordic countries: the next supermodel', the *Economist* magazine in February 2013 argued that politicians from both right and left could learn from the Nordic countries.

current thinking emphasizes the virtues of the Nordic model, the perceptions of the model have historically been characterized by certain 'cycles'. In fact, the demise of the Nordic model has been predicted several times in the past, but the model has always proven to have a strong survival capacity.

The Nordic model does not escape economic crises, but it is resilient. From this perspective, it seems important to focus on the lessons that might be learned from Nordic economies. Is there a distinctive Nordic model that could be usefully followed, by other (small) open economies, in terms of macroeconomic policy design and control, structural reforms, financial market regulation, etc.?

Before engaging in a detailed study of the Nordic model, it seems appropriate to ask what it actually is. The Nordics have much in common, but they also differ in several important respects.[3] For example, there are many differences at the microeconomic level, such as tax structures, unemployment insurance, employment protection legislation, pension systems, etc. In macroeconomic terms there are also notable differences. For example, three different monetary regimes operate: Denmark pursues a fixed exchange rate regime (ERM-2); Sweden and Norway have a floating exchange rate and monetary policy is conducted with a view to achieving price stability; and Finland is a member of the Eurozone. The bottom line is that it is inappropriate to define the Nordic model in terms of a common set of policies.

Despite the differences it is possible to point out a number of similarities within the Nordic countries. For example, they are small and open economies, well-known for their high income levels, high employment rates, organized labour markets, a relatively equal distribution of incomes, large public sectors, etc. Since the key characteristics, including the overarching objectives and supporting institutions, have strong historical foundations, copying and pasting them to other countries is not easily done.

Even though the Nordic experiences are not directly transferable, it seems important to investigate whether they offer some lessons for the design and implementation of economic policy elsewhere. These experiences may add new knowledge about the importance of institutional design, fiscal consolidation, and structural reforms not only for macroeconomic performance but also for how to preserve key objectives such as social balance and equity. Our focus is thus on macroeconomic developments and welfare state structures, and topical areas such as innovation policy, entrepreneurship, etc. are excluded from consideration due to space limitations.

The road map of this chapter is as follows. Section 1.2 provides an overview of the structure and achievements of the Nordic countries. Our focus

[3] Also, the Nordic countries have not always been regarded as a homogenous group. For example, in the 1970s Sweden was the darling, a status Denmark took over in the first decade of this century. More recently, Sweden is again widely regarded as the role model.

is on characterizing the Nordic model in terms of objectives, policies, and institutions, and we discuss the economic achievements in relation to living standards, distribution of income, etc. In Section 1.3 we focus on how the Nordic countries have been affected by and how they have responded to major economic shocks, such as the great financial crisis. Finally, Section 1.4 offers a brief summary of all the chapters presented in this book.

1.2 Structure and Achievements of the Nordic Countries

In policy discussions it is often claimed that there is a particular Scandinavian or Nordic societal model. Typically, the definition hereof is vague, but it often refers to performance measures such as high per capita income, a compressed wage structure, and a relatively equal distribution of incomes.[4] As shown by Figure 1.1, all Nordic countries differ from the OECD average on those dimensions, but the Nordic lead is not with a large margin.

In the academic literature the concept of a Scandinavian welfare model has become known from the work by Esping-Andersen (1990). In Esping-Andersen's definition the model is defined in terms of universal social rights for all; that is, eligibility to welfare arrangements applies equally to all individuals and is independent of contributions as well as social status. These welfare arrangements include the social safety net that gives income support to people unable to care for themselves, and basic welfare services like education, health, and care. Importantly, the social safety net offers a decent living standard to those incapable of supporting themselves, and the welfare services provided should meet the reasonable requirements of most people. The public solution is not second-rate, only used by those who cannot afford otherwise; it is to be used by all. The welfare arrangements are financed via various forms of tax revenue, and in this sense the system is collective.

Despite the concept of a Nordic model, a careful study of policies in the Nordic countries reveals some striking differences.[5] First, there are no unique approaches or solutions adopted in the Nordic countries, as the key policy instruments do not differ from those applied in other countries. It is not the ingredients, but the packaging which makes a difference. Second, there are notable differences among the Nordic countries in specific policy design. For example, Denmark and Sweden have chosen very different paths in the

4 Others stress the institutional structure, in particular a large public sector and organized labour markets, but also an innovative and competitive business sector.

5 In terms of welfare arrangements Finland is usually considered a latecomer to the 'Nordic welfare model', and Iceland, at least before the financial crisis, explicitly stated that it was not opting for the Nordic model. In recent years Norway has become an outlier due to the high importance of oil revenues.

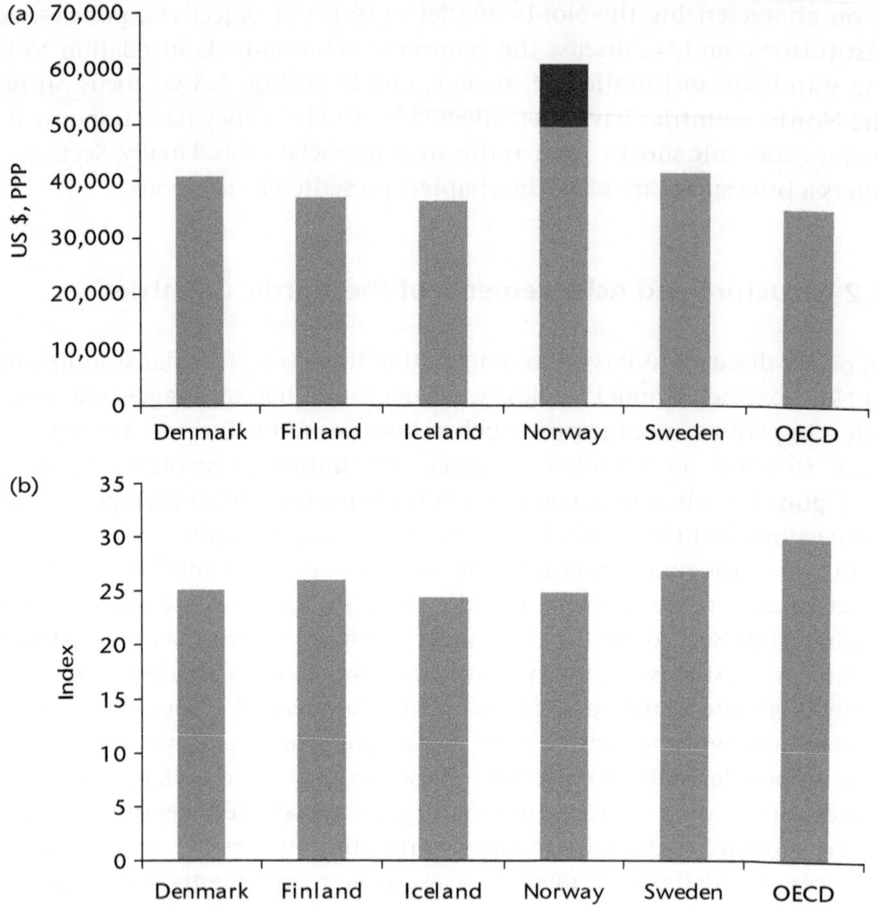

Figure 1.1. Per capita income and income distribution, Nordic countries

Note: (a) Per capita income is given as GDP per capita, US $, current prices, current PPPs, 2011. For Norway the bottom part of the column refers to mainland Norway. (b) Income inequality is based on the Gini coefficient defined over disposable income. The coefficient is defined to be between zero and 100; the lower the coefficient, the more equal the income distribution. Data apply to 2010.

Source: <http://www.OECDilibrary.org>.

design of pension schemes. Similarly, unemployment insurance is voluntary in Denmark, Finland, and Sweden, but mandatory in Norway.

While tax burdens are high in the Nordic countries (except for Iceland), the tax structure differs widely, with Denmark having the larger share of tax revenue accruing from direct income taxes and value-added taxes, while Sweden raises much more tax revenue from social contributions. In terms of monetary regimes the Nordic countries feature the entire spectrum, from floating exchange rates with inflation targeting (Iceland, Norway, and

Sweden) to fixed exchange rates (Denmark) to membership of the EMU (Finland).

These differences in specific policy design underline the point that the package matters more than the specific ingredients. It further implies that the naïve 'copy and paste' perspective often taken in comparative policy discussions focusing on a few policy instruments is misleading, since it overlooks the complementarities between the different policy elements. The Nordic model should not be defined or assessed in terms of specific policy instruments: what matter are the overarching objectives. These have remained stable over time, but the specific policies/instruments to reach them differ across time and countries in the region.

The Nordic countries are small and open economies. Openness to trade has always been important. While trade in the past was mainly inter-industrial (Denmark being an exporter of agricultural products, while Norway, Sweden, and Finland had comparative advantages in wood and minerals), it has become much more intra-industrial, and the Nordic countries have developed new comparative advantages.[6]

There are ongoing discussions about the impact of globalization, but it is important to stress that the Nordics have historically been very explicit about the requirements global competition puts on small and open economies. One prime example of this is the so-called Scandinavian Model of Inflation (e.g., Edgren et al., 1969), which builds on the basic premise that wage determination should be anchored in the competitive situation of the tradable sectors. Non-tradable sectors are not to become wage leaders since that would erode the competitive position of the tradable sector.

The so-called Rehn–Meidner model (Erixon, 2010) stresses that a compressed wage structure presupposes and reinforces a strong ability to make structural changes; that is, less productive firms and sectors must be phased out and labour must be willing to relocate (also geographically) to growing industries. Active unemployment policies are used to re-educate unemployed workers in order to prepare them for new jobs in more productive firms.

While globalization presently takes on new forms and perhaps is more intensive both due to political decisions (further integration) and technological changes (lower information and transport costs), the issue of how to strike a balance between a 'globalized' economy and social concerns has a very strong tradition and has been deeply embedded in the Nordic policy

[6] Adding to the list of notable differences between the Nordics, Denmark has a large number of small and medium-sized firms, while Sweden has historically had many large firms. Norway and Finland are intermediate cases and have historically been closer to Denmark in this respect. More recently, Finland has also been heavily dependent on Nokia, while natural resources are particularly important for Norway.

framework over the years. The Nordic model has not been developed under a shield from international competition but, on the contrary, openness has been regarded a prerequisite for sustaining the welfare state.

The fact about the Nordic countries that most often attracts attention is that a substantial amount of resources are allocated and distributed via the public sector (see Figure 1.2).

The public sector expanded in particular during the 1960s and 1970s, resulting in roughly a doubling of its relative size. Since the 1980s the relative size of the public sector has been constant at about 50% of GDP. However, care should be exercised in making such cross-country comparisons for several reasons, including different tax treatment of social transfers. In some countries social transfers are taxable income, in others they are not (or only partly), and this makes comparisons based on gross rates problematic. This tends to exaggerate tax levels in the Nordic countries since they tend to apply the gross principle more than the average OECD country. For example, Adema and Ladaique (2009) find for 2005 that taxes on social transfers constitute about 4% of GDP in Denmark and Sweden, 2.5% in Finland, and 1.5% in Norway.

Public-sector employment constitutes about 25% of total employment while the EU average is about 18%. Developments in Denmark and Sweden have been rather similar until recently, while growth of the public sector came

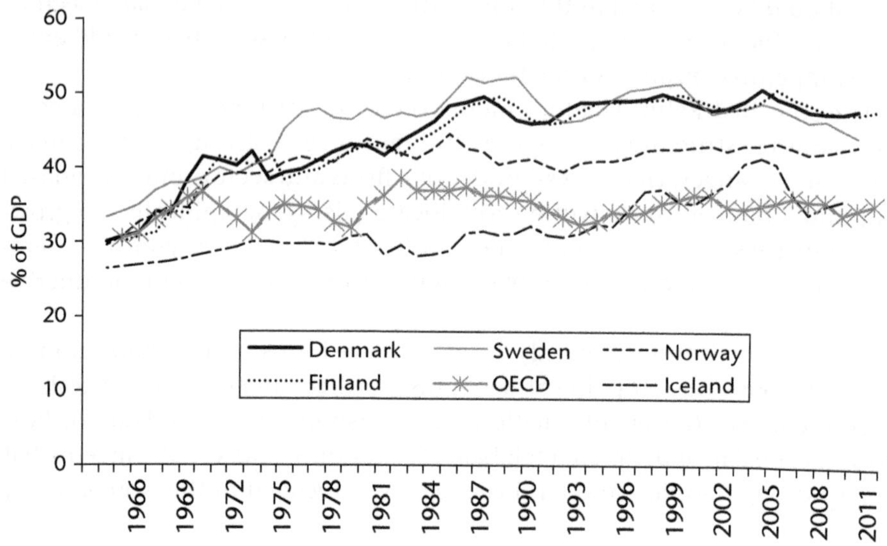

Figure 1.2. Tax burden, percentage of GDP 1965–2011

Note: GDP for Norway includes the petrol sector which tends to bias downwards the expenditure share.

Source: <http://www.OECDilibrary.org>.

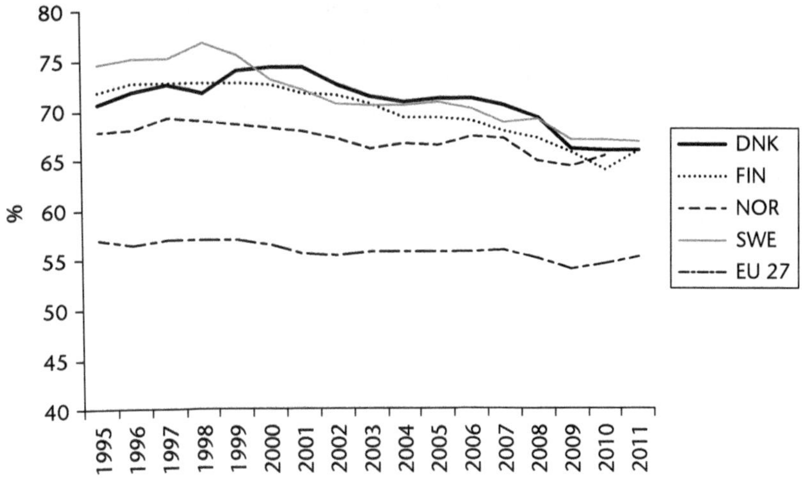

Figure 1.3. Tax wedges for the Nordic countries and EU 27

Note: Total tax wedge given as the sum of the implicit tax on labour income and the implicit consumption tax. Data are not available for Iceland.

Source: Computed based on Eurostat (2013).

slightly later in Finland. Iceland has not seen the same growth in the public sector as the other Nordic countries. Notice that the lower tax burden in Norway is largely attributable to the importance of oil for economic activity.[7]

The large tax burden implies that average taxes on labour are high, and a recurrent theme is the implications of high levels of taxation for labour supply and employment. Taxes cause a wedge between the payment for work received by workers and the costs of workers to employers. The cost of labour to firms is the wage including social contributions, while the purchasing value of the wage to workers is the wage net of direct taxes, social contribution, and indirect taxes. The total tax wedge is thus the sum of social contributions paid by employers and employees, direct taxes, and indirect taxes. The composition on single parts does not matter, but the sum does.

Figure 1.3 shows that the total tax wedge on labour is high for the Nordic countries compared to the EU 27, but also that it has a clear declining trend reflecting a sequence of tax reforms aiming to strengthen the incentives to work and thus increasing labour supply both along the intensive (lower marginal tax rates) and extensive (making work pay) margins. Despite the high tax wedge, the Nordic countries stand out by having a high employment rate for both men and women, although working hours are not high in comparison to OECD countries.

[7] Total GDP in Norway is about 20–25% larger than GDP for mainland Norway. Assessing the size of the public sector relative to mainland GDP leaves a size close to that for Denmark.

The welfare state rests on two important pillars in the public sector, namely the social safety net and the provision of welfare services. Figure 1.4 shows the total public expenditures on these two pillars. Consider first the social safety net (Figure 1.4a). There are several important points to be made. First, social transfers in the Nordic countries are often portrayed as being very generous. Yet, this is a statement which needs to be qualified. For example, considering the average replacement rate for unemployment for the average worker,

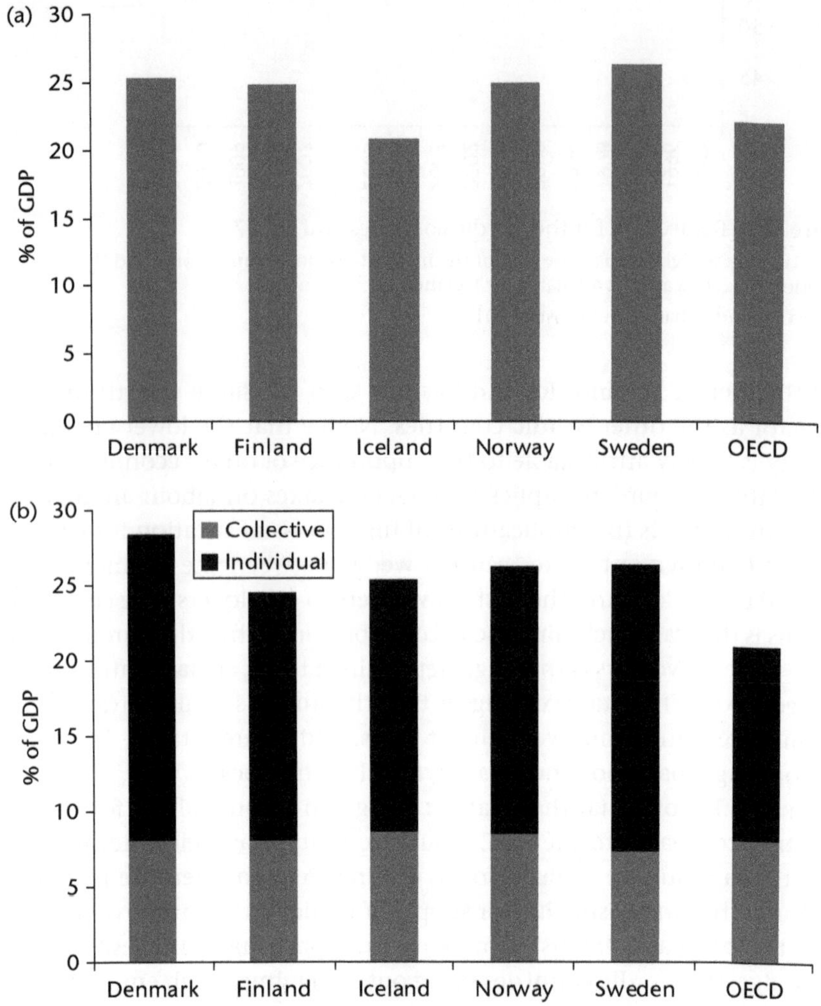

Figure 1.4. The social safety net and public consumption

Note: (a) Includes all forms of social transfer, care, etc. for Norway as a share of mainland GDP. (b) Public consumption as a share of GDP split between individual and collective public expenditure. Data applies to 2011, for Norway as a share of mainland GDP.

Source: <http://www.OECDilibrary.org>.

it is not particularly high in the Nordic countries compared to other OECD countries (Andersen and Svarer, 2007). However, for low-income groups the replacement rate is high. This property carries over to the social safety net in general; that is, the compensation offered to groups with low income and/or marginal attachment to the labour market as well as lack of work capability is comparatively high.

Second, while the system has some universal traits in the sense that eligibility is an individual right independent of contributions[8] and status, it is important to point out that the social safety net in all the Nordic countries has means testing. It is not a passive system equivalent to a 'demo-grant' system. It is also an explicit condition for entitlement that one is not able to support oneself, and there is an active job search requirement as well. The social safety net thus features a number of conditionalities, as part of the eligibility criteria. These are known as the active labour market policies and include requirements on active job search, participation in educational programmes, job training, etc. The active labour market policy has the dual purpose of enhancing qualifications and employability as well as strengthening job-search incentives.

Turning next to public consumption (Figure 1.4b), there is an important distinction to be drawn between collective and individualized expenditures. The former refers to classic public-sector activities like administration, police, legal system, military, etc. The latter refers to solutions provided directly to individuals and which in principle could be offered by the market mechanism, the family, or the civil society (public provision of private goods). The main items are so-called welfare services like education, health, and child- and old-age care. What makes the Nordic countries stand out is the extensive provision of welfare services. These expenditures constitute about two-thirds of total public consumption. Importantly, they are provided on a universal principle since they are available to all and tax financed.[9]

The welfare state is often portrayed as a 'from cradle to grave' model. This popular notion is addressed with the aid of Figure 1.5, based on data for Norway, Sweden, and Denmark.

The figure shows the net contributions between the welfare state and the individual at different ages. In net terms the welfare state is to the benefit of the young and the old, while the working-age population on average constitutes the contributors ensuring the financial balance of the model. This also brings out why the model is an 'employment model'. With an extended welfare state, a decrease in employment has wide public finance implications due to the double budget effect released by larger expenditures on the social

[8] As already noted there are exceptions to this in e.g. the unemployment insurance scheme.
[9] There may be some user charges. This applies in particular to childcare.

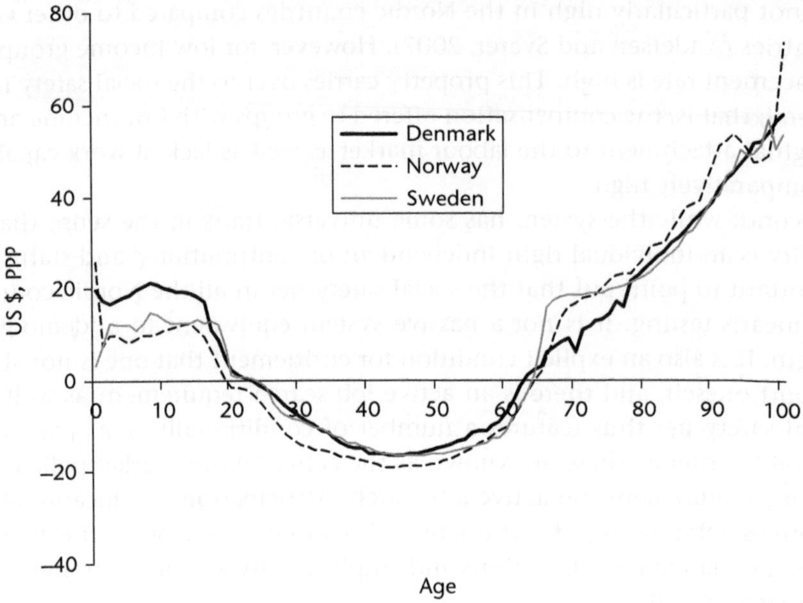

Figure 1.5. Age-dependent net transfers between the individual and the welfare state—Denmark, Norway, and Sweden, 2009

Note: The net transfer is defined as the difference between the value of various services and transfers received and tax payments for an average person at given ages. Non-individualized expenditures are distributed equally over all individuals. Data for Denmark and Norway apply to 2009, and for Sweden 2008. Swedish data is adjusted for wage increases in 2009, and data is presented in US $ using OECD PPP-adjusted exchange rates. Units of 1.000 US $.

Data source: Danish Economic Council (2012), Norwegian Ministry of Finance (2011), Swedish Ministry of Finance (2011), and <http://www.oecd.org>.

safety net and reduced tax revenue. It is hardly surprising, therefore, that OECD (2011) shows that the budget sensitivities to employment changes in the Nordic countries are the highest within the OECD. Since the welfare state is extended, this effect is large. If the (private) employment rate is not high, it will be difficult to ensure the financial viability of the model. As is well-known, in the Nordic countries the employment rate for both genders is high by international standards. This is supported by the welfare state (e.g. via child care and education) but is also a prerequisite for its financial viability. Finally, note that the pattern displayed in Figure 1.5 is found for all OECD countries, but the amplitude is much larger in the Nordic countries due to the more extended welfare arrangements.

In public discourse, the terms welfare state and welfare society are often used interchangeably. The term welfare state may be misleading since it tends to associate all welfare arrangements with the public sector. This is inaccurate since labour market institutions, in particular, are also important. The Nordic countries have a long tradition of strongly organized labour markets with a high degree of unionization; see Figure 1.6a.

This is also related to what is sometimes dubbed a 'consensus tradition' where solutions are sought with the social partners on important issues in relation to business and labour market conditions. Political debates and labour market negotiations are thus typically less polarized than in many other countries—perhaps a reflection of the historic legacy of being small and open countries in fierce international competition.

It may be discussed whether this is a prerequisite for an extensive collective tax-financed welfare state, or whether the welfare state in itself fuels trust (Rothstein, 2001). It has been argued that the Nordic countries have specific traits which are conducive to collective arrangements (Algan and Cahuc, 2009).

It should also be noted that the public sector has a number of 'checks and balances' to ensure that public resources are not mismanaged, but also to ensure that individuals do not evade tax payments. Individuals are identified by a personal number which has to be used when receiving any form of income, etc., which serves to reduce tax evasion. This clearly raises 'big brother' aspects, especially when different registers are combined. In terms of research this may at least partly explain the availability of the detailed individual panel data sets in the Nordic countries. The mutual trust and the expectation that public money is put to good use are thus important, and in the political discussion no one would use phrases like 'feeding the beast' for resources being channelled through the public sector.[10]

Given the large public sector and the centralized labour markets, it may be perceived that the Nordic countries are semi-socialist countries or pursuing 'politics against markets'. Although different meanings can be given to these terms, they do not provide a correct impression of the private sector. Fairly liberal policies have been pursued towards the private sector, and state intervention in the form of state-owned companies and the like have never played an important role. The Nordic countries fit more into the label of a social–liberal model with extensive social objectives catered for through labour market institutions and the public sector and a market-oriented private sector. This point is underscored by Figure 1.6b showing an index of product market regulation and intervention. It is seen that the Nordic countries have less regulation than the OECD average.[11]

[10] In the Transparency International survey on perceived corruption in the public sector covering 177 countries, the four large Nordic countries are all in the top 10 with lowest corruption (Iceland has rank 12), see <http://www.transparency.org>.

[11] The World Bank constructs an index of the ease of doing business based on ten indicators related to how conducive the regulatory environment is to the starting and operation of a local firm. In the 2013 index covering 188 countries, the Nordic countries are all in top 20. See <http://www.doingbusiness.org>.

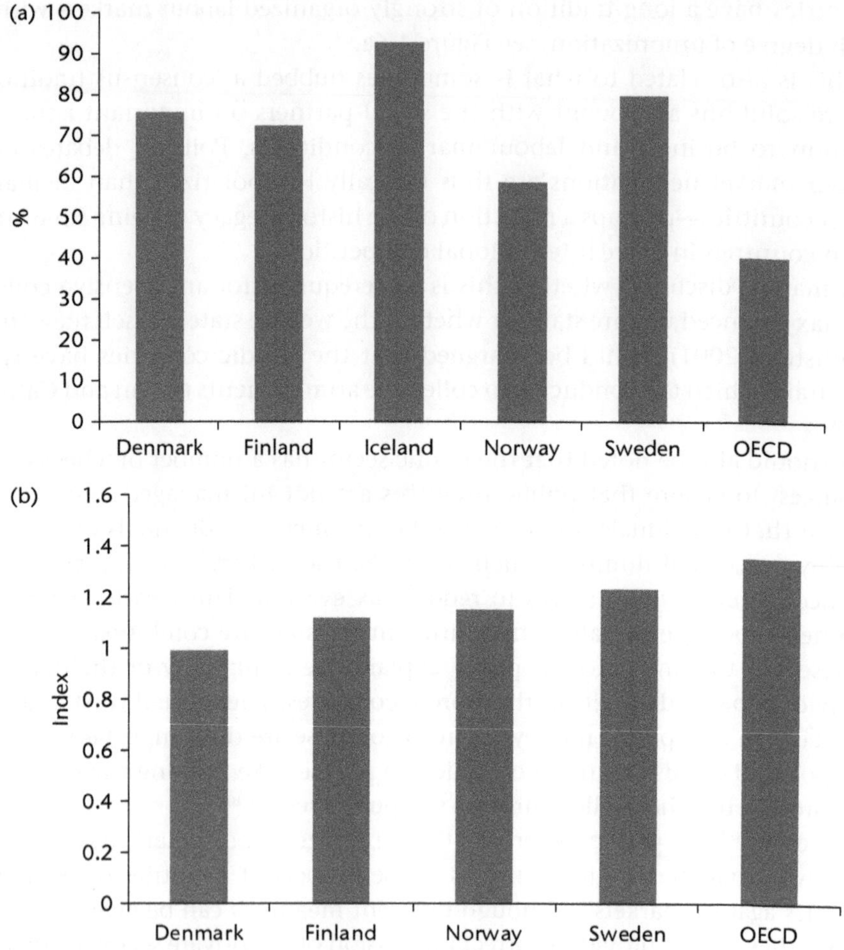

Figure 1.6. Trade union coverage and product market regulation

Note: (a) Number of trade union members as a share of wage earners. Data for 2011 or latest year. (b) Index defined between 0 and 3; the lower the index, the less the regulation. Data applies to 2008. No data available for Iceland.

Source: <http://www.OECDilibrary.org>.

As argued above, the Nordic welfare model combines a large public sector with a competitive private sector and is clearly distinguishable from the Anglo-Saxon, continental European, and Mediterranean models. It is often argued that economic performance, in particular during the recent crisis, has been considerably better in the Nordic countries than in the EU on average. In the next section we compare the macroeconomic performance of the Nordic countries with other mainly EU countries. As we have argued, when looking more carefully at the data we find that the picture may not be as clear as it sometimes appears in the public debate.

1.3 Macroeconomic Performance and Policies in the Nordic Countries

In this section we briefly review recent macroeconomic performance and policies in the Nordic countries. We first look at business cycles, net public lending, and government debt, and then we turn to a more general comparison, also with other European countries, of external and internal imbalances.

Given that the Nordic countries are small, open, and highly integrated economies, it is no surprise that their business cycles are synchronized to a high degree; see Figure 1.7.

The figure shows the percentage change in real GDP in the Nordic countries over the period 1970–2012. The high growth rates observed during the 1970s, over 3% per year on average, have been gradually falling since then. This pattern is in line with other OECD countries. The growth rate in Norway has been considerably higher than in the other three countries since 1970. Even when taking this into account, economic growth in the other three Nordic countries has been around 2% per year on average.

The effects of the banking crises in the late 1980s and early 1990s in Finland, Norway, and Sweden are clearly seen in the figure. Norway had a banking crisis 1988–92, and then both Finland and Sweden experienced banking crises in the early 1990s. As a result, GDP growth rates turned negative in Finland and Sweden. Similarly, we clearly see the effects of the great financial crisis

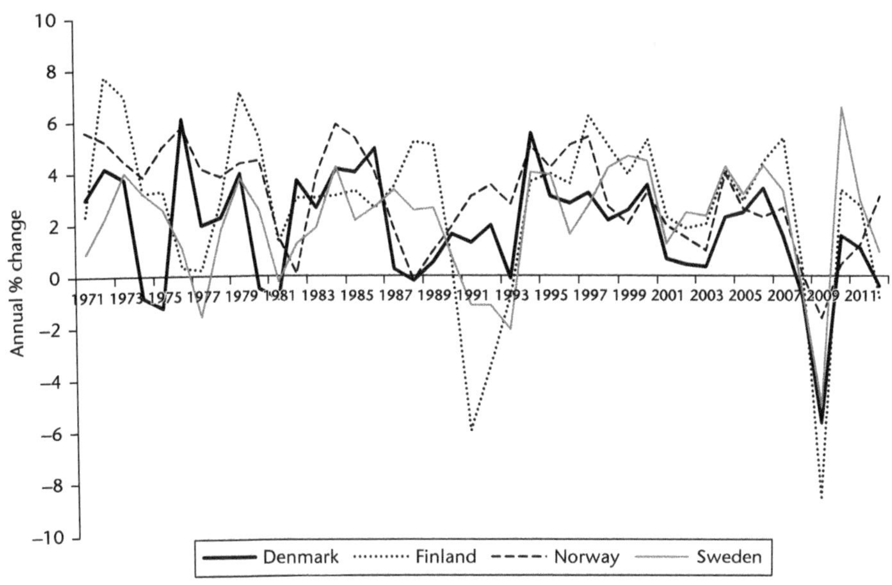

Figure 1.7. Percentage change in real GDP in the Nordic countries 1970–2012
Source: OECD.

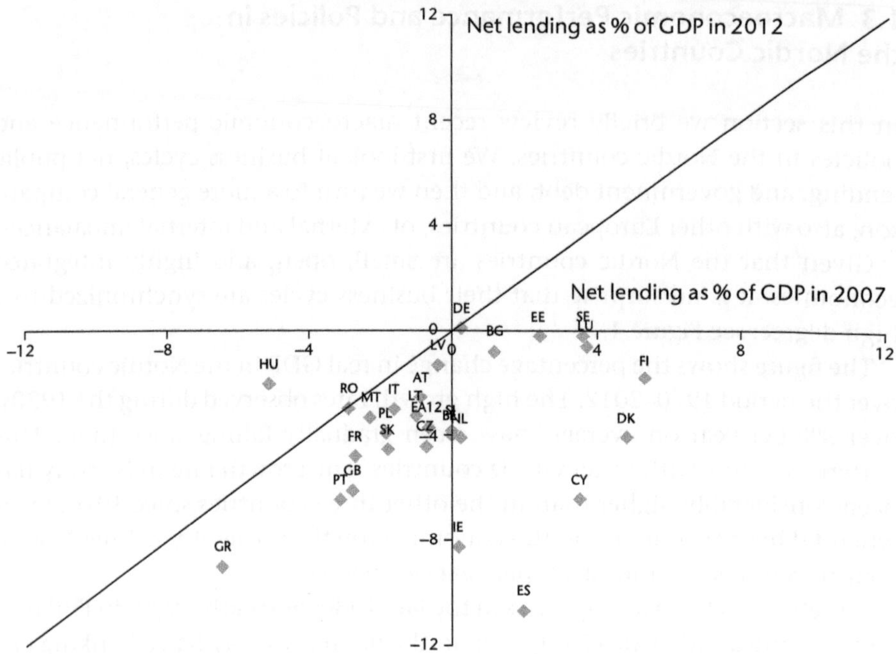

Figure 1.8. Net public lending as a percentage of GDP in EU in 2007 and in 2012
Source: Ameco.

in the period 2007–9. GDP growth fell and all countries had negative growth rates in 2009. The synchronization of business cycles in the four Nordic countries is evident from the figure.[12]

Figure 1.8 reports the development of public net lending from 2007 to 2012 for the EU countries.

As expected, the fiscal situation in most European countries deteriorated considerably during the crisis. There are, however, some exceptions. For example, Germany is close to the 45-degree line, indicating that public finances in Germany have not been affected negatively by the crisis. Countries in a favourable situation in 2007, with net lending surpluses, typically had these turned into deficits in 2012. And for countries entering the crisis period with a deficit, it proved very difficult to reduce the deficit at the same time as the crisis spread throughout Europe.

Finland and Sweden both had net lending surpluses in 2007 and deficits not exceeding the 3% limit in 2012. Denmark had the next highest net lending

[12] More precisely, by computing correlation coefficients we find high correlations between Denmark and Norway and between Finland and Sweden. The Danish business cycle is highly correlated to all other Nordic countries, whereas there seem to be lower correlations between Norway and the other economies.

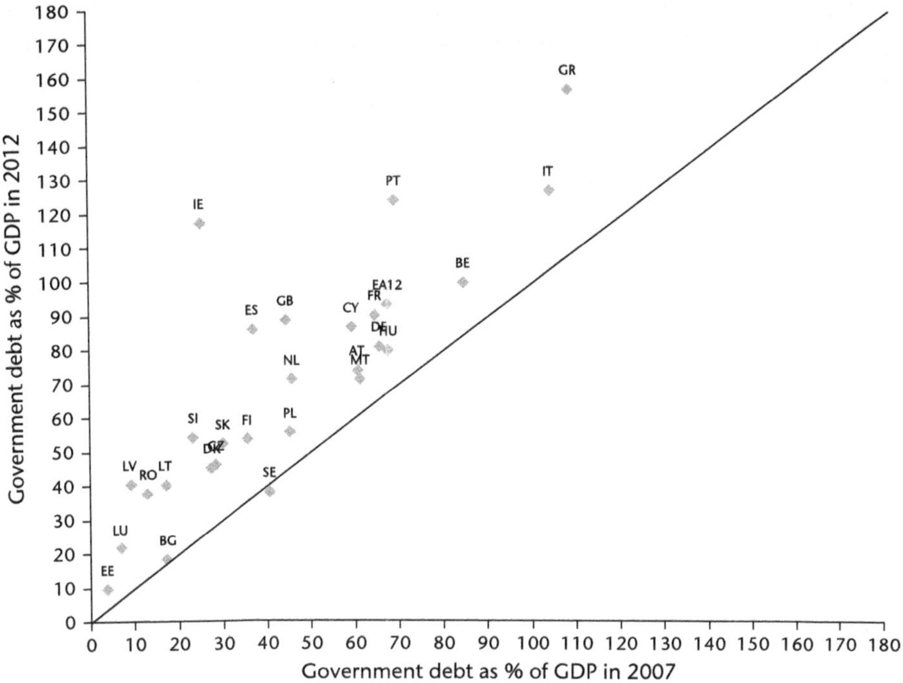

Figure 1.9. General government debt as a percentage of GDP in the EU in 2007 and 2012
Source: Ameco.

surplus of all EU countries in 2007. However, this was turned into a 4% deficit by 2012. The Nordic countries have large automatic stabilizers, due to high tax rates and extended welfare arrangements, and therefore the budget position generally varies strongly with the business cycle.[13] Norway (not included in the figure) is again an outlier, with large net lending surpluses in both 2007 (14%) and in 2012 (17%).

Since public deficits generally have increased, public debt (as a percentage of GDP) has also increased during the crisis; see Figure 1.9. The Nordic countries belong to a small group which managed to reduce public debt prior to the financial crisis, and it is noteworthy that Sweden has even managed to reduce its public debt ratio somewhat during the crisis. Also, it is interesting to note that only the Nordic countries, the new member states (former east-European countries), and Luxembourg comply with the 60% threshold on government debt in the Stability and Growth Pact.

[13] Possible reasons why public finances in Denmark have deteriorated by more than in the other Nordic countries are discussed in Bergman, Hutchison, and Jensen (2015).

What the data underline is that the Nordic countries have relatively strong public finances. They have undertaken major budget consolidations that were successful, sustained, and supported by institutional measures. This put them in a much better fiscal position at the onset of the global financial crisis compared with many other EU countries, particularly in southern Europe. These favourable initial conditions, in turn, allowed them scope to use fiscal policy actively during the economic downturn, moving from large fiscal surpluses to modest deficits without alarming financial markets or creating political upheaval, and hence prevented them from being forced to exercise the severe austerity measures seen in many other European countries.

It could be asked why the fiscal framework in the Nordic countries, and to some extent the large euro area countries in southern Europe, has a better track record than elsewhere in Europe. The answer may be that the northern-European countries have supplemented the supranational fiscal framework, as laid out in the Stability and Growth Pact, with national fiscal frameworks. In fact, the empirical literature suggests that stronger fiscal frameworks at a national level are associated with better performance of public finances.[14]

The current macroeconomic situation in the Nordic counties can be summarized by the scoreboard of indicators used in the Alert Mechanism Report (AMR) to identify internal as well as external imbalances. The AMR is the starting point of the yearly cycle of the Macroeconomic Imbalance Procedure (MIP) and has the aim of identifying imbalances in the EU countries. The AMR does not state whether an imbalance exists, but is used as a guideline as to whether further analysis is required. Yet, the AMR together with the pre-defined thresholds for the indicators used in the scoreboard could give an indication of existing imbalances.

The six macroeconomic indicators used to evaluate internal balances together with the thresholds are shown in Table 1.1. Note that different threshold values apply to some indicators depending on whether a country is a member of the euro area or not. Asterisks indicate whether the value for a country is outside the threshold. As can be seen in the table, the Nordic countries (here represented by Denmark, Finland, and Sweden) show very few indications of internal imbalances. In fact, it is only private-sector debt that exceeds the thresholds. The picture is quite different in other European countries where imbalances are found for both private and government debt as well as for unemployment.

Similar results hold for external balances as well; see Table 1.2. The Nordics here stand out as a group against the other EU countries when comparing five

[14] See, for example, Hallerberg, Strauch, and von Hagen (2007); Debrun, Moulin, Turrini, Ayuso-i-Casals, and Kumar (2008); and Bergman, Hutchison, and Jensen (2013).

Table 1.1. Alert Mechanism Report scoreboard for internal imbalances, EU countries

	% y-o-y change in deflated house prices	Private-sector credit flow as % of GDP, consolidated	Private-sector debt as % of GDP, consolidated	General government sector debt as % of GDP	Unemployment rate, 3 year, average	% y-o-y change in total financial sector liabilities
Thresholds	+6%	14%	133%	60%	10%	16.5%
Denmark	–5.1	6.1	239*	45	7.5	5
Finland	–0.5	9	158*	54	8	–0.2
Sweden	–0.2	1.8	212*	38	8.1	4.4
Germany	1.8	1.5	107	81*	6.2	4.4
Greece	–12.4	–6.8	129	157*	18.2*	–3.4
Ireland	–11.7	–1.6	306*	117*	14.4*	–0.7
Portugal	–8.6	–5.4	224*	124*	13.6*	–3.6
Spain	–16.9	–10.5	194*	86*	22.3*	3.3
Italy	–5.4	–1	126	127*	9.2	7.1

Note: * indicate that the value is outside the limits defined by the threshold.

Source: EU Commission Alert Mechanism Report 2014, November 13, 2013.

Table 1.2. Alert Mechanism Report scoreboard for external imbalances, EU countries

	Current Account balance as % of GDP 3-year average	Net international investment position as % of GDP	Real effective exchange rate % change (3 years)	Export market share % change (5 years)	Nominal ULC % change (3 years)
Thresholds	–4% & +6%	–35%	±5% & ±11%	–6%	+9% & +12%
Denmark	5.9	38	–7.7	–18.6*	1
Finland	–0.5	18	–8.3*	–30.8*	4.8
Sweden	6.2*	–10	10.1	–18.8*	0.7
Germany	6.5*	42	–8.9*	–13.1*	3
Greece	–7.5*	–109*	–4.5	–26.7*	–8.1
Ireland	2.3	–112*	–12.2*	–16.3*	–10.4
Portugal	–6.5*	–115*	–4	–16*	–5.3
Spain	–3.1	–93*	–5.2	–14.6*	–5.6
Italy	–2.3	–25	–6.2*	–23.8*	3.1

Note: When several thresholds are indicated for a macroeconomic indicator, the first threshold refers to euro area countries whereas the second refers to countries outside the euro area. * indicate that the value is outside the limits defined by the threshold.

Source: EU Commission Alert Mechanism Report 2014, November 13, 2013.

indicators of external balances. Comparing both external and internal balances across these countries, we find that for Denmark 9 out of 11 values are within the boundaries defined by the thresholds, and for Finland and Sweden 8 out of 11 indicators are within the thresholds. This can be compared to the GIPSI countries (Greece, Italy, Portugal, Spain, and Ireland) where about half of the variables are outside the boundaries. Germany (as well as France which is not reported in the table) is in between the Nordic countries and the GIPSIs in this respect, with 7 out of 11 indicators within the thresholds. Again, this suggests that the Nordic countries perform very well relative to other EU countries, in particular the GIPSIs.

It should be noted, however, that the scoreboard only presents a snapshot of the current imbalances. Some of the indicators take into account the developments over the last three or five years, whereas the remaining variables only measure year-on-year changes, and even variables such as the most recent changes in housing prices may hide underlying imbalances. For example, the housing markets in all Nordic countries show very similar behaviour with sharp increases, but in contrast to Norway housing prices in Denmark, Finland, and Sweden have fallen during the last year. Even though the particular indicator used in the AMR suggests that there is no imbalance on the housing market (see Table 1.1), the study by Bergman, Sillemann, and Sørensen (2015) suggests that imbalances remain in the Danish and Swedish housing markets.

Looking at the development of current account balances (see Table 1.2), we note a distinct difference between northern (Nordic countries, Germany, and Ireland) and southern Europe, with current account surpluses (some even higher than the threshold) in the north and deficits in the south. The net international position substantially declines in the GIPSIs, whereas it has increased for the Nordic countries, except for Sweden where there is a minor fall. Export market shares have been falling in all countries.

Overall, Tables 1.1 and 1.2 suggest that economic performance is somewhat better in the Nordics but that there are areas in these countries that remain a concern, in particular the developments on the housing market and household debt. That financial instability may pose a threat to the Nordic countries has also been pointed out by the International Monetary Fund (IMF) in their Nordic Regional Report (IMF, 2013). As in the scoreboard above, the IMF notes that the indebtedness of households in the Nordic area may be worrisome.

However, the problems associated with private debt should not be overstressed. In fact, gross debt is not a problem per se, and the criticisms often tend to become overly simplistic. Evidently, there is a huge difference between gross and net debt. Moreover, recent studies indicate that there is only an imbalance between debt and income for a small fraction of households, as reflected by the fact that so far there have been very few private bankruptcies despite the crisis. Of course, there is an exposure for highly indebted households, but advantages associated with easier access to intertemporal consumption smoothing, the housing market for young people, etc. should not be neglected.

IMF (2013) also notes that even though house prices have fallen in Denmark, Finland, and Sweden, it is still an open question whether prices will stabilize in the future or increase again. However, its main conclusion when comparing the economic performance of the Nordic countries is that these four countries have managed to handle the effects of the euro crisis well compared to the average advanced OECD country.

The banking sector is highly integrated in the Nordic countries. There are six major banks operating throughout the Nordic region, comprising around 90% of the total assets of all banks that are publicly listed in the region, and these operate almost exclusively in the region. This poses vulnerability in case the regional banking sector is hit by a negative shock. Until recently, it was an open question if these banks were too big to fail or too big to save. But this has changed with the implementation of the banking union. Those banks are defined as SIFIs (Systemically Important Financial Institution), meaning that they are too big to fail, and therefore subject to specific regulations such as high capital requirements.

While household debt has increased to levels that both the EU Commission and the IMF view as too large, these vulnerabilities should not be overstated. The experience from the Swedish and Danish banking crises is that it was not driven by losses on loans to households but from losses on investments on commercial property. On the other hand, large falls in house prices could have negative effects on aggregate demand, which suggests that excessive increases in household debt should not be ignored.

Finally, it should be stressed that the Nordic model does not escape economic crisis. This applies in general to business cycle fluctuations but also in more structural terms. This has called the overall model into question. For example, Denmark suffered from a prolonged crisis during the 1970s and 1980s, and the other Nordic countries were hit by a deep crisis in the early 1990s. The story about the Nordic model is not a fairy tale about 'living happily ever after to the end of their days'. Rather, it is a story about the need for continuous adaptation to reach overarching goals. This is a process which inevitably involves a lot of trial and error. Perhaps the key reason behind the Nordic success is a strong political and social capital which eventually produces the necessary reforms to maintain the overall objectives.

1.4 The Contributions Made by this Book

The remainder of this book has a collection of twelve chapters, each followed by a brief discussion essay focusing on key macroeconomic aspects of the Nordic economies. The chapters cover a spectrum of empirical and policy-oriented approaches with past, current, and future perspectives. Each chapter contains original and self-contained material on a specific topic. The contributions have been grouped into four main parts, each with a particular focus: labour markets and the welfare state; monetary issues including financial and housing markets; fiscal and public finance issues; and more general studies in a country-specific context.

1.4.1 *Labour Markets and the Welfare State*

The first part of the book, on labour markets and the welfare state, has three interrelated contributions. In Chapter 2, Torben M. Andersen addresses the question why the Nordic countries have been able to achieve both high incomes and an egalitarian distribution thereof. According to traditional reasoning, ambitious redistributive policies and an extended welfare state come at the cost of distorted incentives and thus reduced economic efficiency. A key to explain the Nordic performance is the fact that welfare arrangements not only play a role in terms of redistribution but also in terms of insurance. The latter is associated with direct welfare gains and may also be inductive for a more flexible economy. Disincentive effects of the social safety net are mitigated by eligibility criteria with an active focus on job search and employment.

In Chapter 3, Karl O. Moene and Erling Barth ask: how have the Nordic countries become so egalitarian? It is argued that the political economy of Nordic egalitarianism depends critically on labour market institutions. Both sides of the negotiation table are responsible for the small wage differentials. This essential link may be missing, not only in the minds of the interpreters of the Nordic model, but also in the future of the Nordic countries. Structural change in the form of uneven mechanization across sectors may erode the power of both export-led unions and employers. At the same time it may reduce voters' willingness to pay for redistributive welfare services, thereby threatening the future sustainability of the Nordic model.

In Chapter 4, Michael Svarer considers the role of labour market performance and reforms with reference to Danish experiences. The Danish labour market has been subject to a series of reforms over recent decades, and the reform process is still ongoing. The chapter provides an overview of some of the most important reforms and discusses how they have affected labour market performance. The chapter draws on empirical evidence from recent Danish reforms and from a series of random controlled experiments to test the effectiveness of different active labour market instruments. It is concluded that the labour market reforms have had significant effects on the Danish labour market, although it is an ongoing process to adjust labour market policies in light of new insights and the challenges arising in the labour market.

1.4.2 *Monetary Policy, and Financial and Housing Markets*

The second part of the book is devoted to studies of financial markets in a broad sense, including assessment of monetary policy and the behaviour of housing markets. In Chapter 5, Anders Møller Christensen and Niels Lynggård Hansen document how monetary-policy responses to pressures after the financial crisis differed across the Nordic countries. Notably, the Swedish Riksbank on one hand lowered its policy rates aggressively which resulted in a depreciation of the SEK, while Danmarks Nationalbank raised interest rates to prevent the DKK from depreciating. Based on an analysis of a broad set of macroeconomic data including an econometric analysis of a data set covering 21 OECD countries over the last 40 years, the authors find that whereas monetary policy, unlike other important characteristics, is a distinguishing feature between the Nordic economies, it is far from the main factor explaining the economic performance in different countries in recent years. Instead, differences in performance are mainly attributed to differences in terms of fiscal discipline and stability-oriented economic policies in the years before the crisis. As long as monetary policy is managed consistently, and supported by a stability-oriented fiscal policy, the choice of intermediate target seems to be of minor importance.

In Chapter 6, Hilde C. Bjørnland and Junior Maih focus on a comparison of monetary and exchange rate policies in Norway and Sweden. Both countries have floating exchange rates and inflation targeting. Norway abandoned the fixed exchange rate system in December 1992 and introduced inflation targeting in 2001, whereas Sweden switched to floating exchange rates in November 1992 and inflation targeting from 1995. Comparing the performance of key macroeconomic indicators, the chapter analyses the role of monetary policy in stabilizing the economy and the extent to which monetary policy has contributed to exchange rate stability. It is found that while terms of trade volatility is about five times as high in Norway as in Sweden, other key variables such as inflation and interest rates have about the same volatility in the two countries. This suggests that monetary policy is used more actively in Norway than in Sweden. The empirical evidence supports this conclusion: Norges Bank has actively stabilized the value of the NOK both before and after the adoption of inflation targeting, whereas the Riksbank has, since the adoption of inflation targeting, reduced its response to output and the exchange rate.

In Chapter 7, Michael Bergman, Bjørn Tangaa Sillemann, and Peter Birch Sørensen study the housing market in Denmark and Sweden. As in many other countries, house prices in both Denmark and Sweden increased substantially during the run-up to the current crisis. In Denmark, the increases were followed by a sharp downturn, whereas in Sweden house prices have remained on a historically high level, with small downturns followed by upturns. The authors set out to study the behaviour and determinants of house prices by estimating a theoretical model of the housing market. This model allows them to estimate a fundamental house price that can be used to evaluate whether house prices are over- or undervalued, as well as to analyse the determinants of such over- or undervaluation. They find that there are persistent deviations of actual house prices from their fundamental values. Their estimates suggest that house prices have been overvalued in Denmark since the late 1990s and in Sweden since 2005. In addition, they find evidence suggesting that interest rate changes, credit growth, and household expectations play significant roles for the deviation of actual house prices from the fundamental value. This supports the view that monetary policy cannot bear the full burden of reducing house prices, and that fiscal policy, through its effects on credit growth, also plays an important role.

1.4.3 *Fiscal and Public Finance Issues*

The Nordic countries have attracted a lot of attention due to their ability to combine large public sectors with strong public finances. Two chapters explicitly address the issues of fiscal consolidation, tax and pension reforms, institutional design, etc. In Chapter 8, Lars Jonung analyses fiscal policies from a learning perspective. Jonung characterizes the macroeconomic record of Sweden since the 1970s with special focus on how the design of stabilization policies has changed over time, in particular after the financial crisis in the early 1990s. It is argued that the crisis had a profound effect on the conduct of fiscal policy as well as on the institutional framework for macroeconomic policy. Sweden introduced, as a response to the crisis, new political and administrative institutions designed not only to attain long-term sustainable public finances but also to provide guidelines on the use of stabilization and structural policies. One important element of the fiscal framework is the establishment of a fiscal policy council, in 2007. The chapter discusses the remits of the council and gives a brief evaluation of its reports. The Swedish experience offers an important illustration of the importance of learning from past mistakes.

In Chapter 9, Michael Bergman, Michael M. Hutchison, and Svend E. Hougaard Jensen provide an overview of experiences with fiscal and structural reforms in Denmark and Sweden. First, the experiences with large-scale fiscal consolidations are reviewed, including evidence on the expansionary fiscal contraction hypothesis focusing on the Danish experience in the early 1980s. Second, given the widespread perception that supranational fiscal rules have been ineffective in Europe, the authors study the record of national fiscal rules, fiscal councils, and gradual improvement of public finances, as implemented by Sweden for more than a decade. Third, in view of the challenges raised by ageing populations and future budget pressures in most countries, they assess the experiences with occupational pension schemes in Denmark. Among the important policy conclusions are that longer-term debt sustainability requires symmetry in counter-cyclical fiscal policies—public saving (and debt reduction) during upturns in the business cycle that create room to manoeuvre for a more active policy (and debt accumulation) during bad times; that the fiscal and structural reform process is easier to move forward when the economy is under severe pressure; and that there is no easy way to copy successful fiscal frameworks as the effects and political support of budget consolidations may differ across countries.

1.4.4 *General Country Studies*

In Chapter 10, Erling Steigum and Øystein Thøgersen draw the line between the Norwegian boom-bust cycle and banking crises in the late 1980s and early 1990s, and the succeeding institutional and structural reforms, and strong macroeconomic performance and stability of the last two decades. Comparisons are made to rather similar development patterns in Sweden and Finland and to the somewhat different developments in Denmark. The authors highlight various reasons underlying the ability of the Norwegian political system to learn from previous political mistakes and to reach the necessary consensus and determination to implement necessary reforms. While the recent literature on financial crises indicates that a recession accompanied by a banking crisis may well lead to a 'lost decade', like in Japan in the 1990s, they find no signs of such a lost decade in the three Nordic economies that suffered from systemic banking crises in the early 1990s.

In Chapter 11, Sixten Korkman and Antti Suvanto focus on a comparison of macroeconomic performances in Finland and Sweden. The background is that both these countries experienced deep financial crises in the early 1990s and as a consequence both countries implemented new economic policies and structural reforms, and introduced frameworks to attain long-term sustainability of public finances. Both Finland and Sweden joined EU in 1995 but decided on different approaches to the monetary union; Finland adopted the euro from the start whereas Sweden remains outside and has adopted a freely floating exchange rate and an inflation target. The chapter provides three main conclusions. First, the financial crises created a new political environment allowing for structural reforms to be implemented and more attention to sustainable public finances. Second, the authors suggest that the Nordic model has been successful in combining equity and efficiency. Third, the choice of membership of the monetary union seems less important. There is no clear difference between the macroeconomic performances of Finland and

Sweden and therefore it seems as if it is of less importance whether a country decides to join a monetary union or remains outside.

In Chapter 12, Thorvaldur Gylfason reviews economic developments in Iceland following its financial collapse in 2008, focusing on causes and consequences of the crash. The review is presented in the context of the Nordic region, with broad comparisons also with developments elsewhere on the periphery of Europe; in Greece, Ireland, and Portugal. In some ways, however, Iceland resembles Italy, Japan, and Russia more than it resembles its Nordic neighbours or even Ireland. The chapter also considers the uncertain prospects for reforms and restoration as well as the possible effects of the crash on social, human, and real capital, and on long-term economic growth.

In Chapter 13, using Finland as a case study, Seppo Honkapohja argues that the success of the Nordic model depends strongly on successful macroeconomic performance, especially of exports. Finland currently faces two kinds of difficulties here: adverse structural developments and cost competitiveness problems. In the first, in fact two structural difficulties have emerged. One of them is the rapid decline of IT and electronics caused to a large extent by the difficulties of Nokia. The second problem is the more gradual decline in the paper industry. As regards cost competitiveness, it is an important element in securing good export performance which in turn is needed for the success of the Nordic model. The Finnish labour market failed to maintain cost competitiveness of the economy when the international recession from the global financial crisis hit in 2008–9. The recession and slow growth have worsened the sustainability problems in public finances, which were facing these problems in any case due to the country's ageing population. Finnish public finances are facing major challenges which will require reforms to many aspects of the social welfare system.

References

Adema, W. and M. Ladaique (2009), 'How Expensive is the Welfare State?: Gross and Net Indicators in the OECD Social Expenditure Database (SOCX)', *OECD Social, Employment and Migration Working Papers*, No. 92, OECD Publishing.

Algan, Yann and Pierre Cahuc (2009), 'Civic Virtue and Labor Market Institutions', *American Economic Journal: Macroeconomics*, 1: 111–45.

Andersen, T.M., B. Homström, S. Honkapohja, S. Korkman, H.T. Söderström, J. Vartiainen (2007), The Nordic Model—Embracing globalization and sharing risk, ETLA, Helsinki.

Andersen, T.M. and M. Svarer (2007), 'Flexicurity—Labour Market Performance in Denmark', *CESifo Economic Studies*, 53: 389–429.

Bergman, U.M., M.M. Hutchison, and S.H. Jensen (2013), 'Do Sound Public Finances Require Fiscal Rules or Is Market Pressure Enough?' *European Economy*, Economic Papers 489.

Bergman, U.M., M.M. Hutchison, and S.H. Jensen (2015), 'Shaping the Fiscal Policy Framework: Lessons from Fiscal Consolidations in Denmark and Sweden', Chapter 9, this volume.

Bergman, U.M., B.T. Sillemann, and P. B. Sørensen (2015), 'House Prices in Denmark and Sweden', Chapter 7, this volume.

Danish Economic Council (2012), The Danish Economy—Spring 2012 (Dansk Økonomi—Foråret 2012), Copenhagen.

Debrun, X., L. Moulin, A. Turrini, J. Ayuso-i-Casals, and M. S. Kumar (2008), 'Tied to the Mast? National Fiscal Rules in the European Union', *Economic Policy* 23: 297–362.

Edgren, G., K.O. Faxén, and C.-E. Odhner (1969), 'Wages, Growth and the Distribution of Income', *Swedish Journal of Economics*, 71: 133–60.

Erixon, L. (2010), 'The Rehn-Meidner Model in Sweden: Its Rise, Challenges and Survival', *Journal of Economic Issues*, 44: 677–715.

Esping-Andersen, G. (1990), The Three Worlds of Welfare Capitalism, Princeton University Press, Princeton.

Eurostat (2013), Taxation Trends in the European Union—Data for EU Members States, Iceland and Norway.

Gylfason, T. (2015), 'Iceland: How Could This Happen?', Chapter 12, this volume.

Hallerberg, M., R. Strauch, and J. von Hagen (2007), 'The Design of Fiscal Rules and Forms of Governance in European Union Countries', *European Journal of Political Economy* 23: 338–59.

International Monetary Fund (2013), Nordic Regional Report, IMF Country Report No. 13/274.

Norwegian Ministry of Finance (2011), Nationalbudgettet 2012, Oslo (In Norwegian).

OECD (2011), Employment Outlook, Paris.

Rothstein, B. (2001), 'Social Capital in the Social Democratic Welfare State', *Politics & Society*: 29: 207–41.

Swedish Ministry of Finance (2011), Vårpropositionen, Stockholm (In Swedish).

2

Collective Risk Sharing

The Social Safety Net and Employment

Torben M. Andersen

2.1 Introduction

The financial crisis has shaken beliefs in markets.[1] The causes of the crisis are attributed to market failures and excesses, and market economies have proven not to be crisis-free. Moreover, the economic consequences of the crisis have shown failures in diversifying risks in the market, which has intensified calls for governments to step in.

These developments have revived the debate on the division of labour between markets and the state. This applies both with respect to specific issues on regulation of, in particular, financial markets and institutions, but also more widely in terms of the social safety net. The upshot of this is that individuals carry costs which are too large and consequences of changes which are beyond their control and influence, and therefore there is a quest to expand collective risk-sharing arrangements. The policy focus is shifting from incentives to insurance, and this has caused a U-turn in the debate on the welfare state. Prior to the crisis there was much stress on the fact that globalization called for a leaner welfare state. Increased mobility of goods and factors of production was taken to put pressure on the financial viability of the welfare state both directly via mobility but also indirectly by increasing

[1] This chapter is based on presentations at the DG ECFIN Annual Research Conference, *Governments and markets after the crisis: Finding a new balance*; the XXIII Scientific meeting of the Italian Public Economics Association, *Economic Crisis, Welfare and Growth*; the International Sociological Conference (RC 19) in Oslo; and the Conference on Reform Capacity and Macroeconomic Performance in the Nordic Countries: Track Record and Future Challenges. Comments from M. Bergman, C. Gasper, D. Dreyer Lassen, R. Torres, and A. Watt are gratefully acknowledged. Mark Strøm Kristoffersen provided efficient research assistance.

the distortional effects of taxes. However, the financial crisis, which itself has a strong global element, has shown that there is another side to the debate, namely both the exposure to shocks and the need for insurance arrangements to cope with such shocks.

In debates on the role and scope of the welfare state, reference is often made to the Nordic or Scandinavian welfare model[2] due to its ability to achieve high employment rates and income levels and a relatively equal distribution of income. It is particularly noteworthy that these countries feature large public sectors and an extended social safety net and therefore also large tax burdens. Standard economic theory would predict that countries choosing an extended welfare state and thus high tax rates to achieve distributional and social goals will experience a less efficient economy due to tax distortions. The Nordic countries seem to some extent to have defied these implications. The present chapter takes a look at some of the important mechanisms, explaining how it has been possible to reconcile these apparently contradictory forces.

The chapter is organized as follows. Section 2 provides a brief empirical account of some of the specific achievements of the Nordic countries. Sections 3 and 4 address two key issues in relation to the welfare state. The welfare state has an important build-in implicit insurance element relative to various events which may happen through life (ability to work, health, ability to complete education, etc.). It provides insurance and redistributes at the same time. If private markets offer insufficient insurance options to individuals, it follows that there are welfare gains from public insurance; both directly when agents are risk averse, and indirectly by overcoming market failures. It is an implication that welfare arrangements up to a point may improve both efficiency and equity outcomes. There is not necessarily a trade-off. Section 4 turns to the design of the social safety net and looks at what taxes are financing. The design of the social safety net in the Nordic countries is balancing social concerns with concerns for employment. Hence, the system is not passive but includes a number of eligibility conditions serving to reconcile a generous social safety net with job-search incentives. Along the same lines it is important that a large share of public expenditure is supporting labour supply in both its qualitative and quantitative dimensions. In this sense the welfare state is not just a 'cost' but also important for a well-functioning economy. Finally policy implications of collective risk-sharing arrangements are collected in Section 5.

[2] In the literature some efforts have been exerted on developing classification schemes of welfare regimes building on Esping-Andersen's (1990) seminal contribution. Whether the term 'the Scandinavian welfare model' is well-defined can be questioned. It is used here in the broad sense of universal and generous tax-financed welfare arrangements, with the explicit proviso that this welfare model is not confined to a particular geographical area.

2.2 The Trade-off Between Efficiency and Equity

The trade-off between efficiency and equity is at the core of the discussion of state vs. markets. The quest for economists is to work out the shape of the trade-off (position and slope), leaving it to the politicians to choose based on political preferences. The trade-off arises because taxes and transfers etc. needed to accomplish more equity distort incentives and therefore cause efficiency losses. However, most analyses of policy proposals tend to focus on the incentive and thus efficiency effects of proposals, leaving no or only vague information on the trade-off faced by policy-makers.

2.2.1 *Income Levels and Distribution*

A very broad and aggregate perspective on the trade-off can be taken by exploiting cross-country evidence on economic performance. While this method is obviously crude, the trade-off should show up rather clearly in such data if it is so profound. Accordingly, it is of interest to consider the lessons to be learned from cross-country data.

Numerous measurement problems are clearly at stake, but in a broad perspective efficiency can be associated with per capita income,[3] and equity with the equality in the distribution of income. Rankings of countries routinely use these measures for comparisons. The standard metric of income in international comparisons is per capita GDP (in PPP-corrected US$), and inequality is measured by the Gini -coefficient for equalized disposable income, implying that an equity measure is given as 100- Gini coefficient.

Figure 2.1 gives a cross-country plot of these measures of equity and efficiency for 32 OECD countries based on 2008 data. In this context Luxembourg (financial sector, country size) and Norway (oil) are considered as outliers. There are two striking observations to make from the figure. First, a number of countries manage to have both relatively high efficiency and high equity, including the Scandinavian countries. Second, the simple correlation between efficiency and equity is positive; that is, more equity tends to be associated with more efficiency (the correlation coefficient is 0.3).

It would be misleading to draw policy conclusions from the simple positive correlation observed in the data for several reasons. The data in the figure do not control for various background factors, convergence processes may be at play, and political inefficiencies may be a barrier to reach the efficiency frontier. The best-practice frontier can be assessed by selecting the group of

[3] This is supported by the general finding that tax distortions tend to imply a level of employment that is too low, and thus activity as compared to the social optimum. However, it does not necessarily follow that this gap is increasing in the tax rate, although this is usually taken for granted in discussions.

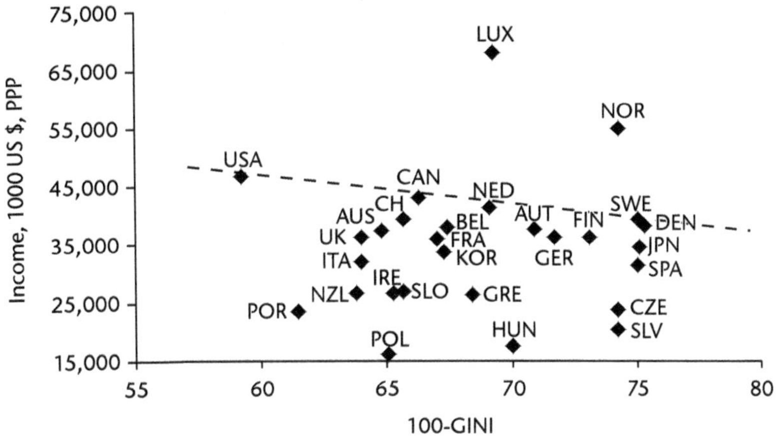

Figure 2.1. The efficiency–equity trade-off—OECD countries 2008

Note: Efficiency is measured by GDP per capita in US$, PPP, and equity as 100-Gini-coefficient, where the latter is computed on the basis of equivalent disposable incomes. Data applies to 2008. The line illustrates the best-practice frontier identified via a data envelope analyses (DEA) analysis.

Source: <http://www.sourceoecd.org>.

countries which have high efficiency for a given level of equity or vice versa. Table 2.1 reports the result of a simple panel estimation based on data for the mid ’80s, mid ’90s, and mid ’00s for seven countries identified to constitute the best-practice frontier.[4]

At the frontier there is a trade-off, and the elasticity of efficiency with respect to equity is approximately –1. The estimated relation is drawn as the straight line in Figure 2.1. In accordance with the parsimonious approach taken here, the overall tax burden is used as a metric of welfare arrangements. According to standard views a higher tax burden should be associated with lower efficiency and higher equity. This is considered for countries at the best-practice frontier in Table 2.1.

These simple regressions confirm the standard interpretation of the mechanisms taken to imply a trade-off between efficiency and equity. A higher tax burden lowers efficiency by an elasticity of about 1/3, while it at the same time improves equity with an elasticity of about 1/3, consistent with the trade-off between efficiency and equity having an elasticity of about –1.

[4] The trade-off is estimated using data for the mid ’80s, mid ’90s, and mid ’00s for OECD countries. Luxembourg and Norway are treated as outliers, and countries are selected such that income per capita is not 25% or more lower than that of the US for any of the periods, and subject to data availability for all three periods. The best-practice frontier is identified by a DEA analysis where efficiency and equity are per capita income and the tax burden the input, and a selection criterion of a NIRS score (decreasing returns) is of no less than 0.99.This leaves seven countries: USA, DEN, NED, BEL, SWE, AUT, and CAN at the frontier.

Table 2.1. Efficiency–equity trade-off and the role of the tax burden

Dependent variable:	Efficiency	Efficiency	Equity
Independent variable:			
Constant	9.32 (0.07)	11.04 (0.24)	−1.62 (0.24)
Equity	−0.93 (0.21)		
Tax burden		−0.37 (0.07)	0.34 (0.03)
Dummy 1995	0.43 (0.03)	0.45 (0.03)	−0.015 (0.012)
Dummy 2005	0.82 (0.03)	0.86 (0.03)	0.027 (0.011)
R2	0.98	0.98	0.91
RSS	0.07	0.05	0.08
DW	1.1	1.0	1.45

Note: Estimated on the basis of data underlying Figure 2.1. The tax burden is total public revenue as a share of GDP. Standard errors in parantheses.

Data: <http://www.sourceoecd.org>.

Note that the dummy variables are significant in the efficiency equation but not in the equity equation. This suggests that the dummy captures a general growth effect which affects efficiency measured by income equally in all countries, but it has no separate effect on equity (for a given tax rate). Hence, this is suggestive that growth implies a parallel upward shift in the best-practice frontier between efficiency and equity. This is consistent with the fact that it has become difficult to pin down a clear effect of the size of the public sector on the growth rate.

Whether the trade-off between efficiency and equity identified here is steep or flat is in the eyes of the beholder. A debate provoked by Prescott (2004) takes the trade-off to be more steep, whereas empirical studies of e.g. labour supply usually find small elasticities suggesting a relatively flat trade-off.[5] In any case one politically interesting issue is the cluster of northern-European countries in the north-east part of Figure 2.1 having both high efficiency and equity in a comparative perspective, and the fact that these countries have extended welfare states. The following focuses on some key mechanisms accounting for the position of the Nordic countries.

[5] In a controversial paper Prescott (2004) assumes a labour supply elasticity of nearly 3. This is significantly larger than in micro studies, which usually find the elasticities to be small and below 1. For other surveys see e.g. Evers, De Moij, and van Vuuren (2005) and Meghir and Phillips (2008).

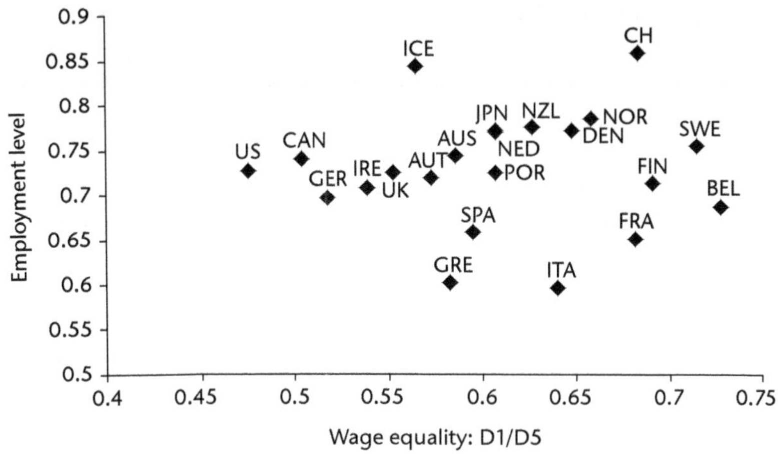

Figure 2.2. Employment and wage equality, 2007
Note: Employment rate for the age group 16–64.
Data: <http://www.sourceoecd.org>.

The trade-off between efficiency and equity can also be considered from a labour market perspective. Clearly measurement problems are at stake, but a basic insight is gained by looking at summary measures of wage inequality and employment rates, as shown in Figure 2.2. Also here it is noteworthy that the cluster of northern-European countries combines low wage inequality in the labour market with high employment rates. This shows that the finding of Figure 2.1 not only reflects that the welfare state repairs consequences of market outcomes, but also that welfare arrangements play a more active role in shaping the distribution of income.

2.3 The Social Safety Net: Insurance vs. Incentives

The debate on efficiency vs. equity usually takes its outset in the deterministic textbook case where more equity can be achieved via redistribution through taxes and transfers, which, however, distorts incentives and therefore has efficiency costs. The key distortion arises from changes in the incentive structure, which tend to cause labour supply to be inefficiently low. This is reasonably straightforward in a deterministic setting.

Modern theories of the welfare state point out that this view is too simplistic. Schemes which redistribute ex-post given income, health, labour market position, etc. do ex ante serve an insurance function. The redistributive schemes are conditional on events like job, income, health, ability to work, etc., and this is ex ante perceived by agents who therefore take into account how the schemes ex post reduce risks. It follows that a sharp distinction cannot be made between insurance and redistribution. In the following, risk diversification or insurance via tax-financed schemes will be denoted social insurance.

Social insurance has important direct and indirect effects. The obvious direct effect is that such insurance has a positive welfare effect for risk-averse agents if risk diversification is achieved at better terms than in private markets (which may offer no such scope). Insurance may also affect behaviour,[6] and much attention is on the adverse incentive effects or distortions (see following discussion). However, risk can be an impediment to adjustment, work, job search, or investment in human capital, and it follows that insurance may be conducive to efficiency (flexicurity).[7] Such behavioural responses to the insurance effect of social insurance are important because they may be counteracting the distortions arising from the schemes.[8]

To clarify this, return to the standard case where a tax causes an inefficiently low labour supply in a deterministic setting. In the presence of risks which cannot be diversified in private markets, the situation is very different. If agents are risk averse, it follows that insufficient risk sharing may cause them to choose a level of labour supply which is inefficiently low. The reason is that while the cost of work is deterministic (disutility from work or opportunity costs of foregone home production) the return to market activities may be risky. In this setting the effects of taxation are much more complicated. Consider a simple tax-transfer scheme; that is, a scheme where a proportional tax on market income finances a lump-sum transfer to all participants (see e.g. Sinn, 1995 or Andersen, 2013). In an ex-post sense this scheme is redistributive since agents with high market income will be net contributors and agents with low market income will be net receivers. In an ex ante sense the scheme reduces the risk associated with income, and this may make risk-averse agents choose to supply more labour to the market. Hence, changing the tax rate has an insurance effect on top of the traditional incentive effect.

The presence of the insurance effect creates a situation similar to the well-known fact that substitution effects are countered by income effects in textbook models of labour supply. In general the insurance effects run counter to the incentive effects, and may even dominate the latter. This implies that the relation between efficiency and equity is not necessarily given by a

[6] See e.g. Domar and Musgrave (1944) and Varian (1980) on taxation; Eaton and Rosen (1980) on education; Sinn (1995, 1996) and Andersen (2010) on tax-transfer schemes; and Agell (2002) and Barth and Moene (2009) on the labour market. See also Barr (2001).

[7] It generally holds, of course, if private markets offer incomplete insurance that social insurance may lead to a Pareto improvement and thus more efficiency. The implicit assertion here is related to activities where agents undertake 'too little' of an activity compared to the social optimum.

[8] By distortion effects are here understood the effects on incentives arising in a deterministic setting where thereby definition is no issue of risk diversification.

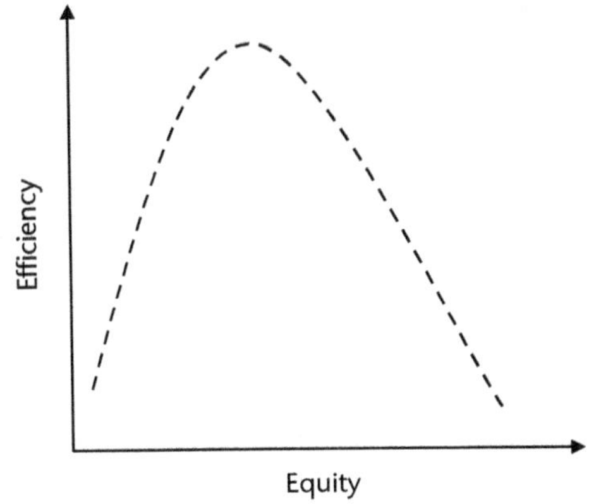

Figure 2.3. Relationship between efficiency and equity in the presence of insurance effects

trade-off, but rather by a hump-shaped relation as shown in Figure 2.3 (see e.g. Andersen, 2013).

In this figure the upward-sloping part (arising when starting from a situation without the social insurance scheme) arises because the insurance effect dominates the distortions; that is, an expansion of the social insurance scheme leads not only to more equity ex post (more insurance ex ante) but also to more efficiency by overcoming a market failure. At some point, a further expansion would cause the incentive effect to dominate the insurance effect, and a trade-off arises in the sense that more equity is achieved at the cost of more efficiency. If political preferences depended positively on both efficiency (e.g. mean income) and equity (a measure of equality in income distribution), optimal policies would situate the economy on the negatively sloped segment of the relationship. It would not be optimal to be on the upward sloping part since both efficiency and equity can be improved by expanding social insurance. However, even though a marginal policy change involves a trade-off between efficiency and equity, it is the case that policy overall has contributed to enhance both efficiency and equity. However, political inefficiencies may cause the economy to be situated on the upward-sloping part, and it is thus possible that countries may end up with similar levels of efficiency but different levels of equity depending on the political system.

The findings illustrated in Figure 2.3 have several important implications, which also point to critical aspects for mainstream policy evaluations. First, in most policy analyses focus is entirely on the distortions. To the extent that risk is important this may be potentially misleading since the insurance effect is neglected. This is illustrated in Figure 2.4 showing a calibration (US data) of the basic textbook labour supply model under standard preferences adopted

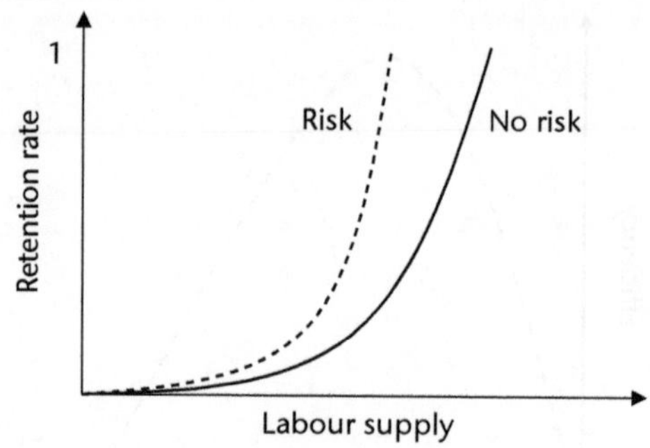

Figure 2.4. Labour supply and taxes—the role of risk and insurance
Source: Andersen (2013).

in the literature,[9] but in the presence of wage risk. The model has a basic tax-transfer scheme where a proportional tax levied on income finances a lump-sum transfer. The dashed line shows in the deterministic case how labour supply depends on the retention rate (one minus the tax rate), while the solid line shows how it depends on the retention rate in the case of risk. As is seen labour supply is, in the presence of risk, fairly inelastic to the tax rate, and the reasons are the counter-balancing insurance and distortion effects of taxation. This has the important empirical implication that low estimated labour supply elasticities may arise due to a failure to distinguish between the disincentive and insurance effects of taxes.

Second, although not always made explicit, standard assessments of incentive effects take a complete capital market structure for given. However, when the initial situation is marred by imperfections the standard trade-off view does not follow. Intervention which explicitly addresses market failures has the potential of leading to a welfare (Pareto) improvement. It is striking that analyses of unemployment insurance are often cast in a deterministic setting or take agents to be risk neutral. Recent events have made it quite clear that simply assuming that risks can be diversified in markets is a very misleading starting point.

Third, it may be questioned whether the above arguments depend critically on an assumption that social insurance can accomplish something which private insurance cannot. Clearly, if such insurance dominance is present, it leaves a clear-cut case for the potential beneficial effects of social insurance. However, even if such dominance is not clear-cut, it should be noted that if there is a political desire to redistribute, it does also imply some insurance, and this does in turn reduce the costs of redistribution (see e.g. Boadway et al., 2006).

[9] The specification implies constant relative risk aversion.

An important element of the welfare state which involves strong capital-market and insurance elements is education. The capital-market function arises because public education is free, but individuals are assumed to use their human capital in the labour market, and hence they will effectively pay back in the form of higher tax payments. The insurance function arises because the 'payment' depends on how successful the education has been in terms of employment and wage prospects. The importance of risk and borrowing constraints as impediments to education are reduced under tax-financed education. In its absence education will presume either previous savings (typically by parents) or borrowing in capital markets. Both are associated with problems since not all parents will have the capacity to save enough for their children's education, and the private market will in general offer insufficient borrowing options for education. Hence, private financing of education may imply an inefficiency in the sense that the human-capital potential of the population is not used appropriately. Since human capital is known to be an important driver of growth, it follows that insufficient education may be evident in lower average income in society.

2.3.1 *Automatic Stabilizers and Persistence*

When discussing social insurance, an individual (micro) perspective is taken for obvious reasons. However, it is important to note that the contingencies implied by social insurance aggregate to the automatic stabilizers stressed in macroeconomics. While for obvious reasons social insurance schemes can diversify idiosyncratic shocks, it is important that aggregate shocks can be diversified over time and thus generations via the public budget. Moreover, this shows that the size of automatic stabilizers tends to arise due to coincidence rather than design as the net product of the design of taxation systems and the social safety net. That is, the design of the welfare state determines the strength of the automatic stabilizers, and it is well known that there is a strong correlation between public-sector size and automatic stabilizers (Van der Noord, 2000). Recent trends in labour and social policies have focused on incentive effects, and while these have had a clear impact, they have also had the side effect of tending to weaken automatic stabilizers (Knieser and Ziliak, 2003).[10] The financial crisis has accordingly initiated a debate on how to strengthen automatic stabilizers (Debrun and Kapoor, 2010).

[10] Using measures from van der Noord (2000) and Girouard and André (2005), there is no significant change in the average size of automatic stabilizers for OECD countries from 2000 to 2005. However, there is some tendency towards levelling in the sense that countries with weak automatic stabilizers in 2000 have tended to get stronger automatic stabilizers in 2005, and vice versa. There are obviously various issues of interpretation here, and the period is very short for identification of trend changes.

While it is a virtue that the automatic stabilizers operate without discretionary policy decisions, they suffer from the problem that they do not distinguish temporary from permanent shocks. Permanent or strongly persistent shocks tend to cause systematic budget imbalances and thus threaten the financial viability of the welfare state. Therefore the persistence of shocks is crucial. It is an important question whether welfare state arrangements accomplish insurance or short-term stability at a long-term cost in terms of more sluggishness or persistence in the adjustment process. Persistent shocks do pose a serious challenge to an extended welfare state, and if welfare state arrangements promote such persistence, it is a serious problem.

Ljungqvist and Sargent (1998) describe a generous welfare state as a 'time bomb' in the sense that it may operate efficiently in tranquil times but be vulnerable to turbulence, which easily translates into persistent unemployment.[11] The latter is caused by weakened job-search incentives and higher reservation wages due to a generous social safety net. In particular, shocks tend to depreciate skills and thus require workers to accept a wage cut to find a new job, but unemployment benefits depending on past wages tend to create inertia in the adjustment of reservation wages. As a consequence the safety net hinders the process of restructuring the economy. It is also an implication of a generous tax-financed social safety net that the level of mobility across jobs is lowered (Ljungqvist and Sargent, 1995). This may contribute to reduce frictional unemployment, but induce higher structural unemployment in a situation with turbulence.

A different explanation of persistence has been advanced by pointing to the role of norms in counteracting the incentive effects of a generous social safety net (see e.g. Lindbeck, 1995 and Lindbeck et al., 2003). A strong norm to be self-supporting counters the economic incentives created by a generous scheme. Allowing for the norm to be endogenous and depending (possibly with a lag) on the number of individuals being self-supporting implies that a generous social safety net can be maintained if the employment rate is high. However, if employment falls due to e.g. a severe business cycle downturn, norms may be eroded and the welfare state caught in a situation with persistent non-employment and fiscal problems.

The empirical evidence that the welfare state tends to produce persistence is not overwhelming. In Andersen (2012) it is argued that there is no evidence that countries with large public sectors and strong automatic stabilizers display stronger persistence than countries with more lean welfare states.

[11] A possibility of multiple equilibria also arises when taking into account the financing of the safety net. Similarly, if incentive problems are countered by costly monitoring, the effectiveness of such monitoring is large at low levels of unemployment, reinforcing this situation, and the opposite in a situation with high unemployment (Ljungqvist and Sargent, 1995).

2.4 Common Pool Problems

Any type of insurance—private or social—suffers from potential problems due to moral hazard and adverse selection. For social insurance some adverse selection problems do not arise since participation is mandatory[12] (enforced pooling equilibrium). However, not all problems are solved since there is still a problem of targeting under incomplete information; that is, to ensure that the scheme only attracts those for whom it is intended.

Moral hazard problems arise for both private and social insurance. In the latter case they are often termed tax distortions. It is worth observing that the debate often stresses the incentive problems arising under social insurance without noting that the same problems would in principle arise if the insurance was organized in a private market. The moral hazard problem arises due to a common pool problem and is in this sense generic. However, this does not imply that one should not take moral hazard problems seriously, but only that the incentive problems arising under social insurance should be evaluated taking into account what the realistic alternatives are.

This is related to the paradox that the Scandinavian countries have high labour force participation and employment rates despite high tax burdens and thus high marginal effective tax rates on work. The latter would in isolation impair work incentives. The Scandinavian experience seems to suggest either that incentives do not matter or that there is a particular preference structure. However, accounting for pro-employment policies in terms of active labour market policies and policies promoting labour force participation like day care, old age care, etc., the apparent puzzle is resolved. Economic incentives also matter in the Scandinavian countries, but other elements in the policy package imply that the net result is consistent with a high employment level.

2.4.1 *Conditionalities in the Social Safety Net*

Policy designs are important for the moral hazard or incentive problems arising from insurance. Such design issues are reflected in actual policy schemes. Most observers are focusing on the generosity of the transfer levels in extended welfare states like the Scandinavian, and they are portrayed as paying people for not working (Rogerson, 2007) or as making work unnecessary (Esping-Andersen, 1990). This effectively amounts to assuming that there is a basic income or demo grant implying an unconditional minimum income for everybody. This is a poor characterization of social insurance in the Scandinavian countries, which includes numerous conditionalities;

[12] Strictly speaking there is an exit option in the form of migration. This is of importance for the scope of social insurance, but it is beyond the scope of this chapter to discuss this aspect.

that is, although eligibility is universal in the sense that all have a formal right, there are conditions to be fulfilled to qualify for the transfers. These conditions apply both to the situation in which the person or family finds itself, but also to behavioural variables like active job search, participation in education programmes, etc. The gateway into more permanent types of support like disability pension is narrowed by medical conditions, external monitoring, etc.

Obviously, this does not completely eliminate moral hazard problems, but it does point to important design issues which are crucial in striking a balance between insurance and incentives. As an example it may be worth highlighting two important dimensions of social insurance in the Scandinavian countries. First, as in most countries, the basic social transfer (social assistance) is means-tested on a family basis. Second, there are crucial workfare elements in the design of social insurance; that is, the right or entitlement to a transfer is accompanied by a duty or requirement to participate in certain activities to receive the transfer. Such conditionalities serve to reduce both moral hazard and adverse selection problems.

These conditionalities include various elements ranging from control/enforcement of job-search and availability criteria to enhancement of qualifications to improve job-finding rates. To see the implications of these conditionalities, consider the limiting case of a participation requirement for an unemployment benefit recipient when programme participation does not affect qualifications but only serves as an availability test. Participation in such a programme increases the opportunity costs of receiving benefits, which reduces both adverse selection problems and the moral hazard problem in individual search activities by lowering the net gains from claiming benefits. As an illustration of how the trade-off between employment (efficiency) and inequality (equity) can be affected by such conditionalities, consider a simple search model of the labour market (Andersen and Svarer, 2013). In this setting unemployment benefits distort search incentives, and if benefits are financed by general taxation, there is a standard common pool or moral hazard problem. Higher benefits (replacement rates) will lower the gain from working and lead to less search and thus reduce employment. Including a workfare element into the scheme implies higher opportunity costs from claiming benefits, which makes unemployed search more for the basic reason that employment becomes more attractive for given benefit levels. Therefore such conditionalities serve to maintain incentives in the labour market and thus support high employment, despite a high level of income insurance (replacement rate). Job-search incentives can thus be strengthened either by a benefit cut or by strengthening of workfare elements. This is illustrated in Figure 2.5, showing combinations of the replacement rate and the workfare requirement

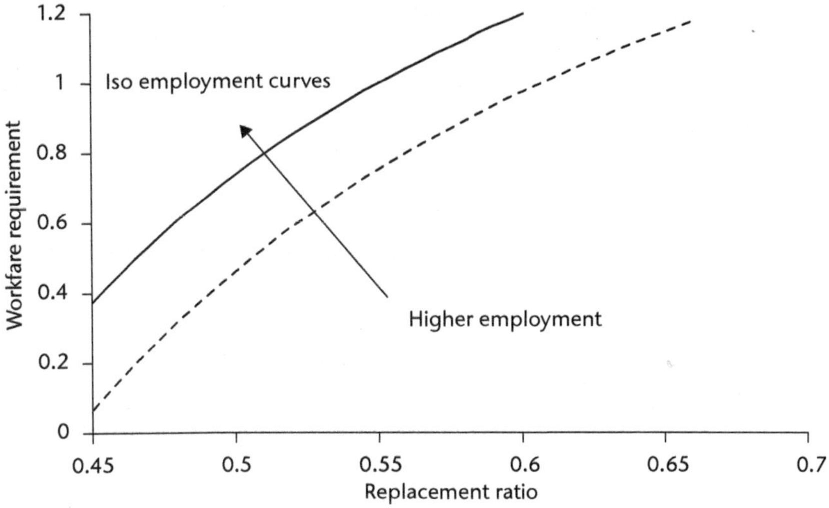

Figure 2.5. The role of the replacement rate and workfare conditionalities in a basic search framework

Note: Workfare requirement is measured as the time requirement relative to normal working hours. The figure is based on a model and simulations in Andersen and Svarer (2013).

(measured in terms of the time requirement relative to normal working hours) delivering the same employment rate (see Andersen and Svarer, 2013).[13]

The important point of this example is that incentives can be strengthened without necessarily deteriorating the level of support offered by the social safety net. Economic deprivation is not necessary to create incentives! This can also be interpreted in the sense that there is a complementarity between replacement rates and workfare requirements, or that the total package matters. From a policy perspective the important lesson is that incentives in the labour market can be maintained without retrenchment of the social safety net (cf. Section 2).

The point is not to deny the incentive problems arising from an extended social safety net. There are many examples of policy designs which have caused large drops in employment rates (including the early retirement scheme in Denmark, and sickness pay in Sweden). The point is that the solution to these problems is not necessarily retrenchment of the social safety net, but design changes which via conditionalities reduce the incentive problems. Thereby incentives can be maintained without increasing income disparities.

[13] In the model the benefit scheme is associated with possible participation in a workfare programme. The programme has two dimensions: the likelihood or share of unemployed people being asked to participate in the programme (the extensive margin) and the work requirement (the intensive margin). The intensive margin is measured as the time requirement relative to normal working hours (Andersen and Svarer, 2013).

Designing active labour market policies involves a number of concerns. Such activities are costly (direct costs of active labour market policies amount to 1.3% of GDP in Denmark), and the shift in the trade-off between incentives and insurance is thus not obtained for free.

2.4.2 *Labour Supply-Enhancing Policies*

The argument that taxes are detrimental to labour supply overlooks the point that it depends on what taxes are financing. Key elements of the welfare state are so-called welfare services like care, education, and health. These provisions are directed at the individual. Public provision serves several purposes including capital market imperfections (e.g. borrowing and paying for education), equal opportunities, and provision of insurance (e.g. health insurance). Provision of these services is not only motivated in terms of social concerns, but may also overcome market imperfections.

A large empirical literature has documented a clear relationship between education and wages, unemployment, working hours, and retirement. In short, at the individual level there is strong evidence that education is associated with higher wages and more labour supply along its various dimensions. Health conditions (mortality and morbidity) are clearly crucial for human capital and hence labour supply. This applies not only in the sense that human capital is maintained and preserved by health activities, but also that better health strengthens the incentive to invest in human capital. Market activities and home production are in some cases close substitutes. The expansion of public day-care and old-age care facilities is a precondition for the increase in female labour force participation rates.

The important conclusion from this is that one cannot infer the implications of an extended welfare state by considering the tax burden only. What the taxes are financing is equally important. In the Nordic countries a large expenditure share (about 1/5 of GDP) may be characterized as active in the sense of expenditure on care, education, and health which has a direct effect on economic performance at the same time as serving social purposes.

2.4.3 *Passive and Active Redistribution*

Most discussions on distribution focus on the role of taxes and the social safety net in redistributing income.[14] The point is that the basis for an equal distribution of income is created in the labour market, as shown in Figure 2.6. Countries which have low inequality in disposable incomes also have low

[14] Universal access to welfare services like care, education, and health has important implications for distribution as well.

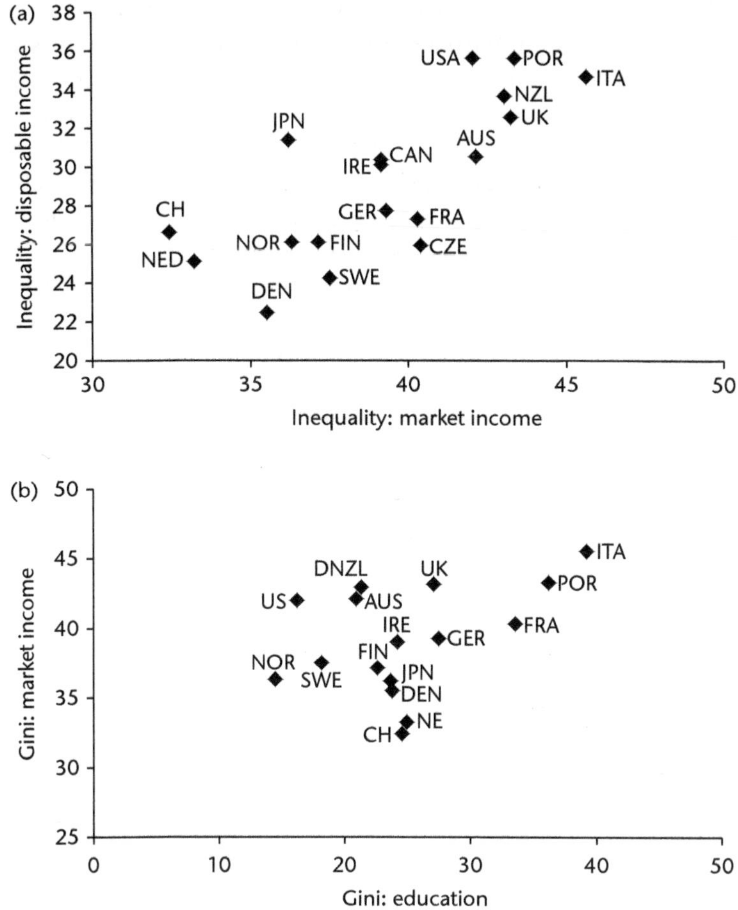

Figure 2.6. Inequality—education and market income

Note: The Gini coefficient for education is for the whole population age group 15 and over in 2000. The Gini coefficient for income is market income before taxes and transfers in 2003.

Source: Vinod, Wang, and Yan (2003) and <http://www.sourceoecd.org>.

inequality in market incomes. This does not imply that taxes and transfers do not play a role in redistribution, but it stresses that the basis of an equal income distribution is created in the labour market. Turning to the latter there is a close relationship between inequality in market incomes and inequality in education (see Figure 2.6).

Strong egalitarian preferences rule out working poor, and thus minimum wages are high.[15] This implies a higher entry threshold in terms of

[15] In the Scandinavian countries minimum wages are determined in labour market negotiations. Clearly the level is related to transfer levels offered in the social system.

qualifications to find a job. To ensure equal opportunities and to make an egalitarian outcome consistent with a high employment level, it is thus a requirement that the qualification structure is reasonably compressed. Maintaining a compressed wage structure and a high employment level requires that the qualification structure is such that supply of low-skilled labour is small[16]. To put it differently, egalitarian outcomes cannot be obtained passively, and an equal distribution of education (qualifications) is a prerequisite for an egalitarian labour market outcome (employment and wages). It is well known that human capital has an important role for growth and thus the level of income. This also stresses the point that the effects of taxes on overall economic performance like average income or income growth cannot be seen independently of what the taxes are financing.

It is worth noting that the Nordic high-tax countries are also among those with the strongest focus on education. That is, the overall level of spending on education is high (and the larger part is public), and the major part is on basic education. This underscores the point that policy designs are important to make high efficiency consistent with low inequality.

2.4.4 *Centralized Labour Markets*

Scandinavian countries are characterized by centralized labour markets and a strong tradition for seeking cooperative solutions (tripartite settlements). In relation to the common pool property of the welfare state, this is particularly important (Barth and Moene, 2009). The common pool problem arises because each single actor perceives that a change in behaviour to its own benefit will have no influence on the whole group (society). When all reason in this way, problems arise, as discussed earlier. However, centralized wage setters will realize that if they change wages or other work conditions, it will have an effect on the whole (or a significant subpart) of the labour market and therefore also the public budget, which in turn will affect workers (Summers et al., 1993). Likewise union leaders will not formulate an agenda where they ask for tax increases to finance a more extended welfare state and at the same time ask for wage increases to compensate for the implied tax increases. In short, centralized wage setters take the effects of their actions on the public budget into account (the common pool problem is partly internalized). This may be one important contributory factor to explain why it has been possible historically to maintain a relatively high labour input despite high taxes. While individuals may perceive that the price of shorter working hours is

[16] Skill bias driven by technology and globalization reduces demand for unskilled labour, and it is important to keep supply low so as to imply that the wage level is in accordance with distribution objectives.

small (the wage after tax), the centralized wage setters will realize that the cost to society is much larger since the lost tax revenue should also be taken into account. Hence, centralized determined working hours will take this into account and tend to be too long as seen from an individual perspective! In a historical perspective it does not seem to be a coincidence that countries with large public sectors are also countries with centralized labour markets.

2.5 Policy Implications

The financial crisis has shown deficiencies in the scope for diversification of shocks. Prevailing welfare arrangements in many countries did not have a proper balance between efficiency and equity, and this has prompted calls for improved collective risk sharing.

When markets are incomplete there is scope for social insurance to make improvements both in terms of efficiency and equity. In the presence of risk it is difficult to separate redistribution and insurance. Collective risk sharing arrangements have direct welfare effects when agents are risk averse but may also have important behavioural effects. With market incompleteness it is possible to improve upon allocation via risk-sharing arrangements, and hence concerns for efficiency and equity need not always conflict, although optimal policies will always feature a trade-off at the margin. The issue for the welfare state is more than a repair of unfair outcomes produced by the market economy.

The latter point is supported by comparative evidence. Empirically this chapter has identified a trade-off between efficiency and equity among the best-practice countries. Whether the trade-off is steep or flat is open for discussion, but a cluster of Nordic countries stand out by having both high income levels and low income inequality. These countries have extended welfare states and thus arrangements for collective risk sharing. Moreover, these effects do not only show up as repairs of market outcome. Considering the trade-off in the labour market, these countries have both high employment rates and a compressed wage structure.

However, collective risk-sharing arrangements imply common pool problems, and the resulting incentive problems may be serious. To counteract these, two active policy arms are crucial. First, the extent of the incentive problems depends critically on policy design. The purpose of the social safety net is to provide temporary and not permanent support. It is therefore essential to build in conditionalities in the safety net with a job focus (job search, labour market programmes, etc.). This makes it possible to maintain relatively generous benefits without jeopardizing the incentive structure. Second, education and qualifications constitute a fundamental factor in making a high employment level consistent with a compressed wage structure. If a large group has no or low qualifications, high wage ambitions (no working poor) will result in permanent unemployment for this group, which in turn will call the financial viability of collective schemes into question. Collective risk-sharing arrangements depend critically on maintaining a high employment rate.

For the same reason, such schemes are vulnerable to persistent shocks. A persistent decrease in employment will, via automatic budget reactions, have serious implications for public finances. It is a virtue of collective risk-sharing arrangements that they can deal not only with idiosyncratic but also aggregate shocks. However, the latter applies only to temporary shocks. Permanent shocks cannot be diversified. Experience shows that persistence in labour markets is strong in many countries. It has also been suggested that social insurance may be contributing to such persistence by making adjustment processes more sluggish. Empirical evidence does not provide support to the hypothesis that the persistence is stronger in countries with extensive collective risk-sharing arrangements. Nonetheless, persistent shocks are a serious policy challenge, and experience from the financial crisis shows that prudence in fiscal policy is important to maintain room in which to manoeuvre in deep crises.

A further aspect is crucial for collective risk-sharing arrangements; namely that the underlying institutions are considered efficient and well-managed and that they have broad political support. It has been beyond the scope of this chapter to discuss these issues, but it is important to stress the role of the institutional set-up as a prerequisite for political support to extensive collective risk-sharing arrangements as seen in the Nordic countries. An important issue is through what mechanisms political support for collective risk-sharing arrangements is established and maintained.

References

Agell, J. (2002), 'On the Determinants of Labour Market Institutions: Rent-sharing vs. Social Insurance', *German Economic Review*, 3, 107–35.

Andersen, T.M. (2012), 'The Welfare State and the Great Recession', *Intereconomics—Review of European Economic Policy*, 206–211.

Andersen, T.M. (2013), 'Income Taxation: Incentives vs. Insurance', *Bulletin of Economic Research*, to appear.

Andersen, T.M. and M. Svarer (2013), 'The Role of Workfare in Striking a Balance Between Incentives and Insurance in the Labour Market', *Economica* 81, 86–116.

Barr, N. (2001), *The Welfare State as Piggy Bank—Information, Risk, Uncertainty, and the Welfare State*, Oxford: Oxford University Press.

Barth, E. and K.O. Moene (2009), 'The Equality Multiplier', NBER Working Paper 15076.

Boadway, R., M. Leite-Monteiro, M. Marchand, and P. Pestieau (2006), 'Redistribution with Moral Hazard and Adverse Selection', *Scandinavian Journal of Economics*, 108(2), 279–98.

Domar, E.D. and R. Musgrave (1944), 'Proportional Income Tax and Risk-Taking', *Quarterly Journal of Economics*, 58, 387–422.

Debrun, X. and R. Kapoor (2010), 'Fiscal Policy and Macroeconomic Stability: New Evidence and Policy Implications', *Nordic Economic Policy Review*, 1, 35–70.

Eaton, J. and H.S. Rosen (1980), 'Taxation, Human Capital and Uncertainty', *American Economic Review*, 70, 705–15.

Esping-Andersen, G. (1990), *The Three Worlds of Welfare Capitalism*, London: Polity Press.

Evers, M., R. A. de Moij, and D. J. van Vuuren (2005), 'What Explains the Variation in Estimates of Labour Supply Elasticities?' CESifo Working Paper 1633.

Girouard, N. and C. André (2005), 'Measuring Cyclically-adjusted Budget Balances for OECD Countries', OECD Working Paper 434.

Knieser, T.J. and J.P. Ziliak (2002), 'Tax Reform and Automatic Stabilization', *American Economic Review* 92, 590–621.

Lindbeck, A. (1995), 'Hazardous Welfare State Dynamics', *American Economic Review*, Papers and Proceedings, May, 1995, 9–15.

Lindbeck, A., S. Nyberg, and J.W. Weibull (2003), 'Social Norms Welfare State Dynamics', *Journal of the European Economic Association*, 1, 533–42.

Ljungqvist, L. and T.J. Sargent (1995), 'The Swedish Unemployment Experience', *European Economic Review*, 39, 1043–70.

Ljungqvist, L., and T.J. Sargent (1998), 'The European Unemployment Dilemma', *Journal of Political Economy*, 106(3), 514–50.

Meghir, C., and D. Phillips (2008) 'Labour Supply and Taxes', *IZA Discussion paper 3405*.

Prescott, E.C. (2004), 'Why do Americans Work So Much More Than Europeans?', *Federal Reserve Bank of Minneapolis, Quarterly Review*, 28 (1), 2–13.

Rogerson, R. (2007), 'Taxation and Market Work: Is Scandinavia an Outlier?', *Economic Theory* 32, 59–85.

Sinn, H.-W. (1995), 'A Theory of the Welfare State', *Scandinavian Journal of Economics*, 97, 495–526.

Summers, L., J. Gruber, and R. Vergara (1993), 'Taxation and the Structure of Labor Markets: The Case of Corporatism', *Quarterly Journal of Economics* 108, 385–411.

Van der Noord, P. (2000), 'The Size and Role of Automatic Stabilizers in the 1990s and Beyond', OECD Working Paper 230.

Varian, H. (1980), 'Progressive Taxation as Social Insurance', *Journal of Public Economics*, 14, 49–68.

Vinod, T., Y. Wang, and F.X. Yan (2003), 'Measuring Education Inequality: Gini Coefficients of Education for 140 Countries (1960–2000)', *Journal of Educational Planning and Administration*. Volume XVII, Number 1, January 2003, New Delhi, India.

Comments on 'Collective Risk Sharing: The Social Safety Net and Employment' by Torben M. Andersen

Andreas Bergh

Torben M. Andersen describes clearly several reasons why countries with encompassing social safety nets need not necessarily suffer from large distortions that hamper employment and growth. Government can minimize the negative effects of high taxes by having a smart structure of benefits and transfers, thereby minimizing the disincentive effects on labour force participation and hours worked. The separation of disincentive effects and insurance effects of redistribution is particularly insightful. The exclusion of background variables such as social trust from the analysis, however, means that important perspectives are lost. In particular, the omission of trust has implications for Andersen's discussion of the efficiency–equity trade-off.

The idea that a line passing through Sweden and the USA (Andersen's Figure 2.1) can be thought of as the efficiency frontier representing the trade-off between efficiency (measured as real GDP per capita) and equity (measured using the Gini coefficient for the annual disposable income distribution) is provocative, interesting, and deserves to be discussed.

After noting that the correlation shown in the figure is actually positive—more equity tends to be associated with more efficiency—Andersen rightly suggests that this correlation should not be used to draw policy conclusions. The reason, he tells us, is that '[t]he data in the figure do not control for various background factors, convergence processes may be at play, and political inefficiencies may be a barrier to reach the efficiency frontier' (p. 28). Andersen goes on to do a data-envelopment analysis (DEA) estimating the best-practice frontier, illustrated by the aforementioned line.

I agree that the bivariate relationship in Figure 2.1 may be misleading if one does not consider the impact of important background factors that potentially creates a bias in the relationship illustrated by the scatter plot. Similarly, the omission of such an important background factor would also affect the interpretation of the DEA analysis.

In this case, the background factor that deserves explicit attention is social trust, a phenomenon typically measured using surveys that ask people if they agree with the statement that most people can be trusted. In a game-theoretic sense, social trust can be understood as a measure of people's beliefs on how agents they do not know will act in situations where they have an incentive to behave opportunistically. Recent research has convincingly shown that social trust has an economically important effect on the variables Andersen is discussing.

First of all, countries with higher social trust tend to have higher economic growth (Algan and Cahuc, 2010). Second, a link has also been established between social trust and welfare state size (Bergh and Bjørnskov, 2011). It should be noted that these papers claim to find that trust causes the outcome variables, and several other papers find similar results.

In line with the first finding, the countries with the lowest efficiency in figure 2.1 are indeed low-trust countries: Portugal (where 20% agree that most people can be trusted), Hungary (26%), and Slovenia (20%).[1] This observation is also consistent with a relatively flat efficiency–equity trade-off, at least for low-trust countries. The second finding means that social trust is important for the sustainability of the welfare state by helping countries to solve the social dilemma created by their welfare systems.

The two findings together have important implications: The comparison between Sweden and the USA is a comparison of a high-trust country with a medium-trust country. As a result, the efficiency–equity trade-off will appear less steep than it actually is. Put another way, Sweden is not the proper counterfactual when USA considers expanding the size of its redistributive sector. Similarly, USA may not be the proper counterfactual when Sweden considers increasing work incentives. When trust matters for both efficiency and equity, inference regarding the efficiency–equity trade-off should be based on cross-country evidence that controls for trust, or—even better—based on variation within countries over time.

On several occasions, however, Andersen discusses the efficiency–equity trade-off and refers to cross-country evidence that does not control for social trust. For example, Andersen describes Assar Lindbeck's hypothesis that endogenous norms create hazardous welfare-state dynamics. The implication of the hypothesis would be that substantial efficiency costs are associated

[1] Trust data are from Bergh and Bjørnskov (2011).

with welfare benefits, and thus a steeper efficiency–equity trade-off. Andersen dismisses the hypothesis by referring to the fact that countries with strong automatic stabilizers do not display stronger unemployment persistence than countries with more lean welfare states.

However, within-country evidence from Sweden (Ljunge, 2012) is very much in line with the Lindbeck hypothesis, and identifies behavioural responses to welfare state benefits that could undermine the long-term fiscal sustainability of the welfare state, resulting in a very steep efficiency–equity trade-off.

As a second example, Andersen mentions that is has been difficult to pin down a clear effect of the size of the public sector on the growth rate. This is true when one looks at all available cross-country evidence. Limiting focus, however, to studies of rich countries that measure total public sector size and use panel data with country-fixed effects, the typical result is a significant negative relationship, as shown in the survey by Bergh and Henrekson (2011). The key methodological issue here is country-fixed effects, which means that the association exists within each country when controlling for time-invariant background factors that matter for growth—such as social trust.

As an alternative to using cross-country comparisons, one could infer about the efficiency–equity trade-off from case studies of countries that have tried different policies. Sweden is a case in point. From around 1970 to 1995, Sweden was a country with a very large public sector by international standards, experiencing large problems concerning economic efficiency and economic growth. Many scholars would certainly agree that the efficiency problems were linked to at least some aspects of government size; in particular tax policy, benefit design, and macroeconomic policies.

In Bergh (2014), I argue that the recent period of relatively high economic growth in Sweden is plausibly a result of smarter and leaner government, illustrated partly by the fact that total tax revenue has decreased to 44% of GDP in 2013 compared to the all-time high of 52% of GDP (in 1987 but also in 2000, according to Statistics Sweden).

Returning to Figure 2.1, the crucial fact is that we have never seen how the USA would perform with tax revenue above 50% of GDP, as was the case for Sweden in the 1980s and still is the case in Denmark. Similarly, we do not know how a country with Nordic trust levels would perform with a public sector of US-size. As a second best we could draw the efficiency frontier between the USA and a country with similar trust levels and higher equity, such as Ireland (with trust at 39%, compared to the USA at 42%).

A central point in Andersen's chapter is that government can minimize the negative effects of big government by (among other things) having a smart structure of benefits and transfers, thereby also minimizing the disincentive effects on labour force participation and hours worked. But it is also true that most countries fail to do so consistently. In many cases, benefits create unearned incomes that worsen the disincentive created by the taxation needed for financing the benefit. The strikingly high levels of inefficiency in Figure 2.1 illustrate that there is substantial political failure in most countries. Understanding the background factors that explain the large inefficiencies in most countries is not only necessary to correctly identify the slope of the efficiency frontier: it is an important question in itself.

References

Algan, Y. and Cahuc, P. (2010), 'Inherited Trust and Growth', *American Economic Review, 100* (December 2010), 2060–92.

Bergh, A. (2014), *Sweden and the revival of the capitalist welfare state*: Edward Elgar.

Bergh, A. and Bjørnskov, C. (2011), 'Historical trust levels predict the current size of the welfare state', *Kyklos, 64*, 1–19.

Bergh, A. and Henrekson, M. (2011), 'Government Size and Growth: a Survey and Interpretation of the Evidence', *Journal of Economic Surveys, 25*, 872–97.

Ljunge, M. (2012), 'The Spirit of the Welfare State? Adaptation in the Demand for Social Insurance', *Journal of Human Capital, 6*, 187–223.

3

Missing the Link?

On the Political Economy of Nordic Egalitarianism*

Erling Barth and Karl Ove Moene

3.1 Introduction

Is Nordic equality the result of egalitarian preferences and homogenous populations? We believe not. Nordic equality is in our view a result of special institutions rather than special populations. If other countries had Nordic institutions, and in particular Nordic labour market institutions, they would have had similar egalitarian outcomes. Yet, many observers miss the link between redistribution of gross earnings in the labour market and the final distribution of disposable income. They overlook how coordinated wage negotiations lead to small wage differentials and a high average wage, fueling the support for further redistribution via generous welfare benefits. In this short essay we emphasize this missing link for three reasons.

First, we want to make clear how the link associates equality with exposure to international competition. The main coalition that has supported the link from the 1930s till today consists of unions and employers in traded-goods industries.

Second, we argue that the link is highly relevant. In fact it must be considered decisive for the political economic equilibrium of Nordic equality. It ties equality of disposable income to wage compression both directly, as wage compression determines the gross earnings distribution, and indirectly, as it raises the political support for redistribution in the welfare state (Moene and Wallerstein, 2001, 2003). In addition come two important feedbacks: one, where higher average wages help sustain the willingness of unions to accept wage coordination

* This article is part of the research at ESOP at Department of Economics, University of Oslo in collaboration with the Institute for Social Research, Oslo (NFR project #199836). ESOP is a research center financed by the Research Council of Norway (179552/v10).

with compression; and another, where a generous welfare state empowers weak groups in the labour market leading to ore wage compression from below (Barth and Moene, 2009; Barth, Moene, and Willumsen, 2014).

Third, we expect that the link may be missing in the future. Having argued that it is necessary for Nordic style equality, we discuss how structural change reduces the number of workers employed in traded-goods industries, weakening the export-led coalition. More labour-saving technical change in commodity production than in service provision (the Baumol effect) may in addition be mirrored by diminishing power to exporting sectors relative to non-tradablesectors. Declining employment in the export sector changes the power inside the union movement and the employer associations, and in politics more generally. All this can threaten the institutional equilibrium. If this occurs, Nordic style equality may paradoxically become less distinct as *less* of the workforce is exposed to international competition.

As we proceed we try to make the mechanism of the missing link clear by addressing some possible objections that may be raised against its importance.

3.2 Which Link Missing—Institutions or Populations?

How do we know that institutions, rather than homogenous populations, are responsible for Nordic equality? How do we know that it is not a peaceful and consensual population with an extraordinary commitment to equality that explains it all? How do we know that the Nordics were not born egalitarians, but rather became egalitarians under new institutions? There are several indications that institutions matter the most. The first is based on observations in the lab.

3.2.1 *Fairness in the Lab*

Compared with other countries one might think that the Nordic population has stronger preferences for equality; that egalitarian fairness norms dominate. Controlled experiments, however, do not provide much support for this. On the contrary citizens in equally rich countries seem to have similar fairness norms even though the inequality within these countries may differ.

For instance, in an international lab experiment of fairness norms (Cappelen, Moene, Sørensen, and Tungodden, 2013) Norway does not appear exceptional at all. The experiment was carried out simultaneously in four countries. Participants from two of the world's richest countries—Norway and Germany—were compared directly with participants in two of the world's poorest countries—Uganda and Tanzania. Each of them first performed a work task and was then invited to share the work revenue in one-way or another in pair-wise connections. Different moral motives come into play. Based on the observed behaviour the authors here estimate the social preferences, emphasizing how people make trade-offs between entitlements, needs, and self-interest.

Participants assigned great importance to individual contributions in their distributive choices. For our hypothesis the similarity between participants across equally rich countries is assuring. Germany is almost as rich as Norway, but otherwise different in many ways. Yet, in the experiment there is no significant difference in the behaviour of Norwegians and the Germans towards other Norwegians and Germans, and between the behaviour of Norwegians and the Germans towards participants in the two African countries. Both Germans and Norwegians are also alike in the sense that they compensate the Africans somewhat for their lack of basic needs fulfillment.

Merging the observations into two groups, the Europeans and the Africans, it is possible to estimate the share of different fairness norms that prevail in the two populations. While the share of egalitarians is estimated at 45% in Africa, it is only 22% in Europe. While the share of meritocrats is 43% in Europe it is only 27% in Africa. Thus the experiment shows that there seems to be little connection between preferences for egalitarian outcomes and the actual income distribution in the country. Europe has more egalitarian income distributions in spite of weaker social preferences for equality per se. The reason why Europe nevertheless has more equality is an indication of the decisive role of institutions, we believe, including of course educational institutions. Both Uganda and Tanzania are more heterogeneous than European countries. Could not the explanation for Nordic equality simply be a high degree of homogeneity in the population?

To learn more, the large difference in inequality between the small homogeneous Nordic countries and the large and heterogeneous United States is a case to explore.

3.2.2 *Strangers in Paradise*

It would be highly misleading just to compare the Nordic countries with the United States. We can learn more about national characteristics and perhaps about the role of institutions by observing how Nordic immigrants to the US do relative to the US population, and how American immigrants to the Nordic countries do relative to the Nordic population.

This is exactly what Björklund and Freeman (1997) have done in the case of Sweden. They developed a refined counterfactual to assess the effects of Sweden's supposedly homogeneous population as opposed to its income-determination system on distributional outcomes. Lacking randomized trials, the best they could do was to contrast the income of people of Swedish descent in the United States with that of people in Sweden and the income in Sweden of Swedes with non-Swedish ancestry with that of Swedes with Swedish-born parents.

They find strong indications that Sweden achieved its egalitarian income distribution largely because of its system of earnings and income determination—its institutions. They conclude that 'the narrow income distribution in Sweden cannot be attributed to an exceptionally homogeneous population: the descendants of Swedes in the United States exhibit as much inequality and poverty as do other Americans, while people of foreign ancestry in Sweden have an income distribution comparable to those of Swedish parentage' (Björklund and Freeman, 1997).

In fact, Swedes in the US look like Americans and non-Swedes in Sweden look like Swedes. This is clear from the numbers. Focusing on the 9th to the 1st decile measure of inequality of hourly earnings (in 1989–91), the inequality of Swedes in Sweden is 2.02, while the inequality of non-Swedes in Sweden is 2.09 and that of non-Nordics in Sweden 1.85. Similarly, the inequality in the US is 5.53, while the inequality among those groups with any Swedish ancestry is 5.59 and those groups with only Swedish ancestry is 5.05. This observation rejects the idea that the more compressed wage structure of the Nordic countries is due to a more homogeneous population, suggesting a strong influence of institutions on the earnings distribution, leading to an American inequality between Swedes in the US and a Scandinavian inequality between Americans in Sweden.

One may assert that the differences in productivity within the group of Swedes in the US and within the group of Swedes in Sweden are similar. If so the numbers indicate that the US institutions magnify these differences into much larger differences in earnings. Similarly, institutions in Sweden mitigate the productivity differences among immigrating Americans to much smaller differences in earnings.

If correct, this just underlines the importance of established institutions. Clearly, it does not prove that Nordic equality cannot be related to Nordic preferences in other ways. Social preferences for equality can of course lie behind the choice of institutions in the Nordic countries. The most important institution of wage compression is the arrangement that takes wages out of market competition and places them in a system of collective decision-making. How was this arrangement established? Was the intention to achieve an egalitarian wage distribution in line with people's preferences? Or were the egalitarian outcomes more unintended?

3.2.3 *New Labour Market Institutions*

The Nordic variant of collective wage-setting was established in the 1930s and formalized in the 1950s under the name of solidarity negotiations (in Sweden and Norway). It involves a mixture of non-cooperative (perhaps competitive) actions and cooperative actions, based on binding agreements. Each big coalition, be it an association, a bargaining unit, or a collection of workers and employers, may agree internally and then play non-cooperatively towards other coalitions. To grasp the missing link we have to understand which equilibrium partition of unions and employers into coalitions is likely to emerge at the intermediate level between complete decentralization in the labour market or complete centralization.

What was the situation in the 1930s, when wage coordination started? Workers who produced for the domestic market were better protected against the collapse in the world market than other workers. These unions, sheltered from international competition, could also be militant. In Sweden and Norway at least, coordinated wage-setting came as a result of a conflict between groups of workers. The strongest union, the metal workers, had most of its members employed in the export sector. They had to take considerable wage cuts in the 1930s to keep their jobs. Workers in non-tradable sectors came under no such pressure. The metal workers were of course afraid that militant unions in the non-tradable sector might increase their wages, implying higher living costs for all. Therefore, the metal workers wanted to control the wages in the non-tradable sector, in particular the wages of construction workers. This was perhaps an action put forward out of solidarity with other workers exposed to foreign competition, but it was also an action in accordance with the narrow self-interests of the metal workers as a group. In any case, their attempts were supported by the employers who always wanted to control wages of militant unions.

Thus, the political coalition that prevailed in the 1950s and established the pattern of coordinated centralized bargaining was comprised of export-oriented unions and employers. High-wage unions in sheltered sectors were prevented from leaving the centralized negotiations by the threat of lockouts. It is unlikely that the low-wage unions and the leadership of the union confederation would have been able to force the high-wage unions to accept an egalitarian wage policy without the backing of employers and the threat of lockouts against recalcitrant unions.

What did the different groups achieve from cooperation? In theory, one might think that if anything near full cooperation emerged, everybody would have obtained at least what he could have achieved alone. Sheltered workers should therefore have obtained at least what they could get in a decentralized system. But this is not so. If another coalition can benefit from blocking decentralization simply by acting together, the outcomes under decentralization have no relevance. This is exactly what happened at the rise of the export-led coalition in the 1930s. Workers sheltered from foreign competition lost out, even though they were among the workers who would have been best off within the old type of wage setting. The distribution of power was changed with the strength of the new export-led coalition.

Based on implicit lock-out threats from employers, the bargaining power of workers in non-tradable sectors was reduced. In practice this meant that the sheltered union followed the pattern of negotiated wages in exporting industries. Interestingly, the 'solution' to the conflicts of interests within the union movement implies class collaboration and implicit threats against the most sheltered workers. As this form of wage coordination reduced the power of workers in the non-tradable sectors to capture monopoly gains in the labour market, the coordination led to a more compressed wage structure. Collective wage coordination leads to smaller wage differentials for other reasons, too.

3.2.4 *Big Institutions for Small Differences*

How does coordinated wage-setting work?[1]

It gives power to large groups: In contrast to non-union labour markets, which are shaped by the preferences and outside options of the most mobile workers whom employers are trying to attract or retain, coordinated collective bargaining is closer to a median voter in elections for union leadership or contract ratification. Thus a mean preserving reduction in wage inequality, which raises the pay received by the median wage earner and all other workers below the mean, would obtain majority support inside the union association given the positively skewed shape of the wage distribution. It alters the influence of different groups, allocating more power to large groups of low-paid workers. Even though the median voter analogy is not perfect, it illustrates how wage coordination changes the distribution of power. Low-paid groups are numerous and can thus exert a high influence in collective decision-making.

It coordinates complementary inputs: In general coordination between complements implies wage moderation (internalization of negative employment effects), while coordination among substitutes implies aggression (all competitors act together). Collective wage coordination of the Nordic type implies that the coordination among workers take place across unions organizing workers who are complements in production, leading to wage moderation among the better paid. Similarly on the employer side: wage coordination across firms and sectors is for them coordination among units that are each others' substitutes, making employers more aggressive in *reducing* wasteful wage premiums.

It implements fairness norms broadly: Wage coordination determines how encompassing the groups are over which fairness norms are applied. The coordination of wage-setting may have a large impact of how existing fairness norms are implemented. In decentralized bargaining, the norm of equal sharing results in a wage structure that depends on the workers' usefulness

[1] See Moene and Wallerstein, 1993, 1997, and Wallerstein, 1999 for more elaborate discussions.

to the firm. With a coordinated wage-setting the same norm of equal sharing results in a pay that depends on the importance of the work force as a whole and its outside opportunities as a group. The larger the fraction of workers who are considered as a group, the more egalitarian the potential of equal sharing rules. When wages are set at the national level, collective bargaining compresses the distribution of wages across firms, industries, and occupations throughout the entire nation. More coordination is associated with less wage inequality.

It involves arguing rather than bargaining: When wages are taken out of local competition worker–employer bargaining is to some extent replaced by worker–worker arguing where it is difficult to utilize the same type of industrial actions as in worker–employer bargaining. This strengthens the power of weak groups. To form a union of workers with different productivity levels implies that the union bargains on behalf of its members who in turn must have a way to distribute the total union rent between themselves.

It alters the pattern of conflicts: Taking wages out of market competition means that unions and employers in practice have a stronger influence on relative wages than on the functional distribution of wages and profits (Wallerstein, 1999, Freeman and Kleiner, 1990, Card, 2001, and Moene and Wallerstein, 1997). It also reduces the incidence of strikes and lock-outs.

3.2.5 *Unexpected Support*

One would think that institutions that increase the power of large groups of workers and at the same time tend to compress wages would meet strong opposition from employers and high-wage earners. It turns out, however, that the model has received implicit support from unexpected sources. The reason likely is that there are gains from coordination to be reaped for more groups than low-wage earners:

It may raise profits: A wage policy that moderates the wages of the high-wage earners and raises that of the low-wage earners may raise profits, as long as employment is kept at a high level, and average wages are adjusted to maintain international competitiveness. In models with heterogeneous firms and homogeneous workers, wage differentials arise because of local rent sharing. Wage compression is then efficiency-enhancing. In models with heterogeneous firms and heterogeneous workers, wage differentials may also arise from competition among firms to obtain more skilled workers. Therefore, even wage differences associated with decentralized wage-setting may be efficient, but also unfair in the sense that the wage distribution is more unequal than the distribution of workers' productivity as firms pay differentials between high- and low-skilled workers that exceed differences in workers' abilities. Compressing wages somewhat would then distort allocation efficiency, but in all cases mentioned above it would increase profits and investments (Moene and Wallerstein, 1997; and Barth, Moene, and Willumsen, 2013). That employers may gain from wage compression is important in understanding the history of wage coordination. Centralized wage coordination was created with active support from employers' associations.

It may raise average income: Reducing the differentials, while maintaining full employment, means that the expected wage costs over the lifetime of new innovations and investments decline. Thus as long as the average wage is kept low enough to clear the labour market, wage compression increases both profits and investments. Higher investments increase the demand for labour, making it possible to raise the pay to low-skilled workers without creating unemployment. As more jobs are created in each vintage, workers become more concentrated in high-productivity enterprises and industries (Barth, Moene, and Willumsen, 2013).

It may raise the average wage: The average wage goes up with more wage restraint at the same time as the expected wage costs for each investment project decline. The explanation is simple: more creative destruction, induced by lower expected wage costs, moves a larger share of the workforce to more productive enterprises, thereby raising average wages. In short, wage compression fuels capitalist investments in the process of creative destruction, increasing the average productivity and the average wage for a constant employment level.

It may benefit skilled workers as well: The higher concentration of workers in more productive workplaces implies that the wages of high-skilled workers can be higher than they would have been without wage restraint, as wage restraint implies that more of the high-skilled workers become employed in more modern firms with higher productivity.

In sum: the missing link redistributes earnings before taxes and transfers. As a consequence, perhaps, one would then expect less redistribution via the welfare state since much of what one wanted to achieve is done prior to welfare spending. Is this so? And, in any case what is the point of redistributing in the labour market before one redistributes via the welfare state? In other words:

3.2.6 *Why Redistribute Twice?*

Consider a system of double redistribution. It has two rounds of voting over the distribution of disposable income. Imagine that each group and each individual have the same power in the second as in the first round of redistribution. Imagine also that the costs and benefits of any redistribution in the second round are just the same as in the first round. Now, if these two restrictive assumptions hold, the second round of redistribution may change nothing. Or, expressed differently, the first round—what we term the missing link of Nordic equality—contributes nothing to the final distribution of disposable income. Any redistribution in the first round would have been done anyway in the second round.

In the Nordic context, however, double redistribution means a first round of wage determination by collective decision-making and a second round based on voting in elections. Even a highly stylized representation of this variant of double redistribution would not satisfy the restrictive assumptions—for several reasons.

The power is not the same. As stated, redistribution in the labour market may give most power to large groups. Since there are a lot of workers just below the mean wage and as long as numbers count in collective decisions, collective wage determination favors groups below the mean. Numbers also count in elections, but if anything the bias in elections benefits more the richer than the poorer groups as long as the political influence is correlated with income via campaign contributions and media access.

The trade-offs are not the same. It is also clear that the efficiency loss of altering the wage distribution in the labour market is similar to the potential dead weight cost of taxation. Yet, they are far from identical. While one can have an individual treatment of different groups in the labour market, one has to apply the same principle to everybody in the tax system.

The provisions are not the same. While redistribution in the labour market is about pay and income only, redistribution in the welfare state is more about services and pay. Thus the welfare state does not just take from the rich and give to the poor. Rather the welfare state provides services that the market, perhaps, does not provide equally efficiently, or maybe not at all. Most of the services the welfare state provides are related to insurance against risk (see eg Barr, 1992) such as health services, and unemployment and disability benefits.

Of the three reasons highlighted, the last may be the most important to expand on.

3.2.7 *Redistribution by Service Provision*

On the cost side, the provisions of the welfare state are offered on redistributive terms where the rich pay more than the poor in the form of taxes. On the benefit side, poorer voters are normally more exposed to risks of income loss and are therefore more vulnerable. For a given exposure to risks, the political demand for welfare state services depends positively on individual incomes in addition to the average income of the country. Thus peoples' demands for services are shaped by their labour market incomes.

There are good reasons to consider most of what the welfare state provides as normal goods. This means that the political demand for welfare spending rises with income. Accordingly, those workers who are favoured by the redistribution in the labour market will also increase their political demand for redistributive welfare provisions by the welfare state. This mechanism of political reinforcement means that less earnings inequality in the labour market gives us even further redistribution in the welfare state. Welfare spending reinforces the distributional changes in the labour market.

This is why the missing link is so decisive. For instance, a mean preserving compression of wages raises voters' support for welfare spending as a majority of workers obtain higher wages. An increase in mean income also increases voters' support for welfare spending. Conversely, higher wage inequality for a given mean should reduce the political support to the welfare state, and economic growth in the welfare support of party platforms.

Do we see this in practice? We have estimated the effects of wage compression in the labour market on the implemented generosity of the welfare state in 18 OECD countries in the period 1976 to 2002 (Barth and Moene, 2009). For instance, a change in wage coordination from the high level in Sweden to the low level of the UK has a direct negative effect on the demand for welfare generosity of 5.3%, which again feeds back to wage inequality as it supports weak groups in the labour market. The end result, taking all feedbacks into account, is an increase in wage inequality of 12.6% and a drop in welfare generosity by 8.1%.

This effect mimics the effect of any exogenous change in wage inequality that would imply 8.3% higher inequality. Examples of such changes could be skill-biased technological change or changes in the direction of more performance-related pay within firms. Again the end result is an increase in wage inequality of 12.6% and a drop in welfare generosity by 8.1%.

Together with Henning Finseraas, we have also estimated the impact of the missing link on party positions on the welfare state issues obtained from the Comparative Manifesto Project data set (Barth, Finseraas, and Moene 2014). Again we find a clear indication of the importance of the missing link, in particular for the left-wing parties in the OECD. Wage compression means that left-wing parties move to the left. More wage equality implies more support for welfare spending.

Economic growth for given level of inequality further stimulates political support to welfare spending. Higher affluence shifts the centre of political gravity towards more welfare spending. As stated, when voters become richer they have more to lose if their income is lost, and they value the extra tax cost less.

Since there is an effect of the corresponding changes in inequality, the total estimated effects of higher income depend on who gets it. If the economic growth is distributed to high-wage groups only (the rich get richer), the effect is weaker than if the growth is mainly distributed to low wage groups. In the latter case the effects of higher average incomes are enhanced by the positive effect of lower inequality. The relationship between wage inequality and economic growth and the political support for the welfare state provides the missing link between institutions in the labour market and the overall generosity of the welfare state (Barth, Finseraas, and Moene, 2014).

3.3 Links Get Missed—High-Productivity Trouble

The export-led coalition that established coordinated wage bargaining in Scandinavia has prevailed for at least sixty years. It has remained stable through shifting governments and shifting political fashions. Recently, however, there have been more tensions in the system than there used to be. This is particularly evident in Norway, where both unions and some employers complain that a group comprising too few workers decides much of the pattern of wage increases for the entire workforce.

These complaints are also related to the dissatisfaction with what are considered the rising costs of the welfare state. The two aspects are likely to have a common cause that might break the essential link to Nordic equality; a link that therefore might be missing in the future.

The potential common cause is structural change caused by productivity growth in the process of creative destruction. As commodity production is much easier to mechanize than service provision, and since the rate of wage growth must be on average the same in all sectors, public provision of welfare services is bound to appear relatively more expensive than private provision of commodities (the Baumol effect). The process creates an impression of declining productivity in the public sector because of the rising productivity in the private sector.

All in all it may lead to the paradox of welfare: the very forces that make the countries richer seem to undermine the ability of the country to finance its welfare provision. The willingness to finance public provision of welfare services is weakened by an increasing ability to finance the provision. We may want to have more services when we become richer, but once we become richer these services appear to be more costly for exactly the same reason that makes us demand more of them.

Like all paradoxes, this one does not have a simple solution. Higher incomes for constant relative prices between public and private goods lead to higher demand for welfare. But relative prices are not constant. Thus voters who become richer may be driven to reduce welfare spending because they perceive that the costs of welfare spending rise when private commodities in reality become cheaper.

Another consequence of the same trends is that an increasing share of the workforce ends in service provision within the welfare state. Thus mechanization implies that more workers become sheltered against direct competition on the world market, making the social forces that back coordinated wage-setting weaker. This may undermine the social conditions for political economic equilibrium since the missing link of wage coordination has been dependent on the organizational strength the export-led coalition. The question is now whether it is equally easy to maintain the system as long as export-led unions are no longer in a majority in the union movement, and as long as the need for international competitiveness is no longer high on the political agenda.

If this is so, one may wonder whether the process of creative destruction with a narrow earnings distribution and a high exposure to international competition will undermine its own achievements. If small wage differentials disciplined by international competitiveness have stimulated the path of creative destruction by a faster elimination of backward technologies and a broader-scale application of modern technologies, high-productivity growth might undermine part of the basis of this development. Nordic equality may be considered a victim of its own productivity success, producing its own slayers in the form of a higher share of sheltered workers.

3.3.1 *The Broad Empirical Picture*

To illustrate the empirical relevance of some of the features emphasized, we draw on data we have collected for a research project with the working title 'Baumol under the northern light', alluded to above. What are the empirical magnitudes of the mechanisms that we have just sketched out? Here we outline part of the empirical pattern that we plan to explore further.

(i) *Manufacturing in decline.* The process of creative destruction is enhanced by the wage compression of coordinated bargaining. Still, there are differences in the scope of innovation and productivity growth across sectors. Figure 3.1 illustrates the differential development of labour productivity with data from the OECD productivity database. The solid lines show the development of labour productivity in manufacturing, exemplified by machinery and equipment manufacturing; the long dashed lines in hotels and restaurants; and the short dashed lines in business services. The large difference between manufacturing and services is particularly pronounced for Finland and Sweden.

Figure 3.2 shows productivity growth in the public sector, as reported by the Danish Productivity Commission. From the year 2000 productivity, using output-based measures, grew by 40% in health, 20% in social services, and

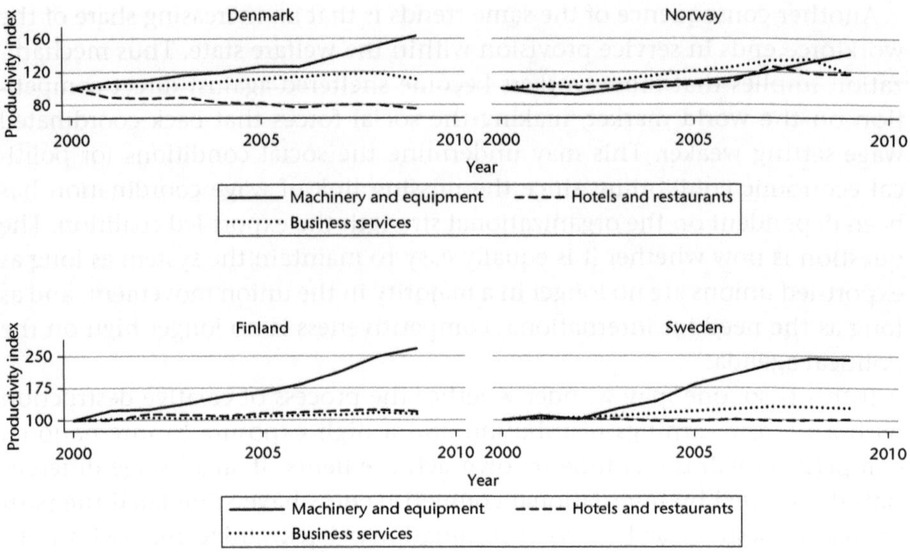

Figure 3.1. Labour productivity by sector

Note: 2000 = 100. Labour productivity indexes calculated from yearly observations of percentage growth reported by the OECD productivity database (see Appendix).

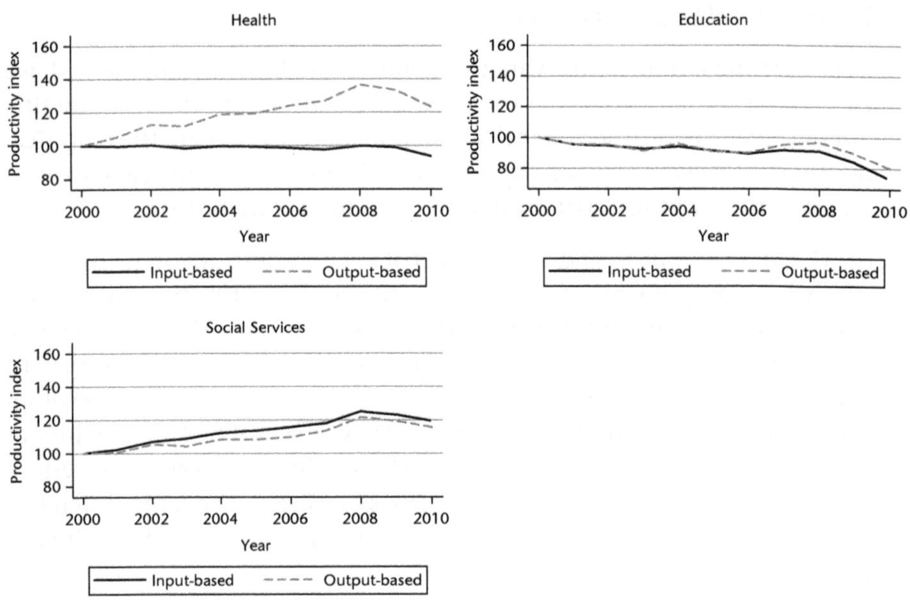

Figure 3.2. Productivity in the public sector

Source: Danish Productivity Commission (see Appendix).

declined in education. Even though it is difficult to measure productivity in the public sector, the figures clearly suggest that productivity growth has also been slower in the publicly provided services, compared to the 60% growth in Danish manufacturing.

(ii) *The vanishing blue-collar workers and their unions.* One important consequence of this differential development is a decline in manufacturing employment, which is thus in heavy decline, mostly driven by the process of creative destruction. This development changes the relative bargaining power of different unions. Even though the Nordic countries have high and relatively stable union membership rates, the composition of union members is changing, simply as a consequence of declining manufacturing employment.

Unions in the manufacturing sectors represent the key interests of workers who produce for the international export markets. This is a cornerstone of Nordic wage coordination, as pattern bargaining and coordination on wage growth constitute crucial links in the Nordic system. As the relative strength of workers in sectors that are sheltered from international competition increases, these links are weakened. Figure 3.3 shows both manufacturing employment and union membership as percentages of the labour force. The

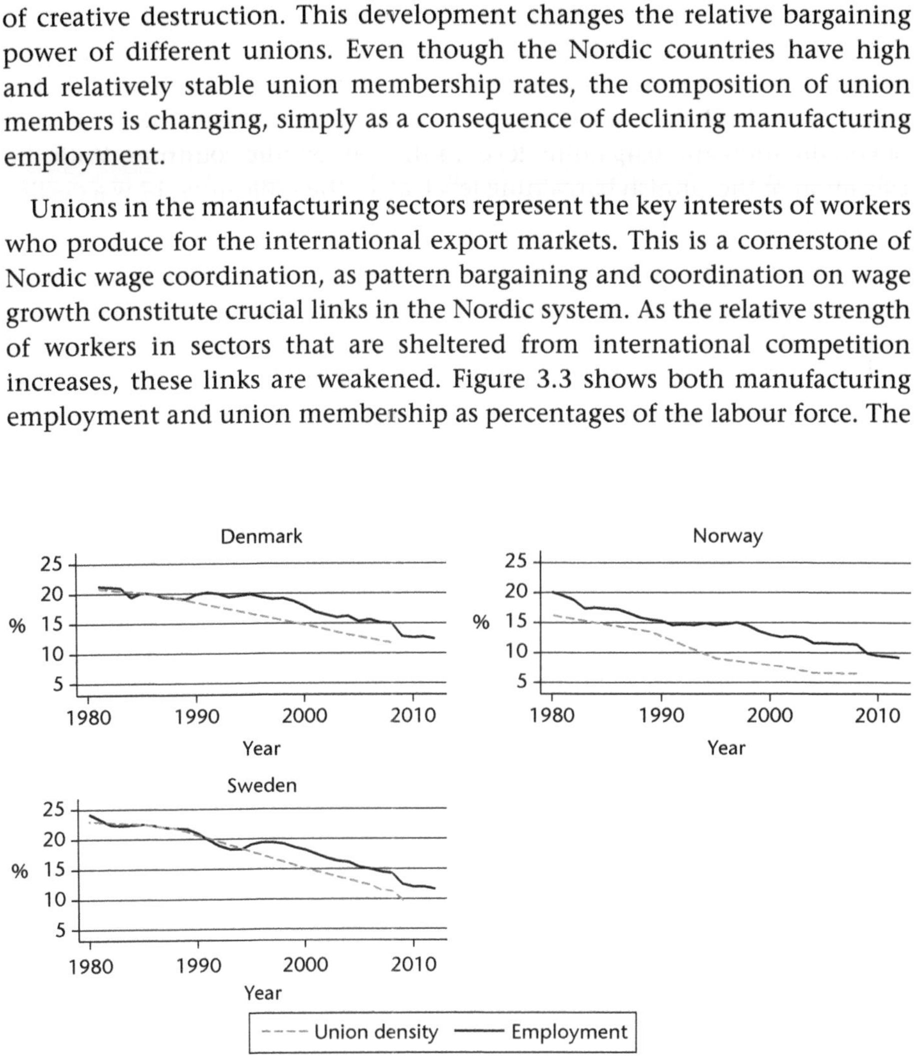

Figure 3.3. Manufacturing employment and union members

Note: Both series as percentages of labour force. The union density line is smoother than the employment line because it is based on less frequent observations.

Source: ICTWSS database (see Appendix).

figure clearly shows the diminishing role of manufacturing union members over time.

In Norway, the part of the labour force that is made up by manufacturing union members drops to 5%, and in Denmark and Sweden it drops to 10%. The declining role of manufacturing unions is thus not due to shrinking membership. Rather it results from deep structural changes eroding manufacturing employment through the process of creative destruction.

(iii) *Less coordination in wage-setting and increasing wage inequality*. The shrinking role of manufacturing may lead to a decline in wage coordination and in a diminished role for pattern bargaining. Figure 3.4 shows measures of coordination and bargaining level in the four Nordic countries. With the exception of the Finnish bargaining level, all of the indicators show a declining pattern.

All in all, these are institutional changes which we would expect to increase wage inequality. In Figure 3.5 we see that wage inequality has been on the rise in all the Nordic countries, particularly after the early 1990s and for the upper part of the wage distribution. Of course, there has been a similar development across many OECD countries, and it may be too early to tease out the exact role of changes in the bargaining systems

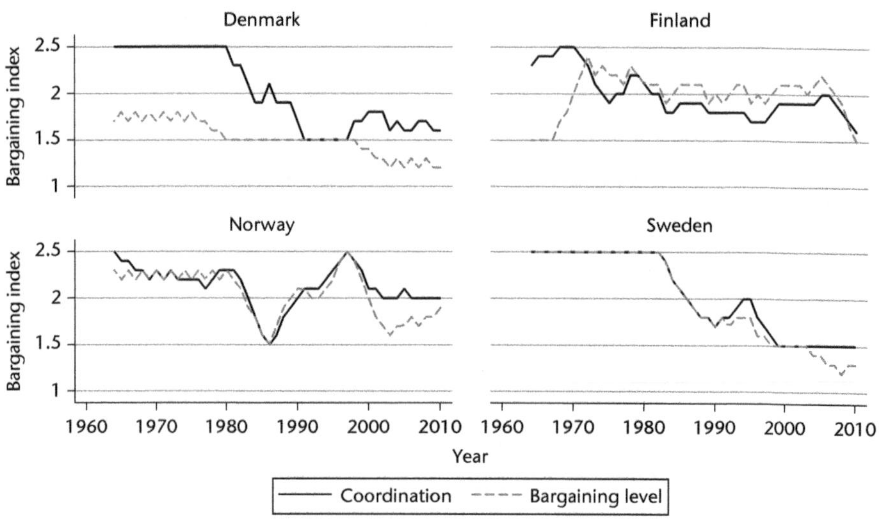

Figure 3.4. Wage bargaining coordination

Note: Coordination is an index of coordination among unions and employers' associations, whereas Level is an index of the bargaining level. Both variables are calculated as the average over the last five years.

Source: ICTWSS (see Appendix).

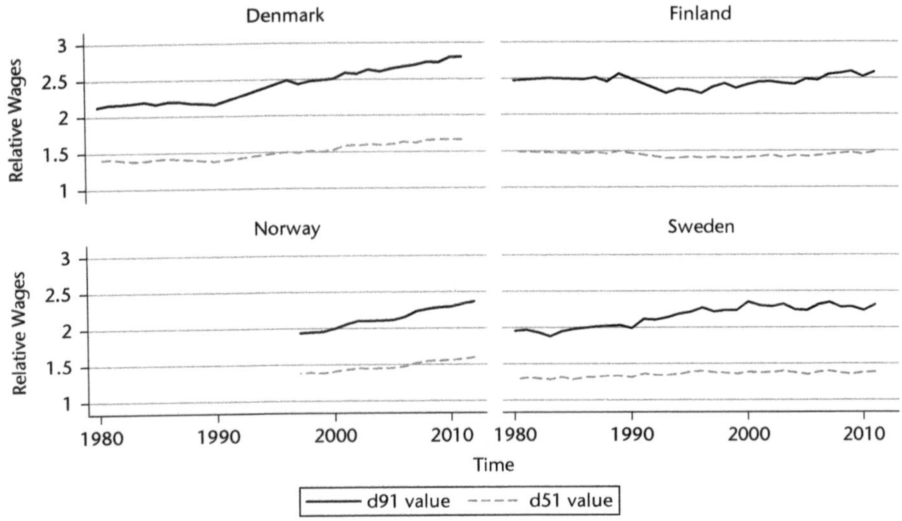

Figure 3.5. Wage inequality

Note: d91 and d51 measures the ratio of the upper decile wages to the wage level of decile 1.

Source: OECD earnings database (see Appendix).

for the recent rise in inequality. Yet, in addition to a direct effect, it also seems fair to assert that these institutional changes may have facilitated the transmission of the same inequality-increasing mechanisms into the Nordic economies as well.

(iv) *Declining welfare generosity*. With the exception of Norway, welfare generosity has been declining in all the Nordic countries over recent decades (see Figure 3.6) where generosity of the welfare state is measured by the overall generosity index provided in the Comparative Welfare Entitlements Dataset.[2] As we have argued, two forces are working for a retrenchment in welfare generosity. The first is increased wage inequality, as we illustrated in Figure 3.5, leading to less demand for welfare generosity by a majority of the voters. The other is the differential in productivity growth between goods provision and the provision of welfare services, as illustrated in Figures 3.1 and 3.2, leading to a change in relative prices. These two mechanisms tend to work against the effect of raising average income on welfare spending, and seem to have dominated the growth effect at least for three of the four countries. Thus over

[2] See Appendix. The index records the generosity of income support in case of illness, unemployment, and/or disability and for old-age pensions of each country for each year. Generosity is constructed by using the replacement ratio, coverage, entitlements, and timing of different schemes, in addition to other scheme features.

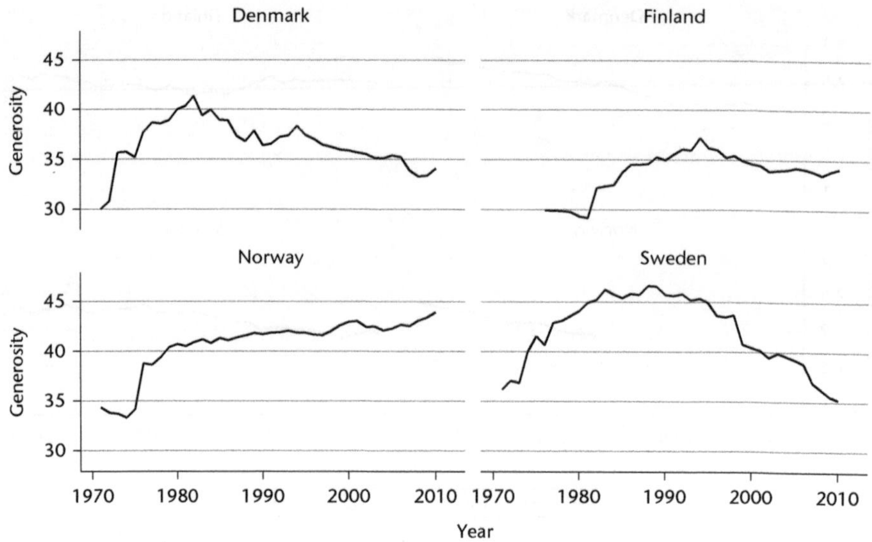

Figure 3.6. Welfare generosity

Note: Welfare generosity is measured by the index developed by Lyle Scruggs, University of Connecticut (see Appendix).

the last couple of decades we have experienced a retrenchment in welfare spending even in Nordic countries.

3.4 Conclusion

This chapter has highlighted three interrelated points.

First, to visualize how Nordic exceptionalism is caused by special institutional arrangements rather than special people one needs to explore how global competition, small wage differentials, large welfare states, and strong capitalist dynamics fit together, constituting a political economic equilibrium.

Second, the final outcome, an extraordinarily low level of inequality in living conditions as measured by the distribution of disposable income in the population, is produced by first compressing the distribution of gross earnings, which in turn generates the political support for generous welfare spending. In this repeated process an essential link, which many observers miss, is the way wages are taken out of market competition and placed into a system of collective decision-making.

Third, this important link may become weaker as Nordic equality seems to become a victim of its own productivity success. Mechanization leads to the paradox of welfare where the willingness to fund the welfare state goes down as the ability to do so goes up. At the same time, and for similar reasons, organized interests become more and more sheltered against global competition. Wage differentials can then become higher and the welfare state smaller because the system does not reproduce its social preconditions.

Appendix: Data Sources

ICTWSS; Database on Institutional Characteristics of Trade Unions, Wage Setting, State Intervention, and Social Pacts, 1960–2011, Jelle Visser, Amsterdam Institute for Advanced Labour Studies AIAS, University of Amsterdam, Version 4.0, April 2013. <http://www.uva-aias.net/208>.

The Comparative Welfare Entitlements Dataset is constructed by Lyle Scruggs at the University of Connecticut. The construction of the index is described in Scruggs (2004, 2007). The dataset is available at <http://sp.uconn.edu/scruggs/wp.htm>.

Danish Productivity Commission on productivity in the public sector: <http://produktivitetskommissionen.dk/media/135939/Baggrundsrapport-om-måling-i-den-offentlige-sektor.pdf>.

OECD Productivity Statistics; OECD iLibrary: <http://www.oecd-ilibrary.org/economics/data/oecd-productivity-statistics>.

OECD earnings database, <http://www.oecd-ilibrary.org/employment/data/earnings-lfs-ear-data-en>.

References

Barr, Nicholas (1992), 'Economic Theory and the Welfare State: A Survey and Interpretation' *Journal of Economic Literature*, vol. 30: 741–803.

Barth, Erling and Karl O. Moene (2009), 'The Equality Multiplier,' NBER Working paper No.1506, Cambridge, MA, June 2009. A revised version is available as 'The Equality Multiplier: How Wage Setting and Welfare Spending Make Similar Countries Diverge' *IZA Discussion Paper 6494*, 2012.

Barth, Erling, Henning Finseraas, and Karl O. Moene (2014), 'Political Reinforcement: How Rising Inequality Curbs Manifeted Welfare Generosity', forthcoming in *American Journal of Political Science*.

Barth, Erling, Karl O. Moene, and Fredrik Willumsen (2014), 'The Scandinavian Model—an Interpretation', forthcoming in *Journal of Public Economics*.

Björklund, A. and R.B. Freeman (1997). 'Generating Equality and Eliminating Poverty, the Swedish Way'. In Freeman, R.B., R.H. Topel, and B. Swedenborg (1997), *The Welfare State in Transition: Reforming the Swedish Model*. Chicago: National Bureau of Economic Research, Inc.

Cappelen, Alexander W., Karl O. Moene, Erik O. Sørensen, and Bertil Tungodden (2013), 'Needs vs Entitlements—an International Fairness Experiment', *Journal of European Economic Association*, vol. 11 (3), 574–98.

Card, David (2001), 'The Effect of Unions on Wage Inequality in the U.S. Labor Market', *Industrial and Labor Relations Review*, Cornell University, ILR School, vol. 54 (2), 296–315, January.

Freeman, Richard B. and Kleiner, Morris M. (1990), 'The Impact of New Unionization on Wages and Working Conditions', *Journal of Labor Economics*, University of Chicago Press, vol. 8 (1), S8–25, January.

Moene, Karl Ove and Michael Wallerstein (1993), 'Bargaining Structure and Economic Performance', in Robert J. Flanagan, Karl Ove Moene, and Michael Wallerstein (eds) *Trade Union Behaviour, Pay Bargaining, and Economic Performance*, Oxford: Clarendon Press.

Moene, Karl O. and Michael Wallerstein (1997), 'Pay Inequality', *Journal of Labor Economics*, University of Chicago Press, vol. 15 (3), 403–30, July.

Moene, Karl O. and Michael Wallerstein (2001), 'Inequality, Social Insurance, and Redistribution', *American Political Science Review*, vol. 95 (4): 859–74.

Moene, Karl O. and Michael Wallerstein (2003), 'Earnings Inequality and Welfare Spending: a Disaggregated Analysis', *World Politics*, vol. 55 (4): 485–516.

Scruggs, Lyle (2007), 'Welfare State Decommodification in Time and Space', in Nico Siegal and Jochen Classen, (eds) *Welfare Reform in Advanced Societies: the Dependent Variable Problem in Comparative Welfare State Analysis*. Cheltenham: Edward Elgar, 133–65.

Wallerstein, Michael (1999), 'Wage Setting Institutions and Pay Inequality in Advanced Industrial Societies', *American Journal of Political Science*, vol. 43: 649–80.

Comments on 'Missing the Link? On the Political Economy of Nordic Egalitarianism' by E. Barth and K. Moene

Niels Blomgren-Hansen

The topic of the chapter by Barth and Moene (B&M)—the interrelationship between institutions and economic outcome in the Nordic welfare states—is challenging and fundamental. How is it that the Nordic states have developed a social model, the 'Nordic model', characterized by a compressed wage structure, high average wage income, and broad political support to generous welfare services and correspondingly high taxes? There is no unambiguous answer. However, B&M's input to the debate is stimulating and reflects their deep insight.

The coexistence of the above-mentioned traits of the Nordic model is puzzling. If the Nordic model is generally considered to be a good one, how come it has not been adopted by other countries? How has it been possible to impose a compressed wage structure on high-wage workers? How is it that the redistribution from high-wage workers to low-wage workers resulting from the compressed wage structure is reinforced by generous tax-financed welfare provisions? How come a wage structure that, presumably, is more equal than the one that would result if workers were paid according to their marginal productivity, is associated with a relatively high average wage rate rather than causing an inefficient allocation of labour and relatively low productivity, as elementary economic theory would suggest?

In social models there is no clear distinction between determining variables and determined variables. Institutions affect economic outcome and economic outcome determines the choice of institutional framework. There might be more (stable) equilibria. What makes an economy end up in one equilibrium or another is generally unexplained, but it is assumed that external political or economic shocks may shift the economy onto a trajectory towards a new equilibrium.

That is what happened during the global depression in the 1930s. B&M explain that employers and employees in the particularly hard-hit export industry reacted to the crisis by colluding with employers in the sheltered sectors to coerce workers in the sheltered sectors (threatening them with lockout) to accept relatively low wages, thereby protecting the competitiveness of the export industry and the purchasing power of industrial workers' wage income. The resulting centralized wage bargaining is the 'missing link'.[1]

In my view, B&M's conspiracy theory is not totally convincing. In Denmark, the tradition for wage bargaining at the level of the central organizations of employers and employees goes back to the end of the nineteenth century. In this respect the crisis in the 1930s did not constitute a break. Equally importantly, the wage-game is not played in a political vacuum. The government and parliament play an important role by determining the rules of conciliation proceedings, notice of conflicts, and ballot among union members, all of which have a clear edge against smaller/militant unions that in the eyes of the majority might abuse their power to hurt the economy and the balance of solidarity. If necessary, parliament may impose a rejected proposal for settlement by law. In addition, the government and parliament might mitigate the negotiation 'climate' and moderate wage demands by passing legislation favoured by the unions. The Danish reaction to the crisis in the 1930s fell within this tradition. In the so-called 'Kanslergade Accord' in 1933 the government and the opposition, with the consensus of the unions and trade organizations, agreed to devalue the Danish krone while keeping wages unchanged; later in the same year the parliament passed a social reform law which was considered a major victory for organized labour and a cornerstone of the welfare state.

As B&M indicate, the conspiracy theory cannot alone explain the compressed wage structure. B&M's narrative reflects that a comprehensive wage settlement requires the acceptance of the rank and file of union members. An acceptable wage structure must be considered 'fair' to pass. A fair wage distribution is less likely to be skewed than one that reflects workers' marginal productivity. The compressed wage structure is the necessary 'side-payment' to the majority of workers earning below the average wage rate.

[1] For a formal analysis of the impact on the economy of various ways of organizing the labour market, see Blomgren-Hansen (2012).

This story poses three questions. First, who pays (voluntarily) for the compressed wage structure? Second, as the Nordic model does not compromise employers' right to manage, how come unskilled workers' unemployment is not higher than in countries with a less compressed wage structure? Third, how is it that a wage structure that is presumably more compressed than the distribution of skills, apparently, has not resulted in inefficient allocation of skills and reduced average productivity? On the contrary, according to B&M the average real wage rate is relatively high.

B&M explain the last puzzle by asserting that predictability of wage development (implicit guarantee of a competitive wage level and absence of conflicts) makes investment in new technology more profitable and encourages structural adjustments ('creative destruction'). As traditionally argued by unions, wage pressure is benevolent to society and, probably, also to employers by forcing them to do their best to raise productivity.

I have doubts that, in fact, productivity is significantly higher in the Nordic countries than in those of our West-European neighbours, particularly taking into account that our populations are very homogenous and the share of underprivileged people correspondingly small.

The compressed wage structure is empirically substantiated. However, that does not necessarily mean that it is more compressed than the distribution of skills. The (un)employment structure does not indicate that to be the case. The solution to the puzzle may be to realize that the skill structure is not exogenous. Labour markets in the Nordic countries are characterized by low wage flexibility and a high degree of functional flexibility. Generous public support to upgrading workers' skills to new functions is an essential feature of the Nordic welfare states. In other words, the discrepancy between the wage structure and the distribution of skills is partly eliminated by adjusting the skill structure to the wage structure.

In conclusion, B&M warn that the Nordic model is threatened. The reason is that the dominant role in wage bargaining of employers and employees in the exporting manufacturing industry is gradually being eroded by the Baumol process (the decline in employment in the goods-producing sectors due to stronger productivity growth in manufacturing than in the service-producing sectors). As a consequence, the competitiveness of the export industry is no longer high on the agenda.

Should we be afraid? Not necessarily. The Baumol effect is not a new phenomenon. In fact it was long ago that workers in the manufacturing industry were numerically dominant. In Denmark manufacturing employment peaked in the mid 1960s. In the Nordic countries the share of the labour force in manufacturing is now down to 5–10%, lowest in Norway (which appears to suffer from the Dutch disease). The development does not substantiate the hypothesis that the defence of the 'competitive state' (a new buzzword) hinges on the power of employers and employees in the export industry to 'discipline' workers in the sheltered sectors. In Denmark the necessity of keeping the economy competitive and avoiding building macroeconomic unbalances is an ever-present theme and is well understood by unions, politicians, and the electorate.

Reference

Blomgren-Hansen, N. (2012), 'Optimum Organization of the Labour Market in a Small Open Economy', *Labour Economics*, 19, pp. 222–31.

4

Labour Market Policies in Denmark

A Story of Structural Reforms and Evidence-Based Policy

Michael Svarer

4.1 Introduction

The Danish government claims to be in a reform frenzy. The validity of this statement is corroborated by a series of labour market reforms, conducted in recent years to combat some of the challenges facing the Danish economy. The most urgent problem has been a deficit in the public balances that followed after the onset of the financial crisis and which is forecasted to prevail for many years. The short-term solution to reduce the deficit has primarily been to slow the growth in public spending, whereas the long-term strategy focuses on reforming the labour market to increase employment and reduce the fraction of the population depending on public support.

The long-term challenge for the public finances was diagnosed much earlier than the onset of the financial crises. Figure 4.1 shows the forecast for the budget balance from the Economic Council in 2005.

The profile clearly indicates that the public finances at that time were not sustainable. The situation was critically worsened by the onset of the financial crisis. To avoid exploding public debt either more income, or less expenditure, or (more likely) both was needed. This can be obtained by higher taxes or lower expenditure or a combination of the two by having fewer people on public support and more in employment.

The current chapter will focus on reforms related to the labour market. This means that perhaps the most important reform in terms of resurrecting budget balances—namely a reform of the early retirement system—will not

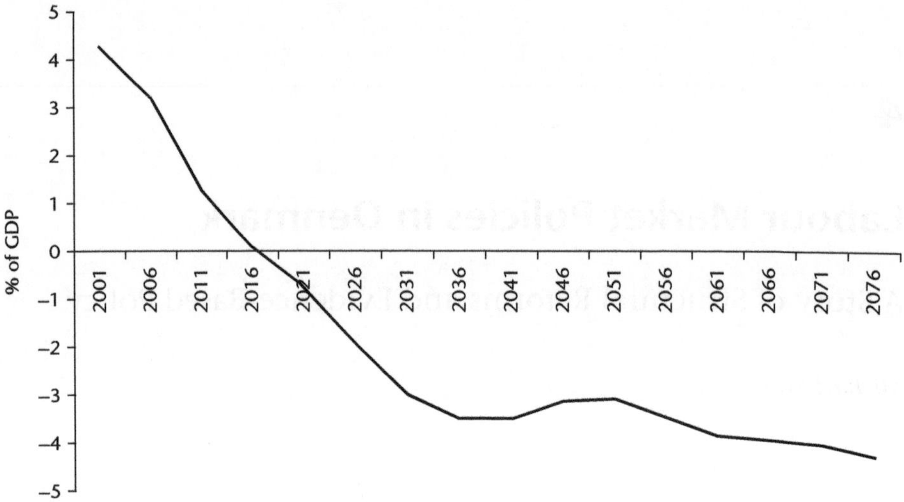

Figure 4.1. Budget balance—forecast from 2005

be addressed explicitly in this article. The main thrust of the early retirement reforms has been to index retirement age to life expectancy and thereby substantially increase the age at which people can withdraw from the labour market while receiving public support. In addition, the reform has reduced the duration of the period of early retirement and increased the general retirement age.

The recent reforms have followed the pattern laid out in the earlier reforms. This chapter describes the recent reforms and relates them to earlier initiatives. In addition, it seeks to illustrate the effects of the reforms on labour market performance.

As an appetizer Figure 4.2 shows the development in the unemployment rate from the early 1990s onwards. It is clear that from a situation with excess unemployment there has been a remarkable development since the early 1990s.

The development in the period from 1993 to the onset of the financial crisis was assisted by a combination of favourable business cycles and a series of labour market reforms that increased incentives to reduce time on public support (see e.g. Andersen and Svarer, 2007).

The structure of this chapter is as follows. First, a short introduction to the Danish labour market is presented. Second, there is a focus on reforms related to the unemployment insurance system. Thirdly, reforms related to active labour market policy are considered, and finally the chapter concludes with a discussion of whether the reforms initiated will solve the problem of unsustainable public finances.

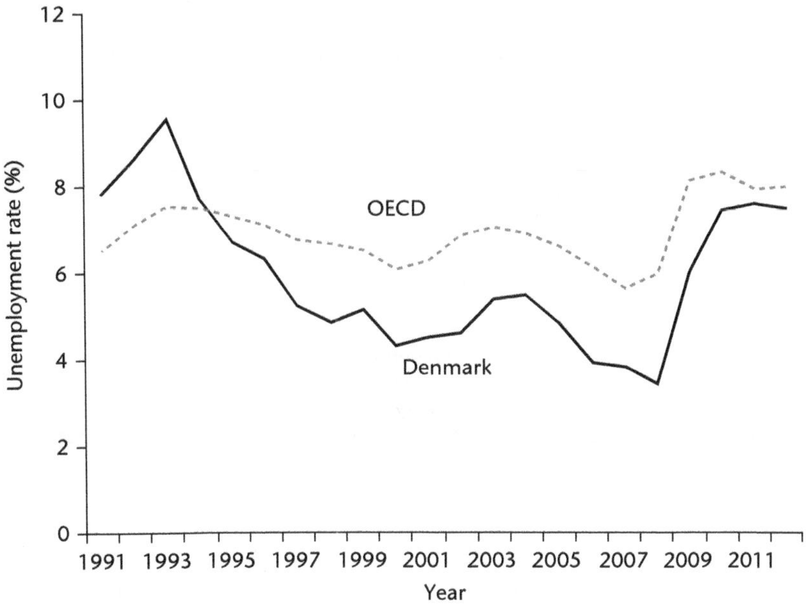

Figure 4.2. Standardized unemployment rates, 1991–2012

4.2 The Danish Labour Market

The short version of the Danish story is the following. Hiring and firing rules are fairly flexible, the unemployment insurance scheme is generous by international standards, and there is an intensive use of active labour market programmes (see Figure 4.3).

A generous social safety net including unemployment benefits and social assistance provides insurance of income for workers. This has a direct welfare effect for risk-averse workers, but it may also be conducive to risk taking and thus labour market flexibility. However, any form of insurance raises problems of moral hazard and adverse selection. These incentive problems have been widely analysed in the literature which has pointed to the detrimental effects of generous unemployment insurance for search incentives, etc. This leaves a political dilemma between insurance and incentives implying that countries weighting insurance high would have incentive problems in the labour market and thus higher unemployment. The Danish experience is a contradiction to this implication.

Active labour market policies broadly interpreted are important in reconciling insurance and incentives. Appropriately designed active labour market policies can be used to strengthen job-search incentives without reductions in benefit levels and the like.

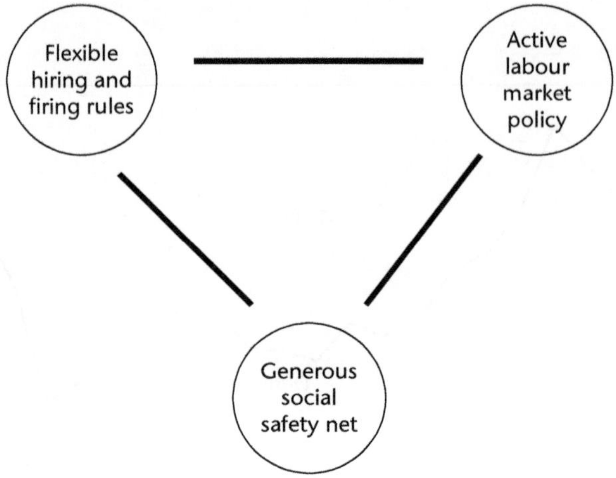

Figure 4.3. The 'Danish model'

Studies of active labour market policies have focused on the direct consequences of programme participation; that is, is there a programme effect which improves the subsequent chances of finding a job? While it is important to consider these direct effects, it is equally important to consider the indirect effects since they may have important implications for the moral hazard and adverse selection problems.

To see this, note that associating some activity requirement with the entitlement to benefits after some duration of the unemployment spell effectively amounts to having a benefit level which is duration-dependent. The dependency arises since the benefit cannot be claimed passively. The work requirement has the role of strengthening incentives in precisely the same way as a declining benefit profile has. It is an implication that the effects of workfare elements should not be evaluated solely from the direct programme effect on the unemployed, but the indirect effect on the unemployed in terms of higher search effort should also be taken into account. Moreover, wage formation will also be affected since the workfare element reduces the value of being unemployed for the worker. Figure 4.4 illustrates with a stylized example the effect on individual utility of a workfare requirement. A more detailed analysis of the effects of workfare in terms of striking a balance between insurance and incentives in the labour market can be found in Andersen and Svarer (2013).

4.3 Reforming the Unemployment Benefit System

A sequence of reforms initiated in the mid 1990s and refined in later years has radically changed the system from having a passive focus on income

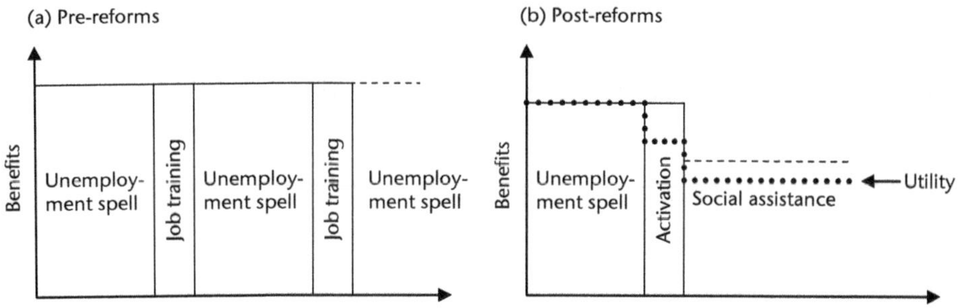

Figure 4.4. Shift in labour market policy: from infinite benefit duration (a) to fixed-time duration with workfare (b)

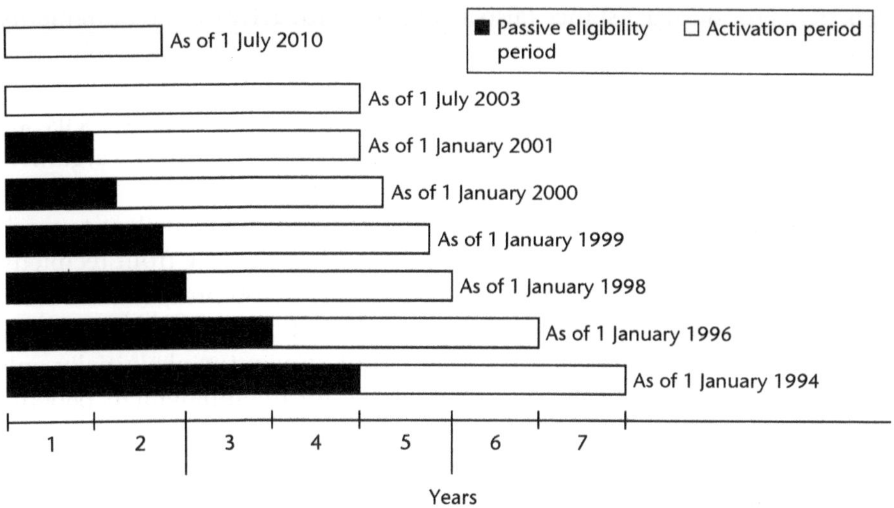

Figure 4.5. Development in the social security system—eligibility and periods of activation

Note: the 'right and duty' principle in the activation period was introduced in 1995. As of 2003 there is no distinction between the two periods.

Sources: Finansministeriet (1999), Arbejdsministeriet (2000), and Beskaefti gelsesministeriet (2002).

maintenance to having a more active focus on bringing the unemployed into employment. The main ingredients of the policy changes are: (i) a shortening of the benefit period, (ii) eligibility for benefits can no longer be regained by participation in activation measures, and (iii) implementation of activation requirements (workfare) both in the unemployment insurance scheme and in the social assistance scheme.

The sequence of reforms is illustrated in Figure 4.5 showing the change in the formal length of the benefit period, and its split into passive and active (workfare) parts.

An important change is that participation in activation measures (job training) no longer qualifies one for remaining eligible for benefits. Before this change the passive period was effectively open-ended since benefits combined with occasional job training would ensure continued eligibility for benefits. As illustrated in Figure 4.4 the system before the reforms effectively implied an infinite benefit period, since despite a formal duration of seven years, a new benefit period could be gained by participating in a job-offer scheme. As a consequence the shift from UI(Unemployment Insurance) benefits to social assistance seldom occurred for people in the UI system. After the reform the benefit period is shorter, activation is compulsory to remain eligible for benefits, and participation does not qualify for fulfilment of the employment criteria to remain eligible for UI benefits, so the transition from UI benefits to social assistance (also associated with activation requirements) is a real option. The profile of compensation offered (including efforts exerted in activation) therefore has a clearer time dependency after reforms.

The shift in labour market policy from a passive to an active focus was launched by appealing to a so-called '*right and duty*' principle. The argument here is that the individual on one hand has a *right* to income support, but on the other hand also a *duty* to actively search for jobs and be willing to work, at the same time as society has a *right* to ask for something from recipients of income transfers but also a *duty* to help improve job prospects. This can be interpreted as reflecting that the welfare state builds on reciprocity and work norms, as we discuss here. The 'right and duty' principle initially only applied to the unemployed who were eligible for unemployment benefits, but in 1998 was extended to also apply to social assistance.

The reform from July 2010 halved the duration of benefit from four to two years, and tightened the re-entitlement conditions so that those unemployed who lost the right to UI benefits had to accumulate 52 weeks of employment within a three-year period, as opposed to 26 weeks in the earlier system.

In an international comparison Denmark is, however, still among the OECD countries with the longest duration of unemployment insurance. The decision to reduce the benefit period was made in combination with an austerity package that was introduced to reduce the public deficit, but whereas the other initiatives in the package had short-term effects, the redesign of UI system was supposed to have long-term effects on structural unemployment.

To illustrate whether or not the reform worked as planned it is useful to see if those unemployed that were affected by the reform found jobs faster than those with longer benefit periods. Since all jobless after July 2010 were affected by the reform, there is no natural comparison group to use as a control. As an approximation it may be useful to compare exit rates to employment for those unemployed with two years of benefit to those unemployed with four years of benefit. This is done in Figure 4.6 for two groups of unemployed.

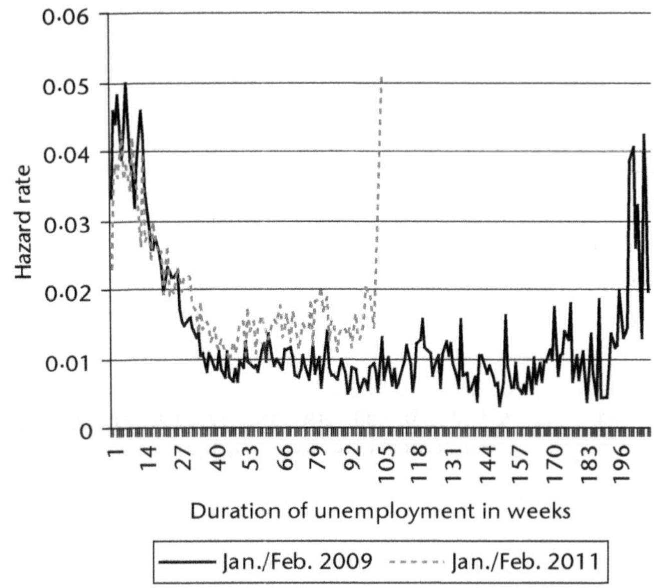

Figure 4.6. Exit rates to employment

Note: based on DREAM data from April 2013. Calculations by the Danish Economic Council.

The darker line shows the exit rates for a group of unemployed who became unemployed in January or February 2009 and therefore had (close to) four years of benefit. For this group the exit rate starts relatively high in the first 13 weeks of unemployment and then sharply drops to a weekly exit rate of around one. It stays at this low level for nearly three years and then sharply rises when the benefit period expires. The exit rate for the group of unemployed who lost their job in January or February 2011 reveals the same pattern, but the sharp rise is now after two years of unemployment. Although it is not a formal econometric test of the effects of the change in the benefit system that is able to correct for observable and unobservable factors that might influence the exit rates, the picture indicates that the reform did affect exit rates to employment close to the moment of benefit exhaustion. Another way to illustrate the effects of shortening the benefit period is to consider those unemployed who have the same duration of elapsed unemployment but are differently affected by the reform.

In Figure 4.7 the survival rates in unemployment for two groups of unemployed that both have had 1½ years of accumulated unemployment in July/August 2011 or July/August 2012 are shown. The former group (darker line) had a remaining benefit period of 1½ years and the latter group (lighter line) had half a year left before benefit expired. For the group with 6 months left around 40% find employment during the six months, whereas around 25%

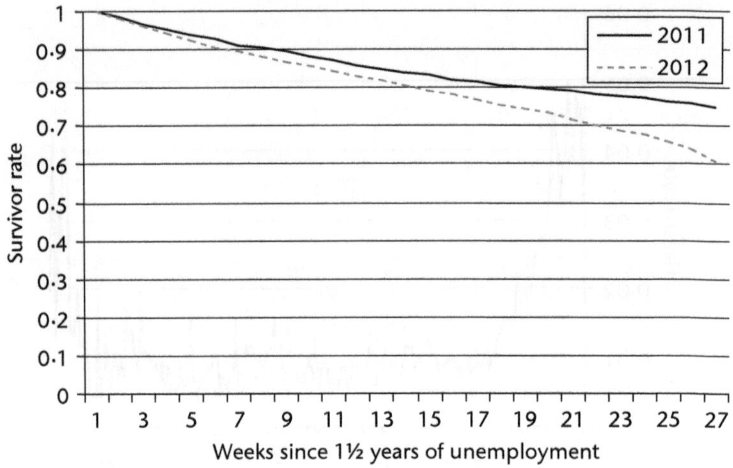

Figure 4.7. Duration of numbers of jobless with 1½ years of elapsed unemployment remaining unemployed

Note: Based on DREAM data from April 2013. Calculations by the Danish Economic Council.

find employment in the group of unemployed with 1½ years of remaining benefits.

The illustrations above support a relatively strong finding from the economic literature, namely that the length of the benefit period is positively related to the length of unemployment spells (see e.g. Card and Levine, 2000; van Ours and Vodopivec, 2006; Card et al., 2007; and Schmieder et al., 2012).

It is an open question whether the reform has also increased economic welfare or improved the functioning of the labour market. Clearly, the insurance aspect of the benefit system has been affected. The number of unemployed that lose their benefits as a result of exhausting their benefit period has increased significantly. In e.g. 2007 (which was a boom year) around 4,000 unemployed exhausted the right to UI benefits. In the first 7 months of 2013 the number is around 25,000 (source: AK-Samvirke). The economic consequence for these individuals is a reduced transfer that is based on the level of social assistance they are entitled to. Social assistance is means-tested and is based on wealth status of the individual and the income level of the spouse.[1] Another aspect is whether individuals that lose their UI benefits transfer to other social support—e.g. sickness benefits.

[1] There have been a number of attempts to reduce the economic consequences for those unemployed that lose their UI benefits, which means that social assistance has been exempted from means testing. It is, however, still the case that the level of income support has dropped.

There are a number of studies that have investigated whether the duration of UI benefits are related to the subsequent job match. At least two competing factors are at play; reducing the benefit period implies less subsidized time to search for employment and hence may result in worse match quality. On the other hand, in a situation with depreciating human capital reducing the length of the benefit period implies that unemployed people find employment earlier, fostering a higher stock of human capital that can support higher income. There is not a strong consensus on the effects of changing benefit periods on subsequent match quality. Card et al. (2007) and van Ours and Vodopivec (2008) do not find that changing the benefit period affects match quality. Le Barbanchon (2012), Gaure et al. (2012), and Caliendo et al. (2013) find that shorter UI periods lead to lower earnings, whereas Degen and Lalive (2012) and Schmieder et al. (2012) find that shorter UI periods lead to higher earnings. There is presumably a trade-off between the length of the benefit period and whether any changes to the benefit system significantly affect efficient job searches.

In sum, the long series of reforms related to the benefit system have all worked in the direction of strengthening incentives and restricting insurance. It appears—although this has not been formally tested—that these changes have helped reduce the unemployment rate shown in Figure 4.2 and in addition have reduced structural unemployment rates. It is interesting that the changes have not resulted in more employment protection. That is, in terms of the internal balance of the Danish flexicurity model the question is whether the current system is sustainable. In a situation where an increasing number of unemployed people lose their benefits and where the alternative income source may be to depend fully on savings or spousal income, the political support to the current system may fade.

Loosening the current system can happen along several dimensions. It has been suggested to make the system business cycle dependent (Arbejdsmarkedskommissionen, 2008; Danish Economic Council, 2012). That is, for example, to have a longer benefit period in downturns than in upturns. A business-dependent benefit period is implemented in countries such as the US and in Canada. There is a growing literature that has investigated the case for business cycle dependent benefits. Andersen and Svarer (2010, 2011) illustrate the case for counter-cyclical benefits, whereas Landais et al. (2013) show that the optimal policy depends crucially on the difference between the micro-elasticity of benefits versus the macro-elasticity. The micro-elasticity is the elasticity of the unemployment probability of a worker whose individual benefits change, while the macro-elasticity is the elasticity of aggregate unemployment when benefits change for all workers. If the micro-elasticity is larger (smaller) than the macro-elasticity then pro-cyclical (countercyclical) UI benefits are optimal.

Given no definitive empirical evidence on the sign of the difference on the micro and macro-elasticity it is, according to Landais et al. (2013), still unclear whether the optimal benefit system should be business cycle dependent.

Another dimension that has been discussed is the trade-off between changing the benefit period and the re-entitlement requirement. From a search angle it is obvious that the two elements of the benefit system can be used as substitutes to design a system that affects aggregate unemployment. In Andersen et al. (2013) a search model is presented that investigates how an optimal unemployment insurance system is affected by e.g. the length of the benefit period and the re-entitlement requirement. The unemployed can either be entitled to UI benefits, or, if they have exhausted their benefits, they can be entitled to social assistance (at a lower level than UI benefits). If social assistance (SA) recipients find employment, the employment relation has to exceed the re-entitlement period before the individual qualifies for UI benefits (UIB). Therefore, shorter benefit duration implies that the UIB-unemployed search more to enhance the chance of finding a job in light of the more dire consequences if this is not successful, and for the SA-unemployed searching becomes less attractive since the value of finding a job leading to UIB entitlement is now lower. A more lax re-entitlement requirement makes the non-entitled unemployed search more, since the value of a job is now higher because it more easily leads to UIB-entitlement; conversely the eligible unemployed search less, since it is less critical to lose entitlement as it can more easily be regained. Figure 4.8 illustrates the iso-unemployment curve in a diagram with benefit period and re-entitlement requirement.

Summarizing on the status of the UI benefit system it is clear that the series of reforms that have been conducted since the early 1990s have implied a convergence of the Danish benefit system to benefit systems in other OECD countries. Before the reforms took place the Danish system was more generous in most dimensions compared to other OECD countries. Now, the different elements of the system are more aligned with systems in other countries. This does not necessarily imply that the reform frenzy has ended. One of the major current challenges to the system is whether it is politically sustainable. The latest reforms have coincided with a significant rise in unemployment incidence and duration and hence many more people are directly affected by the shortening of the benefit period than was the case after earlier reforms. To accommodate the situation of those unemployed who exhaust their benefit and face the risk of not being entitled to any kind of public support, the government has introduced a temporary prolonging of social assistance that is not means-tested and at the same time has proposed the appointment of a commission tasked with investigating the possibilities for further reforms of the benefit system. The commission, which

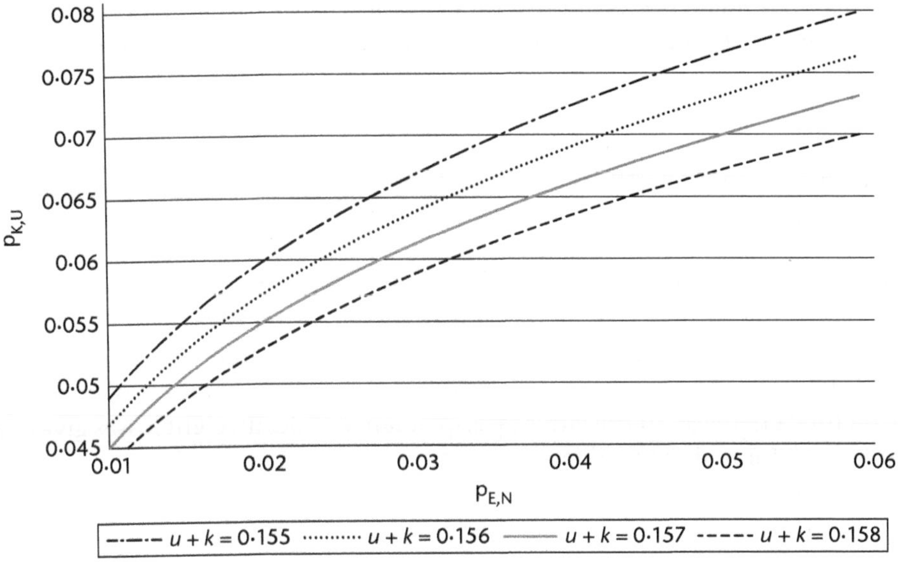

Figure 4.8. Iso-gross unemployment curves—trade-off between UIB duration and re-entitlement requirement

Note: The x-axis shows the re-entitlement criteria. A higher number means that it is easier to regain the right to UI benefits. The y-axis shows the length of the benefit period. A higher number implies a shorter benefit period.

Source: Andersen et al. (2013).

is not appointed yet, is supposed to submit its proposals for reforming the benefit system in 2015.

4.4 Reforming Active Labour Market Policies

The reduction in unemployment implies that active labour market policies have been adjusted over the years to take into account both the effects of policy shifts and also that the composition of the stock of the unemployed has changed with the reduction in the unemployment level.

Designing active labour market policies involves a number of concerns. Such activities are costly (direct costs of active labour market policies amounted to close to 0.7 % of GDP in 2012 in Denmark), and the shift in the trade-off between incentives and insurance is thus not obtained for free. Two aspects are particularly important, namely timing and programme types.

Front-loading of workfare requirements will strengthen incentives the most, but it will also be very costly, and it would entail a large deadweight loss from programme participation for many who in any case would find a job after a short unemployment spell. This is particularly so in a large market with a high incidence of short-term unemployment spells. Hence, workfare requirement should be imposed after some duration of an unemployment spell.

The unemployed group is heterogeneous, ranging from those who have the qualifications and experience that make them readily employable to those who lack these properties (e.g. due to long-term unemployment) and therefore find it very difficult to get a job. For the former group, help with job searches may be sufficient, while for the latter more specific programmes may be needed to directly address the constraints lowering their job-finding rate. In some cases, it may be easy to identify these constraints (e.g. if the unemployed person lacks specific skills) while in others it may be more difficult and also depend on market conditions (qualifications become obsolete due to structural changes). In the latter case, avoidance of deadweight losses gives an argument for making workfare programmes duration-dependent.

These considerations lead to an optimal profile for workfare requirements, as illustrated in Figure 4.9 where the requirements run from general and relatively costless activities to specific and more costly activities, depending on the duration of the unemployment spell. The duration-dependent sequencing of workfare requirements works to minimize deadweight losses and programme costs while maintaining the incentive effects and addressing the more specific programmes to groups for whom they may make a difference.

The selection or targeting of workfare programmes in individual cases may be strengthened by making both participation and the type of workfare programme dependent on some observational characteristics (e.g. extensive educational programmes only available to unemployed without formal education) or by distinguishing between different groups. The latter is done in

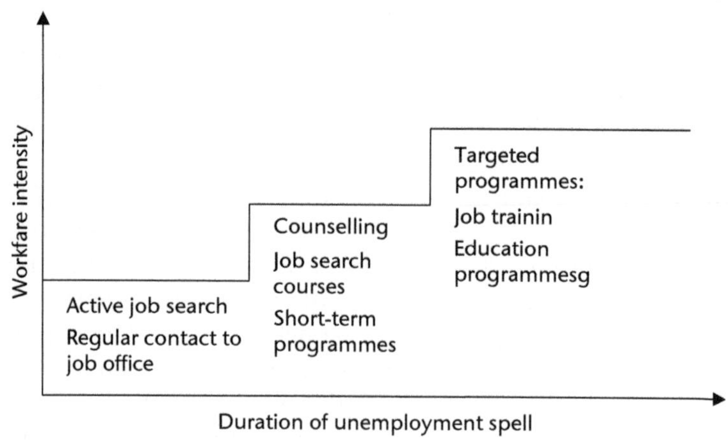

Figure 4.9. Active labour market policy—duration-dependent programme requirements

the Danish social assistance scheme where claimants are divided into three different groups depending on the extent to which they are assessed to be able to work, and the workfare requirements/programme content differ across the groups. A more sophisticated way of targeting programmes is via so-called profiling. Here statistical programmes are used to select which programme (if any) is expected to have the largest effect in reducing the length of unemployment spells for a particular individual with given personal characteristics. The advantage of using statistical tools is that accumulated experience from all previous unemployment spells can be used. Currently, several countries including Germany, Switzerland, and Sweden are considering introducing statistical targeting tools to assist programme selection (Staghøj et al., 2010).

To explain active labour market policies in Denmark, a few institutional details are in order. Unemployment insurance[2] is a voluntary scheme based on membership fees and tax-financed subsidies. Persons not eligible for UIB are eligible for Social Assistance (means tested on a family basis).

All unemployed people are categorized in so-called match groups based on an overall assessment (qualifications, experience, social situation, etc.) of the potential for the individual to be employed.

The system applies to all on unemployment benefits, social assistance, sickness-payment, etc.

- **Group I (job-ready).** An individual with no problems except unemployment. A person who is available for a job and who can become self-supportive within three months.
- **Group II (ready for activity).** An individual who is not at present ready to start working, but is capable of participating in a programme activity aiming at later employment.
- **Group III (temporarily passive).** A person who is neither ready for a job nor for participation in a programme activity aiming at later employment.

Individuals on UIB are automatically in group I. The rules for ALMP (Active Labour Market Programmes) reviewed below apply to all individuals (whether on UIB, SA, or other forms of transfer) in match group I. In the following we distinguish between those unemployed entitled to unemployment

[2] The maximal benefit level is regulated by (i) the fact that the replacement rate relative to past wage income cannot exceed 90%, and (ii) a nominal cap (indexed to wage development). As a consequence the effective replacement rate is declining in the wage and is on average about 65%. Benefit duration has been shortened over the years and since 2011 it has been 2 years (2 ½ years). To remain eligible for unemployment benefits there is a work requirement equal to 12 months within the last 36 months.

insurance benefits—UI unemployed—and those entitled to social assistance and in match group I—SA unemployed. The sum of UI and SA unemployed is denoted gross unemployment.

While the overall focus on ALMP has been strong since the mid 1990s, the specific design has been under more-or-less continuous change. The current system has two key elements (contact and activation):

- **Contact.** An unemployed person (whether on UIB or SA) has to make a CV available on the job centre website within the first four weeks of unemployment, and he/she must participate in interviews on job-search and labour market availability at the job centre at least every third month.
- **Activation.** An unemployed person has a right and duty to activation after nine months of unemployment (duration variable, see below) and thereafter every six months.

The degree of activation (number of people in programmes relative to the relevant target group) and the average duration are shown in Figure 4.10 for both UI and SA unemployed. It is slightly above 20% for the UI unemployed and 35–40% for the SA unemployed. The average duration of programme activities is slightly longer (14–15 weeks) for UI unemployed than for SA unemployed (10–11 weeks).

It is noteworthy that the level of ALMP has been maintained despite the crisis and the increase in unemployment. This is reflected in a clear pro-cyclical pattern for the expenditures on ALMP; see figure 4.11.

ALMP is continuously adjusted in light of the labour market situation and new evidence. In recent years ALMP has shifted more towards focus on job search, counselling, and sanctions. This reflects an adaptation to new research results—some based on natural experiments. We will account here for the changes in ALMP and the empirical research motivating these changes.

In recent years there has been a remarkable focus on implementing evidence-based labour market policies in Denmark. In 2005 the Danish Labour Market Board initiated the first randomized experiment to test the effectiveness of conducting an intensified programme for the newly unemployed. The initiative—which is described in more detailed below—not only led to changes in active labour market policy, but also started a sequence of new controlled experiments. Since 2005 more than six controlled experiments have been carried out and they have all to a smaller or larger extent induced changes in the design of active labour market policies.

In this section we go through a couple of the experiments, report their main findings, and discuss how they have affected policy.

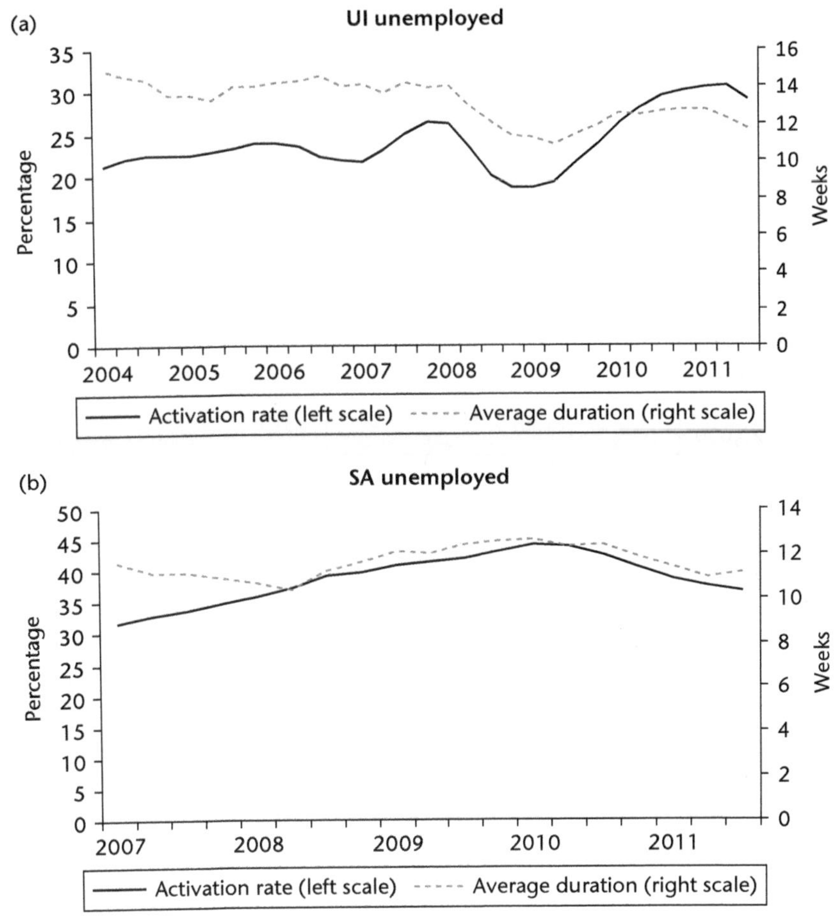

Figure 4.10. Activation rate and average duration of activation activities—UI and SA unemployed

Source: <http://www.jobindsats.dk>.

In terms of evaluating the effects of active labour market policies, random controlled experiments have the advantage that the problem of self-selection into programmes is reduced. At the moment of randomization at least there are—given appropriate implementation—no systematic differences between the treatment and control groups and it is possible to evaluate the effect of the intervention without relying on statistical methods that often require untestable assumptions to identify effects. In this respect random controlled experiments are sometimes viewed as the gold standard of evaluations. In practice there are many challenges when conducting random controlled trials. Besides those relating to extracting effects there are also horizontal equity concerns that might be violated if people facing the

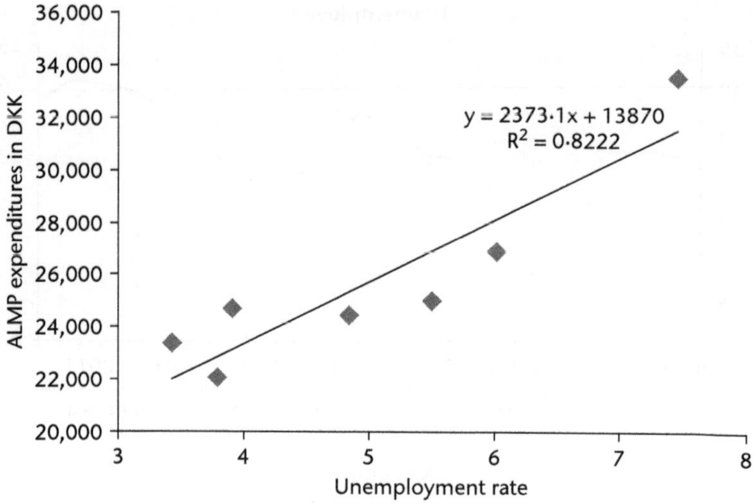

Figure 4.11. Unemployment and gross ALMP expenditures, 2004–10
Source: <http://www.library-oecd.org>.

same problems (e.g. unemployment) are randomly provided with assistance to find employment. This implies that the random control trials have to be carefully designed and ethical concerns have to be faced up front. In the Danish context the general rule is that experiment can only add instruments or intensify already-existing instruments. That is, the control group gets the standard treatment and the treatment group either gets something on top of that or more of the same.

4.4.1 *Quick Back to Work—2005–6*

The first random control experiment was conducted in two counties in Denmark during the winter of 2005–6, and was called Quick Back to Work (QBW). All individuals in the two counties who became unemployed during this period were randomized into a treatment group or a control group based on their birthday. Those born between the 1st and the 15th of the month were given the treatment, and those born between the 16th and the 31st were not. The treatment consisted of a dramatic intensification of labour market policies, involving information, very early mandatory participation in job-search assistance programmes, frequent meetings with employment officers, and full-time programme participation in an active labour market programme for at least three months if they had not found employment before 18 weeks of unemployment. The unemployed were all members of UI funds and therefore had a close connection to the labour market and did not in general have other problems besides being unemployed. Figure 4.12 shows

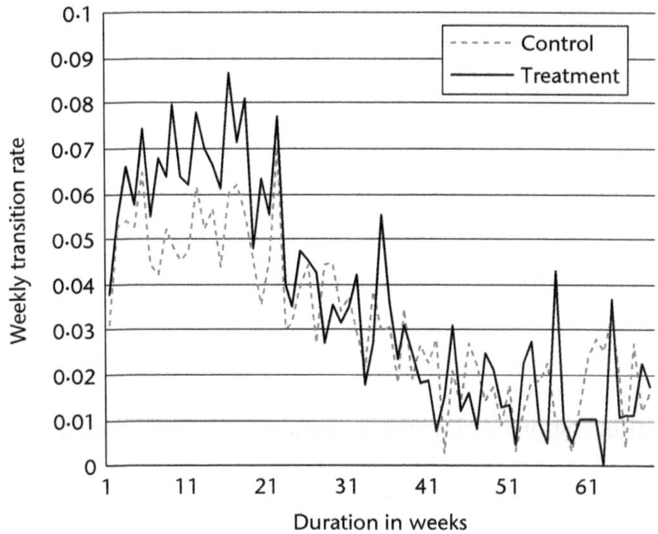

Figure 4.12. Transition rates out of unemployment, QBW
Source: Own calculations based on data from the Danish National Labour Market Board.

the difference in the transition rates from unemployment for the treatment and the control group.

It is clear from the figure that the exit rate is higher for the treatment group in the first 20 weeks of the experiment. Several authors have evaluated the experiment further. Graversen and van Ours (2008) use duration models to address issues of dynamic selection and estimate the effect of the activation programme on exit rates to work. They find that the re-employment rate increases by about 30%, and this effect is the same across age and gender. Rosholm (2008) finds similar results when estimating the effects of the activation programme separately for both counties. Graversen and van Ours (2008), Rosholm (2008), and Vikström et al. (2013) all investigate which elements of the activation programme are most effective. Graversen and van Ours (2008) find that the threat effect and job-search assistance are most effective. A similar conclusion is drawn by Vikström et al. (2013), who construct nonparametric bounds. Rosholm (2008) also finds substantial effects, but he shows too that when controlling for time-varying indicators of treatment all positive effects vanish and some even become negative; the so-called locking-in effect. He finds that the estimated risks of meetings and being activated drive the difference in the job-finding rates between treated and non-treated individuals. Additional evidence for threat effects is provided by Graversen and van Ours (2011). They show that the effect of the activation programme is largest for individuals with the longest travel time to the programme location. Finally, Blasco and Rosholm (2011) analyse long-term effects on post-unemployment employment stability in terms of duration of self-support after leaving the unemployment pool. They find that treatment increases the post-unemployment self-support duration by 10% for men, while treated women show no post-unemployment stability effects.

Although the intensified treatment seems to have been effective for the treated individuals, it might be at the expense of the control group. As case workers meet more often with members of the treatment group, they may suggest job openings to them rather than to members of the control group. To investigate this congestion effect, that is, whether the control persons in the QBW regions had a more difficult time locating jobs than did the unemployed in other regions of Denmark, Figure 4.13 compares the survival rates for the treatment and control groups in the two regions that participated in QBW to the survival rate in unemployment for unemployed in the remaining parts of Denmark.

Comparing the survival curve for the control group with the comparison group of unemployed in other regions of Denmark indicates that in the first 20 weeks of the experiment the control group members in the QBW regions stayed unemployed a little longer, although the difference was quite small. Gautier et al. (2012) took a closer look at the negative externality of the experiment on the control group members and discovered that the they found a

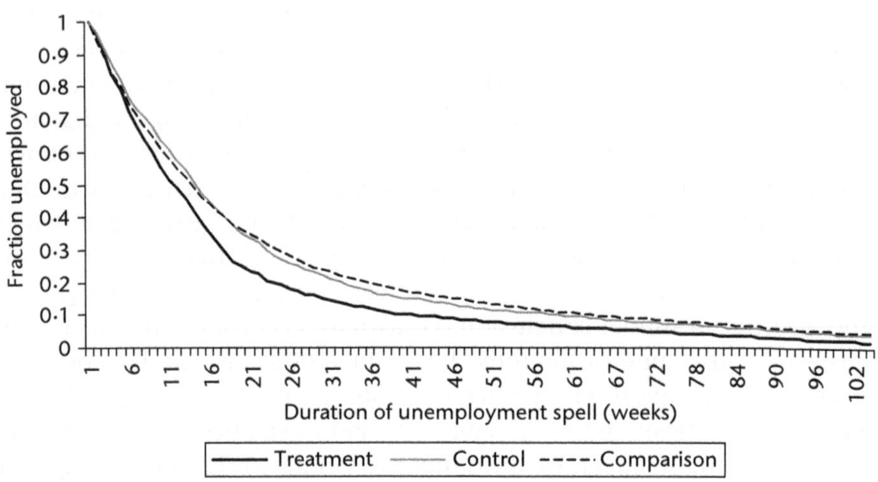

Figure 4.13. Survival rates from unemployment, QBW

Note: The comparison group consists of all the unemployed that entered unemployment in the period November 2005–February 2006 in the remaining regions of Denmark.

Source: Gautier et al. (2012).

job at a somewhat lower rate and hence that the effects reported in the first set of papers that evaluated QBW were slightly overrated.

All in all, the micro-econometric evaluations of QBW suggest that the intensified policy worked both in the short term when focusing on exit rates from unemployment and in the longer term when focusing on return to employment. In addition, a cost–benefit analysis conducted by the Danish Economic Council (2007) demonstrated large net gains from QBW. What is more unclear is what caused these effects of the different instruments in QBW. To evaluate this further a new experiment was initiated in 2008. The new random control experiment was called Quick Back to Work 2 and will be described in the next subsection.

The findings from QBW also affected labour market policies. The lessons that the policy-makers drew from the experiments (of course combined with other types of input) were, first, that early intervention was beneficial for the newly unemployed, and second, that meetings were presumably a more cost-effective tool compared to other types of intervention, e.g. activation. As a consequence activation was moved forward from 12 months to 9 months for those unemployed above 30 years and to 3 months for those unemployed younger than 30. In addition, the first meeting for the jobless under 30 was moved forward from 3 months to after 1 month of unemployment. Although these changes took place before the onset of the Great Recession the policies are still in place, and although there might be reasons to soften the requirements, this has not happened so far.

4.4.2 *Quick Back to Work 2—2008*

As mentioned above, it was somewhat unclear what caused the effects of QBW. To evaluate this further, a new experiment was initiated in 2008. The new random control experiment was called Quick Back to Work 2 (QBW2). It comprised four different experiments, which were designed in such a way that they would yield estimates of the effects of single elements of the QBW package. The treatments consisted of weekly group meetings between a group of unemployed workers and 1–2 case workers (A), bi-weekly individual meetings between one unemployed worker and one case worker (B), early programme participation (C), and a combination of group meetings and early programme participation (D).

Again, the participants were newly unemployed and members of UI funds. They were individuals becoming unemployed between weeks 8 and 29 of 2008. The individuals were randomized into treatment or control groups based on their date of birth. Individuals born between the 16th and the 31st were assigned to the treatment groups, while those born between the 1st and the 15th were assigned to the control groups.

QBW2 has been evaluated by Maibom et al. (2012). They find that the individual meetings in experiment B in particular were effective. Figure 4.14 shows the accumulated difference in the employment rate between the treatment and control groups in experiment B. There were around 400 individuals in the treatment and control groups for both men and women.

Pedersen et al. (2012) find that the meetings between newly unemployed workers and caseworkers on average increase employment rates over the next

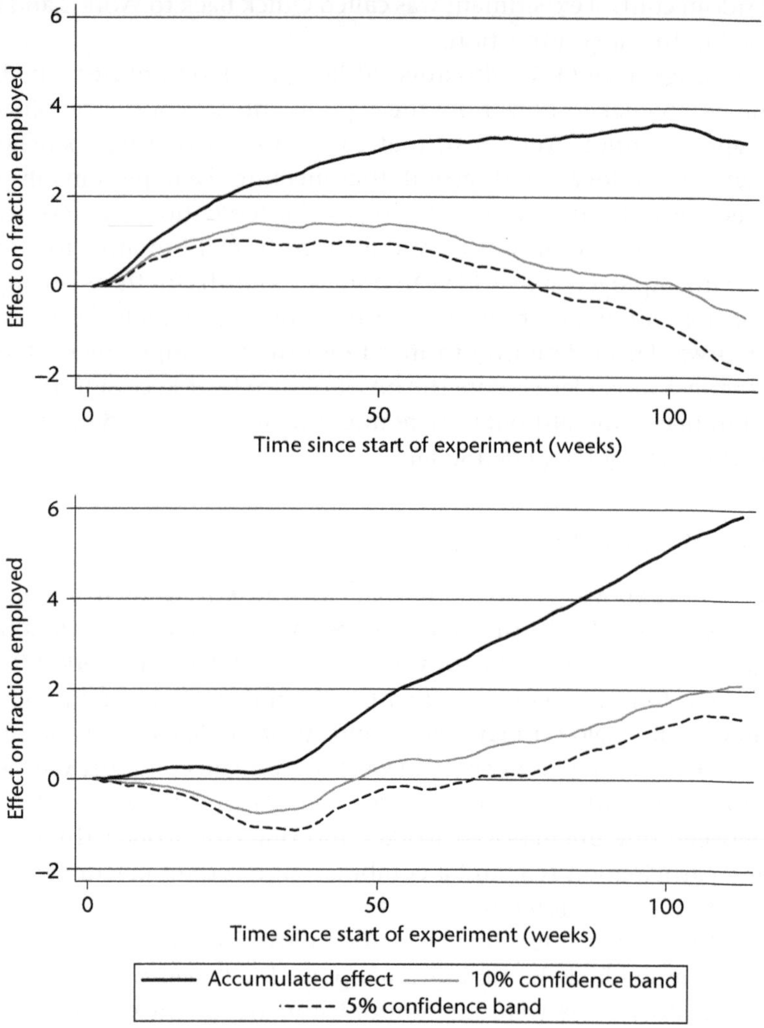

Figure 4.14. The employment effect of individual meetings (experiment B)

Note: The figure shows the accumulated difference in the employment rate between the treatment and control groups. The one-sided confidence bands are obtained by bootstrapping.

two years by 10% corresponding to 5 weeks. In addition, a cost–benefit analysis shows that the surplus per unemployed person is around 4,725 euros.

The group meetings in experiment A were clearly the cheap option, and although the effect of these was quite small, the cost–benefit analysis showed a minor positive return to these meetings.

The early activation experiment (C) showed positive effects for men, especially young men, and especially during more favourable macroeconomic conditions, while for women there was actually a negative effect of early activation due to locking-in effects. The findings suggest that the effect for men arises due to a threat effect (ex-ante effect) and more stable subsequent employment. This evidence on threat effects of early activation for men but not for women corresponds closely to results found by Rosholm and Svarer (2008) based on register data. In addition, the cost–benefit analysis also reports a surplus from the early activation experiment. The final experiment that combined group meetings and early programme participation did not give a statistically significant effect and the cost–benefit analysis showed a deficit from this experiment. In conclusion, QBW2 confirmed that both meetings and early activation were effective—although it also revealed that the early activation programme involved increased costs and increased the risk of prolonging unemployment spells due to the risk of locking-in effects.

Both QBW and QBW2 were targeted at the newly unemployed. To test if the meetings were also effective for the less-employable unemployed, two additional experiments were implemented; one was targeted at long-term recipients of social assistance, and one at sickness benefits recipients.

4.5 Experiments for Social Assistance and Sickness Benefit Recipients

The experiment for the unemployed receiving social assistance was implemented in 2008 and consisted of weekly meetings for 26 weeks. The target population was the unemployed on social assistance that had been out of work for at least 26 weeks. Again, the treatment was randomly given to only a portion of those unemployed in the job centres that participated in the experiment. The group of unemployed people that participated and the control group turned out to be unemployed with an average unemployment spell of around four years. The group therefore consisted of unemployed people with—on average—a very loose connection to the labour market. The experiment was evaluated by Rosholm and Svarer (2009), and the evaluation showed that the meetings did not lead to increased exits to employment for the treatment group. In fact, what happened was that the intensified meeting propensity led to increased activation for the group, and it appeared that in terms of increasing employment the activation for this group was not effective either. In total, the experiment implied a deficit of just over 1,000 euros per participant.

The activation rate for this group of unemployed was in fact relatively high already, and the findings from this experiment together with other Danish studies have led to a significant decrease in the activation rate for those unemployed with long unemployment spells and (in many cases) other problems than unemployment. As a result, the people in group 3,[3] who were labelled as temporarily passive, were no longer required to participate in activation.

The experiment for sickness benefit recipients was implemented in 2009 and targeted at all newly registered recipients of sickness benefits. Again, the setup was a randomized experiment and the treatment was intensified meetings and participation in activation or other health-related activities. The experiment was evaluated by Rosholm and Svarer (2010) and the conclusion followed to a large extent the conclusion from the experiment for social assistance recipients. The intensified treatments did not lead to higher return rates to employment, and since the activation rate went up, the costs of the experiment exceeded the returns and the cost–benefit analysis reported a minor deficit.

In 2009 the government allowed municipalities to use activation for recipients of sickness benefits on the same terms as the ordinary unemployed, and as a consequence to be compensated for active periods. This possibility was partly withdrawn in 2011 when it was required that only the sick-listed who could not be expected to find jobs within the next 8 weeks could be activated on these terms.

4.6 Youth Experiment

As in most countries, youths in Denmark have been disproportionately affected by the financial crisis and the unemployment rate has risen more sharply for this group compared to older persons. This has raised demand for more active policies towards combating youth unemployment. Since many of the unemployed youth lack labour-market-relevant education, a dual strategy seems appropriate. For young people with a qualifying education, the goal is to bring them back into employment relatively quickly, whereas for uneducated youths it might be a better long-term strategy to encourage enrolment in relevant education if they possess the relevant qualifications.

As discussed earlier, the policies aimed at youths are currently quite intensive. To test if it would be helpful to apply even more intensive guidance

[3] As mentioned earlier the Danish labour market system allocates the unemployed into three different groups.

and a stronger focus on education for uneducated youths, a randomized controlled experiment was implemented in November 2009.

The experiment had two branches; one for those unemployed below 30 years of age with some kind of further education, and one for young people without further education. Both consisted of intensified counselling. The educated group had individual weekly or biweekly meetings in the first 13 weeks of the experiment, whereas the uneducated group had individual weekly meetings for the first 32 weeks of the experiment. There was also an increased focus on activation, especially job training, but since the group already participated in activation quite early in the unemployment spell, there was no major difference between the activation rate in the treatment group and the control group.

The major impact of the experiments was counselling, and the evaluation (Maibom et al., 2013) showed that there was a positive, although insignificant, effect on employment rates for the educated group and a positive effect on the exit to education for the uneducated group. For the uneducated group the increased exit to education happened at the expense of exit to employment. In a sense the findings are perhaps not too surprising. The use of meetings is already quite intensive in Denmark towards youth, and the labour market at the time of the experiment was characterized by low job-finding rates and rapidly increasing unemployment. In addition, the treatment population consisted of individuals with quite long elapsed unemployment spells and earlier evidence on the effectiveness of, for example, meetings showed much stronger effects for the newly unemployed. In addition, the analysis found visible effects on the exit to sickness benefits for both groups of unemployed youths.

The conclusion so far from the experiments is that counselling is effective—especially for the newly unemployed. In addition, early activation is in some cases effective since it leads to increased exit to employment before actual participation. It is, however, also clear that activation has a locking-in effect and therefore tends to prolong unemployment spells for those unemployed who participate in activation. On top of this are the costs of running activation programmes. To decrease both the locking-in effects and the costs of programmes there has been a shift from more expensive programmes like classroom training to less expensive programmes like work practice, where the unemployed person has an internship at a private or public firm for on average four weeks on unemployment benefits. Although it has been the intention to implement a more work-related activation policy, it has not been implemented in the experiments in a sufficiently clean way to allow for a test of the effectiveness of the two training schemes against each other.

Finally, as a general comment on most assessments of the effects of ALMPs, it should be noted that they do not consider general equilibrium effects arising via job creation induced by changes in job creation rates due to changed search behaviour or wage effects (see Andersen and Svarer, 2014). The wage effect is potentially important since ALMP affects not only the unemployed and participants in programmes, but also the employed facing a risk of unemployment.

4.7 Concluding Remarks

The reform frenzy evident since 2005 has had a clear impact on the forecast for the budget balance. Figure 4.15 shows a recent prediction by the Danish Economic Council (2013). The assessment is that the fiscal policy is sustainable, which has decreased the necessity of further reforms which strictly focus on improving public finances.

In this respect the reform process in Denmark has tackled the major economic problems without strongly affecting the tax system or the size of the public sector. It remains to be seen whether the predicted effects from recent reforms materialize, but if they do Denmark should stand out as a strong example of how reforming the labour market can contribute to low levels of structural unemployment and sustainable public finances.

There are of course still good reasons for reforming labour market policy to obtain better performance. Obvious areas to focus on are: how to improve

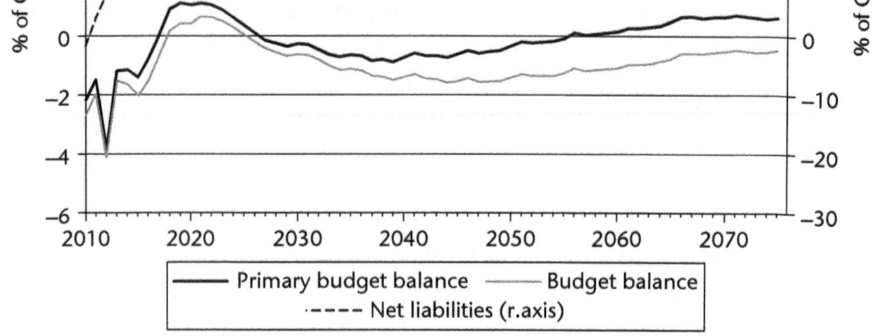

Figure 4.15. Budget balance and net liabilities
Source: Danish Economic Council (2013).

effectiveness of active labour market policies; how to improve employment chances for individuals with low employment potential; and how to ensure that the balance between unemployment insurance and employment incentivesis politically sustainable. The reform capacity of the Danish labour market has proven accommodating in tackling these issues, and future labour market reforms are to be expected.

References

Andersen, T.M. and M. Svarer (2007), 'Flexicurity—Labour Market Performance in Denmark', *CESifo Economic Studies*, 2007, 53 (3), 389–429.

Andersen, T. M. and M. Svarer (2010), 'Business Cycle Dependent Unemployment Insurance', *IZA Discussion Paper 5196*.

Andersen, T.M. and M. Svarer (2011), 'State Dependent Unemployment Benefits', *Journal of Risk and Insurance*, 78(2), 325–44.

Andersen, T.M. and M. Svarer (2014), The Role of Workfare in Striking a Balance Between Incentives and Insurance in the Labour Market, *Economica* 81, 86–116.

Andersen, T.M., M. Kristoffersen, and M. Svarer (2013), 'Benefit Re-Entitlement Conditions in Unemployment Insurance Schemes', Manuscript University of Aarhus.

Arbejdsmarkedskommissionen (2008), Velfærd kræver arbejder, report to the Danish Government (in Danish).

Arbejdsministeriet (2000), *Effekter af aktiveringsindsatsen*.

Beskæftigelsesministeriet (2002), *Flere i arbejde*.

Blasco, S. and M. Rosholm (2011), 'The Impact of Active Labour Market Policy on Post Unemployment Outcomes: Evidence from a Social Experiment in Denmark', *IZA Discussion Paper 5631*.

Caliendo, M., Tatsiramos, K., and Uhlendorff, A. (2013), 'Benefit Duration, Unemployment Duration and Job Match Quality: A Regression-Discontinuity Approach', *Journal of Applied Econometrics*, 28, 604–27.

Card, D. and P. Levine (2000), 'Extended Benefits and the Duration of UI Spells: Evidence from the New Jersey Extended Benefit Program', *Journal of Public Economics*, 78, 107–38.

Card, D., R. Chetty, and A.Weber (2007), 'Cash-On-Hand and Competing Models of Intertemporal Behavior: New Evidence from the Labor Market', *Quarterly Journal of Economics*, 122(4), 1511–60.

Danish Economic Council (2007), Dansk Økonomi, Forår 2007, report (in Danish).

Danish Economic Council (2012), Dansk Økonomi, Efterår 2012, report (in Danish).

Danish Economic Council (2013), Dansk Økonomi, Forår 2013, report (in Danish).

Degen, K. and R. Lalive (2012), 'How Do Reductions in Potential Benefit Duration Affect Medium-Run Earnings and Employment?', Manuscript HEC University of Lausanne.

Finansministeriet (1999), Finansredegørelsen 98/99.

Gaure, S., K. Røed, and L. Westlie (2012), 'Job Search Incentives and Job Match Quality', *Labour Economics*, 19, 438–50.

Gautier, P., P. Muller, B. van der Klaauw, M. Rosholm, and M. Svarer (2012), 'Estimating Equilibrium Effects of Job Search Assistance', *IZA Discussion Paper 6748*.

Graversen, B.K. and van Ours, J.C. (2008), 'How to Help Unemployed Find Jobs Quickly: Experimental Evidence from a Mandatory Activation Program', *Journal of Public Economics*, 92(10–11): 2020–35.

Graversen, B.K. and van Ours, J.C. (2011), 'An Activation Program as a Stick to Job Finding', *Labour*, 25(2): 167–81.

Landais, C., P. Michaillat, and E. Saez (2013), 'Optimal Unemployment Insurance over the Business Cycle', *NBER Working Paper 16526*.

Le Barbanchon, T. (2012), 'The Effect of Potential Duration of Unemployment Benefits on Unemployment Exits to Work and Match Quality in France', *CREST working paper 2012:21*.

Maibom, J., M. Rosholm, and M. Svarer (2012), 'Experimental Evidence on the Effects of Early Meetings and Activation', *IZA Discussion Paper 6970*.

Maibom, J., M. Rosholm, and M. Svarer (2014), 'Can Active Labour Market Policies Combat Youth Unemployment?', *Nordic Economic Policy Review* (issue on youth unemployment), 215–62.

Rosholm, M. (2008), 'Experimental Evidence on the Nature of the Danish Employment Miracle', *IZA Discussion Paper 3620*.

Rosholm, M. and M. Svarer (2008), 'The Threat Effect of Active Labour Market Programmes', *Scandinavian Journal of Economics*, 110(2), 385–401.

Rosholm, M. and M. Svarer (2009), 'Kvantitativ evaluering af Alle i gang', *report to the Danish Labour Market Board (in Danish)*.

Rosholm, M. and M. Svarer (2010), 'Kvantitativ evaluering af Aktive—hurtigere tilbage', *report to the Danish Labour Market Board (in Danish)*.

Schmieder, J.F., T. von Wachter, and S. Bender (2012), 'The Effects of Extended Unemployment Insurance over the Business Cycle: Evidence from Regression Discontinuity Estimates over Twenty Years', *Quarterly Journal of Economics*, 127, 701–52.

Staghøj, J., M. Rosholm, and M. Svarer (2010), 'Choosing the Best Training Programme: Is there a Case for Statistical Treatment Rules?', *Oxford Bulletin of Economics and Statistics*, 72(2), 172–201.

van Ours, J. and M. Vodopivec (2006), 'How Shortening the Potential Duration of Unemployment Benefits Affects the Duration of Unemployment: Evidence from a Natural Experiment', *Journal of Labor Economics*, 24(2), 351–78.

van Ours, J. and M. Vodopivec (2008), 'Does reducing unemployment insurance generosity reduce job match quality?', *Journal of Public Economics*, 92(3–4), 684–95.

Vikström, J., Rosholm, M., and Svarer, M. (2013), 'The Relative Efficiency of Active Labour Market Policies: Evidence from a Social Experiment and Non-Parametric Methods', *Labour Economics*, 24, 58–67.

Comments on 'Labour Market Policies in Denmark: A Story of Structural Reforms and Evidence-Based Policy' by Michael Svarer

Michael Burda

Michael Svarer provides a highly informative overview of the path taken by Danish labour market reforms since the 1980s. In 1983, the jobless rate was 8.4%; by 2008, before the global financial crisis hit, it had declined to 3.4%.[1] In response to the macroeconomic wake-up calls of high unemployment in the 1990s, Denmark witnessed a shift from unconditional benefits with long durations in the 1980s (four years) to shorter durations and increasingly aggressive activation and workfare. This shift was no doubt later accelerated by the financial crisis and the perception of a dynamically unstable fiscal path. The initial Danish reforms served as a model for even more aggressive reform measures in Germany from 2003–5. Recent reform measures were accompanied by a shift to evidence-based active labour market policies.

Labour markets are so important for the functioning of the economy, yet are obviously different from spot markets and thus difficult to reform in crisis mode, when political and social dimensions are most prominent. (In good times, labour market reforms are also difficult, because 'if it ain't broke, don't fix it.') Naïve efficiency goals would keep able-bodied people in work most of the time in the absence of information constraints, yet in a world of imperfect information, a worker may not accept the first job offer that

[1] During the financial crisis the unemployment rate rose again, reaching 7.5%, but has since fallen to 5.5%. Source: IMF WEO <http://www.imf.org/external/pubs/ft/weo/2012/01/weodata/index.aspx>.

comes along, and it may not even be a good idea for them to do so. We would want them to accept 'reasonable' offers and have 'reasonable' expectations of the distribution of wages they will encounter. Yet this penalizes workers with high valuations of leisure time or with poor prospects (e.g. low human-capital endowments), or with uncertain or rapidly changing alternative productivities assessed only under incomplete information. Naturally there is a good argument for generous benefits, so that workers have a fighting chance to deploy their human capital in the best way possible. But there is a race between this aspect and the loss of human capital in the event that the search is unsuccessful, and the situation is further complicated by workers' imperfect knowledge of the value of their skill sets, asymmetric information, and moral hazard in the job-search process.

A little theory can go a long way towards understanding reforms of unemployment benefits, benefit duration, eligibility, and work requirements. Consider the prediction of a standard model of stationary search with on-the-job and unemployed search for the reservation wage w_{it}^R of a risk-neutral worker i who has been unemployed for a spell of t periods (see Rogerson et al., 2005): where:

$$w_{it}^R = b_{it} + \left(\alpha_0(e_i) - \alpha_1\right)\int_{w^R}^{\overline{w_i}} \frac{1 - F_i(w')}{r + \lambda + F_i} dw'$$

b_{it} = value of leisure/non-market work for individual i with duration of unemployment t

α_0 = rate of job arrivals for individual i when unemployed and searching with intensity e_i

α_1 = rate of job arrivals for individual i when employed

λ = rate of match dissolution

r = interest/discount rate

$F_i(\cdot)$ = wage distribution of offers arriving for individual i (possibly also a function of spell duration t)

t = duration of current unemployment spells (time elapsed since last employment).

In the interest of overall macroeconomic efficiency, labour market reform must play several keys of the policy claviature, most importantly, credibly reducing the level of b_{it} and its path as t increases; lifting α_1 by improving information flows to unemployed and promoting mobility, job training, and further skill acquisition; and finally realigning the perceived distribution of wages $F_i(\cdot)$ with reality—which generally means reducing its mean and spread. The Danish labour market model is all about how a high value of b_{it} can coexist with a moderate unemployment rate overall. Two key elements are (1) make b_{it} a decreasing function of t and (2) increase conditionality of benefit on job-search intensity (e). Workers who are 'activated' early on in the unemployment spell may have slightly higher reservation wages initially, but the probability of exit is increased and the economy overall benefits. Furthermore, the 'hassle' associated with activation reduces utility in unemployment, which is tantamount to a reduction of b_{it}, inducing exits from the state.

One feature which I missed in Svarer's analysis was the role of social norms. Social norms modulate the amount of moral hazard and 'light abuse' of the unemployment insurance system, especially at the beginning of unemployment spells (Lindbeck and Weibull, 1999). The Danish evidence cited by Svarer on exits immediately preceding expiry of benefit (e.g. Schmieder et al., 2012) has been well-known since the work of Meyer (1990) and indicates significant intertemporal shifting of exits from unemployment that have little efficiency gain. The remarkable success of Quick Back to Work (QBW) is suggestive of moral hazard at the beginning of an unemployment spell, which may later be offset by loss of human capital and employability signals. Workers often believe they have 'earned' a spell of unemployment upon job loss, especially those who are coming from long employment spells. QBW and its successor programmes seem to go to the source of this problem. Both reforms in Denmark and Germany have addressed this issue, sharing notions of '*Fördern und fordern*' ('to support and to require') as well as '*Pflichten und Rechte*' (duties and rights).[2] Raising the rate of contact of the unemployed with job offers as well as offers of job training and retraining programs are central aspects, as were radical reforms of German job centres and the professionalization of their work. All these aspects contribute towards a societal attitude that considers exploiting the loopholes in the benefit system and moral hazard inappropriate behaviour.

An important point that Svarer makes is the emphasis on the rising influence of modern empirical labour market research on Danish labour market policy. The use of randomized experiments to evaluate the effectiveness of interventions is innovative, and the fact that Danish labour market policies have reacted quickly to empirical findings is similarly impressive. One of the key elements of the Hartz reforms was the introduction of a nationwide

[2] Interestingly, the Danish approach takes the perspective of the state's duties and rights vis-à-vis its subjects, while in Germany the focus has been on rights and duties of workers vis-à-vis the employment office!

databank on job offers, and German labour offices are becoming increasingly concerned about the scientific evaluation of targeted active measures. Yet labour market experiments remain controversial in many continental European countries (especially Germany) because of ethical and fairness concerns.

Unlike the Danish model, German labour markets exhibit much less external flexibility (job protection is much stricter than in Denmark) and unemployment benefits are not particularly generous. The Hartz reforms were instrumental in dismantling the old system of unemployment assistance, which, as in Denmark, had infinite duration (with means-testing). The 'Agenda 2010' programme launched by Chancellor Schröder in 2003 merged the unemployment assistance programme of infinite duration with social welfare, thereby increasing the stigma associated with it. At the same time, an additional 'stick' of activation was introduced where none had been before; even workers in the one-year unemployment insurance window are now expected to check with the employment office and to respond to job offers.

My last remark concerns the general discussion in this interesting chapter and in the Danish policy community. In contrast to Germany, Danish reforms appear more focused on the longer-run behaviour of the labour market at the expense of business-cycle and medium-term aspects. Many of the Hartz and other reforms in Germany were also directed at improving the incentives for enterprises to create jobs, sometimes in a decentralized fashion. The relative success of Germany has shown that the demand for labour is also central, so that those unemployed who become activated actually have jobs to accept. *Kurzarbeit* (short-time work subsidies), increasing flexible forms of employment such as 'Minijobs' and temp agency work (*Zeitarbeit*), working time accounts (*Arbeitszeitkonten*), and concession bargaining (*Arbeitszeitkorridore*) can all be interpreted as measures which support labour demand. These mechanisms are associated not only with wage and non-wage cost moderation before the crisis, but also during the crisis period of 2008–9. They have certainly contributed to the markedly improved employment performance in Germany since 2008, which reflects increasing participation rates among women, older persons, and residents of the eastern states. Works councils were allowed to deviate from national or regional pay agreements, granting wage flexibility to individual production units in distress. Enterprises reduced unit labour costs to manageable levels via 'working time accounts', which have now been adopted by more than a third of all enterprises and are available to more than half of all employees (Ellguth et al., 2013). Figure C4.1 contrasts German and Danish reactions to the Great Recession. One perspective is that Denmark

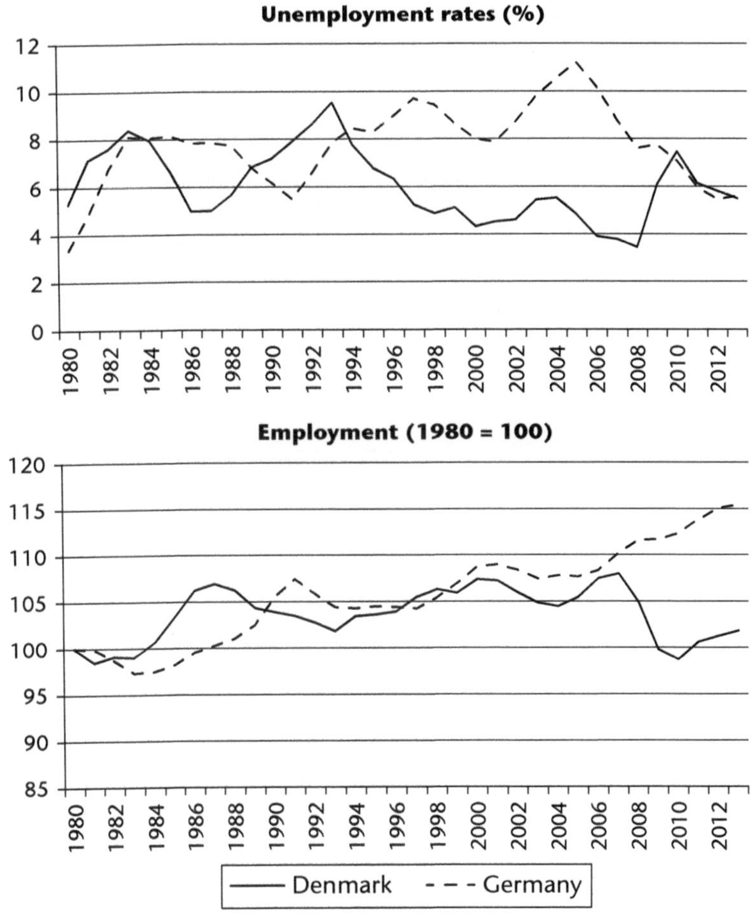

Figure C4.1. Unemployment rates and employment in Denmark and Germany, 1980–2012

has solved this problem and doesn't need to worry about job creation and labour demand. Another more sinister interpretation is that Danish policy may have focused too much on the activation of the unemployed, possibly at the expense of job creation, now and in the future.

References

Ellguth, P., H-D Gerner, and I. Zapf (2013), 'Vielfalt und Dynamik bei den Arbeitszeitkonten' *IAB-Kurzbericht* 3/2013 (Institut für Arbeitsmarkt- und Berufsforschung), Nürnberg.

Lindbeck, A. and J. W. Weibull (1999), 'Social Norms and Incentives in the Welfare State', *Quarterly Journal of Economics* 114: 1–35.

Meyer, B. (1990), 'Unemployment Insurance and Unemployment Spells', *Econometrica*, 58(4): 757–82.

Rogerson, R., R. Shimer, and R. Wright (2005), 'Search-Theoretic Models of the Labor Market: A Survey', *Journal of Economic Literature* XLIII (December 2005), pp. 959–88

Schmieder, J, T. Wachter, and S. Bender (2012), 'The Effects of Extended Unemployment Insurance over the Business Cycle: Evidence from Regression Discontinuity Estimates over Twenty Years', *Quarterly Journal of Economics* 127, 701–52.

5

What Scope for Monetary Policy?

Experiences from the Nordic Countries after the Financial Crisis[1]

Anders Møller Christensen and Niels Lynggård Hansen

5.1 Introduction

In a European context, the Nordic region, apart from Iceland, has performed above average since the outbreak of the financial crisis. Despite a significant drop in economic activity, very large by an international comparison and of almost equal size across the Nordic countries, unemployment has increased only moderately and remained at a low level by most standards. Public finances are generally sound and government debt, although it has increased, is still well below the average in OECD countries. However, some differences in economic performance have also been observed across Nordic economies. The Norwegian economy has outperformed almost every other Western economy, largely due to a favourable development in offshore and related activities. Sweden recovered only a year or so after the crisis, whereas Denmark and Finland have found it more difficult to begin closing the output gap.

Nordic countries have many economic characteristics in common such as size, openness, the approach to the welfare state, and the reliance on the public sector in the economy. At the same time, the monetary policy frameworks

[1] The chapter was prepared as a paper for the conference on 'Reform Capacity and Macroeconomic Performance in the Nordic Countries', Copenhagen Business School, September 20–21, 2013.

Nick Fabrin Nielsen provided valuable research assistance. Furthermore, the chapter has benefitted from comments from and discussions with colleagues at Danmarks Nationalbank, in particular Jens Bang-Andersen, Jesper Pedersen, and Søren Hove Ravn, and with participants in the above-mentioned conference, in particular Jesper Rangvid. Still, the views expressed in the paper are our own and do not necessarily correspond to those of Danmarks Nationalbank.

have been markedly different in the last 20 years and represent a clearly distinguishing feature. Norway and Sweden both have an inflation-targeting framework, whereas Denmark and Finland have given up monetary autonomy, in the case of Denmark through a peg of the krone to the euro within narrow bands around the central rate, whereas Finland belongs to the eurozone.

Monetary-policy responses to pressures after the financial crisis also differed across the Nordic countries. After the meltdown of financial markets in the autumn of 2008 both Sweden and Denmark saw a significant capital outflow, like many other small countries. Sveriges Riksbank responded by lowering interest rates aggressively. This resulted in a depreciation of the krona and a gain in competitiveness. At the other end of the spectrum, Danmarks Nationalbank raised interest rates to prevent the krone from depreciating, and in effective terms the krone appreciated.

In this chapter we investigate whether differences in economic performance can be attributed to differences in monetary-policy responses and frameworks. Are other policies, most notably fiscal policy, of importance as well? The monetary policy of the UK has many similarities with that of Sweden, but the economic performance has been more problematic. The same line of argument goes for member countries of the euro or those with a fixed exchange rate against the euro. A comparatively good performance in the northern part of the euro area and in Denmark stands in contrast to the severe economic problems in several South European countries in the euro area.

As part of the analysis, we revisit our previous analysis (Christensen and Hansen, 2009) of the impact of changes in the monetary-policy regime on different measures of macroeconomic stability. Based on difference-in-difference estimations covering a broad set of countries we found a significant reduction in the volatilities of both inflation and output-gap after the adoption of a consistent fixed-exchange-rate policy, and no such effects from moving to inflation targeting. Both groups of countries saw a decline in the level of inflation after the change of regime. Do these results still hold after the financial crisis? The brief answer is yes. The more elaborate is slightly less straightforward, emphasizing the importance of other policies.

The text focuses mostly on Denmark and Sweden, less on Finland and Norway, and not on Iceland. The next section reviews recent literature on monetary policy in small open economies. In Section 5.3 we look at a series of core macroeconomic variables, including competitiveness and economic stability, as well as monetary-policy responses to the crisis, with an aim of assessing economic performance in the Nordic countries in comparison with other countries. In Section 5.4 we take a closer look at the role of public finances for macroeconomic performance. Thereafter, Section 5.5 contains the econometric analysis of the significance of different monetary-policy regimes for macroeconomic performance. Finally, Section 5.6 concludes.

5.2 Monetary Policy in Small, Open Economies

In all major developed economies inflation has been brought down from chronic high levels in the 1970s to something considered close to price stability. This achievement reflects to a large extent the establishment of strong monetary policy frameworks where monetary policy is delegated to independent central banks with a clear mandate of price stability, i.e. in practice keeping inflation low and stable allowing at the same time for output to be kept close to the potential and hence unemployment close to the natural rate. This reasoning is based on the view that there is no trade-off in the longer run between the level of inflation and the real economy. Different countries have made different choices—*in casu* inflation targeting or exchange-rate targeting—although often not as deliberate choices, but rather as a consequence of the break-down of the previous regime, as was the case for Sweden and the UK in the early 1990s, and in Denmark a decade earlier.

In the academic literature there is no doubt that inflation targeting is generally considered best-practice monetary policy, providing the most favourable trade-off between volatility in inflation and the output gap (cf. the foreword to Cobham et al., 2010).[2]

Inflation targeting was first introduced in New Zealand in 1990 and was soon adopted by countries like the UK, Sweden, Canada, and Australia. More than 20 developed and developing countries have now announced a numerical inflation target. Despite this, the literature on monetary economics mainly focuses on large, closed economies; the prevalent view also on monetary policy in open economies in the period before the financial crisis being that the most suitable monetary-policy regime was flexible inflation targeting, see e.g. Clarida, Gali, and Gertler (2002) and Svensson (2002). One major argument is that under inflation targeting the exchange rate allows exports and imports to adjust to shifts in aggregate demand and hence acts as a 'shock absorber' in the terminology of Friedman (1953). Gali and Monacelli (2005) find in a direct comparison to a regime with fixed exchange rates that social welfare in a small open economy is higher in an inflation-targeting regime with floating exchange rates.

Two assumptions are crucial for this result to hold (cf. Corsetti, Dedola, and Leduc, 2010). The first is producer currency pricing that implies that changes in the exchange rates are fully transmitted to the prices of imported goods. Under local currency pricing price rigidities in the country of destination

[2] 'There is now a strong but not universal consensus among academics and professional economists that central banks should adopt explicit inflation targets and that all key monetary policy decisions, especially those concerning interest rates, should be made with a view to ensuring that these targets are achieved' (Cobham et al., 2010).

imply that changes in the exchange rate are not fully transmitted to the domestic price level and hence lead to inefficient differences between the relative price levels, implying a distortion of demand—the exchange rate is no longer a shock absorber.[3] Optimal monetary policy should weigh this inefficiency against the stabilization of inflation and the output gap, and thus become different from inflation targeting with a freely floating exchange rate. The second assumption is that financial markets should be complete, allowing domestic households access to the international financial markets so that the uncovered interest-rate parity holds. Finally, even under producer currency pricing and complete financial markets some stabilization of the exchange rate might be optimal if there is a home bias in consumption, since domestic consumption will be affected by a change in the terms of trade (see Faia and Monacelli, 2008).

After the outbreak of the financial crisis the inflation-targeting framework has come under critique. The protracted economic recession in many countries has questioned the so-called divine coincidence whereby the inflation-targeting strategy is consistent with stabilization of both inflation and output at the same time. Recent experiences in several countries have shown a clear conflict between pursuing the inflation target and closing the output gap. This has led to suggestions being made to replace the inflation target by e.g. a nominal GDP target which would make it easier to stimulate the economy in the current circumstances with nominal interest rates *de facto* at the zero lower bound by affecting expectations about future monetary policy (see e.g. Carney, 2012, and Wren-Lewis, 2013).

The announcement by the Federal Reserve in December 2012 that interest rates would be kept low as long as the unemployment rate was above 6.5% and inflation remained below 2.5% follows the same line of reasoning. The theoretical arguments were laid out by Michael Woodford at the annual conference at Jackson Hole in 2012. He listed three criteria monetary policy should ideally fulfil in the current situation where monetary policy is constrained by the zero lower bound. First, it is insufficient to have a purely forward-looking monetary policy based on a forecast of inflation and the output gap. Instead, a backward-looking element should be introduced, whereby the central bank would promise to keep interest rates low longer than warranted by the economic development as implied by e.g. a Taylor rule, so as to make up for previous output losses. Second, the announced conditions should be state-dependent and not time-dependent, as a possible postponement of announced increases of monetary policy rates risks being considered by the market as being as if the central bank foresees a worsening

[3] For empirical evidence on the relevance of local currency pricing see Goldberg and Knetter (1997) and Gopinath and Rigobon (2008).

of the economic outlook. Third, the target should be easy to communicate and observe. Such direct attempts at shaping the private sector's expectations about future monetary policy have been dubbed 'forward guidance' (cf. Woodford, 2012b).

When the interest rate is close to its zero lower bound, monetary policymakers may use forward guidance about future policy to stimulate the economy immediately. If policymakers can credibly commit to keeping the interest rate low for a long time—i.e. lower than implied in the 'normal' interest-rate rule—this may push down longer-term interest rates via the expectation hypothesis of the yield curve. In other words, successful forward guidance allows policymakers to operate further out on the yield curve. Obviously, such announcements are subject to the well-known problems of time inconsistency of monetary policy: private agents anticipate that, at some point in the future, monetary policymakers may find themselves tempted to renege on past promises. Although similar in spirit, forward guidance differs from more traditional central bank communication in one important aspect: while central banks traditionally use their communication to enhance transparency and credibility around an already-announced monetary policy strategy, e.g. a path for future policy rates, successful forward guidance during a recession itself acts as additional monetary easing.

Forward guidance can be considered an integral part of inflation targeting (cf. Svensson, 2003). However, a different critique of a narrow focus on inflation stabilization in the short run relates to the fact that inflation signals were muted about the tightening of capacity pressure in many countries before the financial crisis and likewise about the large output gaps in the ensuing recession. Among others, Hall (2013) has emphasized the breakdown of a traditional Phillips curve relationship in US data in recent years, while other authors have suggested that estimated monetary policy reactions to changes in inflation may also have declined in recent years (see e.g. Hofmann and Bogdanova, 2012). Possible reasons for this might be the strengthening of central banks' credibility and successful anchoring of inflation expectations, but also factors like globalization and hysteresis in the labour market may play a role (see IMF, 2013).

Hence, information about capacity utilization should not be conveyed by inflation only. As several countries experienced in the 2000s, inflation might well be low and stable while at the same time financial imbalances are building up. In other words, price stability is no guarantee for financial stability. Borio (2012a, b) stresses that the credible low-inflation monetary policy frameworks along with financial liberalization and globalization of the real economy have laid the ground for renewed financial cycles. These cycles, usually well described by credit and property prices, have a lower frequency than the typical business cycle and coincide closely with financial crises.

One possible way to address financial cycles could be to introduce a longer horizon in monetary policy, beyond the typical two to three years under inflation targeting. This could allow policy to lean against financial cycles—leaning instead of cleaning, in contrast to Greenspan's advice. It is currently an issue if financial stability considerations need to be be taken into account in monetary policy (see the discussion between Woodford, 2012a, and Svensson, 2012). Undoubtedly, the best way to strengthen financial stability is through macroprudential instruments, like loan-to-value and capital requirements. In most advanced countries, including the Nordics, the establishment of frameworks for macroprudential policy is well underway. However, monetary policy influences the development in balance sheets as well.

As indicated above, monetary economics in recent years has focused on aspects of inflation targeting, whereas exchange rate targeting has received little attention. However, as evidenced by the developments in the last three decades, low and stable inflation is, along with a stable progression of the real economy, a feature in countries with both types of regimes. Reductions in the level of and variations in inflation were realized in the second half of the 1980s in countries that successfully adopted a fixed-exchange-rate regime, whereas countries that did not succeed therein were able to obtain similar improvements in the 1990s after adopting an inflation-targeting regime. This observation is in line with the study by Fatas, Mihov, and Rose (2007) who, in a data set of 42 countries between 1960 and 2000, find that the introduction of a well-defined, quantitative goal, be it a money growth target, an exchange-rate target, or an inflation target, leads to lower inflation. In a survey article (Rose, 2011) macroeconomic performance is compared across different exchange-rate regimes,[4] based on a data set spanning 178 countries on a sample from 1974 to 2007, and the conclusion is that macroeconomic outcomes like output growth and inflation are substantively similar across different exchange-rate regimes. This led to the observation that 'Governments of similar countries make different decisions on the exchange rate regime. These views appear to be strongly held and sincere, yet they seem to have neither discernible causes nor visible consequences' (Rose, 2011, p. 671).

A somewhat similar exit line was drawn on the possible argument for central banks to opt for inflation targeting in our previous study based on a difference-in-difference approach (Christensen and Hansen, 2009). The improvement in macroeconomic performance from changing to inflation targeting in a data set comprising 21 OECD countries between 1971 and 2005 was found, if anything, to be inferior to the improvement from changing to a fixed-exchange-rate regime. Another study (Ball, 2010) that

[4] Rose underlines though that it is more correct to talk about monetary policy frameworks, rather than exchange rate regimes.

applied more or less the same methodology and looked at the same set of countries but with a smaller sample between 1985 and 2007 found no significant impact on economic performance from either inflation targeting or from the adoption of the euro. The latter clearly implies a narrower interpretation than ours of a regime where countries have given up monetary autonomy.

With this in mind, it is interesting to see if our results still hold after the experiences from the great recession that followed the financial crisis. It suggests that, at the end of the day, the question of the optimal monetary policy for small, open economies has not been settled. Hence, it is relevant to look at the empirics.

5.3 Economic Development and Monetary Policy in the Nordic Region

Monetary policy frameworks in the Nordic countries have followed diverging paths since the early 1990s. Prior to this, the economic development in Finland and Sweden was clearly unsustainable, and after a severe deterioration of public finances largely due to the banking crises both countries abandoned the fixed-exchange-rate policy in the autumn of 1992 after a period of speculative attacks. Both countries adopted an inflation target framework for monetary policy. Finland joined the ERM in 1996 and later became part of the European Monetary Union from its start in 1998, while Sweden has remained with the inflation-targeting regime with some refinements over time. Denmark suffered from a similarly unsustainable development in the late 1970s and beginning of the 1980s and opted for a stability-oriented economic policy in 1982 where a fixed exchange rate was adopted—this is still in place today. In all three countries the shift in monetary policy regime was accompanied by economic reforms and enhanced fiscal prudence. In Norway the government officially announced the adoption of an inflation target in March 2001. It followed a long period—since the abandonment of the peg against the ECU in December 1992—of stabilization of the Norwegian krone against European currencies though with a gradual move towards more exchange rate flexibility and increased orientation towards domestic inflation.

In a longer perspective, economic growth has moved more or less in parallel in the Nordic countries with Norway as the exception.[5] Real GDP per capita has grown a little faster in Finland and Sweden than in Denmark in

[5] The real income per capita in Norway exceeds that in Denmark by close to 50 per cent.

recent decades, in particular since 1995, reflecting that both Finland and Sweden have caught up after their deep recession, cf. Figure 5.1. Taking the significant gains in terms-of-trade that Denmark has obtained into account along with net foreign income, it turns out that growth rates of per capita income have been very similar across the Nordic countries, and of the same magnitude as in large advanced countries like the UK and US, cf. Figure 5.2.

Compared to most other European countries, the Nordic countries have passed smoothly through the financial crisis. Despite significant drops in real activity, unemployment levels have stayed relatively low, and public finances are generally sound. However, there are also differences in performance across the Nordic region.

In the years prior to the financial crisis, the Nordic region experienced solid growth in real GDP and output gaps were significantly positive, cf. Figure 5.3. In Finland in particular, the rise in activity was steep before the business cycle peaked. As the crisis evolved, the output gap turned negative in all Nordic countries in 2009, but the contraction in Norway was modest. The recovery has progressed at a slow pace in Denmark, while Sweden almost closed the negative output gap in 2010 only one year after the peak of the crisis, and Norway has also seen a fast recovery of real activity.

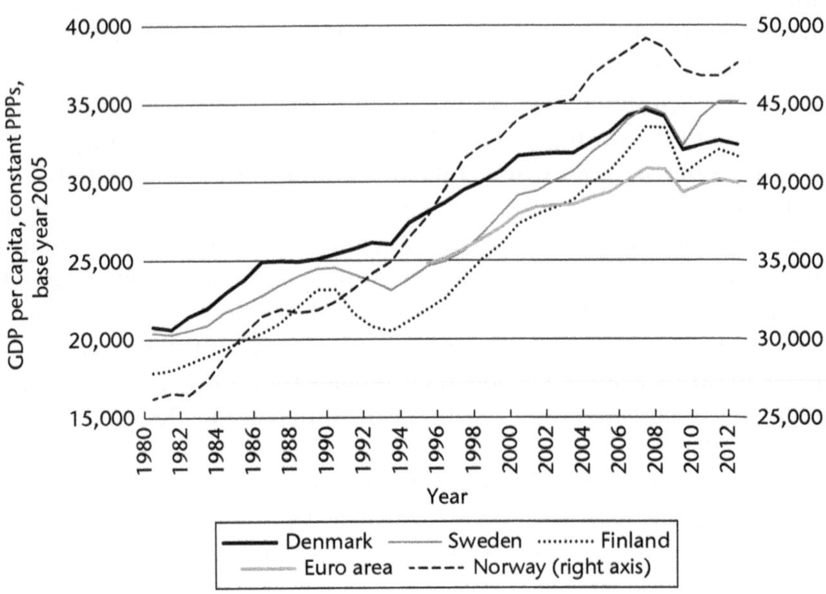

Figure 5.1. Real income levels, PPP-adjusted, base year 2005, 1980–2012
Source: OECD.

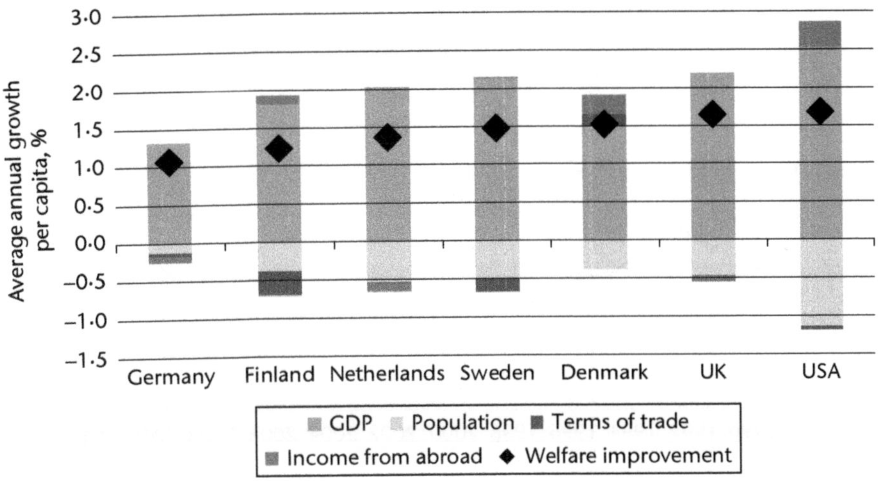

Figure 5.2. Contributions to economic welfare, 1990–2012: average annual growth per capita, per cent

Note: The growth rate of economic welfare has been calculated as the average annual growth rate for GNP per person of working age, adjusted for terms-of-trade effects.

Source: OECD, Eurostat, the IMF, and own calculations.

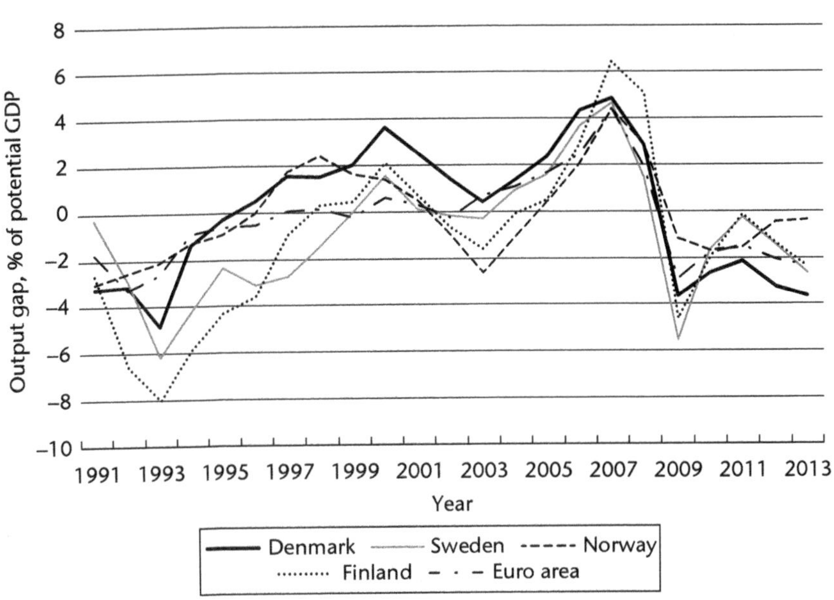

Figure 5.3. Output gap, per cent of potential GDP, 1991–2013

Source: IMF.

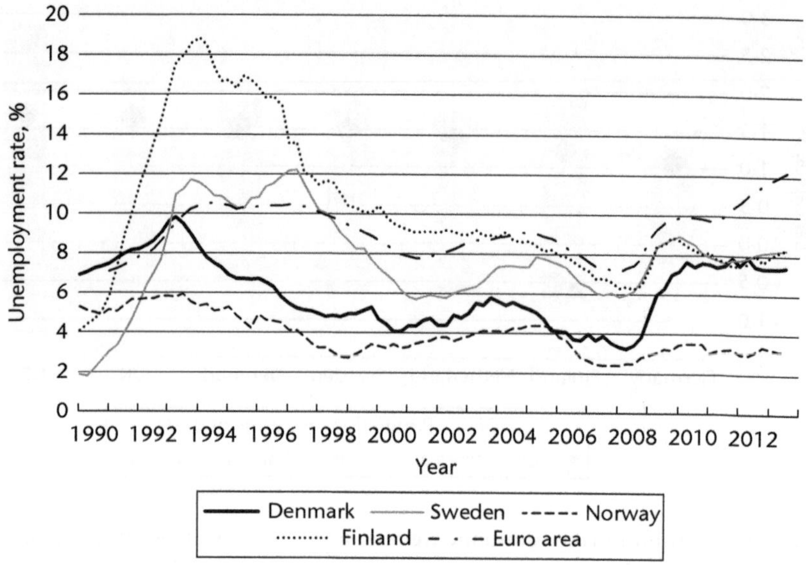

Figure 5.4. Unemployment rate, per cent, 1990–2013
Source: IMF.

The unemployment rate is low in the Nordic countries compared to the euro area, cf. Figure 5.4. In spite of the fast Swedish recovery from the recession, the unemployment rate is still around 8%. The high level of unemployment despite strong growth in economic activity in boom years is an indication of structural problems in the Swedish labour market.

In the years preceding the financial crisis, the Danish economy became overheated with destabilizing forces from fiscal policy due to the combination of a tax freeze and stronger growth in government consumption than warranted. A bubble in the housing market emerged, partly related to a number of liberalizations in mortgage financing and a nominal freeze of property taxes. This development led to losses in competitiveness, cf. Figure 5.5, as real wages increased in excess of productivity gains. The growth rate of unit labour costs has been lower in Sweden than in the other Nordic countries when expressed in local currencies, but taking the appreciation of the Swedish krona since the beginning of 2009 into account, there has been a more parallel development in competitiveness in Denmark, Finland, and Sweden, cf. Figure 5.6.

Inflation has generally been low and stable in the Nordic countries in recent years, cf. Figures 5.7 and 5.8. Even during the peak and subsequent trough of the business cycle from 2007–9 around the financial crisis, volatility in inflation was modest in all countries. Furthermore, inflation expectations in the Nordic region have been well anchored for years. In Sweden, inflation is currently below the target of 2%, just as inflation in Norway until recently was below the target of 2.5%. For Norway, this suggests that keeping

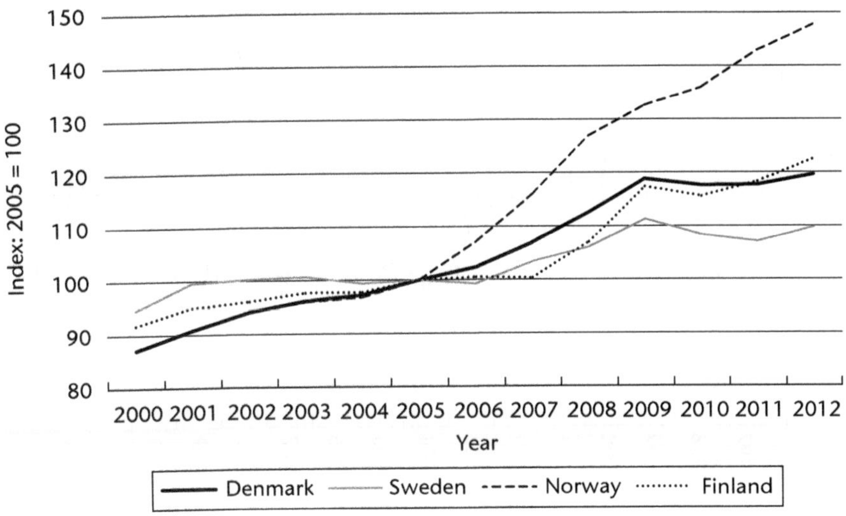

Figure 5.5. Unit labour costs, local currency, 2000–12
Source: OECD.

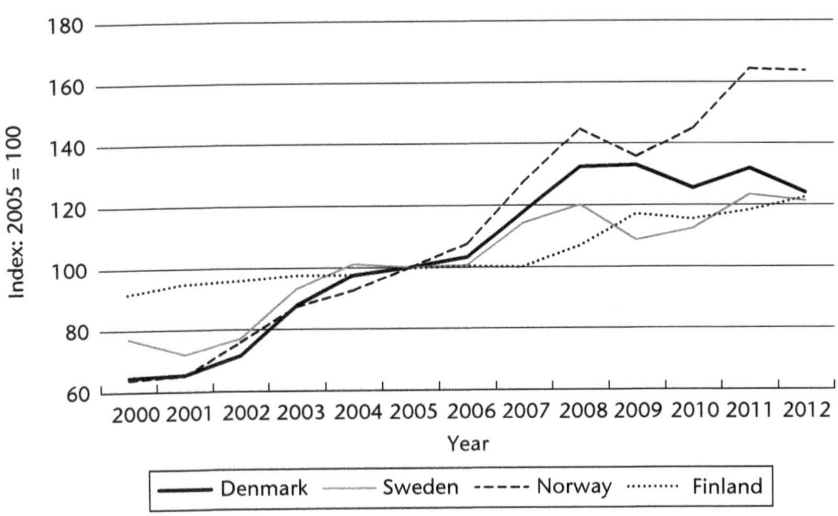

Figure 5.6. Unit labour costs, exchange-rate adjusted, 2000–12
Source: OECD.

the negative output gap close to zero does not pose an immediate threat to price stability. For Sweden, the low inflation rate allows for cuts in the policy rate in order to stimulate growth and reduce unemployment. However, as stated in their recent monetary policy reports, the concern for financial stability due to a continuing rise in house prices and high household debt levels

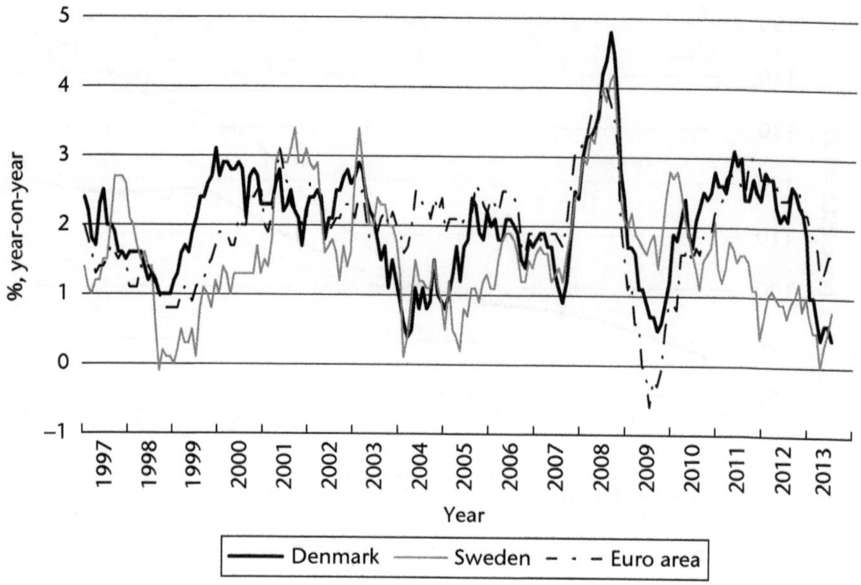

Figure 5.7. HICP Inflation, 1997–2013
Source: Eurostat, monthly data.

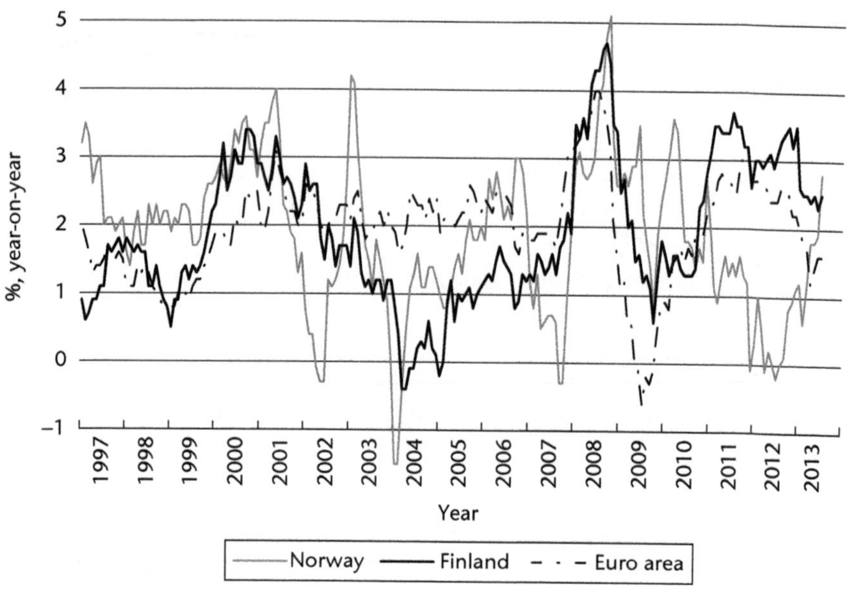

Figure 5.8. HICP Inflation, 1997–2013
Source: Eurostat, monthly data.

makes both Norges Bank and the Swedish Riksbanken cautious of additional lowering of the policy rate, see Norges Bank (2013) and Sveriges Riksbank (2013).

Despite the different monetary policy frameworks, policy interest rates in the Nordic countries have taken remarkably similar paths. In particular the Swedish and Danish policy rates have been close to those of the ECB since 1999, cf. Figure 5.9. Beyond the fixed-exchange-rate policy followed by Denmark, it reflects that business cycles in Sweden and Denmark have been broadly in sync with the euro area for several years. However, amid the financial turmoil in the autumn of 2008, the Swedish Riksbank lowered its interest rate which led to a depreciation of the krona while Danmarks Nationalbank had to tighten monetary policy to stabilize the krone rate. Towards the end of 2008 and throughout 2009, the policy rate was lowered in both Denmark and Sweden.

To counter a sustained inflow of foreign exchange and a tendency for the krone to strengthen, Danmarks Nationalbank lowered the monetary policy interest rates several times in the second half of 2011 and in the first half of 2012. In July 2012, Danmarks Nationalbank lowered its interest rates to historically low levels as a response to ECB's reduction of interest rates. The rate of interest on certificates of deposit in Denmark was reduced to minus 0.20%, which contributed to keeping the krone rate stable. Hence, the transmission from monetary policy interest rates to the krone rate, losing traction during the financial crises, has been well-functioning in recent years irrespectively of the sign of the official interest rates.

In recent years, the Swedish Riksbank has made use of forward guidance by announcing its future monetary policy strategy. To some extent, this may be viewed as a natural extension of the Riksbank's practice of publishing its expected instrument-rate path, which was initiated in 2007 and has been fairly successful at managing market expectations (Svensson, 2010).[6] As discussed in Section 5.2, however, forward guidance differs from more traditional central bank communication in one important aspect: successful forward guidance may provide additional monetary stimulus if the central bank can credibly commit to keeping the interest rate low for a longer period than otherwise expected. Woodford (2012b) finds the Riksbank's recent experiences with forward guidance mixed. For example, in April 2009 the Riksbank cut its repo rate to 0.5%, announcing at the same time that 'the repo rate is expected to remain at a low level until the beginning of 2011'. Paradoxically, this led to an upward jump in the market expectations of the future path for the repo rate. According to the explanation suggested by Woodford (2012b), this announcement led market participants to believe that, in contrast to previous

[6] The Riksbank was preceded by Norges Bank, which had already started publishing its instrument-rate path, in 2005.

expectations, the Riksbank considered 0.5% to be the effective lower bound of the interest rate. Hence, to the extent market participants had expected the repo rate to be cut further in the future, they had to revise their expected path for the repo rate upwards after the Riksbank's announcement. This episode highlights some of the challenges associated with such direct attempts at shaping the private sector's expectations about future monetary policy.[7] Woodford (2012b) argues that other recent forward guidance announcements by the Riksbank have not been successful in affecting market expectations either. On the other hand, countries such as the USA and Canada seem to have had more encouraging experiences with the use of forward guidance.

In theory, the exchange rate typically works as a shock absorber that reduces the need for large interest-rate changes. The Swedish krona and the Norwegian krone fluctuated a lot during the financial crisis, cf. Figure 5.10. However, as indicated by Figure 5.9 this has not been reflected by lower volatility in the policy interest rates relative to Denmark. In the autumn of 2008, international investors withdrew from smaller currencies causing the Swedish krona and the Norwegian krone to depreciate. On the other hand, throughout 2009 and until today both currencies, in particular the Swedish krona, have appreciated against the euro. The strengthening of the krona contributed to bringing inflation down when the Swedish economy was back in recovery after the financial crisis. However, more recently certain voices in the economic debate have advocated the appropriateness of a weaker Swedish krona given the current economic outlook. Similar voices have been absent in the Danish debate for many years, both among politicians and in business circles.

Looking beyond differences in monetary policy frameworks, the financial crisis has provoked a discussion of instruments and objectives of central banks. For example, should central banks care about financial imbalances? Sveriges Riksbank has expressed concerns about household debt. Although macroprudential instruments are better suited for this purpose, the concern could call for a period of higher interest rates than warranted by the inflation-targeting framework as such. Norges Bank has also revealed that it takes financial stability concerns into account, e.g. the strong rise in housing prices and credit growth, by setting interest rates higher recently than suggested by the usual outlook for inflation and the output gap.

In other words, the real interest rate level that is neutral vis-á-vis inflation and output is not necessarily neutral with respect to financial stability. These

[7] Another example of these challenges is provided by the Bank of England's announcement in August 2013 that it intended to keep interest rates low until unemployment has come down to 7 per cent, provided that current and expected inflation remain stable, and financial stability is not jeopardized. This announcement was largely unsuccessful in lowering the market's expected future interest rate path, perhaps because markets had anticipated an announcement of an even more accommodative policy stance or a more unconditional commitment to keep interest rates low.

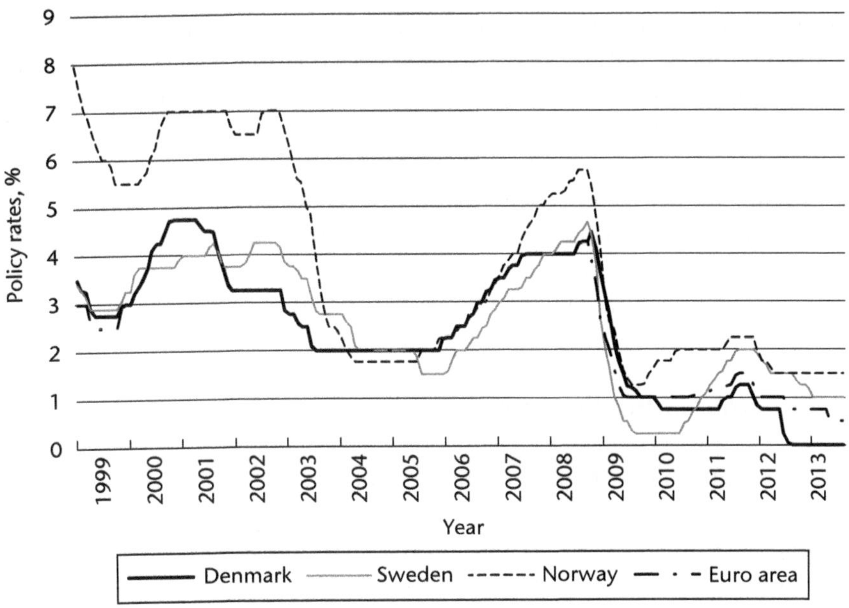

Figure 5.9. Monetary policy interest rates, 1999–2013

Note: Over a large part of the sample the curve for the Danish policy rate covers the one for the euro area.

Source: Danmarks Nationalbank.

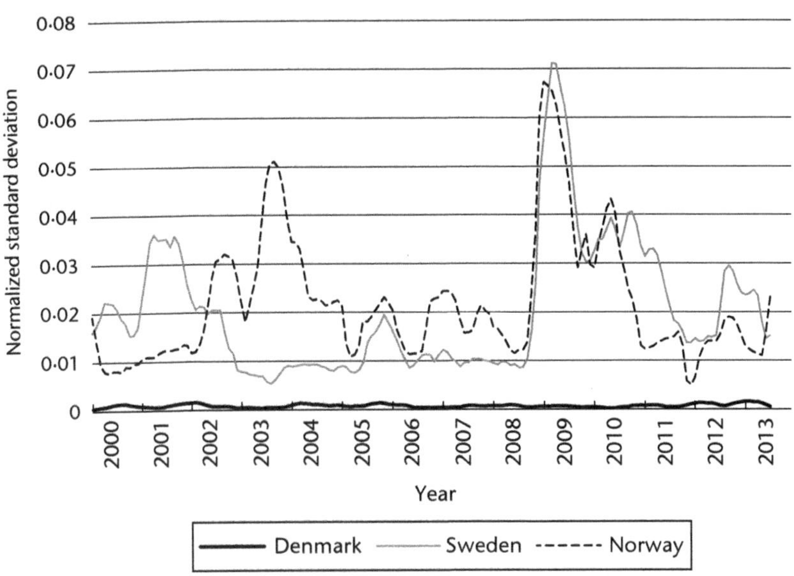

Figure 5.10. Exchange rate volatility, 2000–13

Note: The normalized standard deviation of the exchange rate vis-à-vis the euro is calculated as the standard deviation of the exchange rate divided by the mean of the exchange rate (12-month window).

Source: Danmarks Nationalbank.

considerations reflect that the scope for monetary policy over time has gradually become more ambitious since inflation targeting was introduced in the beginning of the 1990s. A flexible approach to inflation targeting was soon adopted expressing that policy interest rates were set not only with a view to pursue the inflation target but also to stabilize real economic developments. In recent years, the discussions amongst central bankers and scholars in monetary policy have turned to whether central banks with a flexible-inflation-targeting framework should extend its objectives of stabilizing inflation and the output gap to also include financial stability as an objective.

5.4 The Role of Public Finances

Sweden adopted a new regime for fiscal policy in 1997. Government finances would show a surplus of 1% of GDP on average over the business cycle. Nominal expenditures would not exceed a rolling three-year ceiling set by Parliament. The budget contained a buffer as the ceiling included expenditures of a cyclically sensitive nature. The framework has ensured that wishes for new expenditures must be accompanied by proposals for counteracting savings. The mechanism has also ensured that high revenues during boom years do not lead to higher expenditures. In retrospect, the framework has functioned well. The reform has ensured a medium-term-oriented framework for fiscal policy. At the same time this complicates attempts like ours in the present chapter, see below, to single out the impact of a change in monetary-policy framework, as the changes in the conduct of fiscal and monetary policy took place at nearly the same point in time.

As a consequence of the fiscal policy framework and economic development, a severe overheating was avoided in the mid 2000s (cf. Figure 5.3). Government gross debt in Sweden has declined from more than 70% of GDP in the mid 1990s to less than 40%, cf. Figure 5.11.

To put this into perspective, it is interesting for a moment to look at the British development. Swedish and British government debt was similar in 1996, but the British debt has increased to 90% of GDP. Both the UK and Sweden are inflation targeters. There have been some differences in the implementation of the framework, but the similarities are bigger. The pound depreciated more than the krona after the beginning of the financial crisis. The development in debt strongly suggests that the conduct of fiscal policy in the UK with a high degree of spending of windfall revenue gains during the boom has been inferior to Swedish fiscal policy, as the more expansionary fiscal policy has not led to better performance regarding unemployment or output gaps.

The development in government debt, output gaps, and unemployment places Denmark somewhere between Sweden and the UK, and it strongly

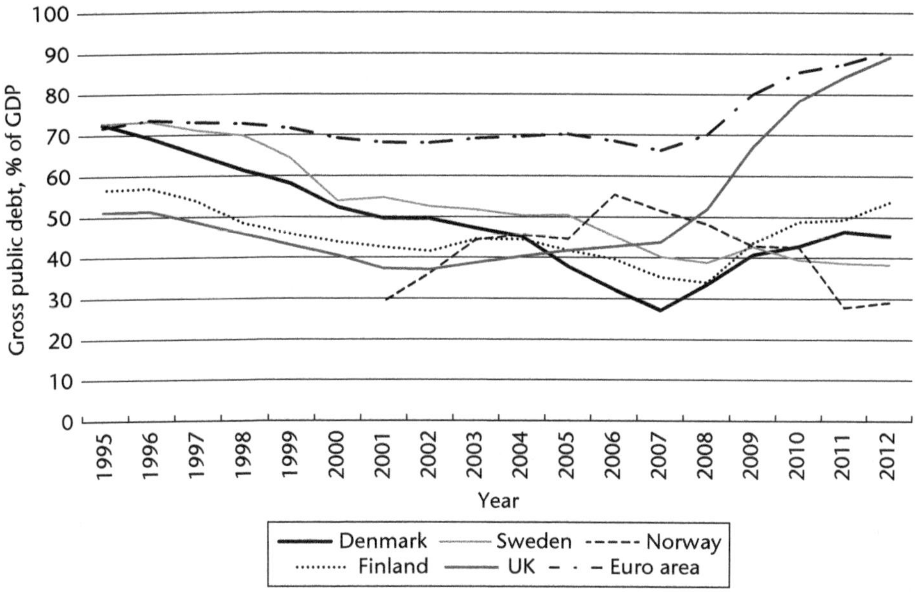

Figure 5.11. Public debt, Nordic countries, UK, and euro area, 1995–2012
Source: Eurostat.

suggests that the differences in monetary policy frameworks are not the main determinant for the actual economic outcome. Differences in the conduct of fiscal policy seem to be far more important. From a Danish perspective, legislation from 2012 on the fiscal policy framework will hopefully prevent government consumption from increasing as it did in the mid 2000s.

Competitiveness is obviously an issue in all regions and countries. The difficulties in achieving economic growth in line with potential have been taken as an indication of problems with gaining competitiveness under a fixed-exchange-rate regime. Unlike the Danish krone, the Swedish krona and the British pound both depreciated. This could be seen as an important help to companies to regain competitiveness, while Danish companies had to struggle with a strong krone, thus prolonging the crisis in Denmark.

On balance, there is not much to that story. International competitiveness is of greater importance in manufacturing than in other sectors of the economy, as the output from manufacturing is tradeable to a larger extent than output from most other sectors. However, production in manufacturing in Denmark has been at least as strong as in Sweden and the UK since the outbreak of the financial crisis, cf. Figure 5.12. Against this, it is our conjecture that just like strong growth in the Danish economy in the years before the crisis was predominantly due to the overheated housing and real estate markets, fuelled inter alia by the introduction of new types of mortgage loans, inadequate property taxation, and insufficient fiscal stabilization, the poorer growth performance in recent years than in Sweden is also attributable to the decline in house prises and thus in household wealth. This is corroborated by the significant drop in construction unlike in the other Nordic countries, cf. Figure 5.13. Investments in residential construction and, via the wealth channel, private consumption are the counterparts to the low growth in aggregate production.

All in all this points to the conclusion that fiscal policy has had a more decisive role for economic performance since the outbreak of the financial crisis than monetary policy.

5.5 Macroeconomic Performance in the Wake of the Financial Crisis

In a previous study (Christensen and Hansen, 2009) we found a significant reduction in the volatilities in both inflation and output gap after the adoption of a consistent fixed-exchange-rate policy, and no such effects of moving to inflation targeting. Estimations covered a broad set of countries on a sample from 1972 to 2005. Subsequently, monetary-policy reactions to the melt-down

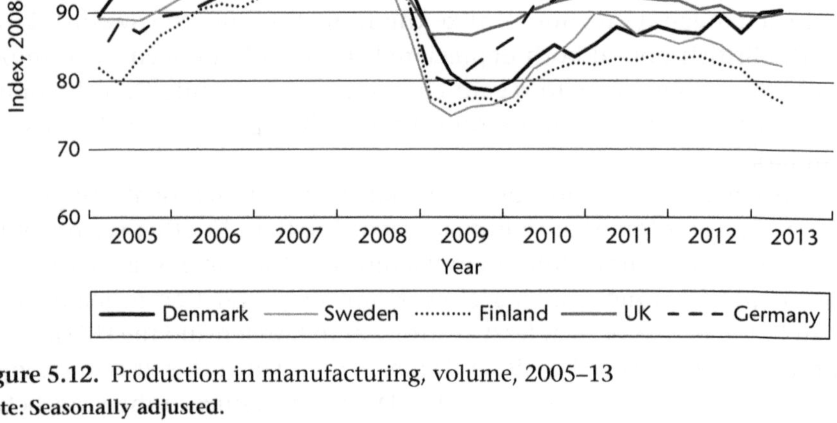

Figure 5.12. Production in manufacturing, volume, 2005–13
Note: Seasonally adjusted.
Source: OECD, Main Economic Indicators, quarterly data.

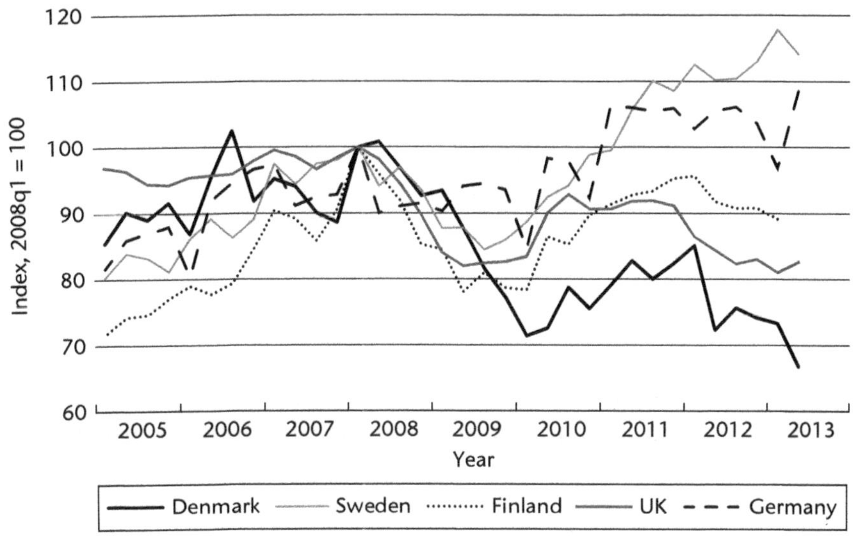

Figure 5.13. Production in construction, volume, 2005–13

Note: Seasonally adjusted.

Source: OECD, Main Economic Indicators, quarterly data.

of financial markets in 2008 and the ensuing economic downturn have varied substantially across countries, partly reflecting the severity of the economic shock and partly differences in monetary-policy regimes, as discussed above. Hence, it is of interest to investigate whether our results still hold after the financial crisis.

As with our previous analysis we apply a difference-in-difference approach to estimate the impact on macroeconomic performance of changing to either a fixed-exchange-rate policy or to inflation targeting. In our sample, which covers the period from 1972 to 2011, we have nine countries that opted for a consistent fixed-exchange-rate policy, seven that opted for inflation targeting, and a control group of six countries that broadly speaking did not alter their monetary-policy regime throughout the sample period.[8] Notwithstanding that any regime classification is subjective and far from unequivocal we consider only changes to a clear and consistent regime.[9]

[8] Countries that changed to a consistent fixed-exchange-rate policy: Belgium (1987), Denmark (1987), Finland (1997), France (1987), Greece (1999), Ireland (1997), Italy (1997), Portugal (1997), and Spain (1997). Countries that changed to inflation targeting: Australia (1993), Canada (1991), Iceland (2001), New Zealand (1990), Norway (1999), Sweden (1993), and the UK (1993). Countries that did not change regime: Austria, Germany, Japan, the Netherlands, Switzerland, and the USA (the years where regime changes are considered to have taken place are in parentheses).

[9] In many cases our judgements are based on discussions with colleagues from the central banks in question. Robustness checks show that in no cases does the classification of any individual country affect the overall conclusions.

The estimation model is as follows:

$$y_{it} = \alpha_i + \beta_t + \gamma_{FER} \cdot I_{FER,it} + \gamma_{IT} \cdot I_{IT,it} + \varepsilon_{it} \quad (1)$$

y_{it} is a variable representing macroeconomic performance, i.e. the level of inflation or the volatility in inflation or output gap, respectively. α_i captures the fixed country effect and β_t the fixed time effect; $I_{FER,it}$ is an indicator, that takes the value 1 if country *i* at time *t* pursues a fixed-exchange-rate policy, and otherwise the value 0; $I_{IT,it}$ is an indicator that equivalently expresses whether a country pursues an inflation targeting strategy; and γ_{FER} and γ_{IT} are the respective coefficients that measure the (treatment) effect of having changed to the regime in question. ε_{it} is an error term assumed to be independently and identically distributed with the mean value of zero.

The model presupposes that the developments in the different measures of macroeconomic performance have a common, underlying time trend. With the exception of the recurrent Icelandic experiences of very high and volatile inflation, this is indeed the case.[10] In general, the rate of inflation decreased from in many cases two-digit levels in the 1970s to low levels consistent with price stability in all countries in the latter part of the sample. In some countries, in particular the core countries of the ERM, low levels of inflation were obtained during the 1980s, while this happened only towards the mid 1990s in countries that in the 1990s joined the ERM or opted for inflation targeting. Inflation volatility that is highly correlated with the level of inflation shows a similar pattern. Regarding the variability in the output, country differences are in general less marked. The variability of the output gap was clearly higher in the first part of the sample than after the mid 1990s, but it rose again significantly in all countries after the financial crisis. Strikingly, the inflation rate in advanced economies has not been much affected by tight capacity before the crisis, nor by the sharp drop in resource utilization subsequently. This indicates that longer-term inflation expectations have become more firmly anchored across regimes in the past decade whereby inflation has become less responsive to changes in economic capacity, see e.g. IMF (2013).

For changes in monetary-policy regimes to have a positive impact on macroeconomic performance they must give rise to an improvement beyond the observed global improvement. Figure 5.14 shows the common trends across countries in inflation levels and variability of inflation and output gap.

To have unbiased econometric results, changes in monetary-policy regime must be exogenous with respect to the development in the dependent

[10] For that reason, Iceland is kept out of the econometric estimations below.

variables, i.e. the measures of macroeconomic performance. This is a questionable assumption since in particular the development in inflation is likely to be a cause for considering changes in regime, see e.g. Gertler (2005) on the importance of inflation for decisions to change to inflation targeting. Oppositely, it might also be the case that regimes changes are prepared by obtaining sufficient economic stability in advance. Like e.g. Persson (2005), we address the problem of a possible bias due to endogeneity by investigating whether the estimated effects of a change of policy are robust to the introduction of a dummy variable for five years up to a regime change.

Finally, serial correlation may lead to an underestimation of the standard deviation of error terms, though not to any bias in the estimated effects of a change of policy. We take account of this by also showing variances based on robust methods allowing for both heteroscedasticity across countries and random serial correlation between the error terms within each country as proposed by Arellano (1987).

The estimated impact of changes in monetary-policy regimes are shown in Table 5.1. Regarding the impact on inflation, both the level and its volatility, adding information about the period 2006–11, i.e. the years around

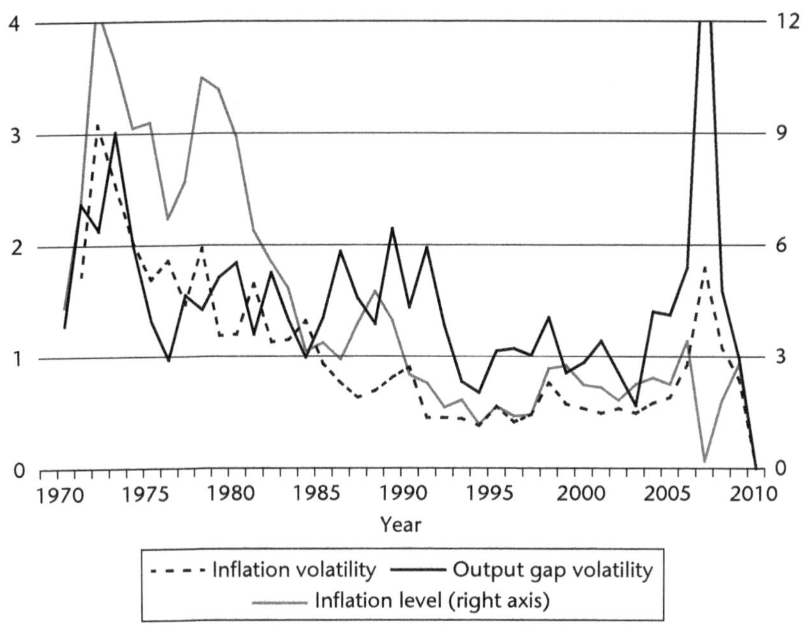

Figure 5.14. Inflation level and volatility in inflation and output gap—estimated common trend across countries, 1972–2011

Note: The graphs depict the estimated time effect, β_t, that follows from estimations of equation (1).

the financial crisis and the economic recession does not alter results in any noticeable way. As in our previous analysis, changing to either inflation targeting or fixed exchange rates has led to a significant reduction in the level of inflation. However, the additional reduction in the annual inflation rate was more marked in countries that changed to fixed exchange rates, 4 to 5% compared to an average reduction of around 2% beyond the global trend in countries that moved to inflation targeting.

Furthermore, inflation volatility has fallen significantly after the change to a consistent fixed-exchange-rate policy, whereas there are no significant effects from the change to inflation targeting. On average the reduction in the volatility, i.e. the standard deviation of annual inflation, in countries that adopted a fixed-exchange-rate policy was around 0.5–0.7% higher than the general tendency of a decline in inflation volatility across all countries from

Table 5.1. Significance of the monetary-policy regime to macroeconomic performance, difference-in-difference estimation, 1972–2011

	Dependent variable					
	Inflation level		Inflation volatility		Variability in the output gap	
	(1)	(2)	(1)	(2)	(1)	(2)
Fixed exchange rates, indicator	−3.65	−4.86	−0.50	−0.67	−0.12	−0.24
	(−9.63)	(−11.9)	(−3.81)	(−4.67)	(−0.72)	(−1.25)
	[−3.71]	[−3.81]	[−2.13]	[−2.05]	[−0.69]	[−1.15]
Inflation targeting, indicator	−1.98	−2.39	−0.09	0.02	−0.04	−0.10
	(−4.67)	(−5.26)	(−0.62)	(0.12)	(−0.23)	(−0.51)
	[−2.42]	[−3.35]	[−0.33]	[0.08]	[−0.17]	[−0.35]
Fixed exchange rates, historical		−3.65		−0.64		−0.27
regime dummy (5 years before)		(−7.39)		(−3.73)		(−1.21)
		[−3.54]		[−2.14]		[−1.30]
Inflation targeting, historical		0.59		0.69		−0.07
regime dummy (5 years before)		(1.03)		(3.43)		(−0.30)
		[0.59]		[1.68]		[−0.35]
R2	0.77	0.78	0.49	0.51	0.40	0.40
#obs	861	861	840	840	752	752
#countries	21	21	21	21	21	21

Note: Inflation is the percentage annual change in CPI, and inflation volatility is the standard deviation of the annual change in CPI for the last 24 months up to the end of the year. For Australia and New Zealand CPI is only available on a quarterly basis. This is of almost no significance to the calculation of the standard deviation. Output gap volatility is the absolute annual change in the output gap in per cent of GDP. (1) and (2): basic model excluding Iceland. Model (1) is estimated without historical regime dummies (measured as the policy regime five years before), model (2) is estimated with historical regime dummies (measured as the policy regime five years before). Conventional t-values in round brackets. Robust t-values in square brackets.

Source for estimation data: OECD Main Economic Indicators and OECD Economic Outlook 92.

around 1½% in the second half of the 1970s and in the 1980s to around ½% in the 1990s and 2000s, see Figure 5.14.

These results are robust to the introduction of indicators for the period preceding the change of regime, despite the fact that these indicators in some cases are significant, and hence cannot be seen as a result of inverse causality. For fixed-exchange-rate countries the coefficient to the dummy for the last five years up to the regime change is negative, reflecting that the level and volatility of inflation were low before adopting fixed exchange rates, whereas the opposite applies to the inflation-targeting countries. This suggests that inflation was brought down in an orderly way in advance of changing to fixed exchange rates, while changes to inflation targeting were in many cases enforced rather than chosen due to an unfavourable economic development, including in inflation.

Changes in monetary-policy regimes have no significant impact on the variability of the output gap. The estimated impact is negative, being largest in the case of changes to a fixed-exchange-rate regime, but numerically smaller than estimates in our previous study, where there was a significant reduction in variability from changes to a fixed-exchange-rate regime. This structural break is no surprise in view of the depth of the economic recession following the financial crisis irrespective of the monetary policy regime.

It is noticeable that including the very exceptional experiences of the recent crisis has not altered the conclusions from our previous study in any fundamental sense. Inflation has declined beyond the global trend following the adoption of both a fixed-exchange-rate policy and inflation targeting. Likewise, there has been a significant reduction in the inflation volatility beyond the global trend after changes to fixed exchange rates, whereas we observe no such effect from a move to inflation targeting. Regime changes have not lead to any significant reduction in the variability of the output gap beyond the global trend.[11] These conclusions are at odds with much of the existing literature on monetary policy and inflation targeting. Hence, it raises questions about the adequacy of some common model assumptions, such as whether the exchange rate in practice acts a shock absorber or as a shock creator, and whether it makes sense to disregard the role of fiscal policy as an active instrument in models of monetary policy.

[11] Overall, the results are not sensitive to the classification of the individual countries, nor driven by experiences in any single country. Robustness checks (not shown) where data for every country are omitted in turn show that no individual country was decisive for the results. Similarly, altering some of the questionable classifications of monetary-policy regimes, as in our previous study, does not impact our estimates qualitatively.

5.6 Conclusions

In this chapter, we have investigated monetary policy in the Nordic countries and macroeconomic outcomes. There are significant differences across the countries with respect to the design of monetary policy, including e.g. the approach to the constraint implied by the zero lower bound, and hence how monetary policy interferes with other types of policy, in particular fiscal and macroprudential policy. In contrast, differences in macroeconomic performance are less distinctive.

Monetary policy over the last 20 years has shown that the inflation-targeting framework is still under development. It started with an objective of price stability and was soon extended to also include a target of real economic stability. In the most recent years considerations to extend the objectives of price and output stability and pay more attention to financial developments, e.g. real estate prices and credit growth, have been made. Monetary policy in Norway and that in Sweden are both cases in point in that respect. Unsurprisingly, the academic interest in this matter is substantial. On the other hand, the fixed-exchange-rate framework applied by Danmarks Nationalbank has remained practically unchanged for decades and continued to show its virtues—completely outside the academic spotlights—even under the severe stress test implied by the financial crisis and the overheating of the Danish economy. It implies a clear distribution of responsibilities where policy interest rates are set to stabilize the exchange rates whereas stability of inflation, output, and the financial system are left to other policies.

Our analysis shows that monetary policy is far from being the main factor in explaining the economic performance of different countries in recent years. Stability-oriented economic policies and sound public finances based on medium- and long-term objectives before the crisis have been a more important determinant. In a longer perspective, a well-designed monetary policy based on a stable nominal anchor, *in casu* the exchange rate or an inflation target, provides the best framework for a stable development in prices and output. As long as monetary policy is managed consistently, and supported by a stability-oriented fiscal policy, the choice of intermediate targets seems to be of lesser importance.

This is at odds with much of the academic literature on monetary economics where inflation targeting is considered best-practice monetary policy. This may be explained by the fact that models for monetary policy analysis often disregard fiscal policy as an instrument for economic stabilization. Furthermore, it is typically assumed that the exchange rate can be determined by the uncovered interest-rate parity implying that exchange rate changes act as a shock absorber that reduces the need for large interest rate changes.

However, this is generally not supported by the empirics, as illustrated by the Nordic experiences in recent years, as discussed, where the larger fluctuations of the Norwegian krone and Swedish krona were not matched by a lower volatility in policy rates in Norway and Sweden than in Denmark.

After all, monetary policy is to a large extent about managing expectations, or to use a well-known quote (Woodford, 2005): 'Not only do expectations about policy matter, but [. . .] very little else matters.' This article is a testimony that monetary authorities in Denmark, Finland, Norway, and Sweden have succeeded in that respect over a longer period, and most notably, that this has been achieved in rather distinct monetary-policy regimes.

References

Arellano, M. (1987), 'Computing Robust Standard Errors for Within-Groups Estimators', *Oxford Bulletin of Economics and Statistics*, vol. 49, no. 4, pp. 431–34.

Ball, L. M. (2010), 'The Performance of Alternative Monetary Regimes', in B. M. Friedman and M. Woodford (eds), *Handbook of Monetary Economics*, vol. 3, pp. 1303–43.

Borio, C. (2012a), 'The Financial Cycle and Macroeconomics. What Have We Learnt?', BIS Working Paper, no. 395, December 2012.

Borio, C. (2012b), 'On Time, Stocks, and Flows: Understanding the Global Macroeconomic Challenges', lecture at the Munich Seminar series, CESIfo Group and Süddeutsche Zeitung, 15 October 2012.

Carney, M. (2012), 'Guidance'. Speech, CFA Society, Toronto, 11 December.

Christensen, A.M., and N.L. Hansen (2009), 'The Monetary-Policy Regime and the Development in Central Macroeconomic Variables in the OECD Countries 1970–2005', *Danish Journal of Economics*, vol. 147, no. 2, pp. 216–49.

Clarida, R., J. Gali, and M. Gertler (2002), 'A Simple Framework for International Monetary Policy Analysis', *Journal of Monetary Economics*, vol. 49, pp. 879–904.

Cobham, D., Ø. Eitrheim, S. Gerlach, and J.F. Qvigstad (2010), *Twenty Years of Inflation Targeting. Lessons Learned and Future Prospects*, Cambridge: Cambridge University Press.

Corsetti, G., L. Dedola, and S. Leduc (2010), 'Optimal Monetary Policy in Open Economies', in B. M. Friedman and M. Woodford (eds), *Handbook of Monetary Economics*, vol. 3, pp. 861–933.

Faia, E. and T. Monacelli (2008), 'Optimal Monetary Policy in a Small Open Economy with Home Bias', *Journal of Money, Credit and Banking*, vol. 40, pp. 721–50.

Fatas, A., I. Mihov, and A. Rose (2007), 'Quantitative Goals for Monetary Policy', *Journal of Money, Credit and Banking*, vol. 39, pp. 1163–76.

Friedman, M. (1953), 'The Case for Flexible Exchange Rates', in *Essays in Positive Economics*, University of Chicago Press, Chicago, IL.

Gali, J. and T. Monacelli (2005), 'Monetary Policy and Exchange Rate Volatility in a Small Open Economy', *Review of Economic Studies*, vol. 72, pp. 707–34.

Gertler, M. 'Comment on Ball and Sheridan (2005), "Does Inflation Targetting Matter?"', in *The Inflation-Targeting Debate*, edited by B. S. Bernanke and M. Woodford, NBER-Studies in Business Cycles, Chicago: The University of Chicago Press, pp. 276–81.

Goldberg, P. and M. Knetter (1997), 'Goods Prices and Exchange Rates. What Have We Learned?', *Journal of Economic Literature*, vol. 35, pp. 1243–72.

Gopinath, G. and R. Rigobon (2008), 'Sticky Borders', *Quarterly Journal of Economics*, vol. 123, pp. 531–75.

Hall, R. (2013), 'The Routes into and out of the Zero Lower Bound'. Presented at the annual Jackson Hole Conference, August 2013.

Hofmann, B. and B. Bogdanova (2012), 'Taylor Rules and Monetary Policy: a Global "Great Deviation"?', *BIS Quarterly Review*, September, pp. 37–49.

IMF (2013), 'The Dog That Didn't Bark: Has Inflation Been Muzzled Or Was It Just Sleeping?', *World Economic Outlook* (Chapter 3), April 2013.

Norges Bank (2013), Monetary Policy Report, 3/13, September.

Persson, T. (2005), 'Forms of Democracy, Policy, and Economic Development', CEPR *Discussion Paper* No. 4938, February 2005.

Rose, A.K. (2011), 'Exchange Rate Regimes in the Modern Era: Fixed, Floating, and Flaky', *Journal of Economic Literature*, vol. 49, pp. 652–72.

Svensson, L.E.O. (2002), 'Monetary Policy and Real Stabilization', in *Rethinking Stabilization Policy*, Proceedings of a Symposium Sponsored by the Federal Reserve Bank of Kansas City, Jackson Hole, Wyoming, 29–31 August, 2002.

Svensson, L.E.O. (2003), 'What Is Wrong with Taylor Rules? Using Judgment in Monetary Policy through Targeting Rules', *Journal of Economic Literature*, vol. 41, pp. 426–77.

Svensson, L.E.O. (2010), 'Policy Expectations and Policy Evaluations: The Role of Transparency and Communication', *Sveriges Riksbank Economic Review 1*, 2010.

Svensson, L.E.O. (2012), 'Comment on Michael Woodford, "Inflation Targeting and Financial Stability"', *Sveriges Riksbank Economic Review 1*, 2012.

Sveriges Riksbank (2013), Monetary Policy Report, July.

Woodford, M. (2005), 'Central-Bank Communication and Policy Effectiveness', in *The Greenspan Era: Lessons for the Future*, Kansas City: Federal Reserve Bank of Kansas City, pp. 399–474.

Woodford, M. (2012a), 'Inflation Targeting and Financial Stability', *Sveriges Riksbank Economic Review 1*, 2012.

Woodford, M. (2012b), 'Methods of Policy Accommodation at the Interest-Rate Lower Bound', in *The Changing Policy Landscape*, Kansas City: Federal Reserve Bank of Kansas City.

Wren-Lewis, S. (2013), Written evidence for the House of Commons Treasury Committee, hearing on the appointment of Mark Carney as Governor of the Bank of England, January. <http://www.publications.parliament.uk/pa/cm201213/cmselect/cmtreasy/944/944we05.htm>.

Comments on 'What Scope for Monetary Policy? Experiences from the Nordic Countries After the Financial Crisis' by A. M. Christensen and N. L. Hansen

Jesper Rangvid

This chapter does three things: it gives an overview of recent theories on monetary policies in small open economies; it discusses recent macroeconomic performance in the Nordic countries; and it updates the analysis in Christensen and Hansen (2009) to include the years surrounding the 2008–9 financial crisis and its aftermath.

I have nothing to say about the overview of recent theories on monetary policy: it's a fine small review. Hence, I will concentrate my remarks on the latter two parts of the chapter.

C5.1 Effects of Exchange Rate Regimes

Christensen and Hansen (2009) investigated whether changes in monetary policy regimes (e.g. switching from a floating to a fixed exchange rate regime) matter for subsequent levels of inflation, inflation volatility, and output gap volatility for 22 OECD countries over the 1970–2005 period. The chapter found that countries that switched to inflation targeting (IT) or exchange rate targeting (ERT) experienced lower levels of inflation after the change. In addition, it found that countries switching to ERT experienced lower levels of inflation volatility and output gaps (the results with respect to the output gap were borderline significant, though), whereas no such effects were found for countries switching to IT. Christensen and Hansen ask in this chapter whether the results remain robust if extending the data to 2011, i.e. to include the years surrounding the crisis. Christensen and Hansen find that the results on inflation levels and inflation volatility remain robust, whereas the results with respect to output-gap volatility are no longer significant, i.e. in the extended sample output gaps cannot be shown to be significantly lower after countries switched to ERT.

The questions asked are interesting and important, and the econometric procedure well-executed. Are we surprised by the results, then? From a theoretical point of view, the authors argue that we should be, but from an empirical stance I would argue that we are probably not.

There is a large body of empirical work conducted by in particular A. Rose and co-authors, starting with the by now classic Flood and Rose (1995) text that showed that volatility of macroeconomic variables do not differ much between fixed and floating exchange rate regimes. This result was interesting, and controversial, as it implies, on one hand, that the choice of exchange rate regime is not crucial for macroeconomic volatility but also, on the other hand, that exchange rate volatility can be brought down without increasing volatility elsewhere in the economy. More recently, Rose (2011) surveys the literature and concludes that 'similar countries choose radically different exchange rate regimes without substantive consequences for macroeconomic outcomes like output growth and inflation'. Breedon, Pétursson, and Rose (2011) focus on small open economies and find that there is only weak correlation between the choice of exchange rate regime and macroeconomic volatility, and Pétursson (2013) shows that there is no systematic difference in export performance after the 2008 crisis between countries with floating or fixed exchange rates. The sample of countries studied in the present Christensen and Hansen chapter is a subset of a fuller set of countries (21 OECD countries are studied here) and the econometric procedure, I would argue, more elegant than procedures sometimes used in the literature, as the difference-in-differences used here gets us closer to identifying 'causality', but the overall result that the exchange rate regime does not matter for real variables (output gaps) is in accordance with existing results. It is comforting to know that other samples or econometric procedures do not change this result.

Regarding inflation, this chapter shows that inflation and inflation volatility are lower after switching to ERT. This seems to be somewhat different to results in Flood and Rose (1995), Rose (2011), and Breedon et al. (2011). It is not 100% clear from the chapter why this is so. It would have been interesting if the present Christensen and Hansen chapter had discussed what could have caused this difference in results in more detail.

C5.2 Macroeconomic Performance

The overall conclusion in the chapter by Christensen and Hansen is that the performances of the Nordic countries are, to a large extent, similar, and not dependent on monetary policy. Christensen and Hansen show that long-term growth in 'welfare', inflation, unemployment, etc. have, overall, been rather similar, with the exception of the special circumstances relating to Norway. I can only agree with this interpretation.

Regarding the post-2008 performance, however, there is one dimension that I would like to draw attention to: the impact of the financial crises on the financial sectors in the different countries has been very different, with the Danish financial sector being particularly hard hit. Rangvid et al. (2013) analyse the causes and consequences of the financial crisis in Denmark, and compare it to other countries, not least some of the Nordic countries.

Figure C5.1 shows that loss impairments were very large in Danish banks, and also large in the total Danish financial sector which includes both banks and specialized mortgage institutions. Figure C5.2 shows that lending growth after the crisis has been low in Denmark, and in particular in Danish banks. In contrast, the Swedish and Norwegian financial sectors have been less affected by the crisis and have continued lending after the crisis.

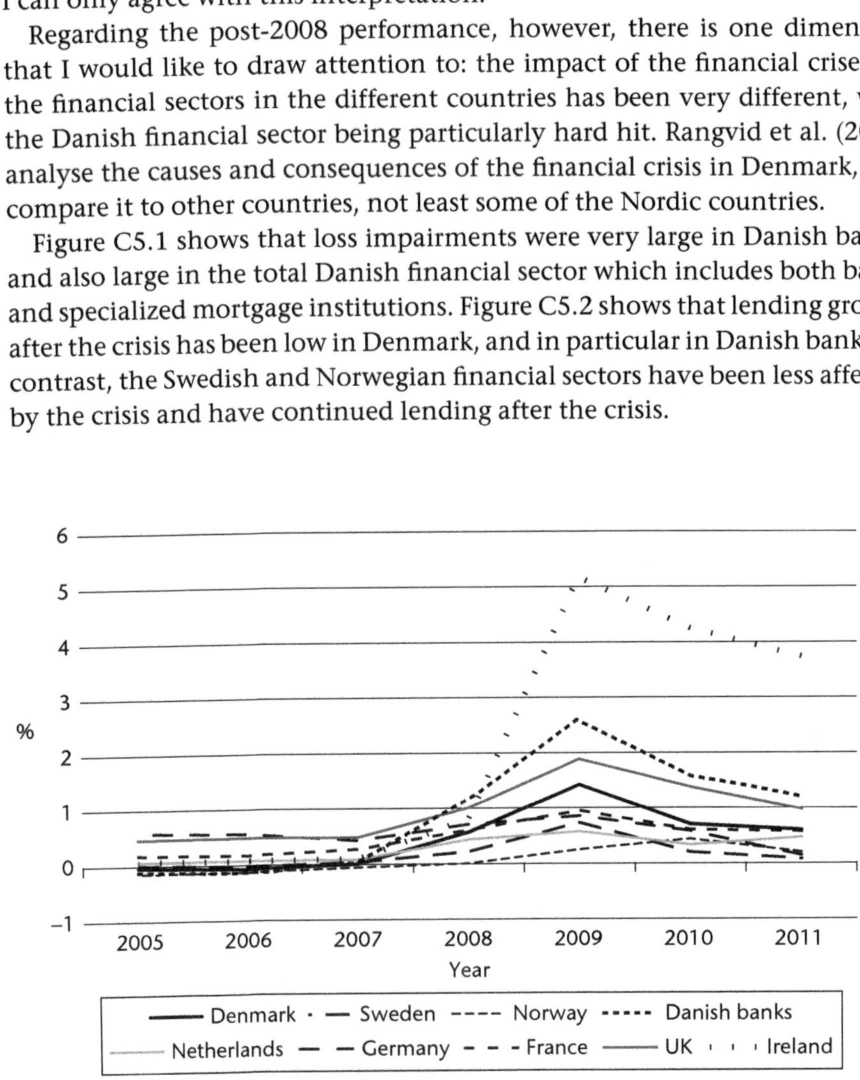

Figure C5.1. Loss impairments in per cent
Source: Rangvid et al. (2013).

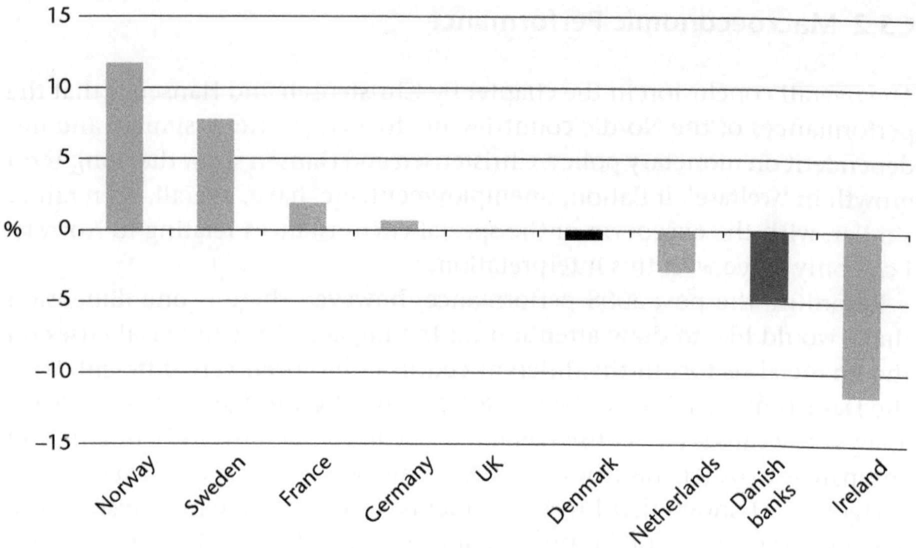

Figure C5.2. Lending growth after the crisis (2008–11) *Source*: Rangvid et al. (2013).

It is difficult to prove causality, but it seems reasonable to speculate that the relatively low economic growth in Denmark after the crisis has at least something to do with the size of the blow to the Danish financial sector: banks experiencing losses hold back on lending which reduces economic growth which then leads to new losses in banks, etc.

Has this something to do with monetary policy, then? On one hand, the fixed-exchange-rate policy in Denmark implied that the Danish central bank could not raise interest rates in the run-up to the crisis, which would have been helpful given the size of the real-estate bubble in Denmark before the crisis. On the other hand, it is not clear that countries with floating exchange rates and overheating real-estate markets before the crisis performed significantly better (e.g. Iceland and the UK compared to Denmark). It is also relevant to remember that in a fixed-exchange-rate regime, fiscal policy becomes relatively more important for stabilization-oriented economic policy. In this regard, it was unfortunate that fiscal policy in Denmark was too loose before the crisis, as Rangvid et al. (2013) and Christensen and Hansen conclude. In any case, at least, there are lessons to be learned from the Danish experience in the sense that Denmark was hard hit by the crisis, and stabilization-oriented macroeconomic policy, in a broad sense, thus should have been adhered to more thoroughly before the crisis. It can also be learned, again, that financial-sector excesses can have important shorter-term consequences for the real economy.

References

Breedon, Francis, Thorarinn Petursson, and Andrew Rose (2012), 'Exchange Rate Policy in Small Rich Economies'. *Open Economies Review*, vol. 23, issue 3, pages 421–45,.

Christensen, A.M. and N.L. Hansen (2009), 'The Monetary-Policy Regime and the Development in Central Macroeconomic Variables in the OECD Countries 1970–2005'. *Danish Journal of Economics*, vol. 147, no. 2, 2009.

Flood, Robert and Andrew Rose (1995), 'Fixing Exchange Rates: a Virtual Quest for Fundamentals', *The Journal of Monetary Economics*, vol. 36, issue 1, pages 3–37.

Jesper Rangvid, Anders Grosen, Finn Østrup, Peter Møgelvang-Hansen, Hugo Frey Jensen, Jens Thomsen, Peter Schütze, Julie Galbo, Christian Ølgaard, Niels Kleis Frederiksen, and Birger Buchhave Poulsen. 'The Financial Crisis in Denmark—Causes, Consequences and Lessons'. *Danish Ministry of Business and Growth*, 2013.

Pétursson, Thorarinn. 'Spot the Difference: Economic Performance and Currency Regimes in the Global Financial Crisis'. Speech given at the 23rd Economic Forum, Krynica Poland, 3–5 September 2013

Rose, Andrew (2011), 'Exchange Rate Regimes in the Modern Era: Fixed, Floating, and Flaky'. *Journal of Economic Literature*, vol. 49, issue 3, pages 652–72.

6

Monetary Policy and Exchange Rate Stabilization in Norway and Sweden

Hilde C. Bjørnland and Junior Maih

6.1 Introduction

Norway and Sweden have both formally adopted inflation targeting as their framework for monetary policy.[1] Sweden switched to inflation targeting in the early 1990s after currency crises and the collapse of its fixed-exchange-rate regime to the ECU in the autumn of 1992.[2] The country has had a policy of not intervening systematically in the foreign exchange market since then.

Norway abandoned the fixed-exchange-rate system in December 1992, and the foreign exchange regime thereafter became more flexible. Monetary policy was still oriented towards maintaining a stable exchange rate in relation to European currencies, although without defining a central exchange rate with fluctuation margins that would be defended by interventions. Eventually, in early 2001, a formal inflation-targeting framework was adopted.

In this chapter we analyse in detail the economic performance of key economic variables in two small open economies: Norway and Sweden, prior to and after implementing inflation targeting as their framework for monetary policy. Having established some stylized facts, we investigate the role of monetary policy for stabilizing economic performance. Specifically, we analyse to what extent monetary policy has contributed to stabilizing the exchange rate (and thereby also inflation) over the period examined.

[1] The views expressed in this chapter are those of the authors and do not necessarily reflect the views of Norges Bank. We thank Michael Bergman, Roberto Billi, and the participants at the conference 'Reform Capacity and Macroeconomic Performance in the Nordic Countries' for constructive comments.

[2] The Swedish inflation target was announced in January 1993 and became operative in 1995 (Berg, 2005).

To examine this question, we build on previous work by Alstadheim, Bjørnland, and Maih (2013), who have developed a model that allows for regime changes in the monetary policy responses and shocks that hit small open economies. With this framework we explore the extent to which the inflation-targeting central banks in Norway and Sweden put the same emphasis on stabilizing the exchange rate throughout the period, independently of the known regime changes and the volatility of shocks that occurred over the period. Furthermore, we analyse whether the effects of terms-of-trade shocks on output and inflation are exacerbated in countries that respond strongly to the exchange rate.[3]

We have three main findings. *First,* we find that volatility has declined over time for all the key economic variables except GDP in Sweden and the exchange rate in Norway. Hence, good policies (and maybe also good luck), have made the Scandinavian economies overall more stable. The exception is the financial crisis when output in Sweden was hit hard.

Second, turning to the recent inflation-targeting period, we find that the interest rate and terms of trade are substantially more volatile in Norway than in Sweden, while the other domestic variables (including the exchange rate) have about the same volatility. This suggests that monetary policy could have a role in stabilizing the exchange rate (and subsequently inflation) in Norway, in particular when terms of trade shocks are a major source of disturbance to the economy.

Third, we find that the central bank in Sweden has put less weight on stabilizing the exchange rate, as measured by the response to the nominal effective exchange rate, since inflation targeting was adopted in the early 1990s. For Norway, we do not observe a systematic change in the response to the nominal effective exchange rate. In fact, the interest-rate response to the exchange rate has remained high throughout the period analysed. This could explain why the exchange rate remains relatively stable in Norway despite high volatility in the terms of trade. We also show that by responding strongly to the exchange rate, the adverse effects of terms-of-trade shocks on the exchange rate and subsequently output are lessened. Monetary policy therefore contributes to exacerbate a terms-of-trade-led boom in the economy, by boosting instead output and inflation.

The remainder of the chapter is structured as follows: in Section 2, we present some stylized facts of business cycles in Norway and Sweden, comparing with other countries wherever relevant. Section 3 briefly describes the small-open-economy New Keynesian model, while the estimation procedure is briefly described in Section 4. Section 5 presents the data, while in Section 6 we report the results. Section 7 concludes.

[3] To analyse this question we use new solution algorithms developed by Maih (2012).

6.2 Economic Performance in Norway and Sweden

We start by examining volatility of key economic variables in the period prior to and after inflation targeting was adopted in Norway and Sweden. Definition of variables and their sources is described in the Appendix. To be able to compare the two countries, we split the sample in 1999. That is, Table 6.1 displays the standard deviation of key variables for the period 1983–99, while Table 6.2 displays standard deviations from 2000–11. Although Norway adopted inflation targeting formally in 2001, monetary policy was already geared towards stable inflation rates, from 1999 (Gjedrem, 2001). Hence, splitting the sample at 1999 seems reasonable. Sweden had an operative inflation target in place from 1995 (Berg, 2005). However, splitting the sample in 1995 would not change the results much for Sweden, hence we keep the same sample for the two countries for ease of comparison.

Focusing first on the volatility of the domestic variables, GDP, annual inflation, the interest rate, and the nominal effective exchange rate, we find that volatility has fallen over time for most variables.[4] One exception is for GDP in Sweden and for the exchange rate in Norway, where volatility is substantially higher in the inflation-targeting period. Hence, good policies (and maybe also good luck), have made the Scandinavian economies more stable over time. Yet, there are some exceptions which merit some further analysis, that we will discuss in the end.

It is also interesting to note that for the early sample 1983–99, volatility of both inflation and the exchange rate are higher in Sweden than in Norway. This suggests one reason for why Sweden switched to an inflation-targeting framework earlier than Norway. The fixed-exchange-rate regime did not provide overall stability in the Swedish economy, at least compared to Norway.

Turning to the recent inflation-targeting period, among the four variables mentioned above, only the interest rate seems to be substantially more volatile in Norway than in Sweden (almost twice as volatile). This is actually quite extraordinary, as the terms of trade are about five times more volatile in Norway than in Sweden (see Tables 6.1 and 6.2), suggesting that inflation and the exchange rate should also be much more volatile.

This is not the case. The fact that the interest rate and terms of trade are more volatile in Norway than Sweden, while the other domestic economic variables have about the same volatility, motivates us to examine the role of monetary policy in stabilizing economic performance.

[4] GDP and the nominal effective exchange rate are transformed to first differences (quarter-on-quarter changes) to be stationary.

Table 6.1. Norway and Sweden: volatility (1983–99)

	GDP	Inflation	Interest rate	Exchange rate	Terms of Trade
Norway	1.28	2.19	3.76	1.59	5.48
Sweden	0.64	3.18	3.44	2.75	1.19

Table 6.2. Norway and Sweden: volatility (2000–11)

	GDP	Inflation	Interest rate	Exchange rate	Terms of Trade
Norway	1.01	1.15	2.02	2.76	5.59
Sweden	1.06	1.10	1.33	2.54	1.18

6.2.1 *Economic Performance in the Inflation-Targeting Period*

Having established some overall stylized facts prior to and after the inflation-targeting period, we now turn to examine in more detail economic performance in the last decade or so (i.e. the inflation-targeting period).

The Norges Bank Watch report from 2011 (Bjørnland and Wilhelmsen, 2011) concluded that many central banks in small open economies, including Norges Bank and Sveriges Riksbank, have successfully implemented their policy within an inflation-targeting framework as best reflected in a consumer price index (CPI) inflation that has moved around the target. This is confirmed in Figure 6.1, which graphs annual inflation in the last decade (2000–11).

Compared to the other countries analysed here, an average inflation rate in Norway of 2% is neither exceptionally low nor high, with the US experiencing the highest average inflation rate of 2.4% and Sweden, with 1.5%, the lowest. However, Figure 6.1 also illustrates that CPI inflation fluctuates a lot in all countries.

Annual growth rates for GDP in mainland Norway have been 2.3% on average in the inflation-targeting period, which of the countries compared here, is only surpassed (marginally) by Sweden (see Figure 6.2). Figure 6.2 also illustrates that throughout this period, the Swedish economy experienced a serious recession in 2008/2009 following the international financial crisis. However, the recession in Norway turned out to be relatively mild. Whether this is primarily due to good policies (an active monetary and fiscal policy) or good luck (being an oil exporter when terms of trade increase) is an issue we will discuss later in more detail.

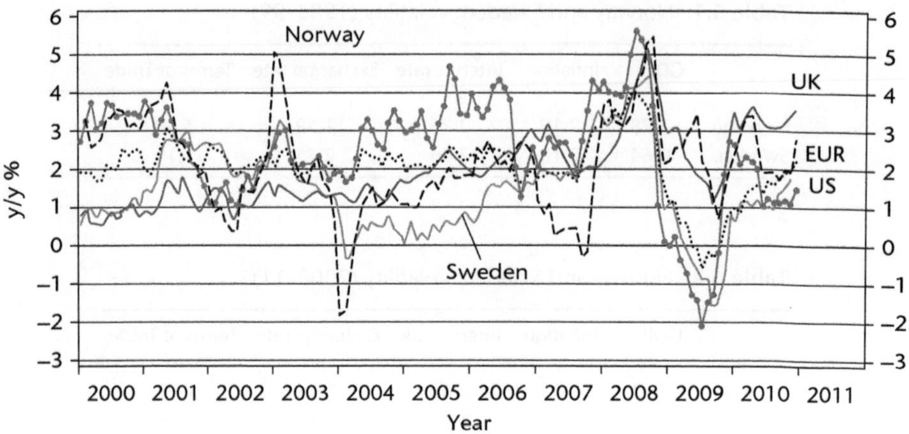

Figure 6.1. CPI inflation in selected countries
Source: Bjørnland and Wilhelmsen (2011).

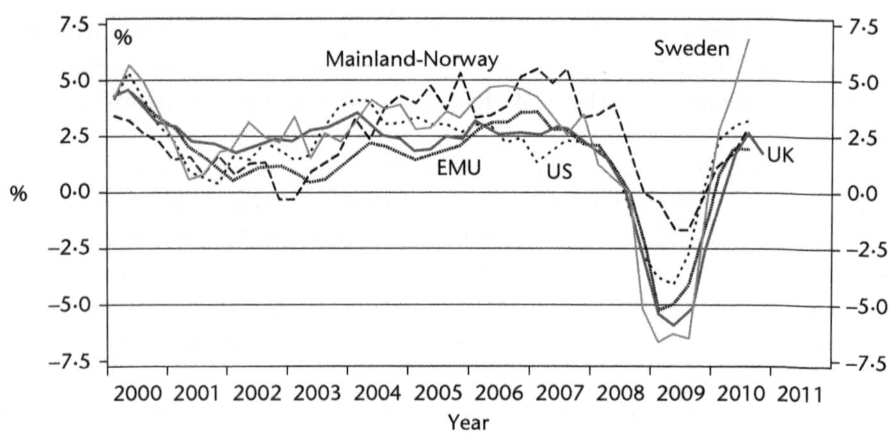

Figure 6.2. GDP in selected countries
Source: Bjørnland and Wilhelmsen (2011).

The main instrument in monetary policy is the interest rate. One important issue to explore with regard to monetary policy is how frequently and by how much the central banks have altered interest rates. Large and frequent (aggressive) interest rate changes can be beneficial if they bring about better economic performance, such as stable inflation and a lower inflation risk premium. On the other hand, large variations in interest rates increase the interest risk premium.

To evaluate the aggressiveness of monetary policy, one can look at the range of interest rates used, as well as the frequency and size of interest rate changes.

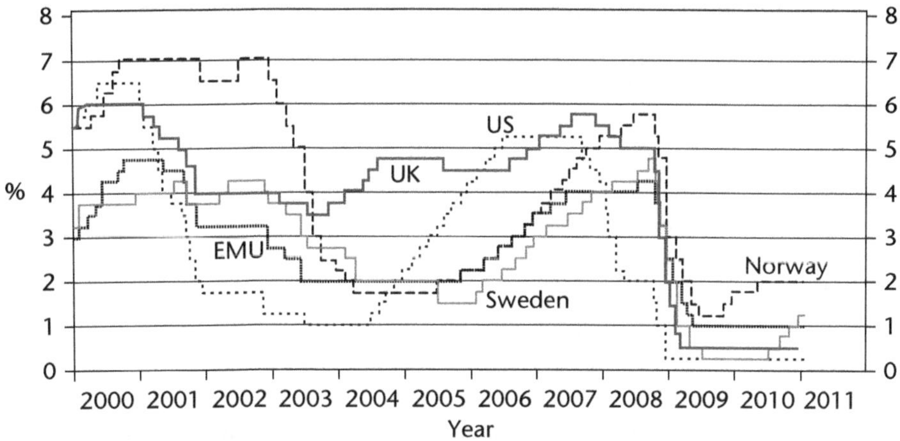

Figure 6.3. Interest rate in selected countries
Source: Bjørnland and Wilhelmsen (2011).

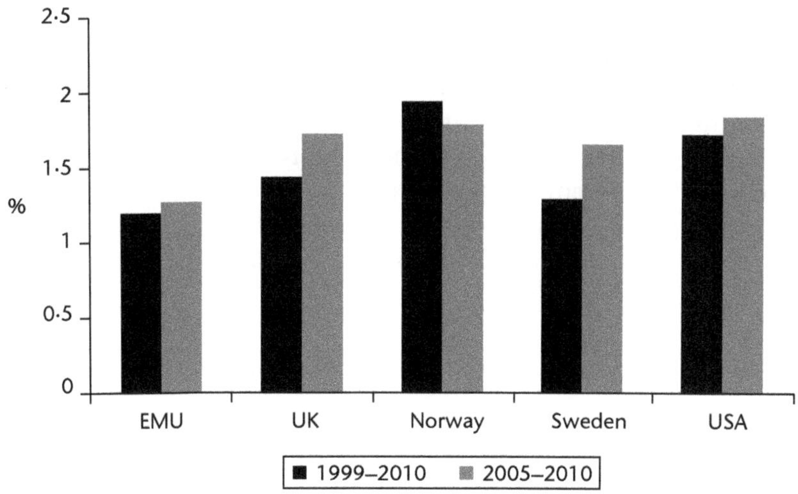

Figure 6.4. Interest rate volatility

Figure 6.3 presents the ranges, whereas Figure 6.4 presents the standard deviation of the annual changes of these interest rates.

In the period where Norges Bank has targeted inflation (informally from 1999 and then formally from 2001) Norges Bank ranks as one of the most aggressive central banks with regard to interest rate volatility (in this sample of countries, but also including other small resource-rich open economies such as Australia and New Zealand). This could reflect that Norway is exposed to more sizeable shocks/impulses or has less emphasis on gradualism, or it might also be a sign of more frequent policy errors.

The Norges Bank Watch report from 2011 believes that some of the volatility of the policy rate in Norway can be explained by the more aggressive interest rate changes in 2001–3—a period when, one could argue, policy errors may have played a role. Redoing the analysis from 2005 brings the volatility in Norway more in line with the other countries, although Norway still ranks high on volatility.

Another reason for the higher volatility of the interest rate could be that Norges Bank has a more flexible inflation target, contributing also to smoothing fluctuations in output, employment, and the exchange rate, while other central banks may tend to focus more on the stabilization of inflation. If that is the case, one would expect the growth rates in GDP and the exchange rate to be more stable in Norway than in many other countries.

This is partly confirmed. For the period 2001–11, the fluctuation in GDP has been less volatile in Norway than in countries such as Sweden and the UK. Compared to the EMU, however, Norway has only marginally more stable growth rates.

Figure 6.5 also shows that the nominal effective exchange rate in Norway appears to have been among the most stable (least volatile) exchange rates of the countries analysed here, although it has appreciated over the sample (10% since 1998). One exception to the stability is the period 2001–3, when the interest rate differential changed by a lot, thereby also contributing to exchange rate fluctuations (the exchange rate first appreciated sharply when interest rates increased, only to depreciate substantially when the interest rate was quickly brought down).

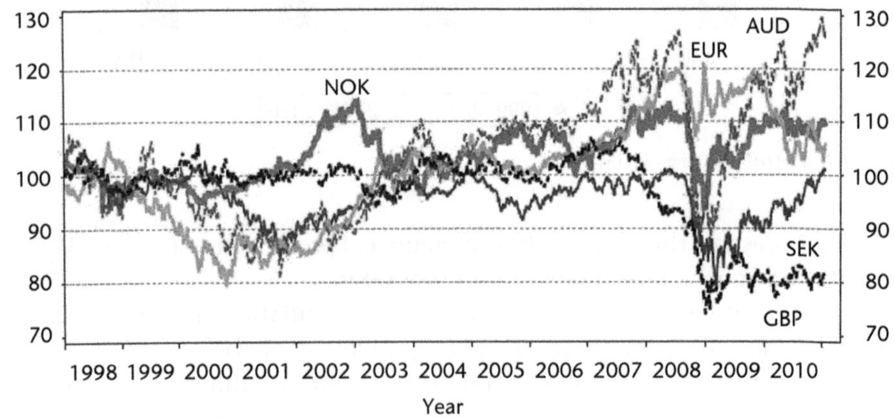

Figure 6.5. Exchange rate in selected countries (indices: 1998 = 100)
Source: Bjørnland and Wilhelmsen (2011).

The same picture of stability emerges if the nominal effective exchange rate in Norway is deflated by relative consumer prices (see Bjørnland and Wilhelmsen, 2011). The real exchange rate has appreciated slightly, particularly over the last decade, but compared to the mean of the period 1970–2010, the appreciation of the real exchange rate is modest. This could reflect the low inflation rates experienced in Norway due to the favorable terms of trade (low prices for imported consumer goods, combined with high prices for the commodities exports), preventing the real exchange rate from appreciating any further. It could also reflect that the central bank also stabilizes the exchange rate, which we will examine in more detail below.

This favorable picture changes somewhat if the nominal exchange rate is deflated by relative wages (see Bjørnland and Wilhelmsen, 2011). The resulting real exchange rate shows clear evidence of declining competitiveness in Norway compared to countries like Sweden in the inflation-targeting era. Hence, notwithstanding the low inflation rates, labour costs have not remained stable in the period. In fact, Norwegian labour costs, measured by relative unit labour costs, have reached an unprecedented high level and competitiveness has thereby weakened (see Figure 6.6).

Although some of the increase in labour costs could reflect increased productivity (having a highly productive petroleum sector), it illustrates a feature of the Norwegian economy that has become more prominent in the last decade: high

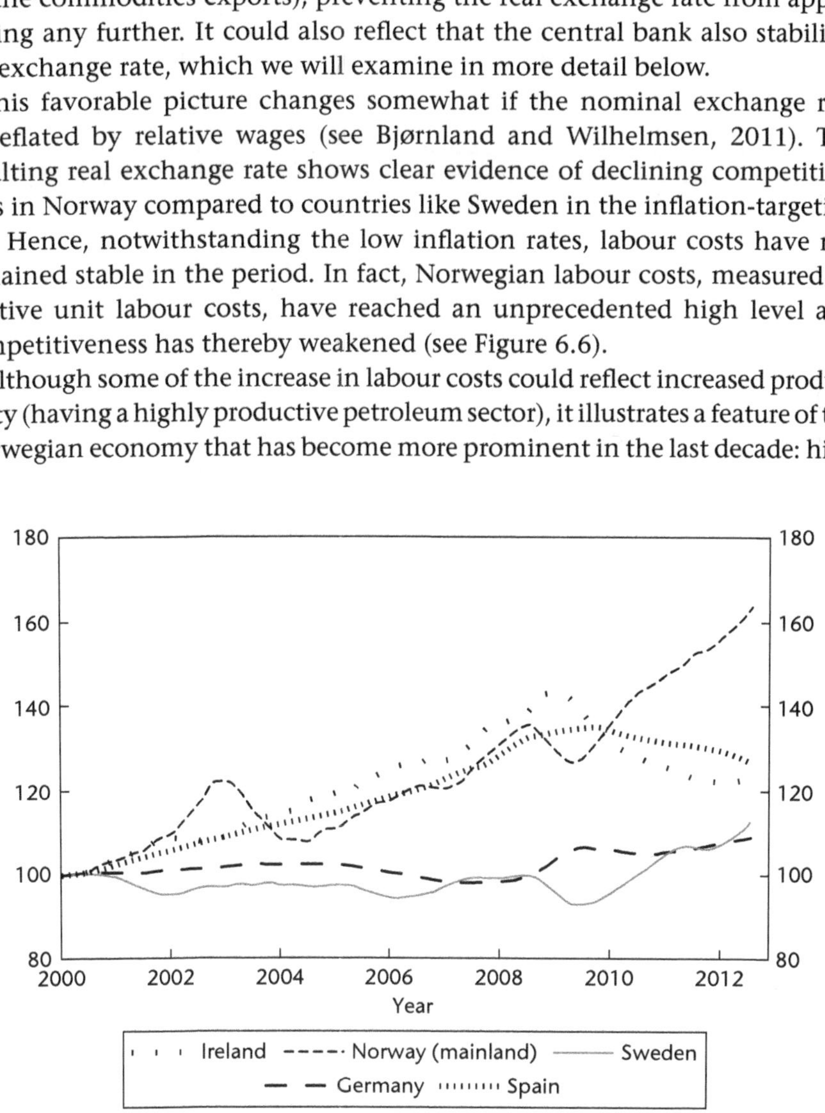

Figure 6.6. Unit labour cost in selected countries (indices: 1998 = 100)
Source: Norges Bank Annual Adresss (2013).

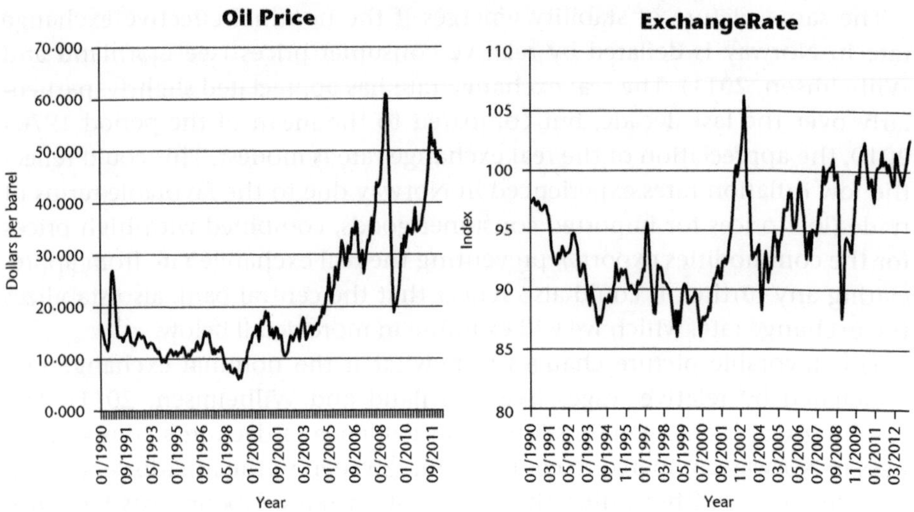

Figure 6.7. Real oil price and real exchange rate in Norway
Source: OECD.

growth in employment in the public sector has come at the expense of employment in the manufacturing sector, where there has been a gradual decline. While 1/3 of the labour force in Norway today is employed in the public sector, only 10 per cent of the labour force is employed in manufacturing industries. Although there has been a decline in manufacturing employment in many other industrial countries, the combination of the public sector's high share of employment, and the low share of employment in the manufacturing sector is unique for Norway. For instance, relative to Norway, Sweden's share of employment in manufacturing is twice as big. This has likely impacted upon wage formation and incentives.

Hence, we have shown that while both Norway and Sweden have had inflation rates close to the target and overall stable economic conditions, there are also differences between the countries in the inflation targeting-era. In particular, Norway has observed higher volatility in interest rate setting than Sweden, but volatility in inflation and the exchange rate is about the same. Furthermore, there is clear evidence of declining competitiveness in Norway compared to countries like Sweden. Hence, notwithstanding the low inflation rates, labour costs have not remained stable in the period.

Clearly, this is not all about monetary policy. Figure 6.7 shows the clear link (or at least correlation) between the real oil price (Brent prices) and real exchange rate in Norway.[5] A higher oil price has gone hand in hand with an

[5] Note that an increase is an appreciation.

appreciated exchange rate. However, if this is a concern for the central bank, stabilization of the exchange rate could be a motivation in itself.

6.3 A Structural Small Open Economy Model

In order to answer the simple question, if monetary policy has contributed to stabilizing the exchange rate, we examine a simplified version of the model in Galí and Monacelli (2005) which is adapted by Lubik and Schorfheide (2007). The model consists of a standard forward-looking (open economy) IS equation, a Phillips curve, an exchange rate equation, and a monetary policy (interest rate) rule. For a full description of the model, see Alstadheim, Bjørnland, and Maih (2013). Here we will only specify the equation for the nominal exchange rate and the policy equation, which are the focus in this chapter.

Following Lubik and Schorfheide (2007), we introduce the nominal exchange rate via the definition of consumer prices. Assuming that relative Purchasing Power Parity (PPP) holds, we have:

$$\Delta e_t = \pi_t - (1-\alpha)\Delta q_t - \pi_t^* \tag{1}$$

where e_t is the nominal exchange rate, π_t^* is world inflation, π_t is domestic inflation, and q_t is the terms of trade. In our set-up, the nominal exchange rate, domestic inflation, the terms of trade, and foreign inflation are observable variables. Of these, the exchange rate and domestic inflation rate are endogenous, while the other variables will be exogenous and follow AR-processes. From equation (1) we see that terms of trade can affect the exchange rate directly via the coefficient α, which measures the degree of openness (the import share). Hence, if $\alpha = 0$, the nominal exchange rate is determined by the inflation differential so that PPP holds.

Monetary policy is described by an interest rate rule where we assume that the central bank can adjust its instrument in response to inflation, output, and possibly a nominal exchange rate depreciation:

$$r_t = \rho_r r_{t-1} + (1-\rho_r)\left(\gamma_\pi \pi_t + \gamma_y y_t + \gamma_e \Delta e_t\right) + \varepsilon_{r,t} \tag{2}$$

We assume that the policy coefficients γ_π, γ_y and $\gamma_e \geq 0$. We also allow for a smoothing term in the rule, with $0 < \rho_r < 1$. $\varepsilon_{r,t}$ is the exogenous monetary policy shock, which can be interpreted as the unsystematic component of monetary policy (deviation from rule). With this set-up, the policy coefficients γ_π, γ_y, and γ_e should be interpreted as long-run responses—with high interest rate persistence, the estimated γ's may be quite large, and still entail small immediate responses.

Finally, we follow Lubik and Schorfheide (2007) and add a law of motion for the growth rate of the terms of trade to the system:

$$\Delta q_t = \rho_q \Delta q_{t-1} + \varepsilon_{q,t} \tag{3}$$

6.4 The Markov-Switching DSGE Model

All the algorithms used for the computations in this chapter are done using RISE, an object-oriented Matlab toolbox for solving and estimating Markov-switching rational expectations (MSRE) models.[6]

In the estimation, we will allow for two Markov chains, each with two states (for a total of four regimes). One of the chains governs the switching in the variance of shocks (high or low volatility), and the other one governs switches in the monetary policy parameters (high or low exchange rate response). The probabilities of going from one state to the other and vice versa are estimated.

Solving a general Markov-switching rational expectations model is not straightforward. The traditional solution methods for constant-parameter DSGE models cannot be used, since the solution in each state will be a function of the solution in all other states and vice versa.

In order to estimate the model, the likelihood has to be computed. Because of the presence of unobserved variables and unobserved states of the Markov chains, the likelihood has to be computed using a filtering procedure.

The chapter uses a Bayesian approach for estimating the models. In particular, we combine the likelihood with the prior density of the parameters, thereby forming the posterior kernel which we maximize to get the mode of the posterior distribution. While the estimate of the mode represents the most likely value, it also serves as a starting point for initializing the Markov chain Monte Carlo (MCMC) procedure aimed at constructing the full posterior distribution and computing the marginal data density (MDD).

Even for simple models as the one considered here, finding the mode is computationally challenging given that the posterior kernel has many peaks.

[6] RISE is the acronym for 'Rationality In Switching Environments'. It is available free of charge at <https://github.com/jmaih/RISE_toolbox> and is being developed by Junior Maih.

Our optimization strategy is to use a stochastic grid search algorithm, which is derivative-free, to locate areas of the parameter space in which the global peak may lie and then use a Newton-based optimization procedure to climb to that peak, see Maih (2012) and Alstadheim, Bjørnland, and Maih (2013) for more details.

6.5 Empirical Implementation

We proceed with a discussion on the data and a description of the choice of parameters in the model that are allowed to switch.

6.5.1 *Data*

We use quarterly data for the period 1982:2–2011:4.[7] For both countries, there are four observable domestic variables: domestic real GDP, inflation, nominal effective exchange rate, and the short-term interest rate. In addition we include the terms of trade for each country and common foreign output and inflation (see Alstadheim, Bjørnland, and Maih, 2013 for how to include the foreign observables into the model). All data except the nominal interest rate and the exchange rate are seasonally adjusted.

Output growth rates are computed as log differences of GDP and multiplied by 100 to convert them into quarter-to-quarter percentages. Inflation rates are defined as log differences of the consumer price indices and multiplied by 400 to get annualized percentage rates. We approximate foreign output and inflation based on US GDP and CPI inflation respectively. We use the log differences (multiplied by 100) of the trade-weighted nominal effective exchange rate to obtain depreciation rates[8]. Percentage changes in the terms of trade are computed as log differences and multiplied by 100 while the nominal interest rate is measured in levels. All series are demeaned prior to analysis. For further details on data and the sources, see Appendix A.

Figure 6.8 plots the four domestic variables used in the analysis for Norway and Sweden over the sample 1983–2011. The picture described above is confirmed in this longer sample. First, there is definitely co-movement between

[7] The start date reflects data availability for the interest rate series in Sweden.

[8] Note that in order to make an increase correspond to a depreciation rate, we invert the exchange rate.

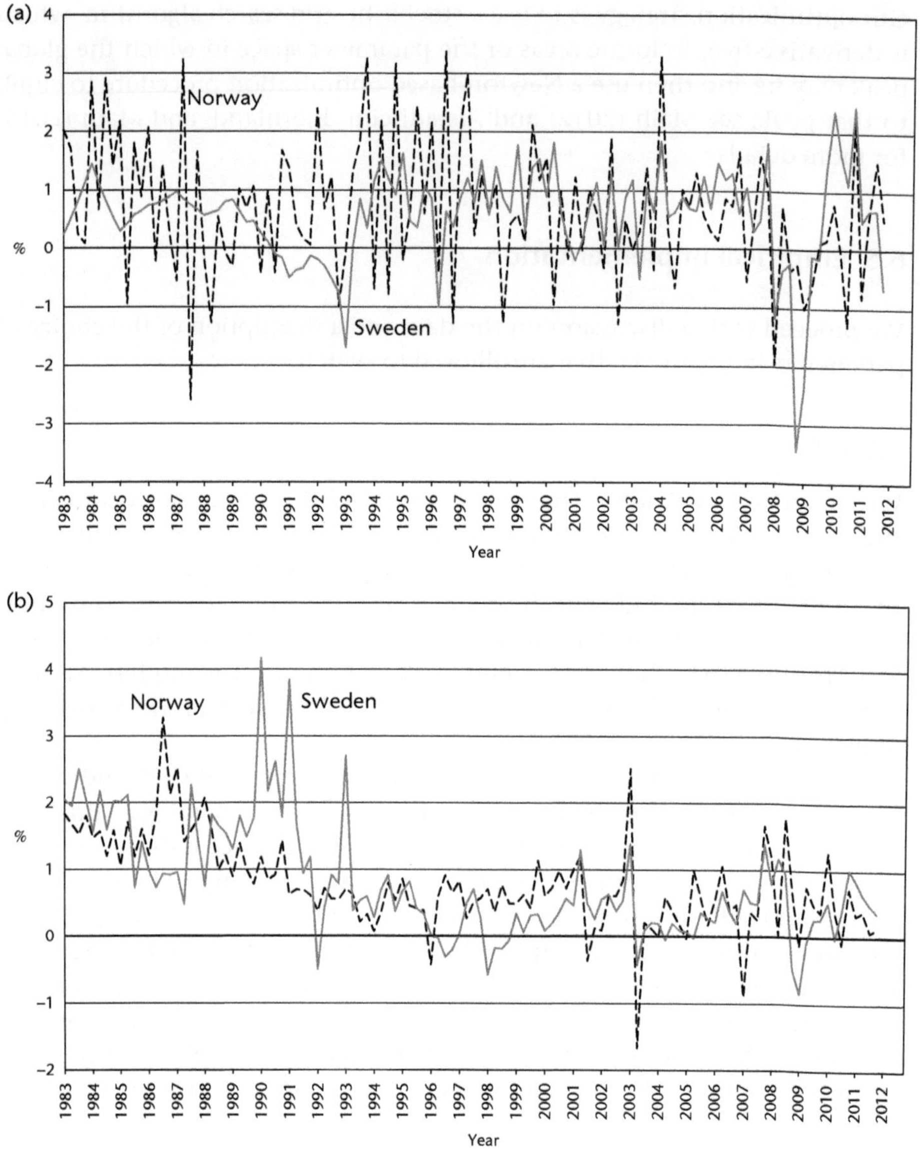

Figure 6.8. Data in the analysis, per cent changes; a) GDP and b) inflation

the series in the two countries. In particular, the interest rate series drift together across the two countries. A similar pattern is also found for inflation, although there is some variation across the two countries. Second, GDP growth in Norway is much more volatile than GDP growth in Sweden, with the possible exception of the latter part of the sample (the inflation-targeting period).

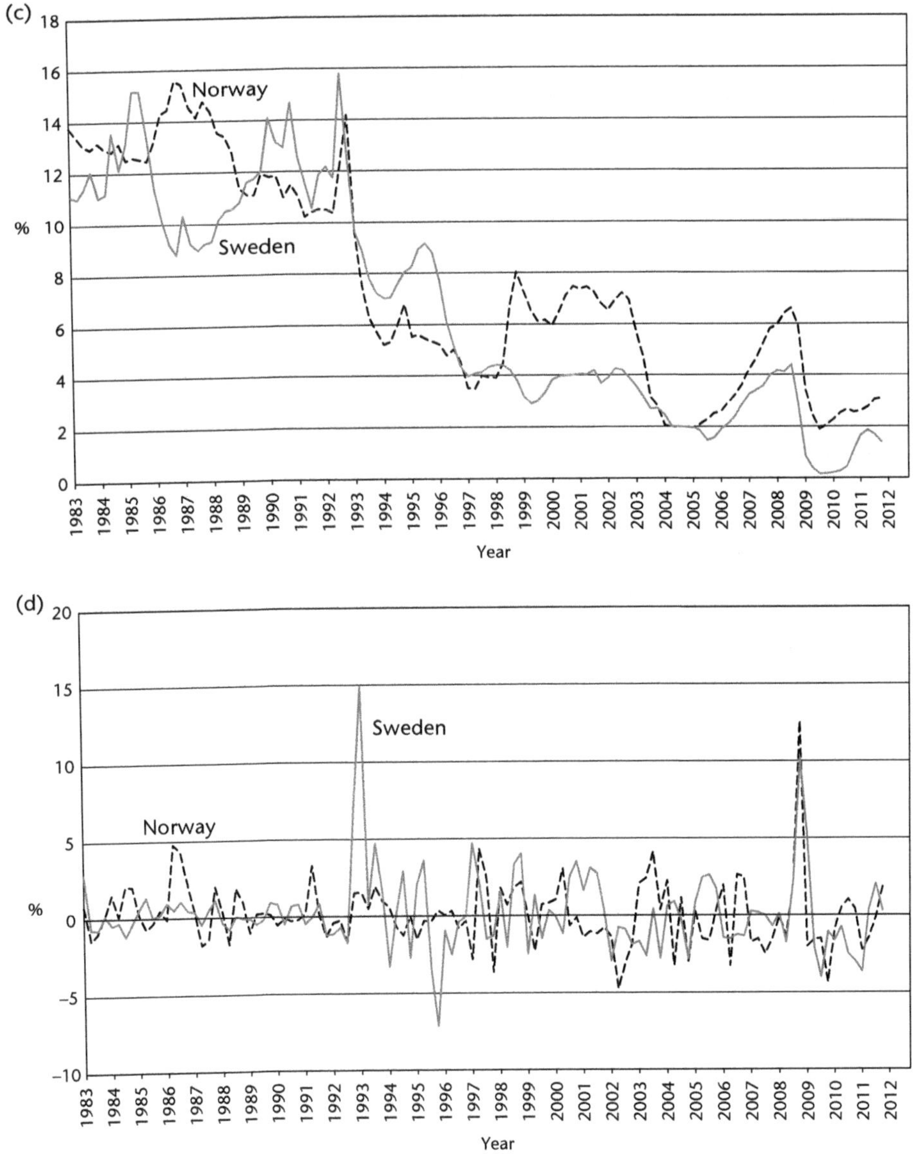

Figure 6.8. Continued; c) interest rate and d) exchange rate

Finally, the exchange rate displays more idiosyncratic movement across the two countries, being clearly more volatile in Sweden prior to the break-up of the fixed-exchange-rate regime in 1992/3.

We next set out to investigate whether empirical evidence of regime shifts and spurs of volatility can be extracted from the data, given our model framework.

6.6 Results

The structural parameters that are switching are presented in Tables 6.3 and 6.4 along with the estimated posterior mode.[9]

For each country, we will use a Markov switching model that allows for (independent) switches in volatility and parameters in the monetary policy rule. That is, we allow the parameters ρ_r, γ_π, γ_y, and γ_e to follow an independent two-state Markov process, where we denote the low-response regime as $(policy, low)$ and the high-response regime as $(policy, high)$. For a systematic comparison between the two countries, we normalize the high-response regime $(policy, high)$ to be the regime where the central bank responds strongly to the exchange rate, i.e. $\gamma_e(policy, low) < \gamma_e\ (policy, high)$.

Furthermore, we allow for regime switching in the volatility of shocks, by letting all structural shock variances follow an independent two-state Markov process. We denote the low-volatility regime as (vol, low) and the high-volatility regime as $(vol, high)$. Again, to compare systematically across the two countries, we normalize the high-volatility regime $(vol, high)$ to be the regime where the volatility (in productivity) is highest, i.e. $\sigma_z(vol, low) < \sigma_z(vol, high)$.

The choices of prior distribution for the structural parameters in the policy rule are presented in Table 6.3, along with the estimated posterior mode for the parameters. We find that the size of policy responses has not stayed constant during the sample period (1982–2011). For both countries, there is a substantial difference between the high and low policy responses.

In particular, there is clear evidence that the central banks have responded strongly to the exchange rate in the high-response regime, while the response to inflation is highest in the low-response regime. Interest rate smoothing is more pronounced in the low-response regime in Sweden, while in Norway it is more pronounced in the high-response regime. However, both countries respond more strongly to output in the high-response regime.

Hence, the low-response regime can be characterized by high inflation response, while the high-response regime is characterized by high exchange rate and output gap response. Note that, between the two countries, Norway has by far the strongest interest rate response to the exchange rate.

Regarding the Markov state processes for volatility (Table 6.4), comparing Norway and Sweden, volatility seems to be of the same size for productivity and output in the high-volatility regime. The two countries differ, however, with respect to the interest rate and the terms of trade, which have

[9] For a full treatment of the model with results, see Alstadheim, Bjørnland, and Maih (2013).

Table 6.3. Estimated policy parameters in two regimes

Parameters	Prior distribution	Prior probability low–high	Norway	Sweden
ρ_r (policy, low)	Beta	0.05–0.95	0.07	0.95
ρ_r (policy, high)	Beta	0.05–0.95	0.97	0.10
γ_π (policy, low)	Gamma	0.5–3.0	0.85	0.13
γ_π (policy, high)	Gamma	0.5–3.0	0.51	0.12
γ_y (policy, low)	Gamma	0.1–3.0	2.11	2.00
γ_y (policy, high)	Gamma	0.1–3.0	2.94	3.15
γ_e (policy, low)	Gamma	0.05–3.0	0.001	0.001
γ_e (policy, high)	Gamma	0.25–3.0	4.069	0.061

Note: See equation (2) for parameter definitions.

Table 6.4. Estimated volatility in two regimes

Parameters	Prior distribution	Prior probability low–high	Norway	Sweden
σ_r (vol, low)	InvGam	0.005–1	0.003	0.001
σ_r (vol, high)	InvGam	0.005–1	0.008	0.002
σ_q (vol, low)	InvGam	0.005–1	0.064	0.010
σ_q (vol, high)	InvGam	0.005–1	0.039	0.019
σ_z (vol, low)	InvGam	0.005–1	0.003	0.003
σ_z (vol, high)	InvGam	0.005–1	0.011	0.009
σ_y (vol, low)	InvGam	0.005–1	0.007	0.002
σ_y (vol, high)	InvGam	0.005–1	0.009	0.007
σ_π (vol, low)	InvGam	0.005–1	0.019	0.015
σ_π (vol, high)	InvGam	0.005–1	0.008	0.039

Note: σ_r is volatility of a monetary-policy shock, σ_q is volatility of terms-of-trade shock, σ_z is volatility of a productivity shock, σ_y is volatility of a demand shock (from the IS equation), and σ_π is volatility of inflation/cost-push shock (from the Phillips curve).

much higher volatility in Norway, and for inflation, which has a substantially higher volatility in Sweden. This confirms what we discussed earlier, in Section 2.

Norway also stands out in the low volatility regime (again as emphasized above) by observing higher volatility in its terms of trade and in the interest rate than Sweden. This is most likely due to the relative size of the petroleum sector in that country. There is also some evidence that the variance of output is higher in Norway than in Sweden in the low-volatility regime. We will discuss possible reasons for this when we examine the terms-of-trade shocks below.

Figure 6.9 displays the smoothed probabilities in Norway and Sweden together (Norway has a dotted line, Sweden a solid line). The figure displays in the upper panel the smoothed probabilities of being in high-policy-response regime $(policy, high)$ and in the bottom panel, the probability of being in a high-volatility regime $(vol, high)$.

The figure emphasizes that the central bank in Sweden switched from primarily responding strongly to the exchange rate in the 1980s to responding more to inflation shortly after inflation targeting was implemented in the early 1990s.

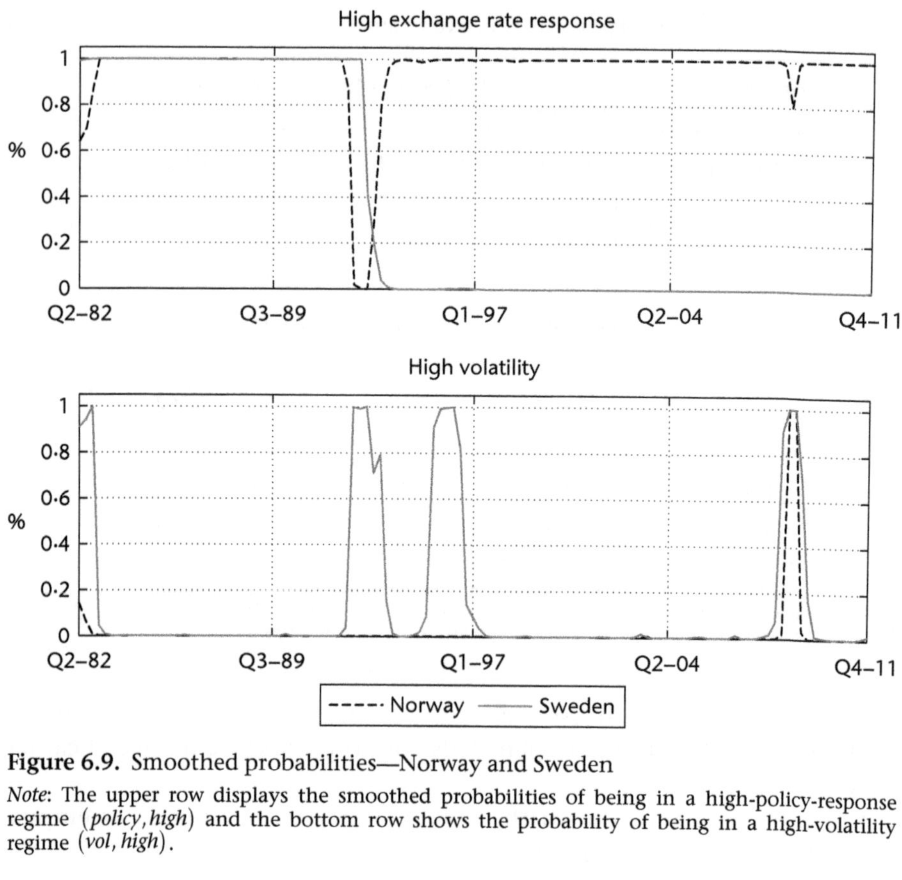

Figure 6.9. Smoothed probabilities—Norway and Sweden

Note: The upper row displays the smoothed probabilities of being in a high-policy-response regime $(policy, high)$ and the bottom row shows the probability of being in a high-volatility regime $(vol, high)$.

The results for Norway are different. With the exception of the brief period in 1992/3, the central bank has responded strongly to the exchange rate both before and after implementing inflation targeting (in 2001). Recall that this regime also involves high-output response. In 1992/3 Norway stopped intervening in the foreign exchange market to defend the fixed-exchange-rate regime, and left the strict exchange rate peg. This is being picked up as a regime switch by the data, and for 1–2 years there is virtually no exchange rate response. The year after, the policy rule in Norway is again best described by a high response to the exchange rate (as well as a concern for output stabilization).

A high monetary policy response to the exchange rate is consistent with the findings in Bjørnland and Halvorsen (2014). But why does monetary policy in Norway respond so much to the exchange rate relative to inflation? First, and as noted earlier, Norway was the country that last formally adopted inflation targeting. Second, terms-of-trade shocks are much more volatile in Norway than in Sweden. As emphasized, they also contribute to much of the exchange rate appreciation of the last decade, which the central bank in this period has tried to stabilize, thereby also stabilizing inflation.

Hence, Norway observes high exchange rate response in the interest rate both before and after authorities stopped intervening to peg the exchange rate. In one way, that is not so different from Sweden. There the interest rate has become more persistent in the inflation-targeting period.

Turning to the lower panel of Figure 6.9, there is a striking similarity in the timing of the switch between the high- and low-volatility regimes in the inflation-targeting periods, although the weights in the policy rule vary. In particular, independently of the chosen policy rules, the probability of staying in a regime of low volatility was high from the mid 1990s and until 2007 (the period of the great moderation). There is also a high probability of staying in a high-volatility regime in the period of the financial crisis in both countries. The period where the countries vary the most is the early 1990s, when Sweden experienced high volatility, as discussed extensively earlier.

6.6.1 *Terms of Trade*

Given the focus on openness in this chapter, we now study the response to a terms-of-trade shock (which increases export prices relative to import prices) in Norway and Sweden. Figures 6.10 and 6.11 display the impulse responses (averaged over all the regimes) to the terms-of-trade shock in Norway and Sweden respectively. The impulse responses are constructed from the regime-specific responses. That is, we have four possible regimes: (Regime 1): low exchange rate response and low volatility; (Regime 2): low exchange rate response and high volatility; (Regime 3): high exchange rate response and low volatility; and (Regime 4): high exchange rate response and high volatility.

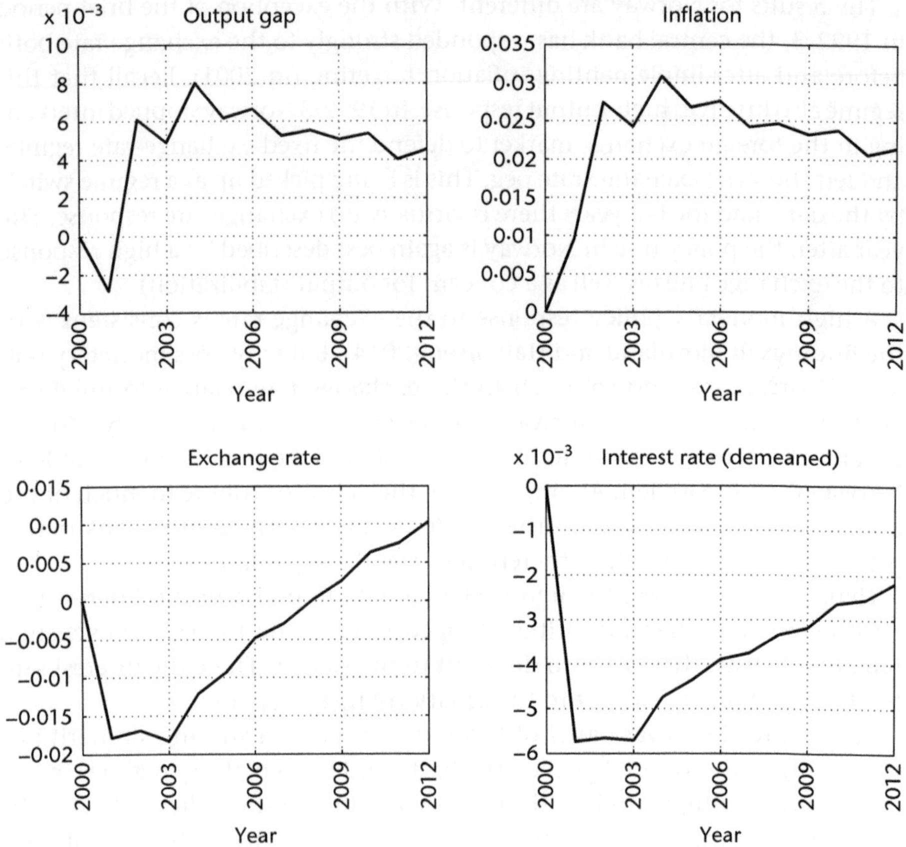

Figure 6.10. Norway: impulse responses to terms-of-trade shocks

Based on the four regime-specific impulse responses and the duration of each regime, we can construct the generalized impulse responses. Appendix B explains in more detail how the impulse responses are constructed and also displays the regime-specific responses.

The impulse responses emphasize that responding strongly to the exchange rate will exacerbate the effects of a terms-of-trade shock on both output and domestic inflation. In particular, a favorable terms-of-trade shock appreciates the exchange rate and increases output on impact. Since both the terms of trade and the real interest rate enter the model through expectation terms, the effect on output (and inflation) will depend on the expected interest rate response.

If the central bank is in a policy regime of high interest rate response to the exchange rate (*regimes 3 and 4*) the exchange rate will appreciate by much

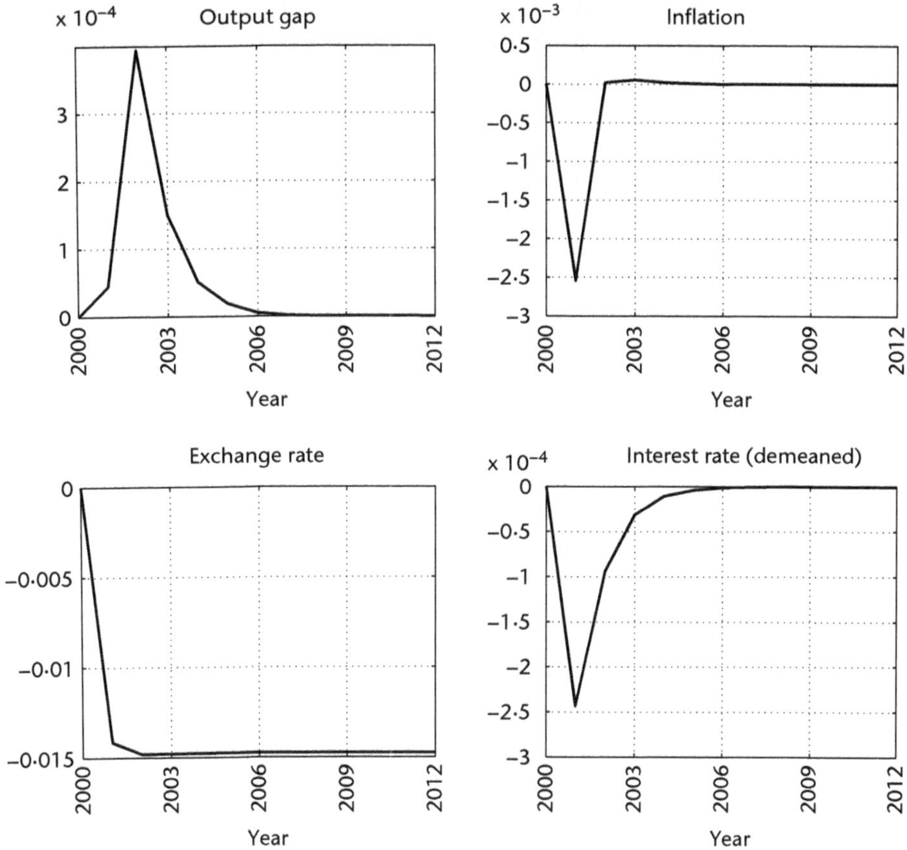

Figure 6.11. Sweden: impulse responses to terms-of-trade shocks

less, as the interest rate will also take into account the fact that the exchange rate has appreciated. This will reverse the initial exchange rate response and push up output and inflation relative to a regime of no interest rate response (see in particular the differences between high- and low-response regimes in Norway and Sweden in Appendix B).

Hence, the exchange rate response reinforces the effect of the terms-of-trade shock on output (and to a certain extent for inflation), and may explain why output was also more volatile (in the low-volatility regime) in Norway than in Sweden, as discussed above. On the other hand, if the central bank is mostly in a regime of low response to the exchange rate, it will ignore the exchange rate and set the interest to curb the effect on inflation.

The different responses are seen clearly in Figure 6.10 and Figure 6.11 for Norway and Sweden respectively. Norway has remained in a regime of high exchange rate response in most of the sample, and the effect of the terms-of-trade shocks on output and inflation are therefore clearly exacerbated relative to Sweden.

On a final note, recall from above that volatility of the terms of trade (and output) is much higher in Norway than in Sweden, which is most likely due to the size of the petroleum sector. Given this volatility, and a formal regime of inflation targeting, it may seem surprising that the terms-of-trade shocks do not explain even more of the variance in the nominal exchange rate in Norway than they do. The fact that the central bank in Norway has stabilized the exchange rate somewhat may have contributed to this.

6.7 Conclusion

We analyse and compare key economic variables in Norway and Sweden before and after the inflation-targeting implementation. Having established the stylized facts, we investigate the role of monetary policy for stabilizing economic performance. Using a Markov-switching DSGE model explicitly allowing for parameter changes, we find that while the central bank in Sweden reduced its response to the exchange rate (and output) shortly after inflation-targeting was implemented, the central bank in Norway has responded strongly to the exchange rate both before and after the inflation-targeting implementation. This could explain why the exchange rate remains relatively stable in Norway despite the high volatility in the terms of trade and also while the interest rate is much more volatile than in Sweden. Finally we show that by responding strongly to the exchange rate, the adverse effects of terms-of-trade shocks on the exchange rate and subsequently output and inflation are lessened. Monetary policy therefore contributes to exacerbate a terms-of-trade-led boom in the economy.

Appendix A: Data and Sources

We use the trade-weighted nominal effective exchange rate, NEER, from the IMF's IFS database for both countries. Note that in order to make an increase correspond to a depreciation rate, we invert the NEER. For the other series, we use the following:

Norway

Terms-of-trade data are from Statistics Norway, seasonally adjusted (SA).
The interest rate is three month NIBOR interest rate, Norges Bank.
CPI is from Statistics Norway, SA.
Real GDP data is from Statistics Norway, SA.

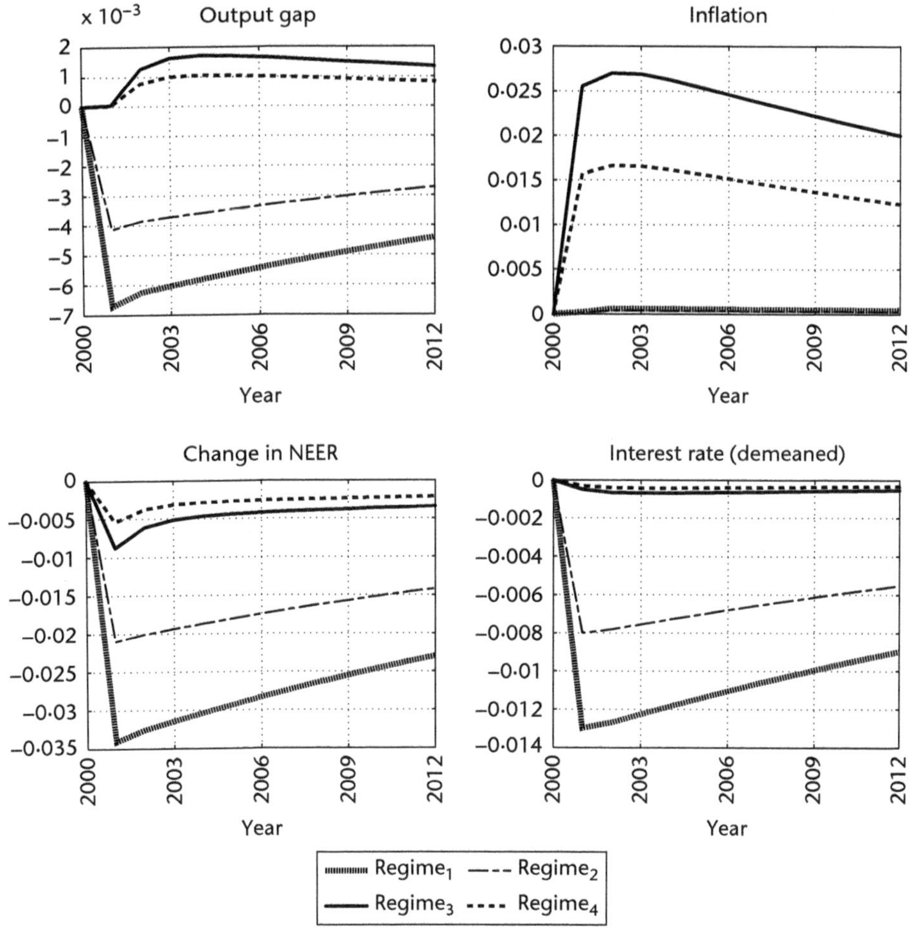

Figure 6.12. Norway: regime-specific impulse response to terms-of-trade shocks

Note: (Regime 1): low exchange rate response and low volatility; (Regime 2): low exchange rate response and high volatility; (Regime 3): high exchange rate response and low volatility; and (Regime 4): high exchange rate response and high volatility.

Sweden

Terms-of-trade data are from Statistics Sweden, SA.

The short-term rate is average quarterly short-term rate from the Swedish Riksbank from 1982.

The CPI data is from Statistics Sweden, SA.

Real GDP is from OECD MEI, we have seasonally adjusted it.

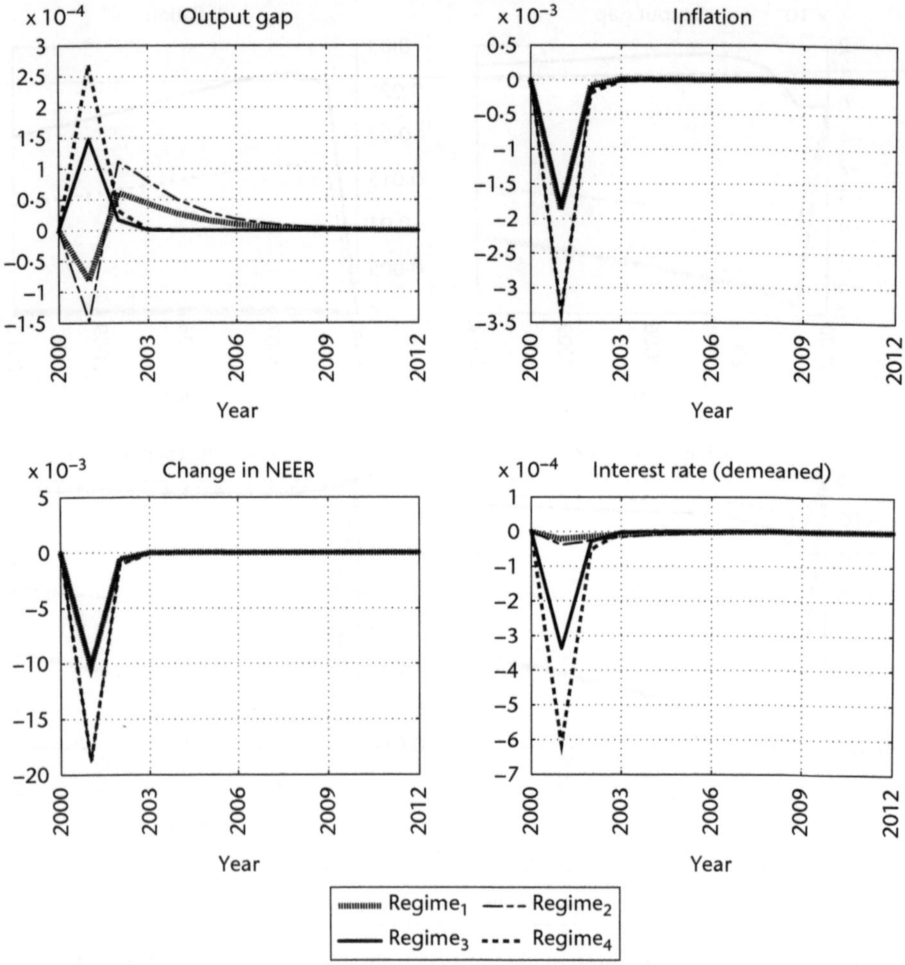

Figure 6.13. Sweden: regime-specific impulse response to terms-of-trade shocks

Note: (Regime 1): low exchange rate response and low volatility; (Regime 2): low exchange rate response and high volatility; (Regime 3): high exchange rate response and low volatility; and (Regime 4): high exchange rate response and high volatility.

Foreign GDP and Inflation

For the foreign variables, we use US data.

Real GDP is US: Gross Domestic Product (SAAR, Bil.Chn.2005$), from the Bureau of Economic Analysis, SA.

The CPI is from the Bureau of Labor Statistics, SA.

Appendix B: Regime-specific impulse responses

We would like to compute the impulse responses (*irf*) for a given horizon $t + h$, conditional on the information at time $t - 1$:

$$irf(h,d,|I_{t-1}) = E(x_{t+h} | e_t = d) - E(x_{t+h})$$

1) At time *t*, a shock *e* hits the system with a magnitude *d*.
2) We randomly draw shocks in all directions (the whole vector of shocks) that are going to hit the system from period *t+1* onward.
3) We compute the path followed by the system after the initial shock in direction *e* (period *t*) and the 'all directions' shocks for the subsequent periods.
4) We compute a second path, where we do not shock the system in the first period, but shock it in the subsequent ones with the same 'all directions' shocks.
5) The impulse is computed as the difference between the first and second paths.

We repeat steps 1 to 5 *N* times and average the results obtained in step 5.

Figures 6.12 and 6.13 show the results.

References

Alstadheim, R., H.C. Bjørnland, and J. Maih (2013), 'Do Central Banks respond to exchange rate movements? A Markov-Switching structural investigation'. Norges Bank Working paper 24/2013.

Berg, C. (2005), 'Experience of Inflation Targeting in 20 countries. *Sveriges Riksbank Economic Review* 1/2005.

Bjørnland, H.C. and J.I. Halvorsen (2014), How does monetary policy respond to exchange rate movements? New international evidence. *Oxford Bulletin of Economics and Statistics*, vol. 76(2), 2014, 208–32.

Bjørnland, H.C. and B.R. Wilhelmsen (2011), An independent evaluation of monetary policy in Norway. Technical report, Norges Bank Watch 2011.

Galí, J. and T. Monacelli (2005), Monetary Policy and Exchange Rate Volatility in a Small Open Economy'. *Review of Economic Studies 72*, 707–34.

Gjedrem, S. (2001), 'Norwegian Monetary Policy in the Age of the Euro'. Speech at the conference on EMU and the euro hosted by the European Commission, Euro-Info Centre and NHO, Oslo, 30 October 2001, Norges Bank.

Lubik, T.A. and F. Schorfheide (2007), Do Central Banks Respond to Exchange Rate Movements? A Structural Investigation'. *Journal of Monetary Economics 54*, 1069–87.

Maih, J. (2012), 'New Solutions to First-Order Perturbed Markov Switching Rational Expectations Models'. Mimeo, International Monetary Fund.

Comments on 'Monetary Policy and Exchange Rate Stabilization in Norway and Sweden' by Hilde C. Bjørnland and Junior Maih

Roberto M. Billi

The chapter written by Bjørnland and Maih is, in my opinion, an informative study that sheds light on the role of the exchange rate in the conduct of monetary policy in Norway and Sweden. The two small open economies formally adopted inflation targeting as their framework for monetary policy. Sweden switched to inflation targeting first in the early 1990s, while Norway waited until the early 2000s. Using a Markov-switching setup that explicitly allows for regime changes in the monetary policy responses and the shocks that hit the two economies, the chapter supports the view that the adoption of inflation targeting has contributed to an overall improvement in economic performance in both Norway and Sweden. In addition, as the authors argue, the central bank has put more weight on stabilizing the exchange rate in Norway rather than in Sweden, likely in response to the declining competitiveness of Norway compared to other countries like Sweden. In my brief comments, I will appraise the study in four steps, namely by raising four questions: Why is the analysis relevant? How do the authors proceed with their investigation? What do they find? And, what else is there to consider in further analysis?

By shedding light on the role of the exchange rate in monetary policy, the analysis is relevant both from theoretical and empirical perspectives. In theory, international trade can lead central banks to explicitly take into account the exchange rate in setting policy. Intuitively, foreign shocks, such as the terms of trade, can alter domestic business-cycle fluctuations which may lead the monetary authority to explicitly take into account international variables. Thus, central banks may have a specific interest in explicitly reacting to and smoothing exchange rate movements as a predictor of domestic volatility. But whether central banks, in actuality, react systematically to the exchange rate to stabilize the business cycle is clearly debatable from an empirical perspective. In a recent line of research, available empirical evidence suggests that some inflation-targeting central banks do respond to the exchange rate while others do not. Namely, Lubik and Schorfheide (2007) argue that, for instance, Bank of Canada and the Bank of England include the nominal exchange rate in their policy rule, while the central banks of Australia and New Zealand do not.

To proceed with their investigation of monetary policy and exchange rate stabilization in Norway and Sweden, the authors estimate a simple structural model of a small open economy. Thus, rather than estimating policy reaction functions in a single variable setting, the authors pursue a multivariate approach and estimate the entire structural model of the economy following the recent strand of research. The structural model is accordingly based on Lubik and Schorfheide (2007) and, in turn, on Galí and Monacelli (2005). In brief, the model consists of a forward-looking (open economy) Euler equation and a Phillips curve, which explain respectively the demand and supply side of the economy. Monetary policy is described by a simple interest rate rule, while the exchange rate is introduced via the definition of the consumer price index (CPI) and under the assumption of purchasing power parity. Thus, overall, the structural model is not very different compared with earlier studies in this line of research. But the empirical implementation is innovative. The important technical novelty is that the estimation procedure allows for regime switching. Both the policy rule coefficients and the variability of the structural shocks hitting the economy are allowed to change over time in the estimation. Because estimating the model is not as straightforward as in earlier studies, the authors face a computational challenge in estimating the regime-switching model.

The results stemming from the estimation of the structural model indicate that economic performance in Norway and Sweden is quite similar in some aspects, yet rather different in other ways. Regarding similarities, foremost, both countries have successfully implemented their policy within an inflation-targeting framework. This success is reflected in CPI inflation that has not moved far from the target. Regarding differences in economic performance, however, the business cycle has generally become more stable in Sweden since the adoption of inflation targeting. The exception is clearly the financial crisis when output in Sweden was hit hard. As a further difference, the interest rate and terms of trade have been substantially more volatile in Norway than in Sweden, which suggests that monetary policy could have a more explicit role in stabilizing the exchange rate in Norway. Furthermore, the central bank in Sweden has put less weight on stabilizing the exchange rate since the adoption of inflation targeting. In Norway, by contrast, the interest rate response to the exchange rate has remained high throughout the period analysed. In sum, while both Norway and Sweden have had inflation rates close to the target and overall stable economic conditions, there is clear evidence of declining competitiveness in Norway compared to other countries including Sweden.

Though the analysis is carefully executed and the results are clearly presented, some additional tests may help clarify the relevance of the empirical findings. In particular, the structural model imposes cross-equation restrictions in the estimation of the policy rule, while by contrast a statistical model would not impose such restrictions. The statistical model abstracts from considerations of the more detailed description of the functioning of the economy. The authors could therefore compare their model-based estimates to estimates from statistical models, along the lines of Lubik and Schorfheide (2007). Such a comparison can help assess the role of the cross-equation restrictions. To be clear, I am certainly not suggesting the presence of any shortcomings in the investigation. Rather, the authors' interesting findings would seem to motivate them to continue with this interesting and promising line of research.

References

Galí, J. and T. Monacelli (2005), 'Monetary Policy and Exchange Rate Volatility in a Small Open Economy'. *Review of Economic Studies* 72, 707–34.

Lubik, T. A. and F. Schorfheide (2007), 'Do Central Banks Respond to Exchange Rate Movements? A Structural Investigation'. *Journal of Monetary Economics* 54, 1069–87.

7

House Prices in Denmark and Sweden

U. Michael Bergman, Bjørn Tangaa Sillemann, and Peter Birch Sørensen

7.1 Introduction

Fluctuations in the housing market often play a key role in the business cycle.[1] This was particularly the case during the recent international financial crisis, which was triggered by a downturn in the US housing market. Many other countries, including Denmark and Sweden, also experienced a long period with strong increases in real house prices in the run-up to the crisis. In Denmark this was followed by a sharp downturn, whereas Swedish house prices have so far remained at a historically high level. At the time of writing, many observers worry that the Swedish housing market may be seriously overvalued and that a future fall in house prices may threaten the country's economic and financial stability. In Denmark some economists also fear that the adjustment in house prices has not been completed so that further drops in real house prices will remain a drag on economic recovery.

This chapter tries to improve our understanding of the drivers of real house prices. It does so by offering estimates of the evolution of fundamental house prices in Denmark and Sweden and by analysing the relationship between fundamental and actual house prices. By studying the evolution of the gap between actual and fundamental house prices, we can identify episodes where positive or negative 'bubbles' in the housing market seem to have been at play. In particular, we can throw some light on the issue of whether house prices in Denmark and Sweden are currently overvalued.

[1] This is a revised version of a paper that was originally prepared for the conference on 'Reform Capacity and Macroeconomic Performance in the Nordic Countries' at Copenhagen Business School, 20–21 September 2013. We thank our discussant Niels Arne Dam and other conference participants for valuable comments on the earlier draft but remain responsible for all errors and shortcomings.

Our method of analysis allows us to answer questions such as the following: What are the determinants of fundamental house prices? Do actual house prices tend to move towards fundamental prices? If so, how fast is the adjustment towards fundamental house prices? What are the factors driving the gap between actual and fundamental prices? Can economic policy help to reduce fluctuations in the house price gap, thereby contributing to macroeconomic stability?

Inspired by the work of Campbell and Shiller (1987, 1989) on fundamental stock prices, several authors such as Hott and Monnin (2008), Campbell, Davis, Gallin, and Martin (2009), Hiebert and Sydow (2011), Costello, Fraser, and Groenewold (2011), Ambrose, Eichholtz, and Lindenthal (2013), the European Commission (2012), and Bergman and Sørensen (2013) have recently attempted to estimate fundamental house prices by various methods. In this chaper we will use the method for estimating fundamental house prices laid out in detail by Bergman and Sørensen (2013). We will extend the analysis in that paper by offering confidence intervals for fundamental house prices and by studying the drivers of the gap between actual and fundamental prices.

The remainder of the chapter is structured in the following way. In Section 2 we describe the developments of house prices in Denmark and Sweden against the international background. Section 3 discusses whether real house prices are likely to display an upward secular trend—an issue which is important for evaluating the sustainability of recent house price developments. Section 4 applies the method of Bergman and Sørensen (2013) to estimate fundamental house prices in Denmark and Sweden, and compares the evolution of fundamental and actual house prices. In Section 5 we analyse how macroeconomic factors, including monetary policy, affect the gap between actual and fundamental house prices. Section 6 offers concluding comments and some reflections on the policy implications of our findings.

7.2 The Evolution of House Prices in Denmark and Sweden

Figure 7.1 shows the evolution of quarterly real house prices in Denmark and Sweden since 1970. Several episodes stand out from the graph. The first is the sharp and persistent increase in Danish house prices from around 1993 up until 2007. The rise in real house prices in Denmark was extremely steep in 2005–6. We also note the sharp downturn in 2008–9 and the further fall in 2011. A natural interpretation is that Denmark experienced a genuine housing bubble in the middle of the last decade. Consumer surveys as well as casual evidence suggest that the acceleration of house prices in 2005–6 was driven by exuberant expectations of future capital gains on houses and that consumers became quite pessimistic about future price developments after

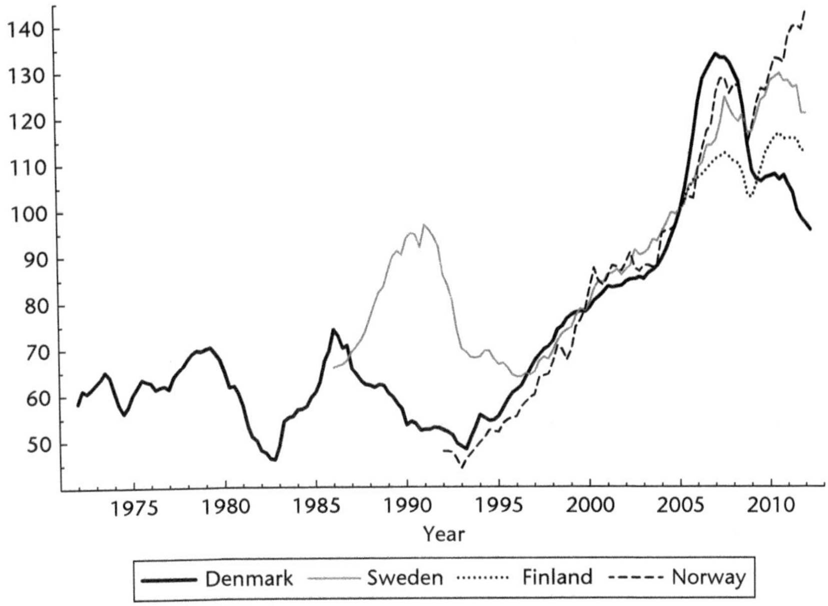

Figure 7.1. Quarterly real house prices in Denmark, Finland, Norway, and Sweden 1970:1–2012:2 (2005:1=100)

Source: Statistics Denmark, Statistics Sweden, and OECD.

the subsequent downturn. Such rapidly shifting expectations seem to be characteristic of most bubble episodes across countries and time.

The soaring Danish house prices in the mid-2000s stimulated consumer demand (through its positive impact on household wealth) and housing investment, and contributed significantly to the overheating of the Danish economy in 2006–7. As a result of record-low unemployment, wage inflation accelerated, undermining the international wage competitiveness of Danish firms. When the housing bubble burst, construction activity and consumer confidence collapsed at the same time as Danish net exports suffered from the combination of the international economic crisis and weaker cost competitiveness. Concerns among international investors that the Danish housing market had become seriously overvalued also made it more difficult for Danish banks to obtain international funding as the international financial crisis unfolded. Thus the Danish housing bubble undoubtedly helps to explain why the growth of the Danish economy has been so anaemic over the last few years.

Second, the soaring house prices in Sweden in the run-up to the banking crisis in the early 1990s are clearly visible in the graph. After the banking crisis real house prices returned to the pre-crisis level in the mid 1990s, but they have increased steadily since 1997. The boom was interrupted by the international economic crisis of 2008–9, which caused a temporary downturn in the Swedish housing market. However, the market quickly recovered and although house prices have recently showed some signs of weakening, they remain at a very high level from a long-term historical perspective.

The same is still true for Danish house prices, although they have fallen by significantly more than Swedish house prices during the last few years. The fact that house prices in both countries are still very high by historical standards explains why many observers worry whether a further downward adjustment is needed in the years to come.

In Figure 7.1 we also compare house prices in Denmark and Sweden to prices in two other Nordic countries, Finland and Norway. House prices in Finland seem to behave like house prices in Sweden to a large extent. Norwegian house prices increased strongly from 1992 and up until the international crisis of 2007–8 and have rebounded vigorously in recent years. It is interesting that all four countries experienced rather similar house price developments up until 2007 whereas developments have been very different since then, especially in Denmark and Norway.

Figure 7.2 shows house prices in two countries (Ireland and Spain) that experienced a housing bubble during the last decade. Like Denmark, Spain and

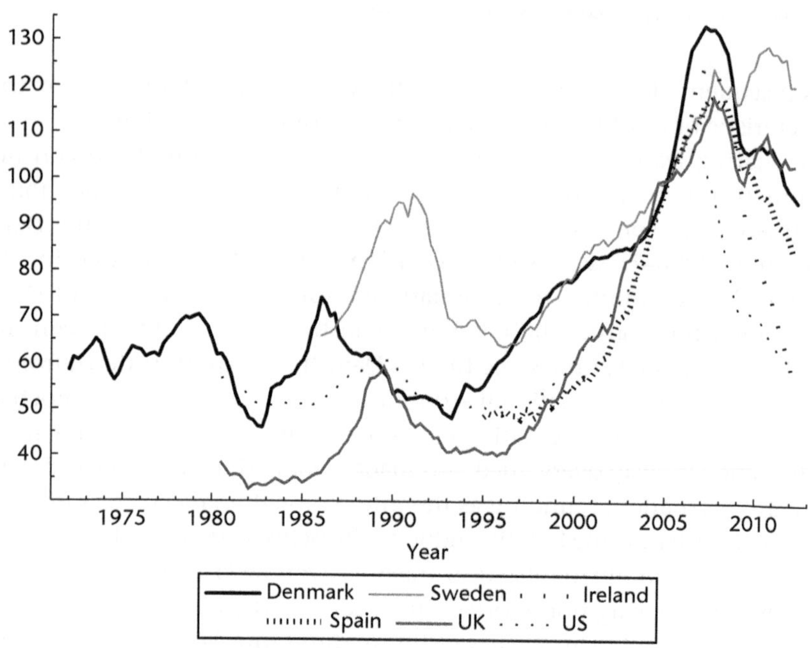

Figure 7.2. Quarterly real house prices in Denmark, Sweden, Ireland, Spain, the UK, and the US, 1970:1–2012:2 (2005:1=100)

Source: Statistics Denmark, Statistics Sweden, and OECD.

in particular Ireland have suffered from a serious housing market downturn since 2007, whereas Sweden stands out with a much better performance.

Figure 7.2 also compares house prices in the two Nordic countries to those in the UK and the US. The housing bubble in the US is clearly outlined in the graph. Again we note the similarity of house price developments across countries in the years preceding the international crisis, with the proviso that the US market started to turn down before markets in the other countries. In the aftermath of the crisis, the Anglo-Saxon and the Danish housing markets have struggled to recover, whereas the Swedish market has so far been much more robust.

7.3 Do Real House Prices Trend Upwards?

In the run-up to the international financial crisis there were sharp increases in house prices in all the countries considered above, and in many countries prices are still very high by historical standards. This raises the question whether there are still 'bubbles' in some housing markets. The answer depends in part on whether one can expect a sustained upward long-run trend in real house prices. Several of the graphs above might suggest that there is indeed an underlying tendency for real house prices to increase, but the time span considered seems too short to allow a final judgement.

There is no consensus on this issue in the international academic literature. Shiller (2007) has argued that there is no evidence of a positive long-run trend in real house prices. Using long historical time series for house prices in the Netherlands, Norway, and the US, Shiller shows that there are several prolonged cycles during the century from around 1890 to the early 1990s, but there is no clear upward or downward trend. The boom in house prices since the mid 1990s and up until the recent financial crisis was quite extraordinary in a long-run historical perspective.

Many other economists share Shiller's view that real house prices are likely to remain constant over the long term. The argument is that, in a long-run equilibrium, the price of existing houses must equal the cost of building new houses of similar size and quality. If construction costs evolve in line with the general price level, it follows that nominal house prices must rise at the same pace as consumer prices.

However, two key components of the cost of supplying a new house are the price of the land on which the building is erected and the cost of the labour needed to build the house. The hypothesis that real house prices must stay constant in the long run implicitly assumes that land prices do not increase more than other prices and that labour productivity in the construction sector increases in line with productivity in other sectors.

Consider first the likely evolution of land prices. Since the total supply of land is fixed, it may be hard to increase the supply of land used for housing purposes without driving up the relative (real) price of land. Moreover, the long-run output growth in other sectors is also likely to raise the total demand for land, thereby driving up its relative price. For both of these reasons we would expect a long-run tendency for real house prices to increase due to a rise in real land prices.

Furthermore, if productivity growth in the building industry is relatively slow, we would expect that industry's unit labour costs to rise at a faster rate than elsewhere in the economy, assuming that the wages of construction workers must increase at the same rate as the average wage level (since construction firms could not otherwise attract labour). Construction costs would then tend to rise at a faster pace than the general price level.

Figures 7.3 and 7.4 show that construction costs (excluding the price of land) have indeed increased at a faster rate than consumer prices in Denmark and Sweden in recent decades, and that land prices have increased at a much faster pace in both countries. In such an environment the total real cost of

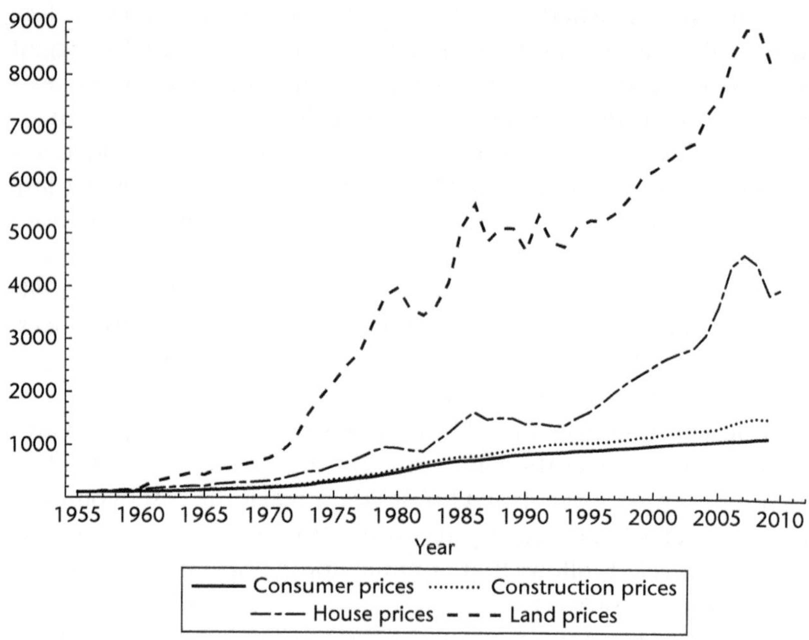

Figure 7.3. Consumer prices, house prices, land prices, and construction costs in Denmark (1955=100)

Note: Construction costs include wages, materials prices, and overhead costs. All prices and costs are measured in nominal terms. The land price is the price of building plots.

Source: Figure 5.5 in Dam et al. (2011), based on data from Statistics Denmark.

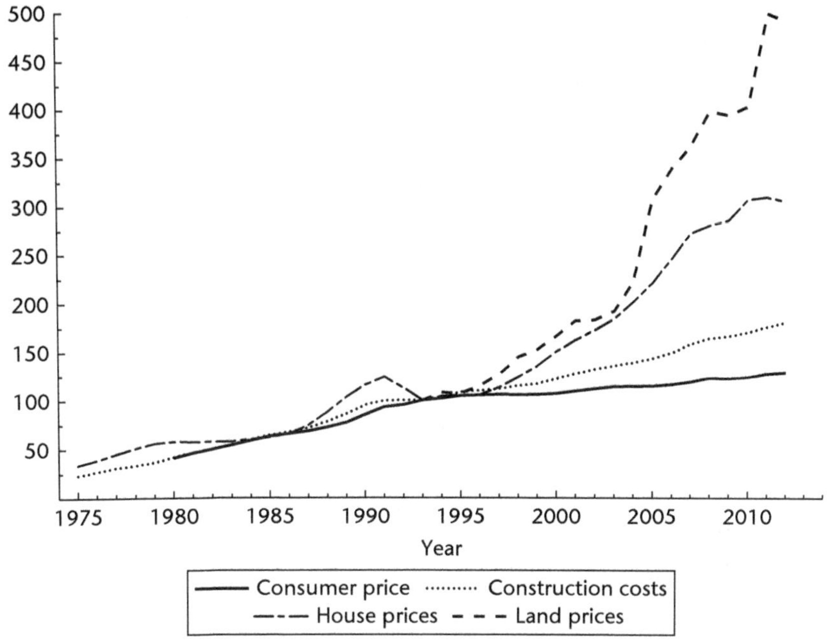

Figure 7.4. Consumer prices, construction costs, house prices, and land prices in Sweden (1993=100)

Note: Construction costs include wages, materials prices, and overhead costs. All prices and costs are measured in nominal terms. The land price is the price of agricultural land.

Source: Statistics Sweden.

supplying a new housing unit will tend to increase over time, generating an upward trend in real house prices. In Denmark, such a trend has been visible since around 1960. In Sweden, the tendency for real input costs and real house prices to go up is only manifest in the relatively short time span since the mid 1990s, allowing no strong conclusions.

The secular trend in the price of housing land depends on the overall scarcity of land in the country and on factors such as zoning laws and urban planning practices influencing the elasticity of the supply of sites for house-building. A country like the USA may still have large areas of vacant land that could be used for housing. Moreover, whereas countries like Denmark, Sweden, and some other European countries have experienced relatively poor productivity growth in the construction sector, productivity in the American building industry seems to have evolved more favourably. The costs of construction in the USA have also been kept in check by the stagnating real wages of common labour in America in recent decades (Shiller, 2007, p. 5). Since all these determinants of the cost of new housing may evolve in different ways in different countries, it would be surprising if real house prices displayed identical long-run trends across countries. In particular, the relative abundance of land in the USA may make sustained increases in real house prices less likely in that country.

To assess whether permanent increases in real house prices could really be sustainable, we may also consider the following simple model of the housing market, where *c*, *P*, and *H* denote the user cost, the real house price, and the real housing stock, respectively, *Y* is real disposable income, and *B* is the share of expenditure on (owner-occupied) housing in household budgets:

$$\text{Housing supply } H = H(P) \tag{1}$$

$$\text{Housing demand } D = D(cP, Y) \tag{2}$$

$$\text{Equilibrium } H = D \tag{3}$$

$$\text{Budget share of housing } B = \frac{cPH}{Y} \tag{4}$$

Equation (1) assumes that housing supply $H(P)$ is an increasing function of the real house price. The demand for housing is given by the function $D(cP, Y)$ in (2), indicating that housing demand depends (negatively) on the cost of housing services, *cP*, and (positively) on disposable income. Equation (3) is the condition for equilibrium between housing demand and housing supply, and (4) defines the budget share of housing expenses. Since the user cost *c* depends on interest rates and tax rates, it may be expected to be stationary in the long run, so in a long-run perspective we may assume $dc = 0$. Using equations (1) through (4) we then find that

$$\frac{dP}{P} = \left[\frac{\varepsilon_Y}{\varepsilon_H + \varepsilon_R}\right]\frac{dY}{Y}, \tag{5}$$

$$\frac{dB}{B} = \left[\frac{\varepsilon_H(\varepsilon_Y - 1) + \varepsilon_Y - \varepsilon_R}{\varepsilon_H + \varepsilon_R}\right]\frac{dY}{Y}, \tag{6}$$

$$\varepsilon_R \equiv -\frac{\partial D}{\partial cP}\frac{cP}{D}, \quad \varepsilon_Y \equiv \frac{\partial D}{\partial Y}\frac{Y}{D}, \quad \varepsilon_H \equiv \frac{dH}{dP}\frac{P}{H},$$

where *dX* indicates the absolute change in variable *X*, ε_R is the numerical elasticity of housing demand with respect to the cost of housing services, ε_Y is the elasticity of housing demand with respect to real disposable income, and ε_H is the price elasticity of housing supply.[2]

[2] In other words, ε_R measures the percentage decrease in housing demand in case of a 1 per cent increase in the real housing cost, ε_Y is the percentage increase in housing demand generated by a 1 per cent increase in real income, and ε_H is the percentage increase in housing supply induced by a 1 per cent increase in the real house price.

On average in the long term, the growth rate of real income, dY/Y, is positive. The income elasticity of housing demand is also positive, and the numerical price elasticity of housing demand is generally a finite number. According to equation (5) the long-run growth rate of real house prices will then be positive unless the supply of housing is infinitely elastic in the long term (that is, unless $\varepsilon_H \rightarrow \infty$).

However, if economic growth creates a growing scarcity of building sites, the elasticity of housing supply is likely to be finite. In that case equation (5) predicts a secular increase in real house prices. But wouldn't secularly increasing real house prices imply that housing expenses would absorb an ever-increasing share of household budgets and hence be unsustainable? According to equation (6) the answer is: not necessarily. For example, if the income and price elasticities of housing demand are both equal to 1, it follows from (6) that the budget share of housing expenses will be constant over the long run even if the elasticity of housing supply is finite.[3]

As mentioned, equations (5) and (6) assume that the real user cost of housing is stationary over the long run. In Figure 7.5 we show the evolution of the real user cost of owner-occupied housing in Denmark and Sweden. We use the real after-tax interest rate on five-year mortgage loans plus a constant risk premium (assumed to be 7% in both countries) as a proxy for the real user cost of owner-occupied housing.

According to the upper graph in Figure 7.5 the real user cost in Denmark varied around a level of 6% during the ten years from 1974 to 1984. From the mid 1980s the mean value seemed to increase permanently, but after a peak in 1987 the Danish user cost fell slowly over time until 2012. There were three main drivers behind these developments. First of all, the rates of nominal interest and inflation came down significantly after 1982 as a consequence of Denmark's shift to a hard currency peg.[4] Since the tax code allows full deductibility of nominal interest expenses, a parallel drop in the nominal interest rate and the rate of inflation will drive up the real after-tax interest rate. This helps to explain the rise in the Danish user cost between 1983 and 1987. Second, the tax rate on capital income against which mortgage interest expenses can be deducted was substantially reduced as a result of a tax reform taking effect in 1987. This explains the sharp increase in the user cost in that year. Third, the downward trend in international real rates of interest since that time has tended to reduce the user cost in recent decades.

[3] According to the empirical estimates in Brusewitz (1998), the income and price elasticities are indeed close to 1 in Sweden.

[4] See Bergman, Hutchison, and Jensen (2015) for a thorough analysis of this change in the Danish policy regime.

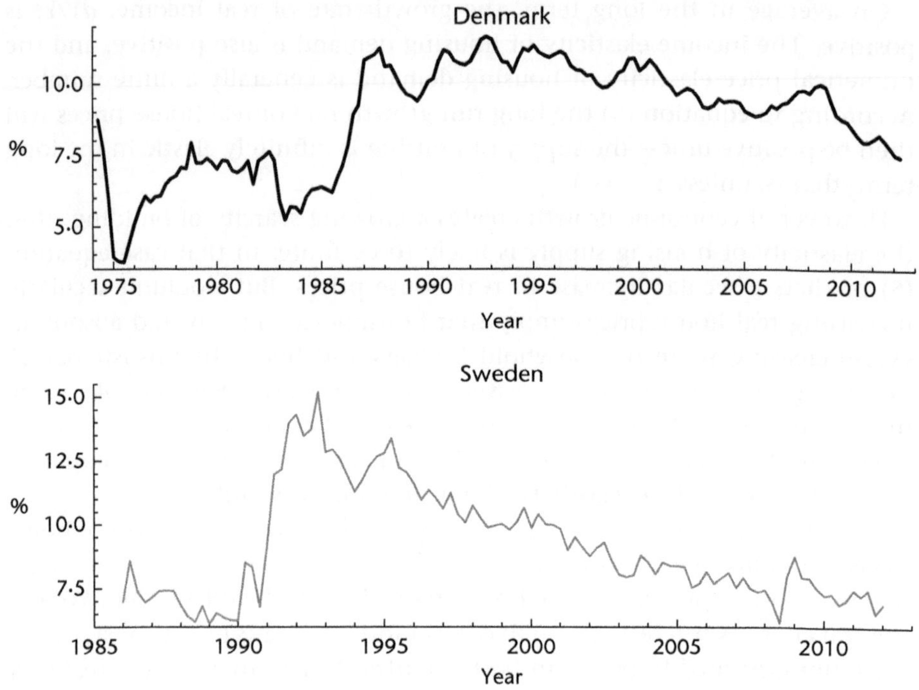

Figure 7.5. The real user cost of owner-occupied housing in Denmark and Sweden (percentage points)

Note: We have assumed that the risk premium is equal to 7 per cent.

In Sweden we see that the user cost rose sharply in the early 1990s. This was due to a special combination of an increase in the nominal interest rate triggered by a foreign exchange crisis, a sharp drop in the expected inflation rate, and the significant cut in the capital income tax rate implied by the ambitious tax reform of 1990–1. However, since the early 1990s the user cost has tended to move back towards the level prevailing in the 1980s, due to a continued fall in the nominal interest rate.

Overall, we consider the Danish and Swedish evidence to be consistent with the theoretically well-founded idea that the user cost is stationary in the long run.

More generally, the analysis in this section suggests that neither economic theory nor the available evidence implies that real house prices should necessarily remain constant over the long run. The mere fact that real house prices in Denmark and Sweden have risen substantially in recent decades does not allow us to conclude that housing markets in the two countries are currently overvalued. To resolve this issue, we shall have to dig deeper.

Next we shall therefore attempt to estimate fundamental house prices in Denmark and Sweden and compare them to actual house prices. This will enable us to evaluate more formally whether there have been bubbles in the two housing markets and to analyse the drivers of the gap between actual and fundamental house prices.

7.4 Estimates of Fundamental House Prices in Denmark and Sweden

In this section we present estimates of the level of fundamental house prices in Denmark and Sweden. The analysis underlying the results presented below is documented in detail in Bergman and Sørensen (2013).

The fundamental house price is defined as the equilibrium house price that would prevail if households had rational expectations about the underlying fundamental determinants of house prices. Those fundamental variables such as the future levels of income, interest rates, and housing supply determine the future value of the housing service delivered by a house.

The fundamental house price may deviate from the actual house price, partly because consumers may not always have realistic (rational) expectations about the future fundamentals that determine the future value of housing services, and partly because of various frictions that prevent an instantaneous adjustment of the house price to its equilibrium level, i.e., its fundamental value. However, economic theory suggests that the actual house price should move towards its fundamental level over the long run.

The fundamental house price can be derived from the following expression for the imputed rent in period t (R_t^H), defined as the real cost of the housing service flowing from a physical unit of owner-occupied housing:

$$R_t^H = \left[i_t(1-\tau_t^j) - \pi_t + \eta\right]P_t - (P_{t+1}^e - P_t). \tag{7}$$

Here i_t is the nominal mortgage interest rate, τ_t^j is the capital income tax rate, π_t is the expected rate of inflation, η is the sum of the effective property tax rate, the real rate of depreciation of the housing stock and a premium for risk and credit constraints,[5] P_t is the real price of a unit of owner-occupied housing, and P_t^e is the expected real price at time $t+1$ given the information available at time t. In the case where the housing investment is fully debt-financed, the term $\left[i_t(1-\tau_t^j)+\eta\right]P_t$ is the homeowner's nominal cash expenses whereas

[5] Sørensen (2013, Appendix) sets up a formal model of the user cost that explains the determinants of the premium for risk and credit constraints.

$\pi_t P_t + (P^e_{t+1} - P_t)$ is the expected nominal capital gain. Rearranging the expression above, we obtain

$$P_t = \frac{R^H_t + P^e_{t+1}}{1+\gamma_t}, \quad \gamma_t \equiv i_t(1-\tau^i_t) - \pi_t + \eta, \tag{8}$$

where γ_t is the user cost of owner-occupied housing, *excluding* the expected capital gain. This equation shows explicitly how the current house price depends on the house price expected to prevail in the next period. But next period's house price will in turn depend on the expected house price in period $t + 2$, which will depend on the house price expected to prevail in period $t + 3$, and so on. Using this insight, Bergman and Sørensen (2013) show that

$$P_t = E_t\left[\sum_{i=0}^{\infty} \frac{R^H_{t+1}}{\prod_{j=0}^{i}(1+\gamma_{t+j})}\right]. \tag{9}$$

This equation defines the fundamental house price. We see that the fundamental house price equals the discounted value of the current and the expected future imputed rents. The relevant discount rate is the user cost of housing excluding the expected real capital gain. Note that we assume that there are no 'bubbles' in the fundamental house price given by equation (9).[6]

The expected future imputed rents are not directly observable, so we need a model to pin down the expected future values of R^H_t. There are different ways to proceed, but here we will consider the so-called supply–demand model discussed by Hott and Monnin (2008). In particular, assume that imputed rents adjust in order to equilibrate the supply of and demand for housing services and that the demand for housing services (D_t) depends on aggregate real disposable income and the imputed rent in the following way:

$$D_t = BY_t^{\varepsilon_Y}(R^H_t)^{-\varepsilon_R} \tag{10}$$

where B is a constant, ε_Y is the income elasticity of housing demand, and ε_R is a price elasticity measuring the numerical elasticity of housing demand with respect to the imputed rent. The aggregate supply of housing services is proportional to the aggregate housing stock (H), and the proportionality

[6] While we assume that there are no bubbles in the *fundamental house price*, we do not rule out that there may be occasional bubbles in the actual house price. The gap between the actual and the fundamental house price can be used to assess whether there are prolonged deviations from the fundamental value and to provide an estimate of the degree of overvaluation or undervaluation.

factor may be normalized at unity by appropriate choice of units. In housing market equilibrium we thus have $H_t = D_t$. This implies that

$$R_t^H = B^{1/\varepsilon_R} Y_t^{\varepsilon_Y/\varepsilon_R} H_t^{-1/\varepsilon_R}. \tag{11}$$

Using this equation and an appropriate procedure for forecasting Y_t and H_t, one can estimate the expected future imputed rents, provided one has realistic estimates of the elasticities ε_R and ε_Y.

When forecasting the future discount rates γ_{t+j} and the variables needed to calculate the expected future imputed rents, Bergman and Sørensen (2013) assume that households act as if they were using a Vector Autoregression (VAR) model describing the historical interaction of the variables Y, H, γ, and the actual real house price as well as actual real rents in the rental housing sector (this is the sense in which expectations are assumed to be rational). Bergman and Sørensen (2013) describe in detail how the VAR model is specified and estimated. The estimation procedure assumes that the average level of actual real house prices observed over the estimation period corresponded to the average level of fundamental house prices over that period. In other words, it is assumed that there was no systematic under- or overvaluation of house prices over the estimation period taken as a whole. The model was estimated using Danish and Swedish quarterly data. The sample period for Denmark is 1974:1–2012:2 and for Sweden it is 1986:1–2012:1. The starting point for the estimation period was dictated by data availability. Bergman and Sørensen (2013) provide a detailed definition and description of data sources. The Danish data we use were taken from Statistics Denmark while the Swedish data were provided by Statistics Sweden.

To apply the supply–demand model of the housing market, one needs to choose specific values for the income and price elasticity of housing demand. As mentioned by Englund (2011), most international studies indicate that the income elasticity of housing demand is around 1 whereas the numerical price elasticity is below 1. The bulk of the international studies surveyed by Girouard et al. (2006) also find that house prices react more than proportionally to changes in housing supply, implying that the numerical price elasticity of housing demand is less than one. On the other hand, using Swedish micro data, Brusewitz (1998) found that the income and price elasticities were both very close to 1. Given the uncertainty regarding the true parameter values, we will illustrate the sensitivity of our results to variations in these elasticities.

Figures 7.6 and 7.7 show our estimates of fundamental (dashed line) and actual real house prices (solid line) as well as 90% confidence bands for the fundamental price (dotted lines). The confidence bands were computed from a standard bootstrap on the VAR model that is used to forecast the variables determining the fundamental house price. Exploiting the estimates from the VAR model, we use a non-parametric bootstrap with 500 replications to estimate the uncertainty of the VAR-based forecasts. There are four graphs in each figure, corresponding to four different combinations of the income and price elasticities of housing demand (ε_Y and ε_R).

Consider first Figure 7.6 showing actual and estimated fundamental house prices in Denmark. The fundamental house price is falling until around 1990 and then increasing again. The main reason is that the user cost increased significantly during the 1980s whereas it followed a slightly declining trend in the 1990s and 2000s, as we saw in Figure 7.5. According to our estimates

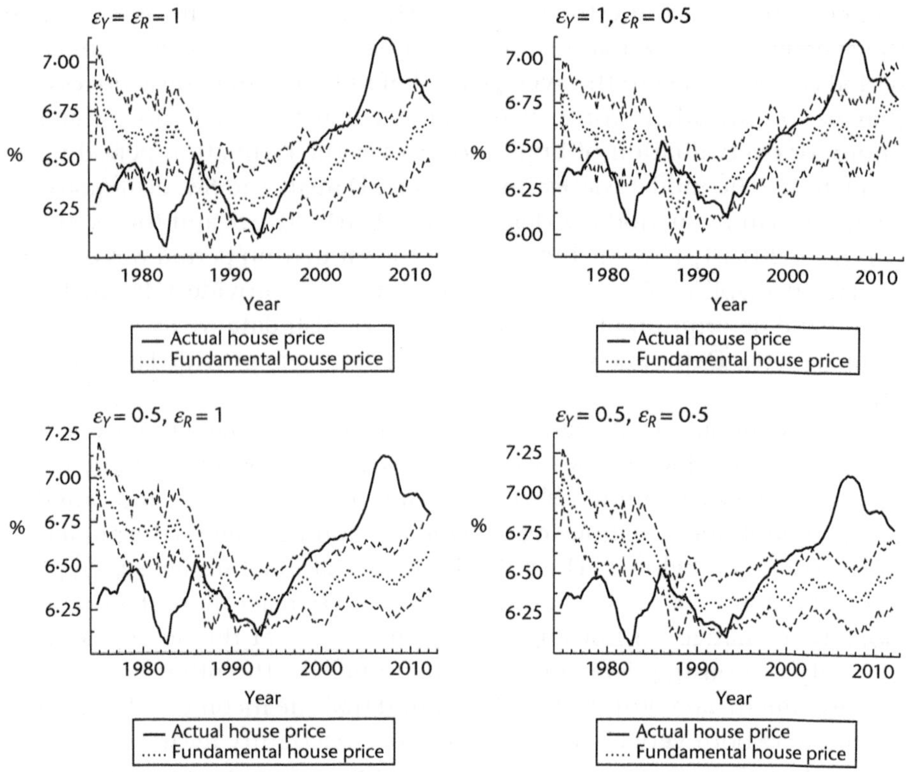

Figure 7.6. Denmark: actual house prices and estimated fundamental house prices with 90% confidence bands

Note: Dotted lines represent the 90% confidence band around the estimated fundamental house price computed using bootstrap simulations with 500 trials.

Source: Bergman and Sørensen (2013).

actual house prices undershot the fundamental level during most of the 1980s and again in the early 1990s. This was followed by a period where actual house prices were not significantly different from the fundamental level, but from the late 1990s and onwards Danish house prices became significantly overvalued. This conclusion is relatively robust to alternative assumptions concerning the income and price elasticities of housing demand, although the degree of undervaluation or overvaluation differs. In 2012 Danish house prices were significantly overvalued (outside the confidence band for the fundamental price level) in two cases, i.e. for $\varepsilon_Y = 0.5$ and $\varepsilon_R = 1.0$, and when $\varepsilon_Y = \varepsilon_R = 0.5$.

Figure 7.7 shows the actual and the estimated fundamental house prices for Sweden. The fundamental house price fluctuated more sharply than the actual house price during the crisis years of the early 1990s, reflecting that

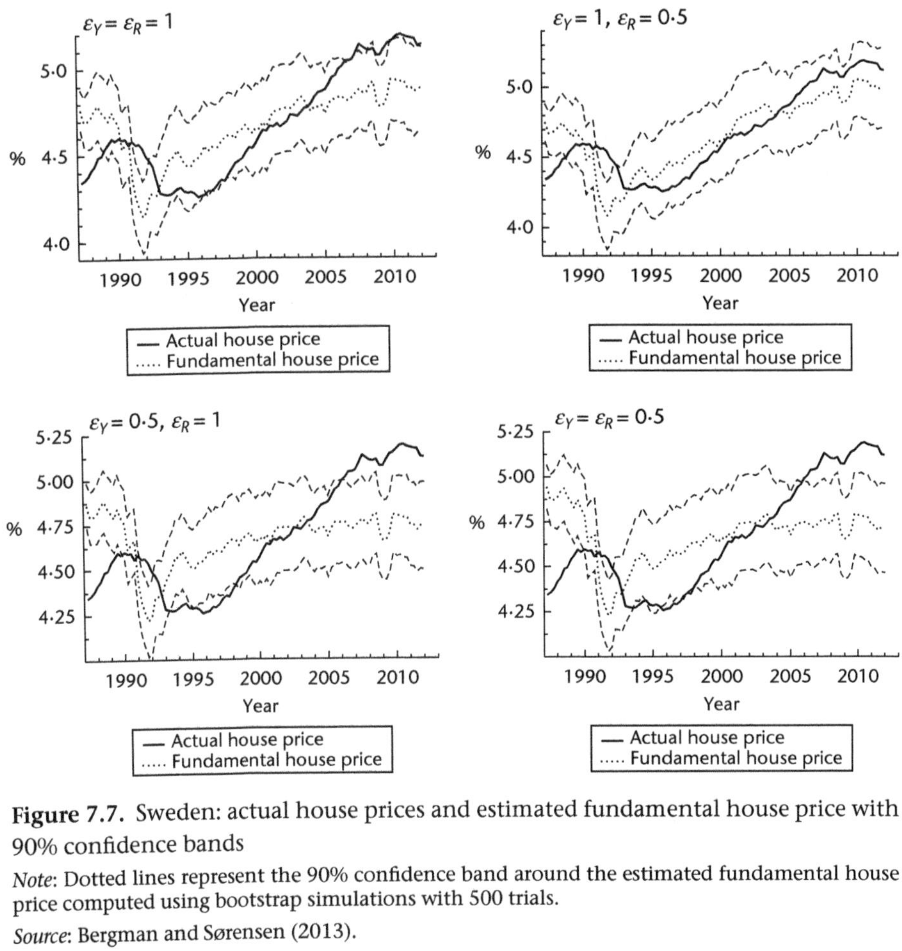

Figure 7.7. Sweden: actual house prices and estimated fundamental house price with 90% confidence bands

Note: Dotted lines represent the 90% confidence band around the estimated fundamental house price computed using bootstrap simulations with 500 trials.

Source: Bergman and Sørensen (2013).

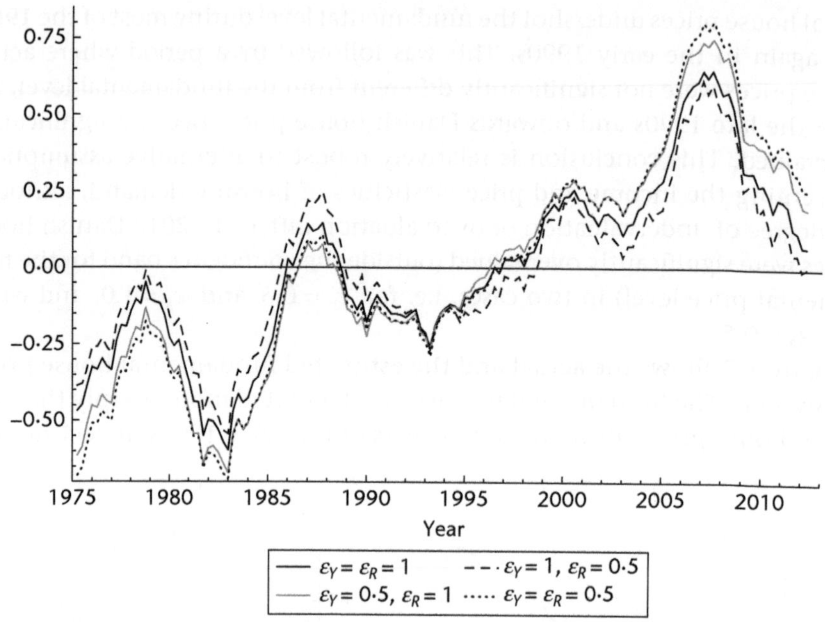

Figure 7.8. The gap between actual and fundamental house prices in Denmark
Source: Bergman and Sørensen (2013).

actual house prices only adjust gradually to shifts in housing demand and supply, due to the market frictions explained in Sørensen (2013, Section 3.1). We also see that, in contrast to actual house prices, fundamental house prices do not appear to have risen very much since the mid 1990s. The estimates suggest that Swedish real house prices were overvalued in the first quarter of 2012, although actual house prices were within the confidence band for the fundamental price level in the case where $\varepsilon_Y = 1.0$.

Figures 7.8 and 7.9 show the estimated gaps between the actual and the estimated fundamental house prices (the logarithmic difference), taken from Figures 7.6 and 7.7 above. We see that for an income elasticity of housing demand equal to 1, which is probably the most plausible case, a lower price elasticity of housing demand implies a smaller current overvaluation of housing markets in both countries. The reason is that, with a lower price elasticity of housing demand the strong income growth since the mid 1990s would require a larger increase in house prices to equilibrate housing demand and housing supply. In this way lower price elasticities would justify a higher level of current house prices.

According to figures 7.8 and 7.9 the price elasticity of housing demand does not have much influence on the size of the house price gap when the income elasticity is as low as 0.5. In this case fluctuations in income induce smaller shocks to (fundamental) housing demand, and the robust income growth

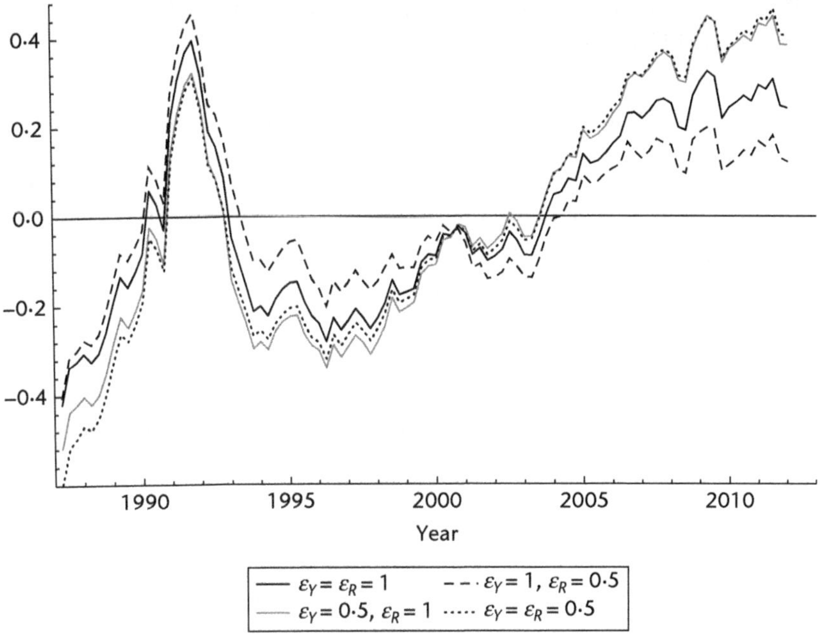

Figure 7.9. The gap between actual and fundamental house prices in Sweden
Source: Bergman and Sørensen (2013).

since the mid 1990s therefore provides a smaller boost to fundamental house prices. As a consequence, lower income elasticities of housing demand imply a higher degree of current overvaluation of housing markets in both countries.

One interesting question is whether the actual price tends to converge towards the fundamental price. The underlying theoretical model of the fundamental house price used in the calculations states that the fundamental house price equals the discounted value of expected future imputed rents. In the short and medium term actual house prices may deviate from the fundamental price level due to various frictions and due to temporary house price bubbles, but in the long run one would expect actual prices to converge on fundamental prices. Empirically this would imply that the gap between actual and fundamental prices is mean-reverting. Looking at Figures 7.8 and 7.9 it is not clear whether the estimated gaps are in fact mean-reverting. However, according to the formal tests in Bergman and Sørensen (2013) one cannot reject the null hypothesis that the gaps are stationary.[7] This indicates that the fundamental house price does indeed serve as an anchor for the actual house price.

[7] This conclusion is based on tests of the linear restriction that the gap is stationary within a bivariate vector error correction model including the actual and the estimated fundamental house

7.5 Determinants of the Gap Between Actual and Fundamental House Prices

We now ask whether macroeconomic variables and monetary policy affect the house price gaps depicted in Figures 7.8 and 7.9. The house price gap is defined as $gap_t = p_t^a - p_t$, where p_t^a is the logarithm of the actual real house price in quarter t, and p_t is the logarithm of the estimated fundamental real house price in that quarter. Our aim is to explain why the gap is closed or opened. The analysis is based on the following regression,

$$gap_t = \alpha + \beta X_t + \varepsilon_t \tag{12}$$

where X_t is a vector of explanatory variables and ε_t is the regression residual. The vector X_t contains macroeconomic variables (the business cycle measured as output growth, unemployment, and credit growth), indicators of household views on the current economic situation and expectations about the future development of the economy (measured by various consumer confidence indicators), and a money market interest rate reflecting the stance of monetary policy. The data appendix at the end of the chapter defines all variables.

We expect that households become more pessimistic during an economic downturn and therefore reduce their housing demand. An increase in unemployment or slower output growth would then reduce actual house prices. Moreover, if households tend to become unduly pessimistic during recessions and overly optimistic during booms, business fluctuations may cause larger fluctuations in actual house prices than in the fundamental house prices warranted by rational expectations about the future. In that case slower economic growth and rising unemployment will tend to reduce the house price gap $p_t^a - p_t$, and vice versa.

In our empirical application we measure household expectations using consumer confidence indicators. In particular, we use the composite consumer confidence index and reported household expectations about the economy one year ahead. A more optimistic outlook would raise the demand for housing and might thereby increase the house price gap. The timing is, however, uncertain and therefore we will allow for lagged effects.

There is a current debate among economists as to whether central banks should also focus on financial stability (including the housing market) when designing monetary policy. One issue in this debate is whether there is a direct and strong effect from monetary policy on house prices. The debate is particularly lively in Sweden. A majority of the deputy governors of the Riksbank are arguing that the repo rate should be kept relatively high in

price. Johansen tests suggest that there is one cointegration vector present in the system and that the gap is stationary for both Danish and Swedish data regardless of our assumption concerning the income and price elasticities of housing demand.

order to limit credit growth and therefore also households' high indebtedness. This argument has been challenged recently by a former deputy governor, Lars E.O. Svensson, who argues that a temporary change in the repo rate will have only minor effects on house prices whereas a permanent change will have a substantial effect. Given this controversy, it is interesting to evaluate empirically if there is an effect from interest rates on the house price gap. We therefore include an interest rate in our regressions; CIBOR for the regressions with Danish data and STIBOR when estimating the Swedish model.

Almost all models of financial crises suggest that rising household indebtedness plays a crucial role when explaining soaring asset prices, including house prices. We include a measure of credit growth in our regressions to capture this effect. We would expect that higher credit growth would tend to increase the house price gap since previous research suggests a positive effect on actual house prices.

In the regression above all variables must be stationary. We already know from Bergman and Sørensen (2013) that the estimated gaps for both Danish and Swedish data are stationary regardless of assumptions concerning the two elasticities, ε_Y and ε_R. Prior to running the regression above, we test whether the variables contain unit roots using standard ADF-tests.[8] If we cannot reject the null hypothesis that the variable contains a unit root, we use the difference instead of the level. The results suggest that both the CIBOR and STIBOR interest rates are non-stationary and therefore we include first differences of these variables in our regressions. The Danish unemployment rate is found to be non-stationary (and is included in first differences) whereas the Swedish unemployment rate is stationary (and included in levels). The consumer confidence indicators for both countries are clearly stationary; they measure the fraction of households having a positive outlook on the economy. Output growth is stationary as well. Total credit in the economy, however, shows a clear trending behaviour and is assumed to be non-stationary and therefore we use the growth rate of credit in our regressions. We measure credit growth in Denmark using bank credit to the non-financial sector whereas for Sweden we use bank lending to households.

We have used a general-to-specific estimation procedure starting off with three lags of every variable. Then we remove parameters with the highest p-value, one at a time, until only significant parameters remain in the regression (using the 10% level as a cut-off). However, we always report the point estimates of the most significant lag for each variable in the tables below. The estimated gaps between the actual and estimated fundamental house prices are autocorrelated, indicating that there is autocorrelation in the residuals. We therefore include the lagged gap as an explanatory variable.

[8] The test results are not shown here in the interests of brevity but are available from the authors upon request.

Tables 7.1 and 7.2 report the estimates of the drivers of the gaps shown in Figures 7.8 and 7.9 using the explanatory variables discussed above and the general-to-specific approach. Consider first the results for Denmark reported in Table 7.1. We see that point estimates on all variables have the expected signs except for GDP growth, which is not significant. The results do not seem to be much affected by the choice of income and price elasticities. Looking at the case with unit elasticities, an increase in credit growth by 1 percentage point increases the house price gap by 0.27 percentage points, and an increase in the CIBOR rate by 1 percentage point reduces the gap in the following quarter by about 0.5 percentage points. The gap also responds positively to the consumer indicator. Unemployment turns out to be insignificant (but with the expected negative coefficient).

For Sweden we see that the point estimates have the expected signs as well, except for GDP growth, which is insignificant. The same variables turn out to be significant as in the Danish case, although the STIBOR rate is only borderline

Table 7.1. Estimated effects of macroeconomic variables on the gap between actual and fundamental house prices in Denmark 1976:1–2012:2

	gap_t ($\varepsilon_Y = \varepsilon_R = 1$)	gap_t ($\varepsilon_Y = 1, \varepsilon_R = 0.5$)	gap_t ($\varepsilon_Y = 0.5, \varepsilon_R = 1$)	gap_t ($\varepsilon_Y = \varepsilon_R = 0.5$)
ΔUnemployment rate	–2.162	–2.302	–2.149	–2.297
	(1.604)	(1.608)	(1.753)	(1.647)
	0.00005	0.0007*	0.0004	0.0007**
Consumer confidence	(0.0004)	(0.0004)	(0.0004)	(0.0004)
	–0.0651	0.058	–0.245	–0.0131
GDP growth	(0.266)	(0.265)	(0.294)	(0.274)
	0.274***	0.244***	0.354***	0.282***
Credit growth	(0.085)	(0.084)	(0.095)	(0.088)
	–0.497***	–0.458***	–0.560***	–0.487***
ΔCibor (–1)	(0.157)	(0.156)	(0.175)	(0.162)
	1.111***	1.105***	1.094***	1.104***
Gap (–1)	(0.053)	(0.053)	(0.053)	(0.053)
	–0.150***	–0.136***	–0.144***	–0.135***
Gap (–3)	(0.051)	(0.051)	(0.052)	(0.050)
R^2	0.17	0.16	0.18	0.17
AR(5)	0.457	0.340	0.621	0.404
ARCH(4)	0.137	0.059	0.174	0.196
Normality	0.846	0.676	0.479	0.599

Note: The regressions also include a constant term, which is not reported for brevity. Consumer confidence is measured as the fraction of Danish households having a positive view of their own financial situation over the next 12 months. Credit growth is measured as the change in bank credit to the non-financial sector. R^2 is the coefficient of determination excluding lags of the dependent variable and the constant term. AR(5) is the Ljung-Box test for autocorrelation using 5 lags, ARCH(4) is the LM test for ARCH using 4 lags, and normality is a test whether the residuals are normally distributed. Only p-values are reported for these tests. Robust standard errors are reported within parentheses below each estimate. *** denotes significance at the 1 percent level, ** at the 5 percent level and * at the 10 percent level.

Table 7.2. Estimated the effects of macroeconomic variables on the gap between actual and fundamental house prices in Sweden 1992:2–2012:1

	gap_t	gap_t	gap_t	gap_t
	$(\varepsilon_Y = \varepsilon_R = 1)$	$(\varepsilon_Y = 1, \varepsilon_R = 0.5)$	$(\varepsilon_Y = 0.5, \varepsilon_R = 1)$	$(\varepsilon_Y = \varepsilon_R = 0.5)$
Unemployment rate (–2)	–0.191***	–0.186***	–0.151**	–0.160***
	(0.064)	(0.067)	(0.060)	(0.063)
Consumer confidence	0.001***	0.002***	0.001**	0.001***
	(0.000)	(0.000)	(0.000)	(0.000)
GDP growth	–0.221	–0.185	–0.190	–0.142
	(0.423)	(0.437)	(0.401)	(0.417)
Credit growth (–1)	0.491**	0.530***	0.391**	0.472***
	(0.191)	(0.197)	(0.182)	(0.189)
ΔStibor (–2)	–0.360*	–0.463**	–0.175	–0.377***
	(0.199)	(0.205)	(0.190)	(0.196)
Dependent variable (–1)	0.905***	0.929***	0.883***	0.937***
	(0.022)	(0.018)	(0.028)	(0.018)
R2	0.36	0.40	0.22	0.24
AR(4)	0.233	0.301	0.180	0.261
ARCH(4)	0.246	0.247	0.314	0.256
Normality	0.852	0.831	0.950	0.968

Note: Consumer confidence is measured as the fraction of Swedish households having a positive view on the general economic situation over the next 12 months. Credit growth is measured as the change in bank lending to households. R^2 is the coefficient of determination excluding lags of dependent variable and the constant term. AR(4) is the Ljung-Box test for autocorrelation using 4 lags, ARCH(4) is the LM test for ARCH using 4 lags and normality is a test whether the residuals are normally distributed. Only p-values are reported for these tests. Robust standard errors are reported within parentheses below each estimate. *** denotes significance at the 1% level, ** at the 5% level and * at the 10% level.

significant depending on the elasticities chosen. Looking at the calculations with unit elasticities and comparing to the Danish outcome, credit growth (now lagged one quarter) seems to have a bigger influence on the gap in the Swedish housing market, whereas the money market rate has a smaller influence compared to Denmark. An increase in the unemployment rate by 1 percentage point causes the house price gap to drop by 0.19 percentage points with a lag of two quarters.

The regression results clearly show that credit growth is essential when analysing the housing market. Slower credit growth has a negative impact on the gap between actual and fundamental house prices but higher interest rates also seem to reduce the gap. This suggests a potential for monetary policy to stabilize the housing market.

7.6 Conclusions and Policy Implications

In this chapter we have analysed the housing markets in Denmark and Sweden. The experience of these countries is interesting since they have both gone through two 'bubble-like' episodes with soaring house prices in recent decades. They have also experienced two major financial crises and have managed to turn unsustainable fiscal situations around, enabling them to stimulate the economy during the recent international crisis. Both countries saw a peak in house prices in 2007, but while Danish house prices have fallen significantly since then, Swedish prices have remained at a historically high level.

We presented estimates of the fundamental house price, defined as the price level that can be justified by the current and rationally expected future values of fundamental economic variables such as interest rates, disposable incomes, housing supply, and property taxes. These estimates allowed us to evaluate whether house prices in Denmark and Sweden have been and still are significantly out of line with fundamentals. We found that there have indeed been periods when house prices were substantially overvalued or undervalued. For Denmark house prices were undervalued in the early 1980s and have been overvalued since the late 1990s. For Sweden we found that house prices were overvalued before and during the Swedish banking crisis in the early 1990s (which was triggered by a sharp downturn in the real estate market) and have been since around 2005.

As of 2012, it appeared that house prices in both countries were above their fundamental level, particularly in Sweden. However, on the popular assumption of a unit income elasticity of housing demand, actual house prices in both countries fell within the 90% confidence bands for the estimated fundamental house prices. This statistical uncertainty is testimony to the difficulties of identifying an asset price bubble ex ante.

We also investigated whether macroeconomic variables can explain the behaviour of the gap between actual and fundamental house prices. We found that variables such as the short-term interest rate, unemployment, credit growth, and consumer confidence have the expected impact on the house price gap. Higher interest rates tend to reduce actual house prices relative to their fundamental level in both Denmark and Sweden. This effect is statistically significant in both countries but seems particularly strong in Denmark. Household expectations about the future economic situation also play a role in both countries. It seems as if households consider their own economic situation as well as the general economic development when deciding to invest in housing. Finally, we find that credit growth has a significant positive effect on the house price gap in both countries. This effect is especially strong in Sweden.

Our findings suggest that the monetary authorities have some scope for reducing destabilizing deviations of actual from fundamental house prices, partly through their interest rate policy, and partly via their potential influence on credit growth. If the cycle in the housing market is tightly synchronized with the general business cycle, there is no conflict between the goal of stabilizing the house price gap and that of stabilizing the overall economy. However, our analysis suggests that large deviations of actual from fundamental house prices can persist for a long time, so the goal of closing the house price gap may not always be consistent with the goal of adjusting monetary and financial policy to the current state of the general business cycle.

In summary, our analysis suggests that the potential dilemma for monetary policymakers between pricking an asset bubble and stabilizing inflation is indeed a real one. We also saw that house prices in many European countries have behaved much like those in Denmark and Sweden, so most likely policymakers in these countries face the same dilemma. The recent Spanish and Irish experience sadly illustrates the utmost importance of pursuing a policy that prevents bubbles in the housing market.

Appendix - Variables explaining the house price gap

Denmark	Sample	Source
Real price of one- or two-dwelling buildings	1974Q1–2012Q2	Danmarks Nationalbank
Bank credit to non–financial private sector	1974Q1–2012Q2	Danmarks Nationalbank
CIBOR T/N	1974Q1–2012Q2	Danmarks Nationalbank
Consumer confidence Indicator	1974Q1–2012Q2	Statistics Denmark
Unemployment rate	1974Q1–2012Q2	Danmarks Nationalbank
Gross domestic product	1974Q1–2012Q2	Danmarks Nationalbank
Consumer confidence indicators	1974Q1–2012Q2	Ecowin

Sweden	Sample	Source
Real price of one- or two-dwelling buildings	1986Q1–2012Q1	Statistics Sweden
Banks' lending to households incl NPISH, total, SEK	1986Q1–2012Q1	Ecowin
STIBOR T/N	1986Q1–2012Q1	Ecowin
Unemployment rate	1986Q1–2012Q1	Ecowin
Gross domestic product	1986Q1–2012Q1	Ecowin
Consumer confidence indicators	1986Q1–2012Q1	Ecowin

References

Ambrose, B.W., P. Eichholtz, and T. Lindenthal (2013), 'House Prices and Fundamentals: 355 Years of Evidence,' *Journal of Money, Credit and Banking,* 45, 477–91.

Bergman, M., M. Hutchison, and S.E.H. Jensen (2015), 'Shaping the Fiscal Policy Framework: Lessons from Fiscal Consolidations inin Denmark and Sweden', Chapter 9 in this book.

Bergman, M. and P. Birch Sørensen (2013). 'Estimating Fundamental House Prices in Sweden'. Working Paper, Department of Economics, University of Copenhagen.

Brusewitz, U.H. (1998). Self-selectivity and Kinked Budget Constraints: the Demand for Housing in Sweden. *Journal of Housing Economics*, 7, 243–72.

Campbell, J.Y. and R.J. Shiller (1987), 'Stock Prices, Earnings, and Expected Dividends,' *Journal of Finance*, 43, 661–76.

Campbell, J.Y. and R.J. Shiller (1989), 'The Dividend-Price Ratio and Expectations of Future Dividends and Discount Factors,' *The Review of Financial Studies*, 1, 195–228.

Campbell, S.D., M.A. Davis, J. Gallin, and R.F. Martin (2009), 'What Moves Housing Markets: a Variance Decomposition of the Rent-Price Ratio,' *Journal of Urban Economics*, 66, 90–102.

Costello, G., P. Fraser, and N. Groenewold (2011), 'House Prices, Non-Fundamental Components and Interstate Spillovers: the Australian Experience,' *Journal of Banking & Finance*, 35, 653–69.

Dam, N.A., T.S. Hvolbøl, E.H. Pedersen, P.B. Sørensen, and S.H. Thamsborg (2011), 'Developments in the market for owner-occupied housing in recent years—Can house prices be explained?' Danmarks Nationalbank, *Monetary Review*, 1st Quarter 2011, Part 2, 1–82.

Englund, P. (2011), Svenska 'Huspriser i ett Internationellt Perspektiv'. Chapter I in Sveriges Riksbank (2011).

European Commission (2012), 'Quarterly Report on the Euro Area,' *Economic and Financial Affairs*, Vol. 11, No. 4, December 2012, 31–8.

Girouard, N., M. Kennedy, P. van den Noord, and C. André (2006), 'Recent House Price Developments: the Role of Fundamentals'. Economics Department Working Paper No. 475, OECD.

Hiebert, P. and M. Sydow (2011), 'What Drives Returns to Euro Area Housing? Evidence from a Dynamic Dividend-Discount Model,' *Journal of Urban Economics*, 70, 88–98.

Hott, C. and P. Monnin (2008), 'Fundamental Real Estate Prices: an Empirical Estimation with International Data'. *Journal of Real Estate and Financial Economics*, 36, 427–50.

Shiller, R.J. (2007), 'Understanding Recent Trends in House Prices and Home Ownership'. Paper presented at the symposium on 'Housing, Housing Finance, and Monetary Policy' organized by the Federal Reserve Bank of Kansas City in Jackson Hole, Wyoming, 31 August–1 September 2007.

Sørensen, P.B. (2013), 'The Swedish Housing Market: Trends and Risks,' Studier i Finanspolitik 2013/5, Swedish Fiscal Policy Council.

Comments on 'House Prices in Denmark and Sweden' by U. Michael Bergman, Bjørn Tangaa Sillemann, and Peter Birch Sørensen

Niels Arne Dam

The Danish and Swedish house-price developments in the past twenty years or so are spectacular with regards to the cumulated increase until today and, specifically, the steep rise in the 2000s leading up to the financial crisis.[1] The analysis conducted by Bergman, Sillemann, and Sørensen offers a timely and relevant discussion of this key component in the recent economic history of the two countries. As the authors point out, however, one should bear in mind that similar developments occurred in other advanced economies with quite different housing markets from the two in question. Hence, the underlying causes obviously have a strong global component in addition to country-specific conditions, be they regulatory or market-driven in nature.

The cumulated increase in real house prices is the topic of heated discussions in both countries. The authors offer a solid theoretical argument why long-term increases in real house prices are a plausible outcome, in particular in countries with scarce supply of land for housing purposes. This is indeed a relevant characteristic in the Nordic countries, in particular in their metropolitan areas, (Nissen et al., 2013). In fact, the discussion is perhaps even more pressing in Norway, and it would be interesting to see similar analyses of fundamental house prices conducted on Norwegian data.

[1] The views and conclusions stated are the responsibility of the author and do not necessarily reflect the views of Danmarks Nationalbank.

The authors enter very hazardous terrain; bubbles and fundamentals are inherently difficult to address empirically, even in hindsight. While I welcome such discussions, the question of 'bubble or no bubble' can tend to remove the focus from house-price volatility itself. From a macroeconomic perspective, one has to keep in mind that big swings in house prices markedly affect residential construction as well as private consumption through their impact on household wealth, whether the house-price swings reflect bubbles or not (Dam et al., 2011). Hence, even if the task of identifying bubbles is important—which it is!—we still need to pay close attention to movements in prices and demand, even when their causes can be rationalized by real economic developments. In fact, it is my firm belief that one cannot grasp the Danish business-cycle developments of the past fifty years without a specific understanding of housing demand and its determinants (cf. also my discussion in Dam, 2008).

C7.1 Estimated Fundamental House Prices

The authors apply an interesting approach to estimating fundamental house prices. I will not as such discuss the technical aspects, yet two of the identifying assumptions require attention.

First, the user cost is based on the real after-tax return on five-year bonds. This is a peculiar choice in Denmark, where house purchases in recent years have predominantly been financed with thirty-year loans with either rolling one-year interest rates or fixed interest rates for the entire period. In addition, the expected inflation is (apparently) calculated using the *ex post*-inflation rate with full weight. It is a valid question whether the high and changing inflation rates of the 1970s were perceived as a lasting phenomenon at the time for the long-term-investment decision of house purchases.

Second, the estimation is conditional on the assumption that the sample mean of the actual house prices is identical to the sample mean of the fundamental price. It is not evident to me that this is the right empirical assumption for the sample in question, and I would have liked to see robustness checks of this as well as the assumption regarding expected inflation. I believe that these two assumptions underlie the estimated result that Danish house prices were significantly undervalued in the 1970s and early 1980s. In related work of my own (Dam et al., 2011) where expected inflation is estimated not to have full weight in the effective user cost, we did not find that to be the case.

C7.2 The Role of Credit and Financing Conditions

The authors empirically assess the role of possible determinants of the gap between actual and estimated fundamental house prices. A key finding is that the gap correlates significantly with short-term interest rates and credit growth. In my view, this points to the role of first-year nominal expenditure (including amortization) in the demand for housing. Specifically, the short-term interest-rate effect in the gap estimation may in part pick up the effects of the introduction of adjustable one-year interest rates on the thirty-year mortgage loans for Danish houses in the late 1990s mentioned above.

More generally, the role of credit effects on housing demand and price formation raises questions of whether the pure economic user cost is an adequate and sufficient determinant of housing demand, in the medium to long term, that is, the 'fundamental demand' in the parlance of the authors. Specifically, it raises the question whether financial liberalizations or other permanent changes in financing options can have lasting effects on demand for housing—a question that remains unresolved in the analysis. I refer the reader to Dam et al. (2011) for an elaborate discussion.

References

Dam, N. A. (2008), 'Konjunkturcykler i Danmark og Europa', *Danish Journal of Economics*, vol. 146, no. 2, 135–55.

Dam, N. A., T. S. Hvolbøl, E. H. Pedersen, P. B. Sørensen, and S. Thamsborg (2011), 'Developments in the Market for Owner-Occupied Housing in Recent Years: Can House Prices be Explained?; Danmarks Nationalbank, *Monetary Review*, 1st Quarter, Part 2, 1–82.

Nissen, K. G., M. H. Pedersen, M. H. Rasmussen, and C. T. Thomsen (2013), 'Prices of Flats in Northern European Capitals', Danmarks Nationalbank, *Monetary Review*, 3rd Quarter, Part 1, 73–94.

8

Reforming the Fiscal Framework

The Case of Sweden 1973–2013

Lars Jonung

8.1 Introduction

Swedish public finances stand out as among the strongest in Europe in the mid-2010s.[1] How do we explain this outcome? One reason for the prevailing fiscal caution is found in the fiscal policy framework that was put in place over the past 20 years, since 2007 also including a fiscal policy council. Today, Swedish fiscal policy is rule-based, reined in by a number of restrictions. This state of affairs is in sharp contrast with the fiscal policy of the 1970s and 1980s founded on a Keynesian approach allowing policy makers a wide freedom for fiscal actions. In short, Swedish fiscal policy has moved from one extreme of fiscal laxness to the other of fiscal prudence in the past 40 years.

This transformation is analysed here as the outcome of a long and still ongoing learning process. In short, major economic crises have induced policy makers as well as university economists to rethink the proper conduct of fiscal policy. As a result of this learning process, the fiscal policy regime which covers the goals, the instruments, and the institutional framework for fiscal policymaking has been transformed.

This account is organized in the following way. First, as a background for the narrative, the macroeconomic record of Sweden since the 1970s

[1] Johanna Modigsson has skillfully prepared the tables and charts for this chapter. Fredrik N. G. Andersson, Michael Bergman, Henrik Braconier, Niklas Frank, Oskar Grevesmühl, Per Molander, Tomas Nordström, Joakim Sonnegård, and Hans Tson Söderström have provided constructive comments. The usual disclaimer holds.

is described. After this introduction, two major sections follow. The first focuses on the stabilization policies of the 1970s and 1980s that culminated in the deep financial crisis of the early 1990s. This crisis became the catalyst for fundamental change in fiscal policy. The second section describes the fiscal framework that emerged in Sweden after the crisis of 1992–3 and presents the lessons that can be learned from it so far. The focus is set here on the Fiscal Policy Council as it has attracted considerable interest.

8.2 The Macroeconomic Record

Economic growth in Sweden was weak in the 1970s and 1980s but recovered after the crisis in 1992–3 (Figure 8.1). The financial crisis during these years caused a sharp drop in real income. The crisis forced the Riksbank to abandon the fixed exchange rate of the krona in November 1992, setting off a sharp and long-lasting depreciation. The floating of the currency contributed to a long recovery, lasting up till the Great Recession. The depreciation of the krona had a significant effect on exports. They rose rapidly as measured by the share of exports to GDP, from around 27% of GDP in 1992 to a level around 50% by 2008 (Figure 8.2). The global financial crisis of 2008–10 caused a minor decline in the ratio. The improvement in economic performance since the crisis of

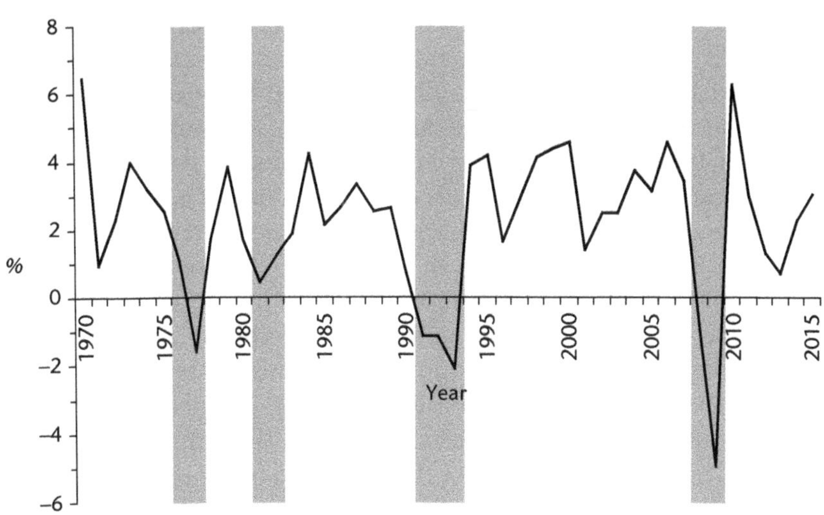

Figure 8.1. Economic growth (annual per cent) in Sweden 1970–2015

Note: The shaded years represent years of recession. Data for 2013–15 is based on forecasts.

Source: OECD Economic Outlook No 94.

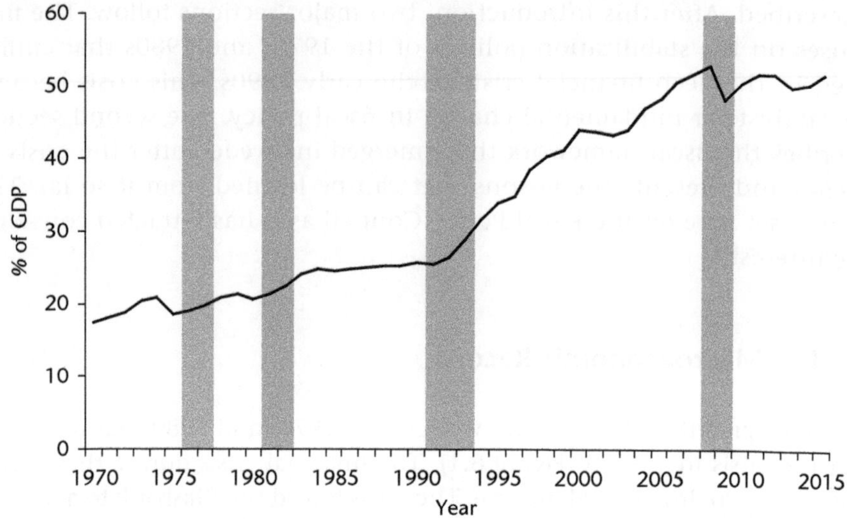

Figure 8.2. Export of goods and services (percentage of GDP, constant prices) in Sweden 1970–2015

Note: The shaded years represent years of recession. Data for 2013–15 is based on forecasts.
Source: AMECO.

the 1990s has been a boon to the Swedish economy during the recent global depression.[2]

The turn-around of the Swedish economy after the crisis of 1992 is also evident in the behaviour of inflation and interest rates. The rate of inflation was high and volatile in the 1970s and 1980s (Figure 8.3). Since the mid 1990s it has been low and more stable. The same holds for the nominal rate of interest (Figure 8.4) displaying the long-term interest rate on government bonds.

The economic growth performance had a major impact on fiscal policy as summarized in Figures 8.5–8.8. Figure 8.5 shows government gross debt to GDP for the period 1970–2013. In the early 1970s, government debt was roughly stable. The two oil price shocks (OPEC I in 1973–4 and OPEC II in 1979–81) elicited an expansionary fiscal policy response with rising budget deficits (government net lending) and thus with rising gross debt (Figure 8.6). In the mid 1980s, the debt ratio started to decline. The financial crisis of the early 1990s set off a sharp and substantial rise in the ratio, which peaked at around 80% in the mid 1990s. Since then the ratio has been falling gradually.

[2] See OECD (2012, p. 9). Many factors contributed to rapid economic growth after the crisis of the 1990s, including a number of major supply-side reforms. For an account see Jonung, Kiander, and Vartia (2009).

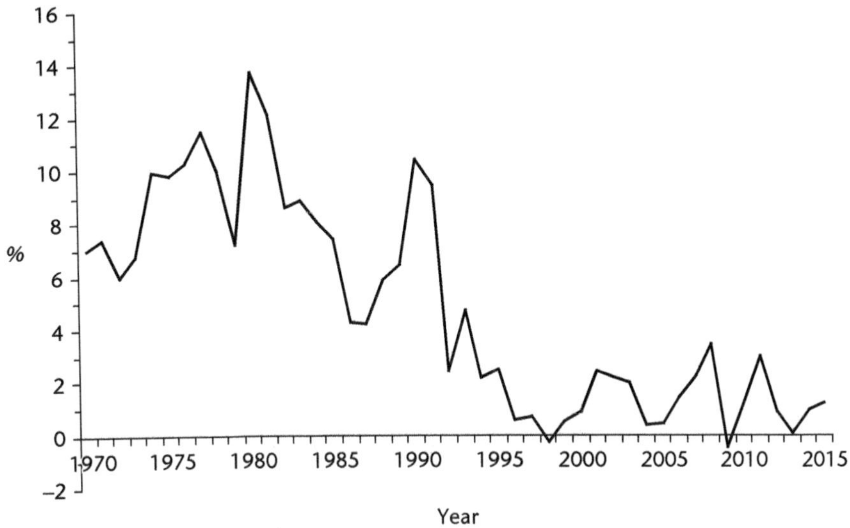

Figure 8.3. Rate of inflation (annual percentage) in Sweden 1970–2015
Source: OECD Economic Outlook No 94. Data for 2013–15 is based on forecasts.

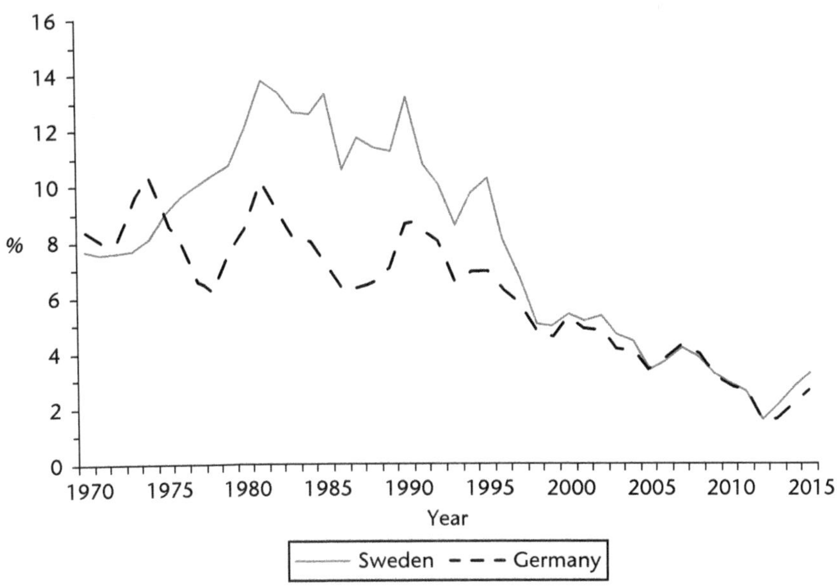

Figure 8.4. Long-term interest rate on government bonds (per cent) for Sweden and Germany 1970–2015
Note: Prior to 1991, the data for Germany refers to West Germany. Data for 2013–15 is based on forecasts.
Source: OECD Economic Outlook No 94.

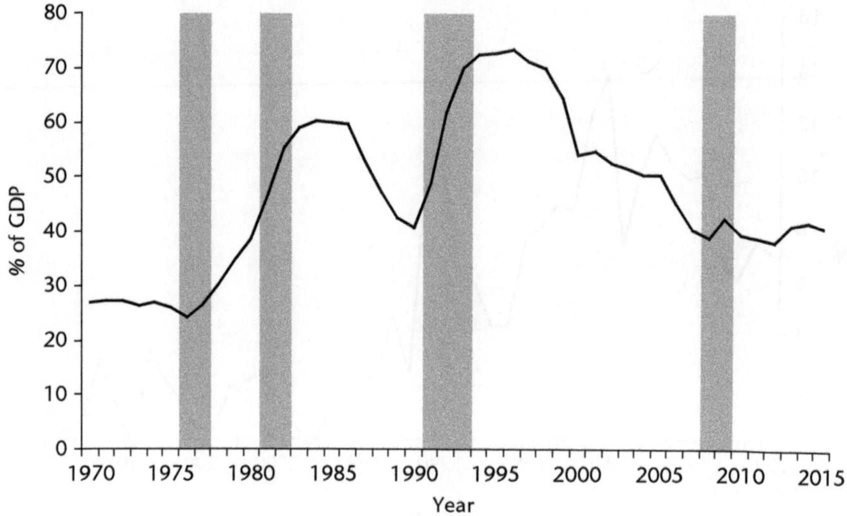

Figure 8.5. General government gross debt (percentage of GDP) in Sweden 1970–2015

Note: The shaded years represent years of recession. Data for 2013–15 is based on forecasts.

Source: AMECO.

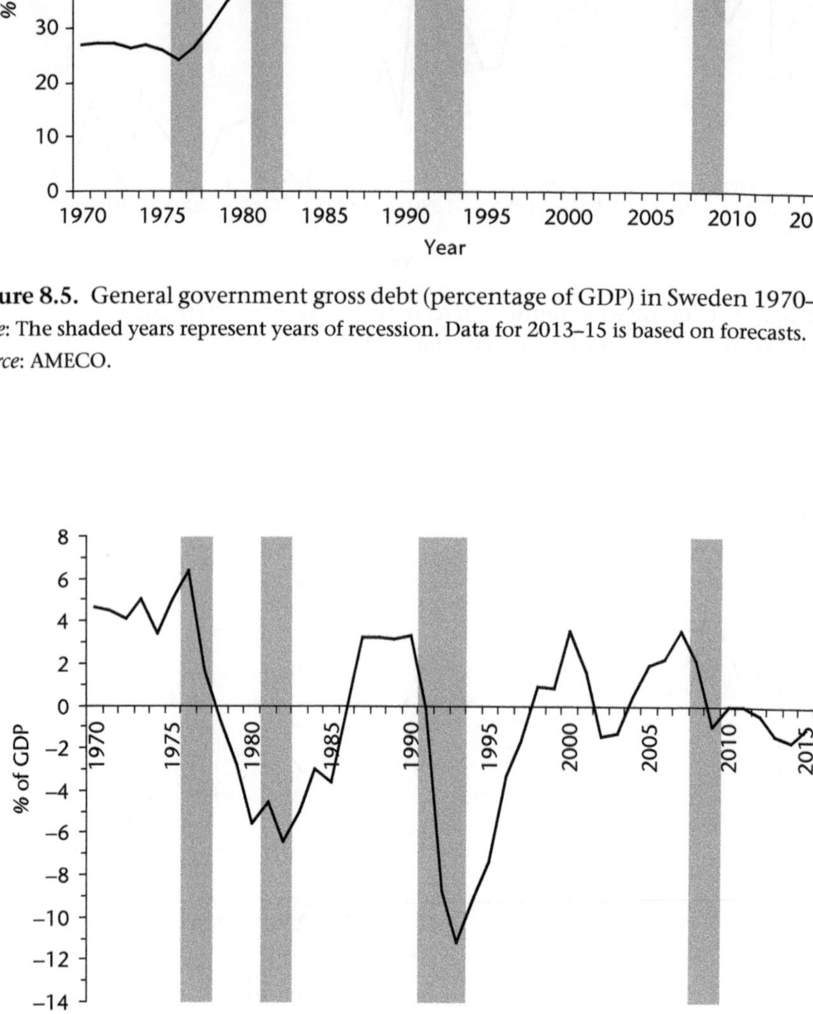

Figure 8.6. General government net lending (percentage of GDP) in Sweden 1970–2015

Note: The shaded years represent years of recession. Data for 2013–15 is based on forecasts.

Source: AMECO.

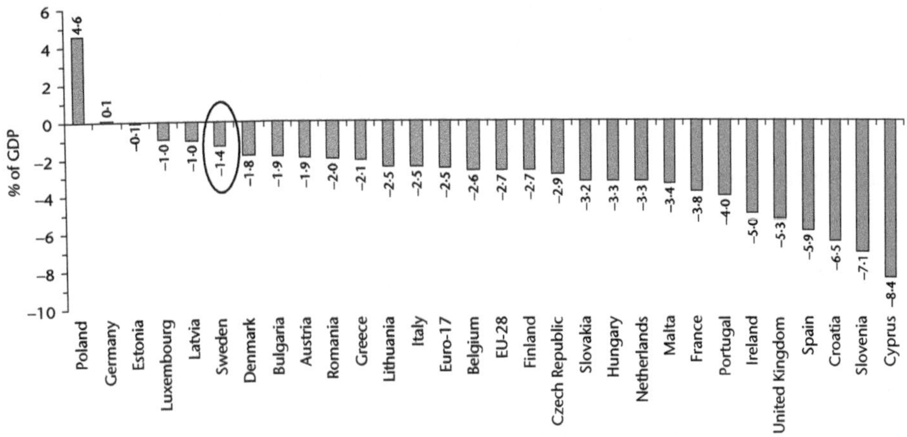

Figure 8.7. General government net lending (percentage of GDP) for EU members 2014
Note: Forecasts for 2014.
Source: AMECO.

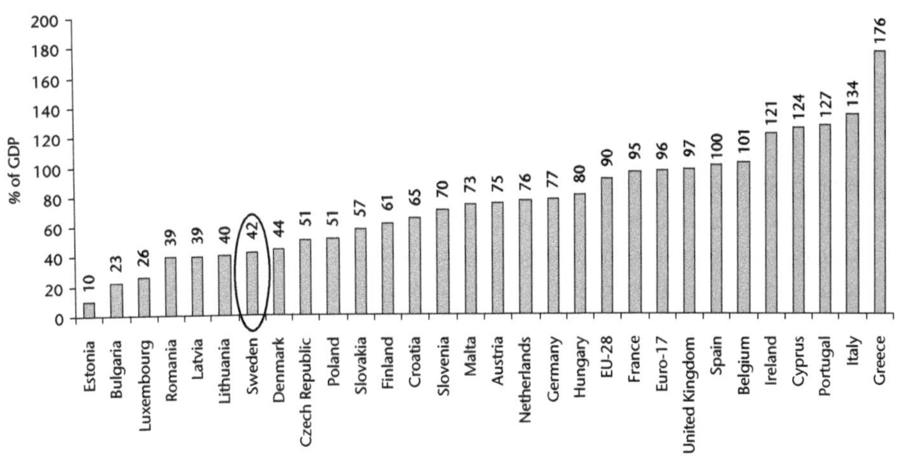

Figure 8.8. General government gross debt (percentage of GDP) for EU members 2014
Note: Forecasts for 2014.
Source: AMECO.

The recent global financial crisis starting in 2008, the Great Recession, is not reflected in any major rise in the debt ratio for Sweden although this crisis caused a sharper fall in economic growth than the crisis of the early 1990s. This is also seen from Figure 8.7 displaying general government net lending as a percentage of GDP for EU member states in 2014, and from Figure 8.8

demonstrating general government gross debt as a percentage of GDP for EU member states in 2014. Figures 8.7 and 8.8 reveal that a large number of countries in Europe are experiencing major problems with high deficits and debts. There are a few exceptions. As noted, Sweden is one of them, actually displaying strong public finances as reflected in a falling debt ratio since the mid 1990s (Figure 8.5).

8.3 Changing the Paradigm for Stabilization Policy 1970–2013

8.3.1 *An Overview*

In the early 1970s, Swedish stabilization policy had a number of goals: a fixed exchange rate for the krona, full employment, low inflation, high growth, and 'low' interest rates. The box of policy tools included a number of selective instruments. The scope of policy action was determined by the fixed exchange rate for the krona and implicit prohibitions against public borrowing from outside Sweden. Capital controls shielded the Swedish financial system from the rest of the world. Due to these external controls, domestic financial markets were extensively controlled by the Riksbank, where the under-secretary of the Ministry of Finance was commonly the chairman of the board of the Riksbank, signifying the power of the Ministry of Finance over the framing of monetary policy. The ruling philosophy of stabilization policy, 'the policy paradigm', was based on Keynesian theory, which emerged as the principal macro-theory after World War II, reinforced by ideas from the Stockholm School of Economics.

Swedish macroeconomic performance in the 1970s, 1980s, and early 1990s turned eventually into a source of disappointment. As noted above, economic growth during this period was lacking. These decades were also marked by large budget deficits, rising government debt and high and volatile inflation and recurrent devaluations of the krona. During the crisis of the early 1990s, unemployment reached a high and persistent level.

Eventually, a new view regarding the proper strategy for fiscal and monetary policy emerged, replacing the view that prevailed prior to the crisis of the 1990s. New goals, new instruments, and a new institutional framework were established after the crisis.

The goals for stabilization policy changed as well as the ranking among the goals. The fixed exchange rate for the krona was replaced by a floating exchange rate in November 1992. Inflation targeting replaced the fixed rate. The monetary policy goal was set as a target of 2% inflation per annum within a band of plus/minus one percentage point from 1995. The target band was abandoned in 2010 while the goal of 2% remained. The primary goal of fiscal policy after the crisis of the 1990s was fiscal consolidation and sustainable public finances. A surplus target of one percent of GDP holds for the general government sector over the course of the economic cycle since 2000.

The old set of stabilization instruments has been replaced by a new one. Selective instruments like the system of investment funds, once receiving international praise, as well as various regulations of the credit and capital market have been scrapped.

The institutional framework for stabilization policy has changed significantly. The Riksbank has been given a role more independent of government. Fiscal policy is managed with the help of new budget legislation as reflected in a new fiscal framework, including a fiscal policy council.

How should this process of changes in the goals, instruments, and institutions for fiscal and monetary policy be explained? The theoretical literature regarding economic policy gives little guidance as traditional theories are based on the analysis of stabilization policy behaviour within given structures and with given policy preferences.

A striking feature of Swedish stabilization policy since the beginning of the 1970s is the close relationship between the policy of the past and of the present. From this perspective, changes in policy, often classified as 'reforms', represent responses to earlier policies. In short, policy makers are involved in policy learning.

Policy learning may be defined in the following manner. Those responsible for stabilization policy learn as they consciously adapt the combination of goals and instruments to new circumstances taking into consideration earlier experiences and new information. From this perspective, policy changes or reforms emerge as a result of learning or, to be more precise, of relearning, that is by revising old notions regarding the proper choice of suitable goals, instruments, strategies, and institutions for stabilization policy.[3]

For several reasons, the Swedish experience of the past 40 years stands out as unique, making it a suitable subject for studying policy learning. First, participants in the stabilization policy process have documented their experiences and views diligently. Second, the structure of the political system has allowed Swedish politicians to test different stabilization strategies more directly than politicians in other countries have been able to do, thereby obtaining rapidly information about policy outcomes. The scope for policy action has been large as well. During the years 1970–95, no formal restrictions on fiscal policy in the form of limits for the budget deficit or the central government debt existed. The Riksbank was subject to close political control by the Government. This institutional framework

[3] This approach is developed in Jonung (1999).

is part of the reason why stabilization policy activism in Sweden became so extensive prior to the 1990s compared to the case in most other OECD countries.

Third, the leading 'activist' stabilization policy approach contributed to Sweden becoming something of a test site for stabilization policy experiments during the last quarter of the twentieth century. This laboratory produced a rich harvest of experiments, which form the central part in the learning process.

8.3.2 *The Learning Process 1970–2013*

The different elements of the learning process during the years 1970–2013 are summarized in Table 8.1. It is based on dividing the sequences of changes in the framing of stabilization policy into four stages. The first stage consists of a macroeconomic disturbance, see column 1, which, with a lag, triggers a policy reaction in the form of fiscal and monetary measures aimed at counteracting the disturbance, see column 2. In this second stage, the policy reaction is extracted from the policy lesson in the period/crisis immediately preceding stage 2. Eventually, the policy response affects the economy in stage 3, see column 3. In due time, and the time lag can be considerable here, economists and politicians reach conclusions when they evaluate the outcome of the policies conducted, see column 4.

Here the politicians learn new lessons when they revise their opinions about the proper future policy reaction. This learning determines the policy reaction when the next macroeconomic disturbance occurs as shown below covering five episodes—each of them defined by an aggregate shock to the Swedish economy during the period 1970–2013.

Episode 1, 1969–72. An outflow of capital from Sweden induced the Government to carry out a tight fiscal and monetary policy to improve the current account. This policy reaction was based on lessons from the Bretton Woods system. Within this institutional framework, a currency outflow required tightening of the domestic economy.

The policy of restraint gave rise to harsh criticism from the opposition parties and from economists. The opposition based its arguments on a Keynesian approach: fiscal policy should be more expansionary in order to counteract the rise in unemployment registered in 1971–2. The criticism contributed to a change towards expansionary policies from the end of 1972.

Episode 2, 1973–4. The next major disturbance was OPEC I, the first oil price shock in 1973–4. The lesson from the 1969–72 episode of tight monetary and fiscal policies decided the policy reaction by the Government. It was reluctant to counteract the OPEC I crisis with a policy of restraint.

Instead, the Swedish policy reaction was based on the idea that the expected international economic downturn after OPEC I could be avoided by expansionary fiscal policy. This 'policy of bridging-over' was likely the most pronounced Keynesian policy experiment among OECD countries in the 1970s.

The attempt of bridging-over eventually failed as it resulted in a growing budget deficit and a deficit in the current account in 1975–6. The acute crisis was brought to an end by two 'defensive' devaluations in 1977.

Episode 3, 1979–80. The next macroeconomic disturbance had its origins in the second oil price shock (OPEC II) of 1979–80. The lessons from 'the policy of bridging-over' triggered a policy reaction different from the response to the OPEC I crisis. Fiscal policy was now tightened. Devaluations were adopted at an earlier stage than during the OPEC I crisis. In 1981, the krona was devalued by 10%. The non-socialist parties in government went to the polls with a programme of fiscal restraint in the autumn of 1982, as opposed to the 1976 election in which their programme focused on expansion.

The social democratic opposition campaigned against the 'belt-tightening'. After winning the 1982 election, the new social democratic government carried out a devaluation of 16% in October 1982 as its first measure. This 'aggressive' devaluation summarized the lessons from the OPEC I crisis. The devaluations in 1981 and 1982 brought about rapidly increasing prices, wages, and profits, which became a major problem during the years to follow.

Episode 4, 1990–2. The experience of the devaluations of 1981 and 1982 contributed to a new view. Economists recommended a fixed-exchange-rate policy that would not accommodate negative disturbances through exchange-rate adjustments. Sweden should convert to a low-inflation strategy by a credible commitment to a fixed exchange rate for the krona, in this way importing the lower rate of inflation assumed to prevail among its main trading partners, in particular in Germany.

The course of events leading to the next deep macroeconomic crisis can be traced back to November 1985, shortly after the general election that autumn, when the decision was taken by the Riksbank to deregulate the domestic credit market. During the following years, the supply and demand of credit increased swiftly. The real rate of interest adjusted for taxes became negative for many borrowers. The prices of capital assets, such as shares and real estate, rose drastically. Prices and wages increased markedly, particularly in 1988–9. Registered unemployment stood at two percent during these years, clearly indicating that the economy was overheated.

Around 1991, the boom turned into bust and deep recession, the most severe in the post-war era. Unemployment increased. The budget deficit accelerated. In real terms, national income declined three years in a row—a unique pattern without parallel in Sweden during the twentieth century. The acute crisis was resolved when the Riksbank was forced to abandon its defence of the fixed exchange rate of the krona in November 1992, allowing the krona to float.

The 1990s crisis contributed to a revision of the policy lessons gained in the 1980s. A new and fundamental lesson regarding monetary policy after the failed defence of the krona was that a fixed exchange rate for the krona is difficult to uphold in a world of deregulated and open financial markets. The old goal of monetary policy, the fixed exchange rate for the krona, was replaced by a new goal in January 1993: a low inflation norm or a price-stability norm.

Fiscal policy was focused on fiscal consolidation after the acute crisis of the 1990s and the large budget deficits following in its wake. Shortly after the crisis, the foundations of a new fiscal framework were established. Balancing the budget became the primary target for fiscal policy against the background of a rapidly increasing central government debt.

Episode 5, 2008–10. The global crisis that started in 2008 following the Lehman collapse in the United States had a major impact on the Swedish economy via international trade. Swedish economic growth fell sharply in 2009, amounting to a decline by five percent in one year, the sharpest annual fall in the post-war period. The crisis was met primarily by an expansionary monetary policy while fiscal policy was largely unchanged.

Policymakers and economists alike blamed much of the crisis on a failure of regulating the financial system properly. The lesson that has emerged so far suggests that the regulatory framework should be strengthened through the use of new macro-prudential instruments. The process of lesson-learning is still ongoing.

Summing up. The different episodes described in Table 8.1 amount to a series of interconnected experiments where the outcomes and the interpretations form the core of the learning process. Each episode is an experiment that results in new lessons. The feedback loops between the present policy and the policy of the past are strong. Stabilization policy is characterized by 'path dependency', although the policymakers probably considered their decision-making situation to be unique during each separate crisis.

Table 8.1 brings out two central features. First, the design of stabilization policy is 'event-driven', that is driven by major macroeconomic disturbances. Second, policy-learning is a continuous process, as indicated in the lowermost part of Table 8.1. When the next crisis hits the Swedish economy in the future, the policy reaction will be determined by the lessons gained from the present global financial crisis.

Table 8.1. The policy learning process 1970–2013: a stylized picture

	Macroeconomic disturbance (1)	Policy reaction (2)	Policy effects (3)	Policy learning (4)
				Lessons from the Bretton Woods system: External balance and a fixed exchange rate.
Episode 1	1969–70: Outflow of foreign reserves. Deteriorating current account balance. Tendency towards inflation.	1970–72: Policy of restraint. Contractive fiscal and monetary policy.	1971–73: Rising unemployment. "The lost years."	
				Lessons of "the lost years": Expansive Keynesian fiscal policy suitable to maintain full employment.
Episode 2	1973–74: OPEC I. Oil price shock. Supply disturbance.	1974–76: Policy of "bridging over". Expansion via fiscal policy.	1977–78: "Costs-crisis." Growing budget deficit and crisis in different industries.	
				Lessons from OPEC I: Expansive fiscal policy creates imbalances. Devaluations "work".
Episode 3	1979–80: OPEC II. Oil price shock. Supply disturbance.	1980–82: Fiscal austerity package. Devaluation in 1981. Offensive "super-devaluation" in 1982.	1983–85: Strong inflationary impulse. Rising profits.	
				Lessons from OPEC II: Rule-bound policy based on a fixed exchange rate. Hard currency policy.
Episode 4	1986–90: Boom due to credit expansion. Overheating. Real interest rate shock.	1990–92: Strong defense of the fixed *krona* rate. Government support to the financial system.	1991–95: Rapidly increasing unemployment and budget deficits. Deflation. Floating *krona* rate.	
				Lessons of the 1990s: Institutional reforms, independent Riksbank, a stricter budget process. Floating *krona* or totally fixed rate.
Episode 5	2008–10: Global financial crisis. Sharp fall in exports. Threats against the banking system.	2008–10: Expansionary monetary policy. Tight fiscal policy. Government support to the banking system.	2011–13: Rapid recovery. Strong public finances. Persistent unemployment.	
				Lessons from the global financial crisis: New regulation and supervision of the banking system. Macroprudential regulation.
Episode 6	The future: Next disturbance or crisis of unknown nature.	Tight fiscal policy. Expansionary monetary policy.	Unknown outcome.	
				New lessons of tomorrow's crisis.

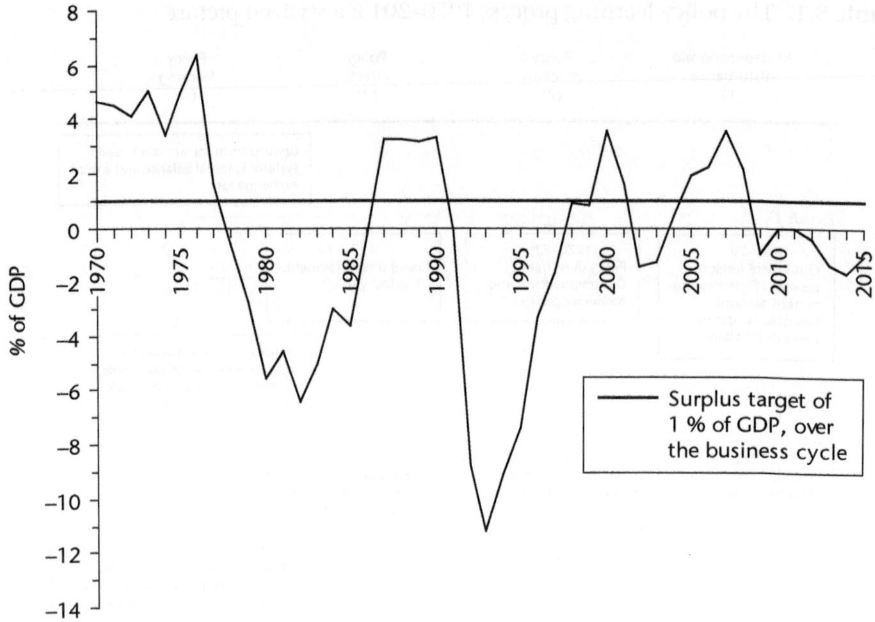

Figure 8.9. General government net lending (percent of GDP) in Sweden and the surplus target 1975–2015

Note: Data for 2013–15 is based on forecasts.

Source: OECD Economic Outlook No 94.

8.4 The New Fiscal Framework After the Crisis of 1992

Eventually, primarily as a response to the crisis of the early 1990s, a fiscal framework was constructed in a political and administrative process covering several years. Actually, this process still continues.[4] A major initial step was a report published in 1992 by ESO, a small research council formally under the Ministry of Finance but independent in its choice of topics to be studied. This study, put together by Per Molander, at that time serving as head of the secretariat of ESO, recommended a top-down approach for the government budget in the Parliament, a stronger position for the Prime Minister's office and the Ministry of Finance in the internal budgetary process, and full coverage for the financing of government expenditures. The ESO report, inspired by a study by Jürgen von Hagen (1992) of the budgeting procedures in 12 member countries in the European Community, demonstrated that the Swedish budgetary process was a weak one in an EC perspective, ranked at the bottom between that of Greece and Italy.[5]

[4] The emergence of the Swedish fiscal framework is covered in several contributions. See Calmfors (2013), Calmfors and Wren-Lewis (2011), Molander (1999), and Molander and Holmquist (2013).

[5] The report, von Hagen (1992), was later extended in von Hagen and Harden (1994).

Table 8.2. The evolution of the Swedish fiscal framework 1995–2011

Since 1995:	*Top-down approach* for the central government budget.
Since 1997:	*Central government expenditure ceiling* (for the third year ahead in the Budget Bill, with a *budget margin* acting as a buffer).
Since 2000:	*Surplus target.* General government net lending is required to show a surplus of 1% over the course of a business cycle. A buffer for economic fluctuations and demographic changes.
Since 2000:	*Balanced budget requirement* for local governments.
Since 2007:	A *fiscal policy council* is established.
Since 2011:	A new instruction for the fiscal policy council is given.

The ESO report contributed to parliamentary reform in 1994 encompassing a top-down approach where the Parliament first decided the total volume of expenditures and then the distribution of expenditures across 27 specific expenditure areas. The calendar year became the basis for the budget. From January 1997 an extended fiscal framework was put in place, including a central government *expenditure ceiling* designed to cover expenditures three years ahead decided by Parliament, the abolishment of open-ended appropriations, and monthly auditing of government expenditures relative to budget.

In 1998, a *surplus target* for general government net lending was introduced, to be implemented from 2000. Public finances were now required to show a surplus of 1% over the course of a business cycle for the whole public sector (Figure 8.9). The surplus target was commonly viewed as a buffer for economic fluctuations and demographic changes. In 1999, a *balanced budget requirement for local governments* was made into law to be implemented from 2000.

The next building block of the fiscal framework was put in place in 2007 when a *fiscal policy council* was established by the center-right government that came to power after the election in the autumn of 2006. The process of developing the fiscal framework has continued. In 2010, the budget act was amended and the use of the expenditure ceiling and the target for general government net lending was made mandatory. The development of the fiscal framework 1995–2011 is summarized in Table 8.2.[6]

By now a fully fledged fiscal framework has been established with the basic aim of fostering a sustainable fiscal policy in the long run. The framework is made up of a few fundamental principles or rules for fiscal policy. Some are

[6] Important changes in the parliamentary budget procedure to strengthen the fiscal framework were also made after the crisis of the 1990s. The Finance Committee of the Riksdag was given a more powerful role. A strict top-down decision model was introduced where the Finance Committee sets binding limits for all expenditure areas that the special committees of the Riksdag cannot exceed, and where any expenditure increase must be financed within the same area and by the same committee.

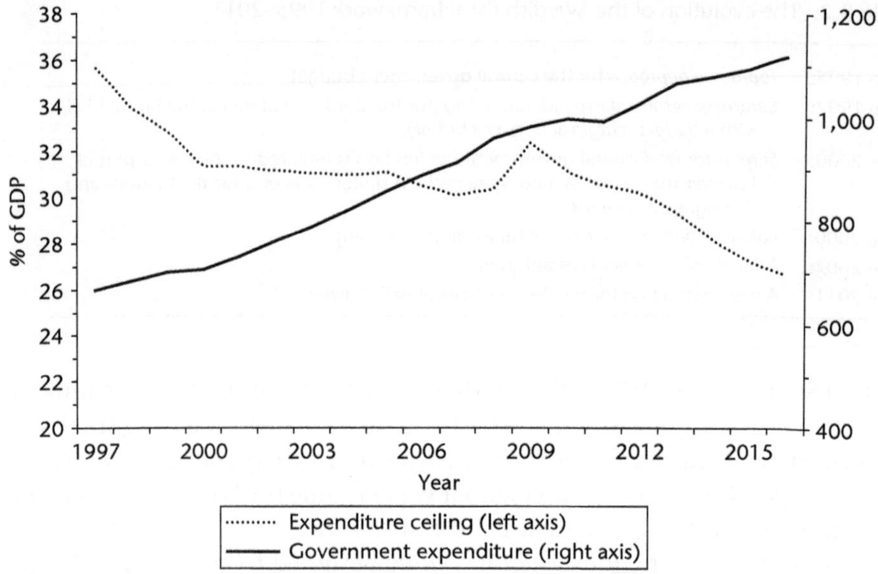

Figure 8.10. The expenditure ceiling (percent of GDP) and government expenditure (billion SEK) 1997–2016

Note: Data for 2014 and 2015 are based on forecasts.

Source: The Swedish Ministry of Finance.

governed by law, as displayed in Table 8.2, while others follow a practice that has emerged over the past 20 years.

The budgetary framework, as set out in the Budget Act, is the core of the legal basis of the fiscal framework. According to this act, the Government is obliged to propose targets for general government lending to the Riksdag. The surplus target is presently defined as an average of 1% of GDP over the business cycle. Under the Budget Act, the Government must propose an expenditure ceiling for the third year ahead in the Budget Bill presented in the autumn to the Riksdag.

The expenditure ceiling has served as a fundamental restriction on the budgetary process. It sets a cap in nominal terms for government expenditures, reducing them measured as a share of GDP (Figure 8.10). So far, the expenditure ceiling has not been revised upwards except for minor technical adjustments. The ceiling has not prevented government expenditure from growing in nominal terms over time (Figure 8.10). Under this ceiling or cap, expenditures are allocated across different spending areas. The main idea is that proposals by members of the Riksdag for expenditure increases in one area should be covered by proposals for expenditure reductions on other activities within the same area.

The balanced budget requirement covers the local government sector which makes up a large part of the Swedish government sector. In 2011, local government expenditure constituted about half of total government spending. They represented slightly more than 20% of GDP. The balanced budget rule stipulates that each municipality and county council must plan for a balanced budget.

The Government has also presented a number of principles or guidelines—not put into law—concerning the design and use of stabilization policies. The most important task of fiscal policy is to maintain confidence in the long-term sustainability of public finances. The task for monetary policy is to stabilize both the rate of inflation at a low level and aggregate demand in the economy under normal demand shocks. Thus, the use of active (discretionary) fiscal measures is ruled out during a normal business cycle. Instead, the main countercyclical effect of fiscal policy is provided via the workings of automatic stabilizers. However, very large demand and supply shocks may allow for an active fiscal policy response to limit the rise in unemployment. Financial crises may also require special measures to maintain financial stability.

8.5 The Fiscal Policy Council

It is probably true to say that the Fiscal Policy Council is the component in the Swedish fiscal policy framework that has attracted most interest in public debate, as its annual report has turned into a major media event, commented on by the government and the opposition. The Council so far represents a major step in a reform process that should properly be classified as a learning process—in short learning from the fiscal crises of the past.

8.5.1 *The Establishment of the Council*

The roots of the Council can be traced back to a government commission reporting in 2002 on the role of fiscal policy in the event of Sweden becoming a member of the euro area and losing the use of an independent monetary policy in the framing of stabilization policies.[7] Here the idea of a Swedish Fiscal Policy Council was discussed for the first time.[8] No legislative step towards a council was taken in response to the report of the government commission, however.

The idea of a fiscal council attracted the liberal–conservative government that came to power in the election of 2006. At the initiative of the Minister of Finance, a fiscal policy council was established one year later. The initiative first encountered negative reactions from the three parties in opposition: the

[7] Accounts of the Swedish fiscal policy council and its impact are found in Calmfors and Wren-Lewis (2011) and Flodén (2013). The role of fiscal policy and the fiscal framework during the recent crisis is discussed by Bergman (2011) and Hassler (2010). See also the report by the Swedish Fiscal Policy Council (2012).

[8] Wyplosz (2002) prepared a contribution on fiscal policy councils for the commission. His piece inspired the commission in its recommendations.

Social Democrats, the Left Party, and the Green Party. The Left Party expected the fiscal council to serve as 'another body providing false scientific clothing for the government's right-wing policy'.[9]

A fiscal council was a novelty for Sweden although similar institutions or authorities have actually existed in countries like the Netherlands and the US for a considerable time. Various forms of fiscal policy councils are now established in about 16 countries. The number is expected to grow in the near future as the EU, IMF, and OECD are recommending the introduction of fiscal policy councils or independent fiscal authorities.

The Swedish Council is set up as an agency under the Government, directly under the Ministry of Finance. Its budget is determined by the Ministry of Finance and thus by the Government. Presently, the Council has a small secretariat made up of five persons. The annual budget is about 9 million SEK; approximately 1 million euros. The Council is thus a very small body by international standards.[10] The Council, however, has the option of asking outside experts to prepare reports on issues of interest. These usually serve as inputs into the annual report of the Council. The Council also arranges a yearly conference where the reports prepared by outside experts commissioned by the Council are presented.

The Council has six members with fixed terms of appointment—it ranges between a maximum of three years for the ordinary members to six years for the chairman. The members hold positions at universities and/or have made careers as policymakers or as high-level civil servants. They serve as members on a part-time (10%) basis, as a supplementary activity to their ordinary jobs or positions. The Council is in principle a self-perpetuating body. It recruits itself in the sense that it proposes to the Government replacements for members who are leaving.

8.5.2 *The Remit of the Council*

The tasks of the Council are defined in a remit framed by the Government. The first instruction was presented in 2007. A new instruction was given in April 2011. It is short, roughly one page long, and states that the main task of the Council is 'to monitor and evaluate the extent to which the fiscal and economic policy objectives proposed by the Government and decided by the Riksdag are being achieved and thus to contribute to more transparency and clarity about the aims and effectiveness of economic policy'.[11]

[9] Calmfors and Wren-Lewis (2011, p. 682).

[10] See the comparison of the tasks of various fiscal councils in Table 2 in Calmfors and Wren-Lewis (2011).

[11] Swedish Code of Statutes SFS 2011:446. This section is a rough translation of this code.

Starting from the Spring Fiscal Policy Bill presented in April and the Budget Bill announced in September, the Council assesses whether the fiscal policy of the Government is consistent with:

1. long-term sustainable public finances and
2. budgetary targets, particularly the surplus target and the expenditure ceiling.

More specifically, the Council has to:

1. assess whether the fiscal policy stance is consistent with cyclical developments in the economy;
2. gauge whether fiscal policy is in line with long-term sustainable growth and leads to long-term sustainable high employment;
3. examine the clarity of bills concerning economic policies, particularly with respect to the arguments for policy measures;
4. analyse the effects of fiscal policy on the distribution of welfare in the short and long terms.

The Council may assess the quality of the forecasts made by the Government and the models on which the forecasts are based. Finally, the Council should foster public debate on economic policy.

This remit represents a broad mandate, in particular the request to examine the consequences of economic policies on the distribution of income and wealth. This was a new task given by the instruction of 2011 as part of a compromise between the Government and the opposition.

The starting point of the remit is the fiscal framework. It requires the Council to examine to what extent the actual measures of the Government are consistent with the fiscal framework. This task facilitates the Council's work by giving it a benchmark to start its evaluation of the economic policies of the Government. The Council is then free to express its opinions concerning any issues it deems of importance for fiscal sustainability, as well as issues it finds to be neglected or ignored by the Government.

The Council is set up at arm's length from the Government. It has no informal or confidential contacts with the Government. It is not involved in policymaking consultations with the Government; it does not provide the Ministry of Finance with any judgments, forecasts, or recommendations except what is made public in the annual report of the Council and the reports prepared for the Council by outside experts. All its communication with the Government thus takes place in the public sphere. It has the authority to ask the Ministry of Finance for information about work underlying Government proposals. So far, the books of the Ministry of Finance have been open to the Council when it has made requests.

8.5.3 *The Council's Reports 2007–13*

Gradually, the Council has by itself established a reputation of being independent. This is probably a major reason why in 2011 a new instruction for the Council was supported by the Social Democrats, the Left, and the Greens, at that time in opposition. It is fair to say that the Council is now well entrenched in the Swedish political system in the sense that it has presently the backing of seven out of eight parties in the Parliament.

The main tool of the Council for communicating its message is the annual report. The first report of the Swedish Council was published in 2008, followed by annual reports since then. It is published in mid May. A few weeks later, the report is presented by a member of the Council, usually the chairman, at a hearing before the Committee on Finance of the Riksdag where the Minister of Finance responds as well. The report serves as an input for the Committee's evaluation of the economic policies of the Government. The Government replies in the Budget Bill to the report of the Council, usually in September the same year.

The six annual reports produced in 2007–13 have focused on a number of issues. One theme is a recurrent plea for increased clarity concerning the surplus target. The Council has asked for explanations of the fundamental objectives of the surplus target as the Government has given various explanations over time. The Council has also made requests regarding how the Government monitors the compliance with the target.

The Council has criticized attempts of circumventing the expenditure ceiling, when actual expenditures have approached the cap set by the expenditure ceiling. It has scrutinized the Government's fiscal sustainability calculations. It requested temporary discretionary fiscal stimulus in the recession of 2009–10. It has questioned the evaluations of the Government's labour market reforms and the economic reporting of the Government. So far, the fiscal policy pursued in recent years has complied with the fiscal framework. However, there is a considerable risk that this will not be the case in coming years. In the report from May 2013, the Council expressed strong doubts about the Government's commitment to the surplus target.[12]

The Council has stressed in several reports that rapidly expanding credit and rising property prices imply macro-financial risks for the Swedish economy. The Council has recommended the Government to decide how macro-prudential regulation and supervision should be strengthened to reduce the risk of future financial crises.

Many of the issues brought up by the reports of the Council have attracted the interest of the media. For this reason several issues remain in public

[12] See the Swedish Fiscal Policy Council (2013).

debate. The annual reports are cited and referred to long after their initial publication.

8.5.4 *The Independence of the Council*

Representatives of the Council commonly describe the Council as a watchdog that barks when fiscal sustainability is threatened by the economic policies of the Government. In other words, the Council tries to serve as an early warning system for threats against fiscal stability. The proper question to ask is, then: How well can it fulfill this function when it is financed by the Ministry of Finance?

It has been proposed that the Council should be organized under the Parliament instead, reporting directly to Parliament, in order to minimize any direct pressure by the Government. So far, the general view is that the Council has managed to remain independent and thus credible in the eyes of the media and the public. This independence is based on various mechanisms, formal as well as informal, some of which may not work or may not be as strong as in other countries.

First, the Council is made up of members who are independent of the Government, as they are recruited from academia or from end-of-career positions. They are taken from outside of the political system.

Second, the Council recruits itself by openly proposing new members to the Government. The Government has so far accepted and supported all proposals.

Third, an important pillar of the independence of the Council is found in the tradition of open public debate in Sweden where the economics profession has a strong and long-standing position. Economists are respected and regarded as important and constructive voices in the public sphere. Some of them have been extremely prolific in writing op-ed articles, serving as journalists and commentators in economics. This tradition goes back to the activities of Knut Wicksell, Gustav Cassel, Eli Heckscher, Bertil Ohlin, and Gunnar Myrdal. They created a platform used by present generations of Swedish economists.

A government that ignores the voice of the Council runs the risk of losing credibility. Such a loss in credibility could also arise if the Government attempts to control or pressure the Council. The cost of such a loss serves to some extent as a guarantee of the Council's independence.

On the other hand, the Council must present professional analyses and well-founded recommendations in order to remain credible. The Council will not be able to maintain a solid brand name if its performance is lacking. High credibility in turn fosters independence.

8.5.5 *The Impact of the Fiscal Framework*

Sweden established a new fiscal framework after the crisis of the early 1990s. This raises questions about its effect on fiscal performance. A cursory glance may suggest that the framework has been successful. Government debt to GDP has fallen from a peak of above 70% in the mid 1990s to a level below 40% today (Figure 8.5). The trend seems to be towards still lower debt levels. The surplus target appears to have been met (Figure 8.8) and government expenditures have been kept below the expenditure ceiling, actually giving rise to a substantial budgetary margin, i.e. the difference between the expenditure ceiling and actual expenditures.

However, causality does not run in a simple unidirectional way from the framework to fiscal prudence. It is more complicated. The fiscal framework has evolved as part of a policy of fiscal stringency and prudence, coloured by the experience of the crisis of 1991–3. The fiscal framework has been established to facilitate fiscal consolidation, by making it easier for the Government to also argue for debt consolidation in good times.[13] The political will across party lines to strengthen the fiscal stance has contributed to the fiscal consolidation and to the establishment of the fiscal framework as well.

The most important building block of the fiscal framework is probably the expenditure ceiling. Once it was introduced, it put an effective lid on the expansion of government expenditures and programmes. Much suggests that it has served as the main instrument for the Ministry of Finance to keep the requests from the spending departments at bay. As it is expressed in nominal terms as a fixed sum, the expenditure ceiling has the advantage of being simple to understand and communicate to parliament and the public. It serves much more as a binding constraint than the surplus target which is defined 'over the business cycle'. Such a concept is more elusive as it allows the Government more leeway in interpreting the degree of adherence to such a goal.

It is too early to make any firm assessment of the impact of the Fiscal Policy Council as it has only existed since 2007. Still, in some areas, an effect may be noticed. The dialogue where the Government responds in the budget of September to the report of the Council from May the same year is one channel of influence. The Government has replied to a number of the recommendations put forth by the Council. As the Council has established a credibility

[13] The impact of fiscal frameworks and fiscal policy councils on macroeconomic performance is the subject of several recent contributions. See for example Debrun, Gérard, and Harris (2012), Schaechter et al. (2012), and Wyplosz (2012).

of its own and is supported by all the political parties, there are likely to be political costs for completely ignoring its views.

It is proper to regard the fiscal framework, which encompasses the Council, as an attempt to create an institutionalized collective memory with the aim of keeping the experience of the large and persistent budget deficits of the early 1990s alive in the minds of present and future policymakers. It is thus a method of preventing a recurrence of the deficit policies of the past. The fiscal framework including the Council represents a new innovation. Time will tell which role it will play. It has not yet been put to serious test in the sense that the Council has openly declared that the Government has made a serious breach of the fiscal framework.

8.6 Lessons Concerning the Fiscal Framework

The record from Sweden suggests the following lessons concerning the new fiscal framework. Lesson-learning is not an exact science. The views below are based on my own reading of the literature on fiscal councils and my own experience with the Swedish fiscal framework from serving on the Council for three years.

1. The fiscal framework including the Fiscal Policy Council was adopted *after* the severe fiscal shock during the crisis in the early 1990s. This shock was the basic cause of the fiscal framework. The task of the framework including that of the Fiscal Policy Council should be to keep the memory of this shock alive in present and future fiscal policy debates.
2. The fiscal consolidation process started *after* the financial and fiscal crisis of the 1990s and has continued since then. Timing is important when introducing a fiscal framework and a fiscal policy council. It should *not* be established in such a way that it prevents an effective response by the fiscal authorities during an acute economic crisis. Actually, a tight fiscal framework during the crisis of the 1990s could have served as a fiscal straightjacket that would have hindered a proper fiscal response to the financial crisis.
3. The fiscal consolidation process has been accompanied by falling long-term interest rates. Thus policymakers have been rewarded by the financial market for their efforts. The task of a fiscal framework including a fiscal policy council is facilitated by a well-functioning financial system that serves as a signalling device concerning the fiscal policy stance. A fiscal framework will under these circumstances represent a pro-market device.

4. A fiscal framework is likely to consist of a number of quantitative fiscal targets and constraints covering various time horizons. Here nominal government spending ceilings specified on an annual basis are likely to be more efficient from a political economy point of view than over-the-business-cycle-defined constraints and targets.[14]

The effectiveness of a fiscal policy council depends on several factors.

5. A fiscal policy council should be part of a fiscal framework. The task of a fiscal policy council is facilitated by the existence of a fiscal framework founded in law and/or in practice. The council can use such a framework as a benchmark for its analysis and recommendations concerning fiscal policy. Without a fiscal framework, a council would face a much more difficult mandate. It would be forced to select the proper fiscal rules to use when judging the fiscal performance of the Government. Whatever it chooses, it will be more open to criticism and counter-arguments than in the case of an existing fiscal framework. It is comparable to a court or authority first writing the rules and then sentencing according to them.
6. The independence of a fiscal policy council is facilitated by the council being at a distance from the Government. Independence is promoted by not being directly involved in current policymaking, for example by supplying the Ministry of Finance with forecasts or other recommendations.
7. Independence is fostered by recruiting a majority of the members of the council from academia, preferably also foreign members. Members could also be selected from policymakers and civil servants who have left active service and are expected to have no further career plans.
8. Consensus in society about a council is facilitated by a strong position of the economics profession in public discourse. The council will then be recruiting members who by themselves have a respected background.
9. A fiscal council can be a strong voice in public debate, serving as an educator of the public and of the political parties on fiscal issues, if the existence of a council is supported across party lines. A council that is viewed as partisan will find it hard—if not outright impossible—to gain credibility. A consensus society like the Swedish one is likely to serve as a better background for a council than a country deeply divided across political party lines.[15]

[14] This is also a lesson from the failure of the Stability and Growth Pact which was designed as a common European fiscal framework. See Larch, van den Noord, and Jonung (2010).

[15] This suggests that a country like the US for the moment lacks an important prerequisite for an effective fiscal council as it is sharply divided politically.

10. The impact of a fiscal policy council depends on the economic policy culture or traditions of governance. If a country has a culture where the public holds a strong trust in public institutions, in government effectiveness and honesty, in the accountability of elected politicians, in the democratic process, and in the rule of law, such an environment makes a fiscal council more effective. A fiscal council per se does not bring about immediate trust in public governance. However, a council may contribute in the long run to trust in the political system.
11. The fiscal framework including the Fiscal Policy Council in Sweden was created *within* Sweden in the domestic political process. Thus, it was not an import forced upon the country by outside pressure, like the present case in the euro area where euro area members are obliged to set up independent fiscal authorities. A fiscal framework that is created domestically is likely to have a wider public acceptance and a stronger impact than one established 'from the outside'.
12. Finally, creating new institutions and making them trustworthy in the eyes of the public is a time-consuming, trial-and-error process. Mistakes will be made. A new fiscal policy council should not be expected to have an immediate impact.

8.7 Conclusion

The Swedish experience of policy-learning and policy reforms since the early 1970s gives rise to a number of conclusions. First of all, policy learning is a continuous process. The process has not ended. It will continue, thus implying that we should expect new reforms concerning the goals, instruments, and institutional framework for macroeconomic policy. New crises and new research will bring about changes.

Second, it is important to have the capacity to learn from past mistakes. The Swedish record suggests that an open debate involving policymakers and economists fosters improvements in fiscal policymaking.

Third, the fiscal experience of Sweden can serve as a source of inspiration for countries now searching for new ways to achieve stable government finances. Of course, the Swedish framework cannot be copied by other countries without paying attention to country-specific institutional circumstances. Still, several lessons can be condensed from the Swedish experience. A basic one is that a fiscal framework is a method for maintaining a collective memory of the dangers of fiscal overexpansion. A fiscal policy council may serve as a guardian that defends and develops the fiscal framework, that warns against the dangers of relying on deficit financing, and that educates the public and politicians about fiscal policies. Serving this task, a council can foster the workings of a democratic society.

References

Bergman, M. (2011), 'Best in Class: Public Finances in Sweden During the Financial Crisis', *Panoeconomicus*, vol. 4, pp. 431–53. <http://www.panoeconomicus.rs/casopis/2011_4/01%20Michael%20Bergman.pdf>.

Calmfors, L. (2013), 'Sweden: Watchdog with a Broad Remit', chapter 10 in G. Kopits, ed., *Restoring Public Debt Sustainability. The Role of Independent Fiscal Institutions*, Oxford: Oxford University Press.

Calmfors, L. and S. Wren-Lewis (2011), 'Fiscal Councils', *Economic Policy*, vol. 26, pp. 651–95.

Debrun, X., M. Gérard, and J. Harris, (2012), 'Fiscal Policies in Crisis Mode: Has the Time for Fiscal Councils Come at Last?', background paper no. 2, OECD Parliamentary budget officials and independent fiscal institutions, 4th annual meeting, OECD, Paris, February 2012.

Flodén, M. (2013), 'A Role Model for the Conduct of Fiscal Policy? Experiences from Sweden', *Journal of International Money and Finance*, vol. 34, pp. 177–97.

Hassler, J. (2010), 'Sweden in Past, Current and Future Economic Crises', report for the OECD Economics Department, Paris. <http://hassler-j.iies.su.se/PAPERS/OECDSwedenAug2010.pdf>.

Jonung, L. (1999), *Looking Ahead Through the Rear-View Mirror: Swedish Stabilization Policy 1975–1995, a Summary*, ESO, Ministry of Finance, Stockholm, July.

Jonung, L., J. Kiander, and P. Vartia, (eds), (2009), *The Great Financial Crisis in Finland and Sweden: The Nordic Experience of Financial Liberalization*, Cheltenham: Edward Elgar, 2009.

Larch, M., P. van den Noord, and L. Jonung (2010), 'The Stability and Growth Pact: Lessons from the Great Recession', European Economy. Economic Papers, no. 429, December, Brussels. ISBN: 9978-92-79-14915-3 ISSN: 1725-3187. <http://ec.europa.eu/economy_finance/publications/economic_paper/2010/pdf/ecp429_en.pdf>.

Molander, P. (1999), 'Reforming Budgetary Institutions: Swedish experiences', in R. Strauch and J. von Hagen, eds., *Institutions, Politics and Fiscal Policy*, 191–214. Boston: Kluwer Academic Publishers.

Molander, P. and J. Holmquist (2013), 'Reforming Sweden's Budgetary Institutions: Background, Design and Experiences', rapport till Finanspolitiska Rådet 2013/1. <http://www.finanspolitiskaradet.se/download/18.11165b2c13cf48416debd6d/1378975262624/Underlagsrapport+2013-1+Holmquist+%26+Molander.pdf>.

OECD (2012), *OECD Economic Surveys: Sweden 2012*. OECD Publishing. <http://www.oecd-ilibrary.org/economics/oecd-economic-surveys-sweden-2012_eco_surveys-swe-2012-en>.

Schaechter, A., T. Kinda, N. Budina, and A. Weber (2012), 'Fiscal Rules in Response to the Crisis: Toward the "Next-Generation" Rules. A New Dataset', IMF Working Paper/12/187.

Swedish Fiscal Policy Council (2012), *Swedish Fiscal Policy*, Fiscal Policy Council Report of 2012, Stockholm. <http://www.finanspolitiskaradet.se/download/18.27ff7b0b138dcbbff3e7067/1377195308466/Swedish+Fiscal+Policy+2012.pdf>.

Swedish Fiscal Policy Council (2013), *Swedish Fiscal Policy*, Fiscal Policy Council Report of 2013, Stockholm. <http://www.finanspolitiskaradet.se/download/18.1b89d9140c56bc4c73b70/1378219272657/Swedish+Fiscal+Policy+2013.pdf>.

von Hagen, J. (1992), 'Budgeting Procedures and Fiscal Performance in the European Communities', *Economic Papers* 96, DGII, European Commission, Brussels.

von Hagen, J. and I.J. Harden (1994), 'National Budget Processes and Fiscal Performance', *European Economy*, no. 3, 311–408.

Wyplosz, C. (2002), 'Fiscal Policy: Institutions vs. Rules', Chapter 5 in *Stabiliseringspolitik i Valutaunionen*, (*Stabilization Policy in the Monetary Union*), 291–328. SOU 2002:16, Fritzes, Stockholm.

Wyplosz, C. (2012), 'Fiscal Rules: Theoretical Issues and Historical Experiences', National Bureau of Economic Research, Working Paper 17884, Cambridge, MA, March 2012.

Comments on 'Reforming the Fiscal Framework: The Case of Sweden 1973–2013' by Lars Jonung

Henrik Braconier

I am happy for the opportunity to comment on and discuss Lars Jonung's chapter 'Lessons from Reforming the Fiscal Framework in Sweden'.[1] As always, he provides a convincing narrative blending a historical perspective, economic analysis, and a thorough understanding of the roles of institutions and individuals in shaping events. As I tend to agree with many of his conclusions, my focus will mainly be to look at future challenges for the Swedish fiscal framework through the prism of the recent crisis and its lingering aftermath.

C8.1 Why Fiscal Rules?

A key reason for why fiscal rules may improve social outcomes is that politicians' preferences may in some ways differ systematically from society's. An excessive focus on short-term economic outcomes and winning elections can generate tendencies for political business cycles, pro-cyclical fiscal policies, and persistent deficits. In addition, weak budgetary rules may put too strong a weight on the short-term benefits of concrete spending proposals relative to negative long-term effects of high distorting tax rates. Fiscal rules can limit the possibilities to pursue such policies—or at least make the public aware of the fact that policies deviate from set-up goals.

Fiscal policies are—and should be—used to accomplish several functions relating to distribution, efficiency, stabilization, and long-term sustainability.

[1] The opinions expressed in this comment are those of the author and do not necessarily reflect the view of the Swedish Financial Supervisory Authority.

This makes any kind of notion of 'optimal' or even 'good' policy contingent on numerous conditions. Well-designed fiscal rules therefore need to be fairly complex in order to bring in these different dimensions. This however makes evaluation more complex and ambiguous, which in turn suggests that some kind of external evaluation of target fulfilment is useful. Many countries have therefore opted for setting up fiscal monitoring institutions—fiscal councils—to assess whether fiscal policies are set in line with existing rules and targets.

C8.2 How has the Swedish Fiscal Framework Performed?

As Lars Jonung describes, the Swedish fiscal framework developed gradually after the severe crisis in the early 1990s, with the setting up of the Fiscal Council in 2007 as the latest major addition. It should however be noted that since the financial and economic crisis starting in 2009, fiscal surveillance and rules at the EU level have increased significantly, adding restrictions and complexity to existing domestic rules.

In trying to evaluate how successful the Swedish fiscal framework has been, it should be acknowledged that Sweden's economic performance since the early 1990s has been strong and that public finances have improved dramatically and are among the strongest in the OECD area. Sweden also weathered the financial crisis well, and strong public finances provided space for manoeuvre which many other OECD countries lacked. However, strong economic performance cannot solely—or even mainly—be attributed to strong public finances and a successful fiscal framework; structural reforms in a number of areas including pensions and the labour and product markets and an improved monetary policy framework have also contributed. An evaluation of the fiscal framework therefore has to look more into how it has dealt with the problems that frameworks are intended to rectify.

The most tangible achievement of the Swedish fiscal framework is probably the persistent and large lowering of public expenditure in relation to GDP which has taken place (See Figure 8.10 in Chapter 8). Interestingly this has never been an explicit target of the framework, and policymakers have rarely identified it either. Without judging on the extent to which this development has been deliberate or a consequence of a combination of tight spending limits enforced through a disciplined budgetary framework and surprisingly strong economic growth, this development has been extraordinary and instrumental in the success of improving the long-term outlook of public finances. This latter improvement is arguably the framework's second feat.

In terms of addressing pro-cyclicality and political–business cycles, the framework's success seems to have been limited. If anything, fiscal policy seems to have become (slightly) less countercyclical since the mid 1990s, while election years tend to be positively correlated with fiscal stimulus. Thus the framework seems to have been better at addressing long-term challenges than stabilization concerns.

C8.3 Lessons from the Crisis and Looking Ahead

The recent crisis has highlighted a number of factors that have a bearing on how the Swedish fiscal framework needs to evolve. From Sweden's perspective the crisis has shown that:

- A neat separation of fiscal, monetary, and financial regulation policies is often not possible. During the crisis it has become clear that fiscal positions can be threatened by imbalances in the financial sector. Fiscal frameworks may need to evolve to accommodate such risks.
- The presumption that monetary policy should be able to manage stabilization by itself has proven wrong. In situations with impaired financial transmission and deflationary pressures, fiscal policy has an important role to play. Fiscal rules and plans need to ensure room for such policies.
- The need for international fiscal coordination has increased. Developed coordination within the European Union could entail further rules, and changing fiscal risks related to potential international obligations.
- There are strong reasons to believe that fiscal institutions like fiscal councils help to support and strengthen fiscal frameworks and performance. In order to perform their role of monitoring the government's performance, independence from direct government intervention is helpful, however. Stronger independence for the Swedish Fiscal Council could be achieved through transferring the responsibility for it from the government to the Riksdag.
- The focus on containing public spending through the budgetary framework has served Sweden well. A weakness is however the lack of strategic focus within the framework, with little strategic prioritization between e.g. public and private provision and financing. Dealing with future challenges—relating to e.g. health, long-term care, or funding large and needed expansions of tertiary education—will likely require such prioritization through structural reforms.

To conclude, Lars Jonung's chapter provides a very valuable exposé on how the Swedish fiscal framework has evolved, driven by economic shocks and new insights. The existing framework has served Sweden well and could—with some adjustments—continue to do so in the years ahead.

9

Shaping the Fiscal Policy Framework

Lessons from Fiscal Consolidations in Denmark and Sweden

U. Michael Bergman, Michael M. Hutchison, and Svend E. Hougaard Jensen

9.1 Introduction

Over the last three decades, Denmark and Sweden have undertaken major budget consolidations that were successful, sustained, and supported by institutional measures.[1] This put them in very favourable fiscal positions at the onset of the global financial crisis compared with many other EU countries, particularly in Southern Europe. These favourable initial conditions, in turn, allowed them scope to use expansionary fiscal policy actively during the economic downturn, moving from large fiscal surpluses to modest deficits without alarming financial markets or creating political upheaval, and hence without being forced into implementing austerity measures as seen in many European countries.

Against that background, this chapter focuses on lessons from Denmark and Sweden in relation to design and operational aspects of fiscal frameworks. We investigate reform experiences in Denmark and Sweden, and attempt to draw lessons as to how other small open-economy countries can introduce and maintain viable public finances. We focus both on short-term adjustment policies and longer-term reforms of public and private policies, including pension reforms.

The chapter is structured as follows. Section 2 reviews the scope and structure of the fiscal balances in Denmark and Sweden in comparison to a select number of other European economies in the run-up to and the aftermath of the financial crash in 2008. Section 3 briefly reviews the international

[1] We thank Steinar Holden and other conference participants for helpful comments.

evidence on large-scale fiscal consolidations, followed by a look at experiences with fiscal consolidations in Denmark (Section 4) and Sweden (Section 5). Given the widespread perception that supranational fiscal rules have been ineffective in Europe, Section 6 studies the record of national fiscal rules, fiscal councils, and gradual improvement of public finances, as implemented by Sweden for more than a decade. Section 7 addresses some particular features of successful structural reforms, focusing on the occupational pension schemes in Denmark. Section 8 draws out some policy lessons.

9.2 The Scope and Structure of Fiscal Imbalances in Denmark and Sweden

Recent developments in public debt and deficits make it clear that European economies do not form a homogeneous region. To illustrate this point, Table 9.1 shows the primary budget balance, the overall budget balance, and public debt, all stated as ratios to GDP, covering both the run-up to the financial crash (2006–8) and the period following the crisis (2009–13). Also, for comparison, numbers are shown for (a) the euro area as a whole (EA); and

Table 9.1. Selected fiscal indicators (as a percentage of GDP)

	2006	2007	2008	2009	2010	2011	2012	2013*
Primary government surplus								
Denmark	5.8	5.3	3.4	−2.4	−2.2	−1.5	−3.9*	−2.5
Sweden	1.9	3.0	1.4	−1.9	−0.8	−0.8	−1.3*	−1.8
Euro area	1.2	1.9	0.5	−3.9	−3.7	−1.5	−0.8	0.0
Greece	−1.3	−2.0	−4.8	−10.4	−4.8	−2.3	−1.2	—
Portugal	−1.3	−0.6	−1.0	−7.5	−7.1	−0.6	−0.8*	−1.4
General government surplus								
Denmark	5.0	4.8	3.3	−2.8	−2.7	−2.0	−4.4*	−2.8
Sweden	2.2	3.6	2.2	−1.0	−0.1	0.1	−0.4*	−0.8
Euro area	−1.3	−0.7	−2.1	−6.3	−6.2	−4.1	−3.6	−2.9
Greece	−6.0	−6.8	−9.9	−15.6	−10.7	−9.4	−6.4	−4.6
Portugal	−3.7	−3.2	−3.7	−10.2	−9.8	−4.4	−4.9*	−5.5
General government debt								
Denmark	32.1	27.5	33.4	40.7	42.7	46.4	50.1*	51.8
Sweden	45.2	40.1	38.8	42.5	39.4	38.3	38.0*	37.7
Euro area	68.6	66.4	70.3	80.0	85.6	88.1	92.9	95.0
Greece	107.5	107.3	112.5	129.3	147.9	170.6	158.5	179.5
Portugal	63.7	68.3	71.6	83.1	93.2	108.0	123.0*	122.3

* Estimates.

Source: IMF, World Economic Outlook Database, April 2013.

(b) Greece and Portugal, two of the weaker EA countries in Southern Europe, often used as 'identifiers' of the European sovereign debt crisis.

The Nordics had substantial primary and general government surpluses, and low debt levels, through 2008. By contrast, Greece, Portugal, and several other European countries had substantial deficits and debt levels going into the global financial crisis. Moreover, the euro area had average government debt levels (70% of GDP) substantially higher than those of Denmark and Sweden in 2008 (ranging from 33 to 39% of GDP).

Fiscal positions deteriorated markedly after 2008 in most countries, and the Nordics were not exceptions. The general government surplus swung from surplus to deficit, reversals of 6.1 and 3.2% of GDP in Denmark and Sweden, respectively. Nonetheless, because of strong initial positions, debt levels remained moderate and the size of budget deficits were not large by international standards after the financial crisis.

The Nordic experience contrasts sharply with Greece, Portugal, and several other European countries. Indeed, several years after the crisis, Denmark was pursuing quite expansionary fiscal policy, with the resultant general government budget deficit at –4.4% in 2012. In Sweden, by contrast, rough balance in the general government budget was restored by 2010 and maintained since that time. It is noteworthy that Denmark had larger budget surpluses than Sweden before the financial crisis, and larger deficits than Sweden after the crisis. This does to a large extent reflect the 'boom–bust cycles' in the Danish economy.

Indeed, deficits in Denmark after the crisis have been moderately large while the budget in Sweden has been roughly balanced. In part this indicates strong cyclical sensitivity of public finances in Denmark, but also a remarkable robustness of public finances to major external shocks in Sweden. The Swedish experience is particularly surprising given that GDP fell by 6% from the first quarter of 2008 to the last quarter of 2009. However, unemployment increases and the swing in the budget position were moderate. Swedish Fiscal Policy Council (2011) suggests that the reason why public finances in Sweden did not deteriorate as much as in Denmark and many other European countries was that employment fell considerably less than normally during periods with large falls in GDP. The fall in employment in the manufacturing sector was to a large extent offset by increases in employment in the service sector, which is labour intensive.

It is striking that the fiscal austerity undertaken in Greece, Portugal, and elsewhere in the euro area is reflected in improvements in the primary budget positions from 2009 to 2012. The primary deficits of Denmark and Sweden are substantially larger than in the Southern European countries. However, due to very high levels of public debt and associated interest payments in the southern part of the euro area, far beyond the thresholds stipulated by the

Stability and Growth Pact (SGP), their overall deficits are still much higher than in the Nordic countries.

Given the stronger initial conditions, both Denmark and Sweden have allowed these two countries to use fiscal policy more actively to combat the economic downturn. Recent estimates provided by the European Commission indicate that Denmark and Sweden both had a cyclically adjusted budget balance (CAB) surplus in 2007. The financial crisis in 2008 led to a fall in the output gap from in both countries but they both managed to maintain a CAB surplus. Our interpretation is that fiscal policy was used for stabilization purposes. Finally, it should be mentioned that Denmark and Sweden are among the few countries which meet the requirements for fiscal sustainability.

9.3 Large Fiscal Consolidations: International Evidence

The deterioration in public finances following the financial crisis has been met by efforts at fiscal consolidation—tax hikes and government spending cuts—by most countries in recent years. Such programmes have in turn led to concerns that economic activity would be adversely affected in countries already facing slow growth or recessionary conditions.

Recent work indicates that these fears are well founded. IMF (2010) and Guajardo et al. (2011) find that fiscal consolidations typically reduce output and raise unemployment in the short term and that these effects will be exacerbated if they occur simultaneously across many countries. Interest rate cuts and a fall in the value of the currency—options precluded for individual GIIPS countries (Greece, Italy, Ireland, Portugal, and Spain)—as well as a rise in net exports usually soften the contractionary impact of fiscal consolidation. The decline in private consumption and private investment is mitigated by a rise in net exports associated with a fall in the value of the domestic currency.[2]

Fiscal consolidation may be less costly, however, when the perceived risk of sovereign default is high, since the default risk and inflation premium on sovereign yields may be expected to decline. Moreover, the GIIPS countries are not experiencing 'normal' fiscal consolidations, such as those typically investigated in simulation studies using conventional (and assumed stable) macroeconomic models. Rather, the GIIPS countries are facing substantial and far-reaching consolidations of a large part of the government sector. These

[2] The exchange rate transmission channel associated with fiscal actions is the focus of the investigation by Beetsma and Giuliodori (2011). They consider consolidations in fixed- and flexible-exchange-rate regimes, and euro area and non-euro area countries, and find that fiscal consolidation under fixed exchange rates and in the euro area in particular has more severe negative repercussions in terms of GDP, unemployment, and consumption than in countries with flexible exchange rates or without the euro.

far-reaching measures may limit the insights derived from most case studies or model simulations. In this respect, international evidence on 'large-scale' fiscal contractions would seem most applicable to the GIIPS countries.

In theory, a major fiscal contraction could lead to the expectation of permanently lower future paths of government consumption and taxation and, in some circumstances, have an expansionary effect on output. This non-Keynesian prediction has been termed the 'expansionary fiscal contraction' (EFC) hypothesis (Giavazzi and Pagano, 1990). Non-linearities in fiscal response functions or 'trigger points' associated with large stabilizations are discussed by Bertola and Drazen (1993), Sutherland (1997), Barry (1999), Blanchard and Perotti (2002), Giavazzi et al. (2000), and others. The basic argument is that large fiscal consolidations lead to a revision in expectations about the future tax burden—future taxes are expected to be lower, which in turn signals a rise in the present discounted value of wealth—and may also induce a supply-side response if taxes are distortionary. A key issue in this context is that the fiscal consolidation is viewed as credible and the reform will be followed systematically.

There is mixed international evidence on the output effects of large-scale fiscal consolidations. Empirical work supporting the EFC hypothesis and finding non-linearities includes Alesina and Perotti (1995), Perotti (1999), Giavazzi et al. (2000), Höppner and Wesche (2000), and, more recently, Alesina and Ardagna (2010). By contrast, Guajardo et al. (2011) find little evidence suggesting that countries with very high interest rates on their debt such as the GIIPS countries are not likely to see beneficial effects from fiscal consolidation on short-term economic growth.

Timing is also an important issue. Blöchliger et al. (2012), for example, review thirteen large and sustained fiscal consolidation packages in OECD countries between 1980 and 2000, including four Nordic cases (Denmark, 1983–6; Sweden, 1981–7 and 1994–7; and Finland, 1993–2000), with episodes extending over several years, during which budgets improved considerably and debt tended to stabilize or decline. They find that growth rates typically picked up before fiscal tightening began in these cases and became relatively robust, with unemployment rates starting to decline slightly after the trough. That is, unlike the cases in GIIPS countries, consolidation was usually implemented in an economic environment that had already turned favourable.[3]

[3] Similar to the IMF (2010) report, Blöchliger et al. (2010) also find that currency depreciations led to a considerable improvement in external positions, which contributed to a gradual improvement of current account balances both before and during consolidation. Fiscal consolidation started on a basis of improving competitiveness and, in turn, favourable growth prospect. By contrast, they find that interest rates only began to decline a couple of years after the consolidation.

The literature suggests that deep and prolonged recessions associated with fiscal consolidation in the GIIPS countries are not unexpected. Key mechanisms of economic expansion following fiscal tightening, such as depreciating currencies, improved competitiveness, and lower interest rates, are not evident in the fiscal consolidations of the GIIPS countries.

9.4 Experiences of Fiscal Consolidations in Denmark

In this context, the large Danish fiscal contraction that was announced in October 1982 with the formation of a new coalition government, and implemented in stages between 1983 and 1986, is a fascinating case study that has, for several reasons, attracted considerable international attention (e.g., Alesina and Perotti, 1996, 1997; Barry and Devereux, 1994, 1995, 2003; Bergman and Hutchison, 1999, 2010; and Bertola and Drazen, 1993).

First, the Danish 'consolidation' was substantial and broad-reaching in that it covered public-sector spending, public-sector wages, taxes, and other features. It was also the most successful budget consolidation experienced in the OECD area at that time. The actual budget deficit improved by 12.5% of GDP and the structural (cyclically adjusted) deficit improved by 9.5% of GDP over the three-year fiscal consolidation period. The actual budget position (structural budget position) was –9.1% (–8.1%) of GDP in 1982—the year prior to the fiscal consolidation—and 3.4% (1.4%) during the last year of the consolidation in 1986.

Second, the economy experienced very strong output and consumption growth and a substantial reduction in unemployment during this period, which provides prima facie evidence of an 'expansionary fiscal contraction'. Real GDP and consumption growth averaged 3.7 and 4.0%, respectively, during 1984–6—the fastest growth period in Denmark since the 1960s. Unemployment also declined by 2.2 percentage points during the period.

Third, the Danish economy's strong performance was totally unexpected, as shown in Table 9.2 (ΔY is the change in real GDP. ΔC is the change in real consumption, and U is the rate of unemployment). It was widely anticipated that the fiscal contraction measures would have a significant adverse short-run effect on the economy in line with standard Keynesian predictions.

The Economic Council in Denmark revised sharply downward (upward) their forecasts of output and consumption (unemployment) following the announcement of the economic package leading to fiscal austerity measures in late 1982. In particular, the real GDP and consumption growth forecast for 1984 were revised downward by 1.7% and 0.6%, respectively between October 1982 and May 1983. Unemployment was expected to increase by 1.5 percentage points.

Table 9.2. Forecast revisions and errors in Denmark, 1982–6

(A) Official forecast revisions for 1984 following fiscal contraction (%)

	ΔY	ΔC	U
Forecast, 1982:10	3.0	2.4	10.4
Forecast, 1983:5	1.3	1.8	11.9
Forecast Revision	–1.7	–0.6	1.5

(B) Official forecast errors following fiscal contraction (%)

	ΔY	ΔC	U
Actual outcome,1984	3.5	2.1	10.2
Forecast, 1983:5	1.3	1.8	11.9
Forecast error	–2.2	–0.3	1.7
Actual outcome, 1985	3.6	4.0	9.2
Forecast, 1984:11	3.0	2.4	10.3
Forecast error	–0.6	–1.6	1.1
Actual outcome, 1986	4.0	5.9	8.0
Forecast, 1985:12	3.4	3.5	8.7
Forecast Error	–0.6	–2.4	0.7

Source: Danish Economy (Economic Council), various periodicals, and Eurostat.

What actually occurred was quite different, as the official forecasts greatly underestimated positive developments in the economy in 1984–6. The year-ahead official forecasts (published in May 1983, November 1984, and December 1985) cumulatively underestimated GDP growth by 3.4% and consumption growth by 4.3% in 1984–6. Similarly, the official forecasts systematically overestimated the level of unemployment during this period. The economy was very strong by historical standards and moving in the opposite direction of what had been anticipated.

Danish households, however, became more optimistic about the future development of the Danish economy. Figure 9.1 shows how households perceived the fiscal consolidation and its effects on the Danish economy.

In the graph we show the net balance of perceptions (the difference between the share of households having positive and negative perceptions) and we have indicated the fiscal consolidation period using a shaded bar. As can be seen from the graph, households were on average rather pessimistic during the crisis. The fraction of households viewing the current state of the economy and expecting a better economic situation was larger than the fraction with optimistic views (net balance was negative). When the government introduced the fiscal consolidation the views changed considerably. Even during the fiscal consolidation, households became more and more optimistic about the economy. They also expected unemployment to fall. These changes in household views may have contributed to both the success of the

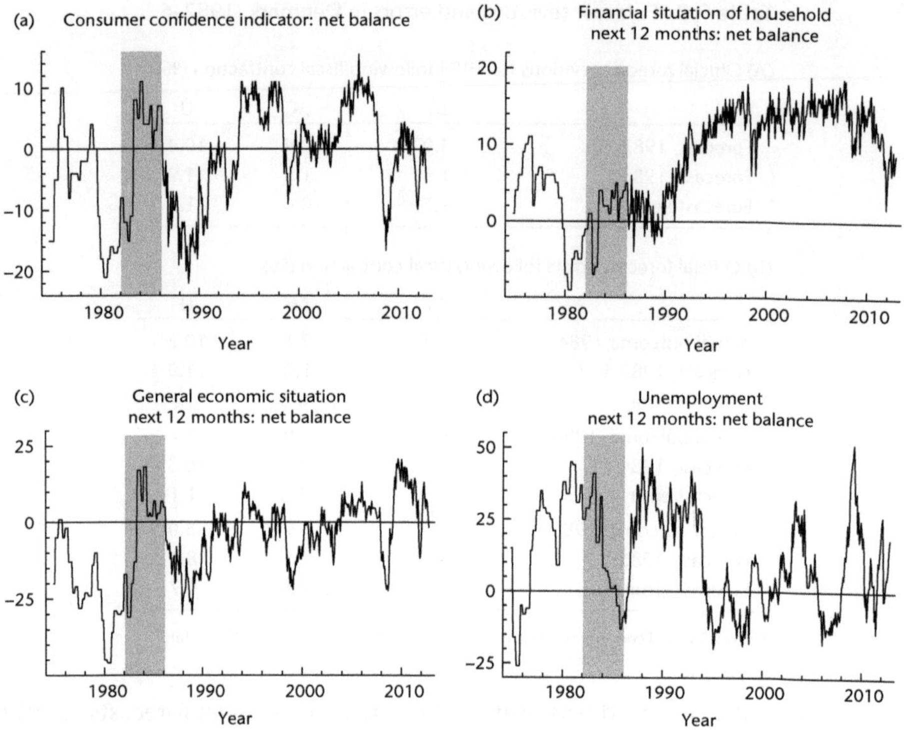

Figure 9.1. Household confidence indicators in Denmark
Note: The shaded bar indicates the fiscal consolidation period.
Source: OECD.

consolidation and the fact that private consumption unexpectedly increased during the consolidation. Such an interpretation is also consistent with the underlying argument behind EFC; expectations about the future development of the economy are crucial for EFC effects to appear.

Although Alesina and Perotti (1995), Perotti (1999), Giavazzi et al. (2000), and others suggest the Danish case is supportive of the EFC hypothesis, this view has not gone unchallenged. Andersen and Risager (1991) and Andersen (1994), for example, postulate another hypothesis for Denmark, based primarily on the idea that the decline in government spending was concentrated on non-tradable goods, which in turn depressed real wages and increased international competitiveness. Similarly, Bergman and Hutchison (1999) find some support for the EFC hypothesis for Denmark, but attribute most of the rise in consumption at the time to a favourable terms-of-trade development and other factors increasing permanent income. Other explanations such as lower real interest rates associated with the adoption of a 'hard currency regime' have also been put forward as alternative explanations.

Bergman and Hutchison (2010) find that the combination of fiscal contraction and institutional reforms in Denmark had simulative effects on both consumption and output. Although controlling for a number of macroeconomic shocks occurring during the period of fiscal consolidation, they emphasize that other structural reforms undertaken at the same time also played a role in the economic expansion.

The Danish case illustrates that economic conditions may improve even during large-scale fiscal consolidations but usually the effects are in line with standard theory. The Swedish budget consolidation is one example of a large-scale budget consolidation that had no expansionary effects. In the next section we discuss the particulars of this consolidation as well as its effects on the Swedish economy.

9.5 Experiences of Fiscal Consolidations in Sweden

The banking crisis that hit the Swedish economy in the beginning of the 1990s quickly transformed into a currency crisis and the Swedish central bank (the Riksbank) and the government were both determined to defend the exchange-rate regime while at the same time resolve the banking crisis.[4] There was a tremendous pressure on the exchange rate and finally the Riksbank had to abandon the fixed exchange rate on 19 November, 1992. The exchange rate anchor of monetary policy was abandoned. The dollar exchange rate depreciated by 7% immediately and by 26% over a three-month period (until 1 March 1993). (The TCW—the total competitiveness weighted average of the exchange rate—set to 100 on 18November 1992, averaged 133 in 1995Q2 and 124 in 1999Q4).

The government and the Riksbank were forced to reconsider the institutional framework for monetary policy and, in January 1993, Sweden became the fourth country to introduce an inflation target, adopted formally by statute in 1999.[5] The new Swedish monetary policy framework has been quite successful. Actual inflation as well as inflation expectations have been reduced and actual inflation has fluctuated closely around the target or, as is currently the case, well below the target. This is in sharp contrast to the very high and persistent inflation rates in the Swedish economy during the 1980s.

[4] Before and during the banking crisis Sweden had a fixed-exchange-rate regime where the currency was fixed against a basket of currencies where the weights were given by the trade weights of its major trading partners.

[5] The banking and currency crisis in Sweden during the early 1990s constituted a major shift in both macroeconomic policy as well as the institutional framework, see Hansson-Brusewitz and Lindh (2005) and Claeys (2008).

The financial crisis, and the policies implemented to resolve the banking crisis, led to a sharp increase in budget deficits and government debt. A political consensus emerged that it was important to implement a budget consolidation after the acute crisis was resolved. The budget consolidation was imposed in 1994 and lasted until 1997. Similar to the Danish budget consolidation discussed in the previous section, the Swedish budget consolidation was substantial. The cyclically adjusted primary balance rose by 10.7% of GDP over five years, with cuts to primary current expenditure accounting for most (about 80%) of the improvement. In particular, transfers to households accounted for almost half of the total expenditure reduction. On the revenue side, social contributions and other income sources rose substantially. It is noteworthy, however, that the value-added tax on food was reduced as part of the programme. The total effect was estimated to be around 7.5% of GDP. Also, similar to the Danish experience, the Swedish krona was substantially depreciated from its value at the beginning of the crisis, allowing the export sector to be very competitive during the fiscal reform period.

The reductions of government expenditures were substantial. Total outlays as a percentage of GDP fell from 68.3% in the quarter just preceding the implementation of the budget consolidation to 58.7% in the first quarter of 1998. Government revenues as a percentage of GDP, on the other hand, did not change much even though taxes were raised. It is also notable that revenues increased over time after the budget consolidation to almost 62% of GDP in the first quarter of 2000. As expected, the budget deficit improved substantially and went from a deficit of 7.9% of GDP before the consolidation to a surplus of 2.1% of GDP after the consolidation. Average growth in output and in private consumption were negative during the period preceding the budget consolidation, even though economic growth had already started to increase during the last quarters before the consolidation was implemented. As expected from standard economic theory, output growth fell during the consolidation and then increased somewhat in the subsequent period. Mirroring output movements, unemployment was relatively high during the consolidation but started to fall in the beginning of 1998. Three years after the consolidation, unemployment was almost halved.

If we compare household perceptions about the likely effects of the fiscal consolidation on the economy with the Danish evidence discussed in Section 3 and reported in Figure 9.1, we find that the fraction of households with a negative view about the future macroeconomic situation increased during the consolidation. Figure 9.2 reports consumer confidence indicators for Sweden. As in Figure 9.1 above, we show the net balance of household perceptions and have indicated the consolidation period with a shaded bar.

The views of the Swedish households during the fiscal consolidation differ markedly from how the Danish households viewed their consolidation.

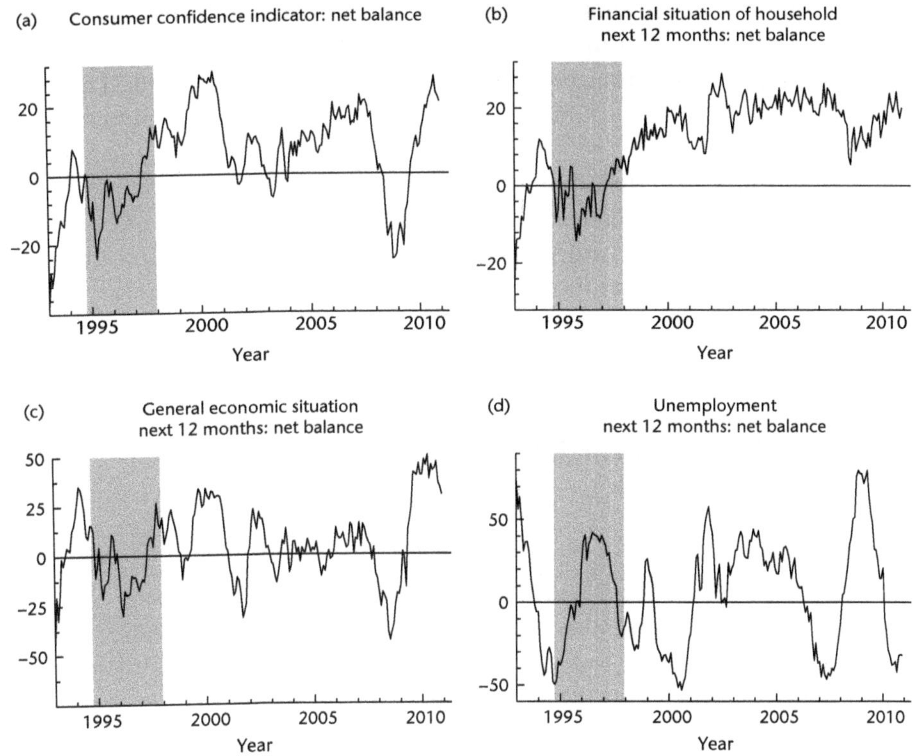

Figure 9.2. Household confidence indicators in Sweden
Note: The shaded bar indicates the fiscal consolidation period.
Source: OECD.

Initially, Swedish households expected a worsened economic situation and higher unemployment. Note the shift in the views about future unemployment in the lower graph on the right-hand side. Overall consumer confidence had started to increase but dropped immediately when the discussion about the need for a fiscal consolidation started in 1994. This is also reflected in the graphs showing household expectations about the economic situation during the next 12 months. As the consolidation period came towards its end (it was publicly announced that the consolidation was to end in 1997), households became more optimistic about the future economy. This stands in contrast to the Danish evidence where we find a more positive view about the economy during the consolidation. In this respect, the Danish case is more in line with what the EFC hypothesis than the Swedish case where pessimistic views about the effects of the consolidation dominated.

However, the gradual Swedish fiscal consolidation was successful in permanently bringing down government expenditures and laid ground for a more sustainable development of public finances. Our interpretation is that the budget consolidation managed to break the pattern of almost automatic increases in government outlays and hence reduce budget deficits. This constituted an important structural break in the pattern of Swedish fiscal finance. We view the Swedish budget consolidation as a specific and atypical event and hypothesize that the links between changes in government expenditures (and taxation) are different during this period. Although not occurring immediately, as the EFC would predict, household expectations about future disposable income and public finances appeared to gradually adjust to the new situation, in turn eventually raising expectations of permanent income and therefore also private consumption.

9.6 Institutional Reform: Fiscal Rules and the New Fiscal Framework

In addition to the fiscal consolidations discussed above, the Swedish as well as the Danish governments reformed the fiscal framework. In Sweden this was motivated by the experiences from the banking crisis. The framework consists of four main parts: (i) a balanced budget requirement for municipalities and county councils; (ii) an expenditure ceiling for the central government; (iii) a top-down budget process where expenditure limits are established first and then the government allocates expenditures within this limit to individual budget areas; and (iv) a surplus target for the entire public sector.[6]

The first pillar, a balanced budget requirement on local governments, was introduced in 2000 and implies that every local government must plan for a balanced budget but is allowed to budget for a temporary deficit under some special circumstances, for example unforeseen events such as large losses on asset holdings.[7] If budget deficits were to occur, these should be corrected within three years. The government conducts surveillance over the financial situation and local governments are required to submit an annual report to the government.

The second part of the fiscal framework is an expenditure ceiling for government outlays that was introduced in 1997 and made statutory in 2009. This ceiling is decided by the Parliament (the Riksdag) for at least three years ahead and refers to all central government expenditures except interest payments on government debt. The expenditure ceiling includes a budget margin (a safety margin) to be used in case there are large unexpected changes in government revenue.

[6] See Ministry of Finance (2011) for a detailed description of the framework. Bergman (2011) provides an analysis of the Swedish fiscal framework.

[7] The balanced budget is a minimum requirement; in general local governments are required to practice what is called sound economic management (equivalent to a 2% surplus).

The third pillar is a top-down budget process. This requires that the sum of all budget proposals lie within the total expenditure ceiling, creating a clear distinction between the total size of the budget and the composition of expenditures. As mentioned above, the expenditure ceiling also includes a budget margin. This budget margin is defined and decided by the government using the guideline that it should be 1% for the current year (year t), 1.5% for year t+1, 2% for year t+2, and 3% for year t+3.

The fourth and last pillar is a surplus target, which was approved by the Riksdag in 1996 and has been fully implemented since 2000. Since 2010 it has been a statutory requirement for the government to propose a surplus target for general government net lending. Under the recent Budget Act, the government proposes a surplus target for general government net lending and then the Riksdag decides. It is important to note that the Budget Act does not require that the target must be a surplus. The target could be balance or a deficit depending on economic developments and the level of government debt. The term surplus target was first used when it was introduced in 1996 probably since it was decided that the target was a surplus. The current decision by the Riksdag is a surplus target of 1% of GDP. The underlying idea is that the expenditure ceiling should complement and support the surplus target.

The surplus target is evaluated using mainly forward-looking indicators and is used in order to assess the scope of reform or as an indicator suggesting future consolidation measures. A potential problem with the definition of the surplus target is that it refers to an average over the business cycle. Since the business cycle cannot be measured precisely there is a need for measurable alternative indicators, see for example Swedish Fiscal Policy Council (2013) for a discussion and evaluation of these indicators.

The fiscal framework is monitored both according to the rules laid out in the Stability and Growth Pact (submission of convergence reports) and by national bodies including the National Financial Management Authority, the National Audit Office, the Fiscal Policy Council, and the National Institute of Economic Research.[8] Each of these has specific responsibilities but is also allowed to focus on all aspects of fiscal policy and the long-term sustainability of public finances.

Denmark also revised their fiscal framework gradually after the crisis and the fiscal consolidation.[9] A target or cap was introduced on real public consumption growth. Since 1992 there has been a balanced budget rule stipulating a target for the structural balance as a percentage of GDP in the medium

[8] The chapter by Lars Jonung (2015) in this volume provides a detailed account of and lessons learned from the Swedish Fiscal Policy Council.

[9] The Danish framework was definitely less well-defined and rigorous than the Swedish one. It mainly consisted of the so-called 2010/2015/2020 plans, and expenditure targets were consistently violated prior to the crisis.

term. There are no escape clauses, but the target has been revised several times. The current target is a structural general deficit of less than 1/2% in 2015 and a balanced structural budget by 2020. Direct and indirect taxes cannot be raised. Exceptions are allowed if a tax rate is raised for environmental reasons or to fulfil Denmark's EU obligations and if extra revenue is used to reduce other taxes. In April 2012 the government proposed a budget law that includes multiannual expenditure ceilings covering all levels of government. The ceilings are to be underpinned by sanctions and monitored by the Danish Economic Council.

What are the lessons for Europe? Both the Danish and in particular the Swedish cases suggest that fiscal frameworks are important and can have substantial positive effects on public finances. The question is whether such a conclusion would also apply for other European countries. The EU Commission publishes a numerical index of national fiscal rules in all EU countries covering the sample 1990 until 2011. In the first graph in Figure 9.3 we show the change between 2000 and 2011 in this national fiscal rules index.

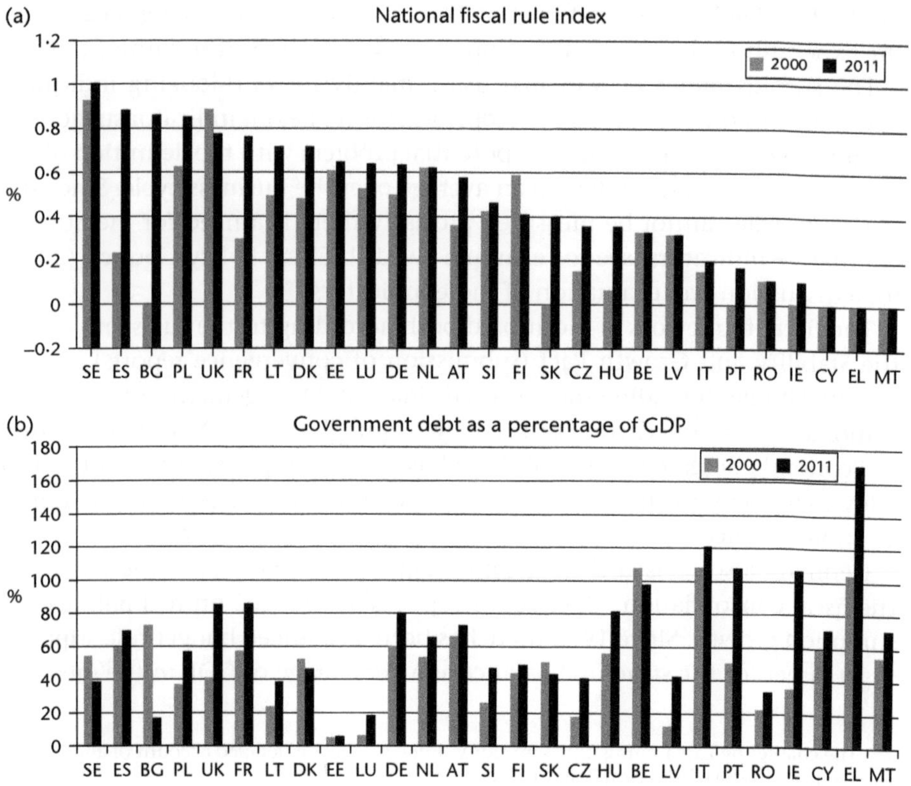

Figure 9.3. Fiscal rules index and public debt level in EU countries, 2000 and 2011
Source: EU Commission and Ameco.

Denmark and Sweden have fiscal frameworks that are stricter than the EU and euro area averages. The second graph shows the change in government debt ratios over the same period using the same ranking of countries as in the first graph. The figure suggests that countries with stricter fiscal frameworks tend to have lower debt ratios than countries with lax fiscal frameworks. This is an argument suggesting that countries experiencing solvency problems should put an emphasis on designing and implementing national fiscal frameworks. However, there may be reverse causality—a country putting more emphasis on long-term solvency may also tend to introduce stricter fiscal rules. At the same time, both the Danish and Swedish experiences suggest that a country experiencing a deep crisis and a fiscal consolidation may be more inclined to impose fiscal rules in order not to experience a new crisis.

In Figure 9.4 we show how the national fiscal rule index has developed since 1990 in Denmark and Sweden compared to Finland, Greece, Portugal, and the euro area as a whole. All of the Nordic countries have introduced stricter fiscal rules than the euro area or in the two Southern European countries. This graph and the deficit/debt ratios presented in Table 9.1 suggest that stronger fiscal rules lead to more restrictive pressure on budget deficits and thereby debt ratios.

It is evident that Denmark and Sweden (as well as Finland, which also experienced a financial crisis in the early 1990s) successfully imposed fiscal

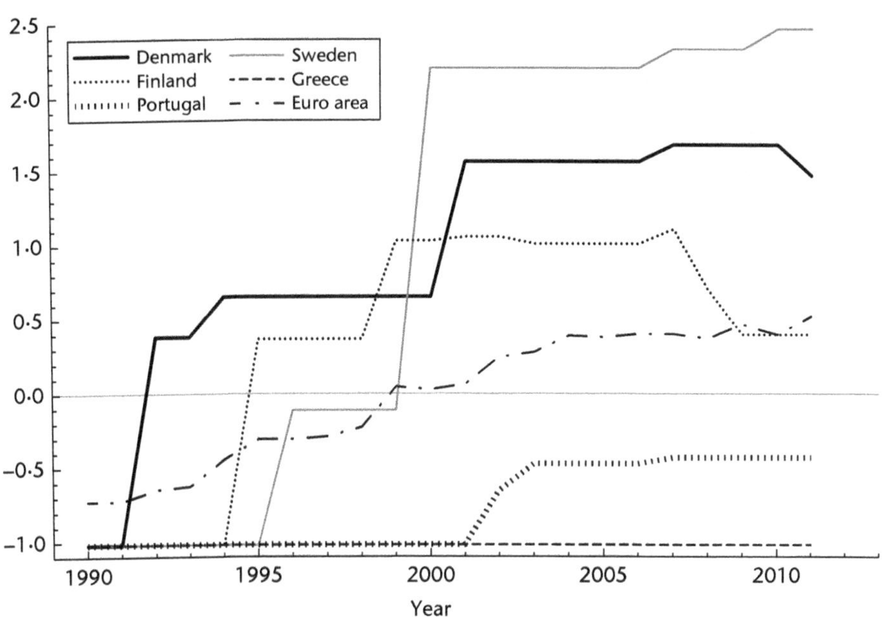

Figure 9.4. National fiscal rules indicator in different countries, 1990–2011
Source: EU Commission.

frameworks as a response to their financial crises occurring in the mid 1980s and in the early 1990s, respectively. Analogously, the Southern European countries currently experiencing solvency crises may be induced to design new fiscal frameworks that could potentially prohibit new solvency crises in the future. The recent focus on new fiscal frameworks in Europe, and the objective of basing these rules on national laws are first steps in this direction. What is an open question, however, is whether these new rules will be credible and enforceable.

It may not only be the existence of national rules that has an effect on public finances; supranational rules (rules that apply to a group of countries) may also be of importance. In an EU context, the SGP rules stipulating that the deficit in net lending as a percentage of GDP must not exceed 3% and the rule that government debt as a percentage of GDP cannot exceed 60% apply to all European countries. Bergman, Hutchison, and Jensen (2014) argue that supranational rules should not be viewed as substitutes for national rules. Their empirical evidence suggests that strict national fiscal frameworks are effective in disciplining budget policy but that supranational frameworks have only limited or no additional effect on public finances. The lesson learned from both the specific Danish and Swedish experiences as well as the empirical evidence suggest that European countries should reform their national fiscal frameworks in order to lay the ground for long-term sustainable public finances.

In the next section we focus on the importance of sustainable pension systems by discussing the particulars of the Danish occupational pension scheme.

9.7 Fiscal Sustainability, Ageing Populations, and Pension Reform in Denmark

The task of achieving long-term fiscal sustainability is to a considerable extent complicated by the fiscal 'overhang' posed by ageing populations and uncovered expected financial liabilities associated with future public-sector outlays to social security and health care. For example, a recent paper by the IMF (2009) has shown that the fiscal stress caused by the financial crash in 2008 was probably only about 10% of that likely to be caused by future age-related spending in economies with a shrinking labour force. This is clearly a major challenge to public finances in many European countries.

Pension reform plays a crucial role in order to restore the sustainability of public finances. Due to space constraints, the remainder of this chapter focuses on pension reform in Denmark, but it should not be neglected that pension reforms have also taken place in other Nordic countries.[10]

[10] For example, Sweden reformed its pension scheme in 1994, by moving away from a pay-as-you-go system to a mixture of pay-as-you-go and funded system with privately managed individual

In Denmark, the pay-as-you-go public pension system has recently been reformed. Most importantly, the so-called 'welfare agreement' across a broad political spectrum of 2006 has increased the statutory retirement ages of early retirement as well as old-age pensions, and indexation of retirement ages to changes in longevity has been introduced. This is widely regarded as being crucial for the fact that the Danish pension system is now approximately fiscally sustainable.

In addition to the adjustments made to the public pension system, Denmark has developed a funded, private pension system, which is based on mandatory occupational pension (OP) schemes covering the blue-collar segment of the labour market. While white-collar and public employees have been covered by OP schemes since the 1950s and 1960s, the blue-collar schemes were introduced in 1993.

The OP system grew out of negotiations between trades unions and employers' federations, as part of the collective wage bargaining, and thereby the system differs from the set-up in most other countries, where OP systems have typically been introduced as part of the legislative process. This unique feature of the Danish design may well have founded the legitimacy of the OP system.

The system has not yet reached a steady state, as contributions (about DKK 120 billion per year) are significantly higher than the benefits received by retired scheme members (about DKK 80 billion per year). The size of the accumulated OP funds currently amounts to 160% of GDP, and is expected to increase to 200% of GDP by year 2040. The non-mature status of the funded pension systems in Denmark has major implications for the tax base of the personal income tax in the transition period. This is because contributions to pension systems are deductible in the personal income tax whereas pension payments from the pension funds are taxable at the personal income tax rate. This feature implies that the personal income tax base is relatively low in an economy with a non-matured pension fund (due to the high contributions and the low pension payment from the fund), and the tax base is increasing through time as the pension fund matures. This has the effect that the government possesses an implicit asset which, for a given initial level of the public debt, serves to moderate the fiscal adjustment needed to meet the projected increase in the age burden.

accounts, and the first benefits under the new system were paid out in 2001, see Palmer (2000), Palmer (2002), Palme (2005), and Sunden (2006) for details of the new pension system as well as of the reform process in Sweden. Similarly, Finland (during the 1990s) and Norway (during the 2000s) have reformed their pension systems. Kangas, Lundberg, and Ploug (2006) provide a comparison of the pension reforms in Denmark, Finland, and Sweden, and Andresen (2006) compares the pension reforms in Sweden and Norway.

The OP schemes are widely regarded as highly successful and they have been acknowledged for having contributed substantially to restoring fiscal sustainability, having helped avert chronic imbalances in the current account, and having reduced poverty among the elderly. For example, compared to the year 2000, the number of poor retirees (defined as people aged 60+ with incomes below 50% of the median income) has fallen by 60%. This is to large extent attributable to the OP schemes, but also to the public pensions including supplements.

The OP system has also contributed to a substantial increase in replacement rates. For example, while the current replacement rate for a blue-collar worker relying exclusively on public pensions is about 65%, it is expected to approach 100% when OP schemes are included in a steady state after 2040 (Forsikring and Pension, 2012).

To illustrate the significance of the OP system, we consider a scenario where contributions to the OP system are gradually abolished, starting in 2013. Phasing out the OC system means that working-age people instead of contributing to a pension fund would have a larger disposable income available for current consumption. Following Arnbjerg and Barslund (2012) and Chetty et al. (2012) we assume that mandatory OP schemes crowd out private saving by 0–30%. In other words, by giving up contributions to the OP system, the empirical evidence suggests that net saving would fall dramatically.

Figure 9.5 summarizes the effects on the government budget (first chart) and the current account (second chart). In order to understand the fiscal effects, it is crucial to understand the model of taxation of the OP system. In the process of saving via an OP system, taxation can appear at different stages, namely when (a) money is contributed to the fund; (b) investment income and capital gains accrue to the fund; and (c) retired scheme members receive their benefits. In the Danish OP system, tax exemption (E) occurs at the time of contribution, while fund income and benefits are taxable (T, T)—hence it is referred to as an ETT regime (Whitehouse, 2005).

In the very short term, public finances will improve, as households do not exempt as many contributions from taxation as in the baseline scenario. Over time, however, tax revenues will fall, simply because the OP tax base disappears. In the baseline there will be a long period characterized by deficits on the primary balance, a trajectory largely determined by the demographic dependency ratio. As Figure 9.5 shows, abolishing the OP schemes would improve public finances for quite a long period, up to the end of the 2030s. In the long term, however, public finances will be significantly stronger with the OP system and the ETT regime in place.

It is thus evident that the OP system plays a major role for the behaviour of public finances in Denmark. It is also evident that a major trade-off is involved: by abolishing the OC system, improvements can be made in the short

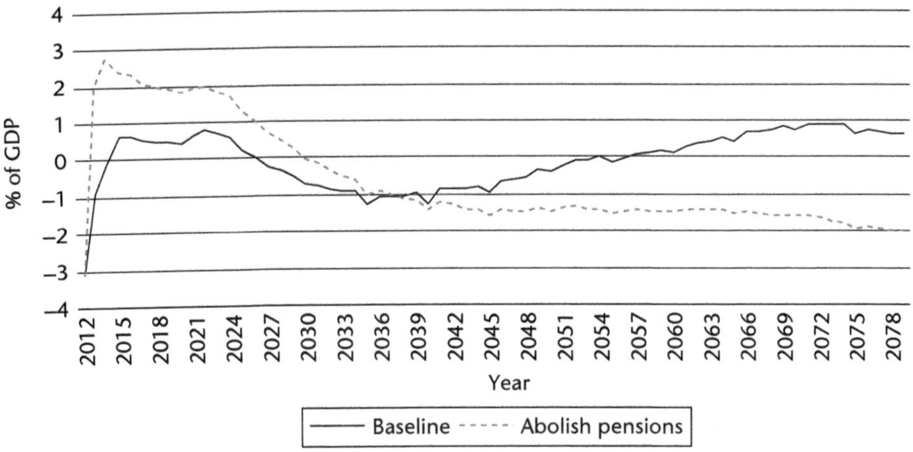

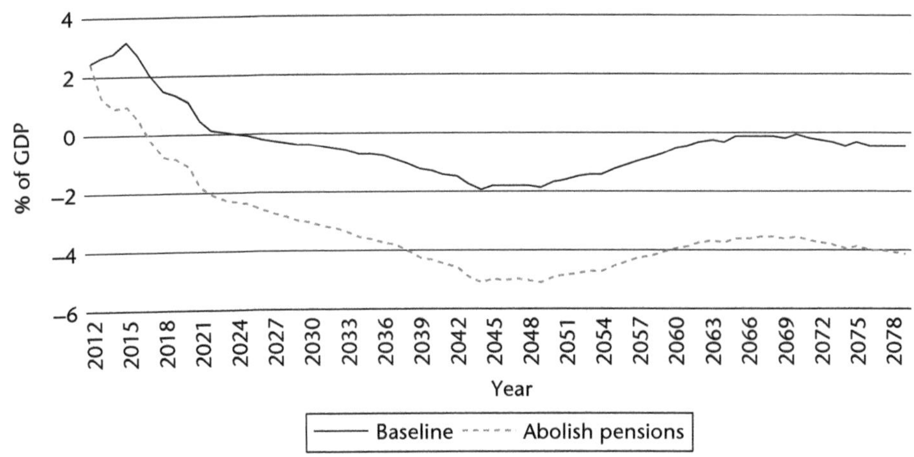

Figure 9.5. Effects on public finances and external balances. (a) Primary government surplus. (b) Current account surplus

term but only at the expense of weaker public finances in the longer term. In a recent study, Hansen and Jensen (2013) find that public finances are basically sustainable if the OP system is implemented whereas in the alternative scenario of phasing out the OP system, the public finances are not sustainable.[11]

Finally, given the challenges raised in several euro area countries of not only high public debt and deficits but also huge external imbalances, it is worthwhile to briefly comment on the impact of OP schemes on the current

[11] See Andersen, Jensen, and Pedersen (2008) for an earlier study of the importance of the OP system for sustainability of fiscal policy in Denmark.

account; see Figure 9.5(b). The reason for this is that if the system is dismantled then consumption increases, part of which stems from imports. The induced wage pressure leads to a deterioration of international competiveness. All in all, for countries struggling with not only fiscal deficits but also deficits on the current account, launching a funded pension system seems to be recommendable.

The OP system in Denmark is one example of a structural reform with major fiscal effects. In addition to fiscal improvements, including a better generational balance, there may be other beneficial effects as well. For example, by having pensions and wages integrated in the same bargain, citizens might find it easier to accept wage moderation. It might simply be a better deal to opt for larger contributions to the pension fund than wage increases which could lead to macroeconomic instability.

The projected development of the occupational schemes will also have a substantial effect on the Danish economy's ability to cope with the demographic changes. For example, the study by Hansen and Jensen (2013) shows that the ETT regime will provide almost simultaneity for (increases in) age-related expenditures allocated to the elderly and tax revenues from the OP system. By changing the tax system towards a TTE system, this property would disappear. Admittedly, if the government saves the revenues collected from front-loading the taxation of OP schemes, the problem does not arise. However, one could be concerned that such a high degree of fiscal discipline would not be present in reality. Thus, keeping the ETT tax system clearly removes an important part of the increase in the tax burden that would otherwise have been placed on future wage earners. It goes without saying that these outcomes are associated with a lot of uncertainty (Alho et al., 2008).

The continued success of the system would most likely be closely linked to the development of the public part (first pillar) of the general pension system. In particular, citizens must feel certain that their private contributions to the occupational schemes will not be fully offset by cuts in their public pension benefits. In this respect, it is essential that key decision-makers (the government and the main political parties) announce to citizens that the basic PAYG benefit will continue to exist.

9.8 Lessons for Fiscal Consolidations and Long-Term Reform Strategies

Despite their recent experiences, Denmark and Sweden have not always been strong fiscal performers. They have had their own crises, which have spurred them to undertake major fiscal consolidations and reforms. These initiatives strengthened the long-run stance of public finances and, very importantly, provided the two countries with strong initial conditions at the onset of the 2008 global financial crisis allowing them to pursue quite expansionary countercyclical policies during the recession following the crisis. The Nordic cases illustrate that restrictive fiscal policies during business cycle upturns provide room for manoeuvre during economic downturns, i.e. allowing fiscal expansions without stressing sovereign debt markets.

The major fiscal reforms in Denmark in the early 1980s were followed by a strong turnaround in the economy. But these reforms were part of a broader package, involving not only budget consolidation but also far-reaching reform of the public sector, wage bargaining, and other measures. Also, they were undertaken together with a sharp devaluation, followed by a credible conversion to a fixed-exchange-rate regime. Tighter fiscal rules were also implemented later in support of fiscal reforms. Fiscal consolidation in Sweden was more gradualist in nature than in Denmark, and implemented amidst a period of slow growth. But Swedish consolidation was also introduced as part of a broader set of reforms—fiscal rules and fiscal reforms that put finances on a sustainable path. Moreover, the Swedish exchange rate had depreciated sharply prior to the introduction of reforms, leading to a very strong and competitive international export position.

On balance, many of the conditions associated with reforms in Denmark and Sweden are missing in the current environment for the GIIPS countries. The positive transmission mechanisms of depreciating currencies, improved international competitiveness, and lower interest rates are not available in the context of EMU membership where monetary and exchange rate policy is set for the system as a whole and not individual countries. The consolidations are also occurring during a period of deep and prolonged recessions.

In addition, there are serious doubts about the long-run sustainability of many of the policy reforms in the GIIPS countries, and whether they have been far-reaching enough. The outright market transactions (OMT) announcements of the ECB are a case in point—the ECB argued that they were implementing the OMT because of widespread market expectation that some GIIPS countries would leave the euro area and that this expectation was making national debt placements difficult and keeping interest rates high on their national sovereign debt. Sustainability of reforms is also challenged by ageing populations in the GIIPS countries and elsewhere in Europe, not least in Denmark and Sweden. Rising pensions and health-care costs threaten attempts to restore fiscal sustainability.

Denmark and Sweden have dealt with this challenge more proactively than most countries, contributing markedly to long-term fiscal sustainability. One concrete example of dealing with ageing is the reform of occupational pensions in Denmark. Overall, the Danish pension system possesses a number of attractive characteristics that other European countries with severe macroeconomic, fiscal, and distributional problems could learn from when designing their own reforms. Although the Danish OP system faces a number of challenges, the reform has clearly relieved some pressure from current and expected future fiscal imbalances.

In part, doubts about the long-run sustainability of reforms are related to the magnitude of the structural problems facing the GIIPS countries, including relatively small traded-goods sectors. Perhaps most important, especially in Greece, is a general distrust in the political process about the consequent income and wealth distributional effects. In Denmark and Sweden, public confidence is enhanced by a transparency of policy and political process. Issues of income and wealth-distributional effects across different segments of society are explicitly addressed and debated. This transparency and confidence in government evident in Denmark and Sweden is lacking in several Southern European countries, making the implementation of fiscal reforms viewed by the public as credible and sustainable, quite difficult. Without strong political support and confidence in the sustainability of adjustment policies, the adverse output and unemployment effects of fiscal consolidations in the GIIPS countries have been extraordinarily high.

References

Alesina, A. and S. Ardagna (2010), 'Large Changes in Fiscal Policy: Taxes versus Spending'. In: Brown, J. R. (Ed.), *Tax Policy and the Economy*, Chicago: University of Chicago Press.

Alesina, A. and R. Perotti (1995), 'Fiscal Expansions and Fiscal Adjustments in OECD Countries,' NBER Working Papers 5214, National Bureau of Economic Research.

Alesina, A. and R. Perotti (1996), 'Reducing Budget Deficits', *Swedish Economic Policy Review*, 3, 115–34.

Alesina, A. and R. Perotti (1997), "Fiscal Adjustments in OECD Countries: Composition and Macroeconomic Effects," *IMF Staff Papers*, 44, 210–48.

Alho, J, S. H. Jensen, and J. Lassila (2008), *Uncertain Demographics and Fiscal Sustainability*, Cambridge: Cambridge University Press.

Andersen, T. M., (1994), 'Disinflationary Stabilization Policy—Denmark in the 1980s', in, Åkerholm, J. and A. Giovannini, (eds), *Exchange Rate Policies in the Nordic Countries*, London: Prentice Hall & IBD.

Andersen, T.M., and Risager (1991), 'The Role of Credibility for the Effects of a Change in the Exchange-Rate Policy', *Oxford Economic Papers*, 43: 85–98.

Andersen, T. M., Jensen, and L. H. Pedersen (2008), 'The Welfare State and Strategies toward Fiscal Sustainability in Denmark', in: R. Neck and J. Sturm (eds), *Sustainability of Public Debt*, Boston: MIT Press.

Andresen, M. (2006), 'Pension Reform in Norway and Sweden,' *Nordisk Forsikringstidsskrift*, 4: 303–11.

Arnberg, S. and M. Barslund (2012), 'The Crowding-Out Effect of Mandatory Labour Market Pension Schemes on Private Savings: Evidence from Renters in Denmark', DØRS Working Paper 2012:1

Barry, F., (ed.) (1999), *Understanding Ireland's Economic Growth*, London: Macmillan Press.

Barry, F. and M. B. Devereux, (1994), 'The Macroeconomics of Government Budget Cuts: Can Fiscal Contractions be Expansionary?', in Robson, W. B. P. and W. M. Scarth, (eds), *Deficit Reduction: What Pain, What Gain?*, Toronto: C. D. Howe Institute.

Barry, F. and M. B. Devereux, (1995), 'The "Expansionary Fiscal Contraction" Hypothesis: A Neo-Keynesian Analysis', *Oxford Economic Papers*, 47, 249–64.

Barry, F. and M. B. Devereux, (2003), "Expansionary Fiscal Contraction: A Theoretical Exploration," *Journal of Macroeconomics*, 25, 1–23.

Beetsma, R. and M. Giuliodori (2011), 'The Effects of Government Purchases Shocks: Review and Estimates for the EU', *The Economic Journal* 121: F4–F32.

Bergman, U. M. (2011), 'Best in Class: Public Finances in Sweden during the Financial Crisis,' *Panoeconomicus*, 58: 431–53.

Bergman, U. M. and M. M. Hutchison (1999), 'Economic Expansions and Fiscal Contractions: International Evidence and the 1982 Danish Stabilization,' in: T. Andersen, S. H. Jensen, and O. Risager (eds), *Macroeconomic Perspectives on the Danish Economy*, London: Macmillan.

Bergman, U. M. and M. M. Hutchison (2010), 'Expansionary Fiscal Contractions: Re-evaluating the Danish Case,' *International Economic Journal*, 24: 71–93.

Bergman, U. M, M. M. Hutchison, and S. Hougaard Jensen (2014), 'Measurement and Effectiveness of National Fiscal Rules and Governance in the European Union,' University of Copenhagen, manuscript.

Bertola, G. and A. Drazen (1993), 'Trigger Points and Budget Cuts: Explaining the Effects of Fiscal Austerity', *American Economic Review*, 83: 11–26.

Blanchard, O. and R. Perotti (2002), 'An Empirical Characterization of the Dynamic Effects of Changes in Government Spending and Taxes on Output', *The Quarterly Journal of Economics*, 117: 1329–68.

Blöchliger, H., D. Song, and D. Sutherland (2012), 'Fiscal Consolidation: Case Studies of Large Fiscal Consolidation Episodes', OECD Economics Department Working Papers 935, OECD Publishing.

Chetty, R., J. N. Friedman, S. Leth-Petersen, T. Heien Nielsen, and T. Olsen (2012), 'Active vs. Passive Decisions and Crowd-Out in Retirement Savings Accounts: Evidence from Denmark', NBER Working Paper No. 18565

Claeys, P. (2008), 'Rules, and Their Effects on Fiscal Policy in Sweden', *Swedish Economic Policy Review*, 15:7–47.

Forsikring & Pension (2012), 'Danskernes Pension: Design i Verdensklasse'. Copenhagen.

Giavazzi, F. and M. Pagano (1990), 'Can Severe Fiscal Contractions Be Expansionary? Tales of Two Small European Countries', in: NBER Macroeconomics Annual 1990, 5: 75–122, National Bureau of Economic Research.

Giavazzi, F., T. Jappelli and M. Pagano (2000), 'Searching for Non-Linear Effects of Fiscal Policy: Evidence from Industrial and Developing Countries,' *European Economic Review*, 44: 1259–89.

Guajardo, J., D. Leigh, and A. Pescatori (2011), 'Expansionary Austerity: New International Evidence', IMF Working Paper 11/158, IMF, Washington DC.

Hansen, J.V. and S. H. Jensen (2013), 'Arbejdsmarkedspensionerne Efter 25 år: En Succes med Udfordringer', *Nationaløkonomisk Tidsskrift*, 150: 201–17.

Hansson-Brusewitz, U. and Y. Lindh (2005), 'Expenditure Ceiling and Fiscal Policy: Swedish Experience', in: Banca d'Italia, *Public Expenditure*, pp. 667–81, Rome.

Höppner, F. and K. Wesche (2000), 'Non-linear Effects of Fiscal Policy in Germany: A Markov-Switching Approach', Bonn Econ Discussion Papers 9/2000.

International Monetary Fund (2009), 'Fiscal Implications of the Global and Financial Crisis', IMF Position Note SPN/09/13, Washington DC: IMF.

International Monetary Fund (2010), World Economic Outlook, October 2010, Washington DC: IMF.

Jonung, L. (2015), 'Lessons from Reforming the Fiscal Framework in Sweden', chapter in this volume.

Kangas, O., Lundberg, U., and Ploug, N. (2006), 'Three Routes to a Pension Reform: Politics and Institutions in Reforming Pensions in Denmark, Finland and Sweden'.

Ministry of Finance (2011), *The Swedish Fiscal Policy Framework*, Government Communication, Skr. 2010/11:79.

Palme, J. (2005), 'Features of the Swedish Pension Reform', *Japanese Journal of Social Security Policy*, 4:42–53.

Palmer, E. (2000) 'The Swedish Pension Reform Model—Framework and Issues', World Bank's Pension Reform Primer Social Protection Discussion Paper No.0012. Washington, DC: The World Bank.

Palmer, E. (2002), 'Swedish Pension Reform: How Did It Evolve, and What Does It Mean for the Future?' in Feldstein, M. and H. Siebert, (eds), *Social Security Pension Reform in Europe*, Chicago: University of Chicago Press.

Perotti, R., (1999), 'Fiscal Policy in Good Times and Bad', *Quarterly Journal of Economics*, 114, 1399–436.

Sunden, A. (2006), 'The Swedish Experience with Pension Reform', *Oxford Review of Economic Policy* 22(1), 133–48.

Sutherland, A. (1997), 'Fiscal Crises and Aggregate Demand: Can High Public Debt Reverse the Effects of Fiscal Policy?', *Journal of Public Economics*, 65: 147–62.

Swedish Fiscal Policy Council (2011), *Swedish Fiscal Policy*, Fiscal Policy Council Report of 2011, Stockholm.

Swedish Fiscal Policy Council (2013), *Swedish Fiscal Policy*, Fiscal Policy Council Report of 2013, Stockholm.

Whitehouse, E. (2005), 'Taxation: The Tax Treatment of Funded Pensions', Washington, DC: World Bank.

Comments on 'Shaping the Fiscal Policy Framework: Lessons from Fiscal Consolidations in Denmark and Sweden' by U. Michael Bergman, Michael M. Hutchison, and Svend E. Hougaard Jensen

Steinar Holden

This is an interesting and valuable contribution. Many OECD countries are now in a difficult position, with high unemployment and large and increasing public debt. The Nordic countries have done better. However, the Nordic countries went through similar crises in the 1980s and early 1990s, and it is interesting to see whether there are any lessons to be learned from those experiences. The present chapter considers the experiences of Denmark and Sweden, focusing mainly on the fiscal consolidations undertaken in these countries in the wake of the crises.

As a sort of additional introduction, Section 3 contains a brief discussion of some international evidence on the so-called Expansionary Fiscal Contraction (EFC) hypothesis. In the policy debate, a number of policymakers, economists, and commentators have argued that fiscal consolidation need not be bad for growth. They have referred to the earlier literature on the EFC hypothesis, see references in Bergman et al. (2014), claiming that these studies show that fiscal contractions can often have expansionary effects. However, as is pointed out in Bergman et al. (2014), more recent studies are more sceptical as to the validity of this conclusion in the current European setting. Most importantly, the crisis countries—here referred to as GIIPS (Greece, Italy, Ireland, Portugal, and Spain)—are in a different economic situation to the countries that have been considered in this literature. Crucially, the GIIPS countries are members of a currency union, so improved competitiveness via currency depreciation, which is a key mechanism in several cases discussed in the empirical literature, is not directly available as a policy option.[1]

The authors also mention the basic theoretical argument in the EFC literature, which is that a large fiscal consolidation leads to a downward revision of the expected future tax burden, inducing a positive effect on output. The authors then note that a key issue is whether the fiscal consolidation is viewed as credible, but they do not conclude on this matter. In the European setting I think the important question is not whether the fiscal consolidations are credible. The GIIPS countries have all undertaken massive consolidations—they had little choice—so focusing on credibility of the consolidation seems less relevant. What is not clear, however, is what the outcome will be in the end, as weak economic growth and 'fiscal fatigue' might lead to persistent weak public finances. More recent studies show that the fiscal multiplier is much larger in recessions (see e.g. Auerbach and Gorodnichenko, 2012; Michaillat, 2014; and Holden and Sparrman, 2013), suggesting that the risk is rather that fiscal policy might have been too tight. Furthermore, there is a question of whether the countries undertake sufficient, and the appropriate, structural reforms. To my mind, the EFC literature has little to offer on these questions.

Section 4 describes the experiences of the fiscal contraction in Denmark in the mid 1980s, from 1983 to 1986. This episode is often viewed as a leading example of an expansionary fiscal contraction. Bergman et al. provide some evidence consistent with this interpretation of events, emphasizing that the strong performance was unexpected, but nevertheless went together with a strong increase in consumer confidence. Yet other and probably more plausible interpretations are possible here, and the authors mention some, for example that international competitiveness was improved via wage moderation.

The fiscal consolidation in Sweden from 1994 to 1997 was different. While the currency also depreciated in the Swedish case, overall economic growth was much weaker. Unemployment increased considerably, and household confidence was weak. Yet I agree with the authors that the consolidation managed to break the trend towards increased public expenditure, laying the foundation for more sound public finances in the future. It is less clear to me why the authors view the Swedish budget consolidation 'as a specific and atypical event', while no such conclusion was expressed for Denmark.

The last sections of the chapter constitute the most interesting parts. Section 6 presents the fiscal framework of Sweden and Denmark, making a good case for these frameworks being important for the subsequent sound evolution of

[1] Leaving the monetary union would be a much more drastic change, and is not discussed in the chapter.

public finances in these countries. The fiscal frameworks were a consequence of the countries learning from their crises. The authors mention that the same was true in Finland, but they could also have added Norway, which also adopted a sounder fiscal framework after the crisis in late 1980s–early 1990s.

Section 7 describes the mandatory occupational pension scheme in Denmark, focusing on the effects for the long-term public budget balance. In the short run, this pension scheme is costly for the government budget, as the contributions are deductible in the personal income tax. In the longer run, when the system matures, the effect will be more favourable, as the pension payments from the fund are subject to personal income tax. The authors present an interesting illustration of how a counterfactual abolishment of this pension scheme would improve the budget balance in the short run, but involve a marked deterioration in the longer run. Considering the long-run challenges of ageing and increasing pension expenditures facing many OECD countries, this is an important property of the Danish system. It would be interesting to know whether other countries have pension schemes with similar properties.

An entirely different aspect, which the authors do not discuss, is that a scheme with high gross pensions and high tax rates might be vulnerable to emigration. If pensioners have the possibility to take a generous gross pension with them to another country with lower taxes and lower prices, the future tax revenues would be considerably lower. This might be relevant for Denmark.

The concluding section provides a nice summing up of the Danish and Swedish experiences, put into a broader perspective. The authors point out that in Denmark and Sweden, public confidence is enhanced by transparency of policy and political process. In contrast, in particular in Greece, the general distrust of the political system makes it more difficult to find a way out of the difficulties.

References

Auerbach, A. J. and Y. Gorodnichenko (2012), 'Fiscal Multipliers in Recessions and Expansions', in A. Alesina and F. Giavazzi (eds) *Fiscal Policy after the Financial Crisis* Chicago: University of Chicago Press.

Bergman, U. M., M. M. Hutchison, and S. E. Hougaard Jensen (2014), Shaping the fiscal policy Framework: Lessons from fiscal consolidations in Denmark and Sweden.

Holden, S. and V. Sparrman (2013), 'Do Government Purchases Affect Unemployment?' Mimeo, University of Oslo.

Michaillat, P. (2014), 'A Theory of Countercyclical Government Multiplier', *American Economic Journal: Macroeconomics*, *6* (1) 190–217.

10

A Crisis Not Wasted

Institutional and Structural Reforms Behind Norway's Strong Macroeconomic Performance

Erling Steigum and Øystein Thøgersen

10.1 Introduction

The systemic banking crises in Norway, Finland, and Sweden in 1991–3 were extremely surprising events, both because they occurred after more than 75 years of financial stability, and because they happened in well-organized Nordic countries, a small corner on Earth where such terrible things were not supposed to happen.[1] Due to financial liberalization, pegged exchange rates, high international capital mobility, and asymmetric shocks, the old stability properties of the Nordic countries' economies had suddenly been undermined, but this was not understood until after the systemic banking crises in Finland, Norway, and Sweden had taken their toll in 1991–3.

Now twenty years have passed, and we are in a position to look back on the post-crisis macroeconomic performance of Finland, Norway, and Sweden. In the literature on financial crises and their real effects, it has been emphasized that systemic financial crises are likely to have seriously negative medium-term effects on the real economy (Reinhart and Rogoff, 2009). If not dealt with properly, they could paralyze the credit system and trigger a depression, or as in the case of Japan in the 1990s, lead to a 'lost decade'.

This chapter compares Norway with Denmark, Finland, and Sweden; the four being rather similar countries along many economic and institutional

[1] We are grateful to Hans Tson Söderström and Arne Jon Isachsen for valuable comments.

dimensions. Denmark is of particular interest because this country avoided a banking crisis twenty years ago. Denmark experienced a similar boom as in Norway in the 1980s, and there were also clear signs of banking distress, but in Denmark the financial deregulation process had started much earlier and was more gradual than in the other three Nordic countries.

Bank losses (relative to GDP and total loans) in Finland were larger than in Sweden, and the bank losses in Norway were smaller than the Swedish ones. One would therefore expect that any short- and long-run effects of the systemic banking crises would be greater in Finland than in Sweden, perhaps even smaller in Norway, and non-existent in Denmark.

In the Nordic countries, it makes good sense to think in terms of a two-sector model in which the sectors produce traded and non-traded goods. It is not controversial to assume that fluctuations in aggregate demand have been important for the booms and busts, and that the financial deregulation policy triggered a huge credit supply shock that increased aggregate demand and asset prices. Large asset price movements released wealth effects in consumption as well as substantial fixed investment fluctuations during the Nordic boom–bust cycles.

Our implicit theoretical framework also includes hypotheses about the political system's reactions to the crisis. The Nordic countries are parliamentary democracies with big governments and powerful, non-elected civil service staff, particularly in the ministries of finance. Norway may now have one of the most powerful Ministry of Finance among OECD countries (relative to the economy's size), and this increase in power of economists in the Norwegian government seems to have occurred about the same time as the banking crisis, if not somewhat earlier.

In the next section, we take a closer look at the Norwegian boom–bust cycle and compare it with what happened in Denmark, Finland, and Sweden. Then we discuss the series of structural and economic policy reforms that took place in Norway, starting with prudential regulations of banks (Section 3), monetary policy (Section 4), and fiscal policy (Section 5), and other structural reforms (Section 6). Section 6 also compares the post-crisis performance of the Norwegian economy with those of Denmark, Finland, and Sweden. Section 7 concludes.

10.2 The Boom–Bust Cycle and Banking Crisis

Norway's dramatic boom–bust cycle started in 1984–5 and ended about 12 years later (Steigum 2009). The bust began in 1988, three years after the dramatic (for Norway) fall in oil price and three years before the systemic banking crisis. Mainland output gap was not closed until 1996–7.

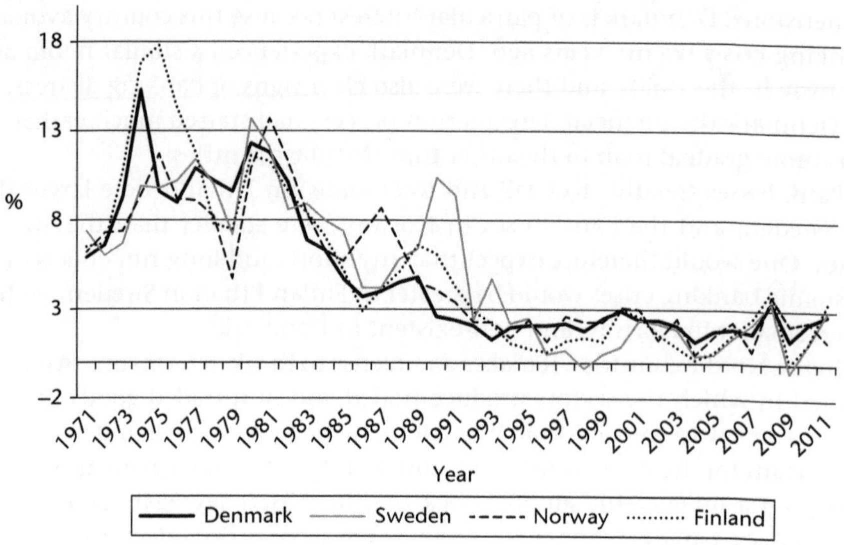

Figure 10.1. Consumer price inflation (CPI) in Denmark, Sweden, Norway, and Finland, 1971–2011

Source: OECD and Statistics Denmark, Sweden, Norway, and Finland.

As Figure 10.1 illustrates, Denmark, Finland, Norway, and Sweden had inherited an inflation problem from the 1970s. All four countries had crawling pegs in the 1970s and1980s, with occasional 'surprise devaluations' intended to improve cost competitiveness of industries exposed to international competition. The central banks were dependent on and took orders from the government. In Norway, the government also told Norges Bank what the interest rates should be, even money market rates. This was a consequence of the popular 'low-interest-rate policy', with roots back to the early 1950s (Steigum, 1992). In all the Nordic countries during the 1970s and part of the 1980s, fiscal and monetary policies became too expansionary to be consistent with fixed exchange rates.

In 1984, the Norwegian government decided to start a financial deregulation process. Financial liberalization in Norway began about four years after Denmark's, but from the start, Denmark's financial sector and monetary policy were to a greater extent based on market-clearing interest rates than Norway's. Moreover, Denmark's banking industry was much better capitalized than Norway's (Vastrup, 2009). By 1984, the Norwegian economy was financially underdeveloped to a considerable extent. Denmark had developed a system of home-ownership finance which protected borrowers from short-term fluctuations in the money market interest rate. In the other three Nordic countries, home owners were much more exposed to short-term interest rate risk.

In Norway, the financial deregulation policy triggered a huge, positive credit supply shock in 1985–7, as Norwegian banks moved into new geographical regions and competed aggressively for market shares by expanding lending and employing new staff. The lending boom triggered excess aggregate demand for goods and services, and increasing inflation in 1986 and 1987, fuelled by the 1986 devaluation and excessive wage increases in 1987.

Sweden and Finland also launched financial deregulation reforms. In Finland and Sweden, the lending boom had similar macroeconomic effects as in Norway, and they lasted longer.

The Norwegian government lost its majority in Parliament in the 1985 election, and in the spring of 1986, *after* a dramatic fall in the oil price, the central wage settlement resulted in huge wage increases and shorter working hours. In 1986, the rate of (registered) unemployment was 1.8% and declining, see Figure 10.2. The current account went from +4.8% of GDP in 1985 to -6.2% in 1986, and the rate of inflation was high and increasing; see Figure 10.1.

As a consequence of the 1985–6 oil price shock Norway's terms of trade deteriorated by about 25% and national income declined by about 10%. After 1986, inflation increased in Finland, Norway, and Sweden. Inflation was not

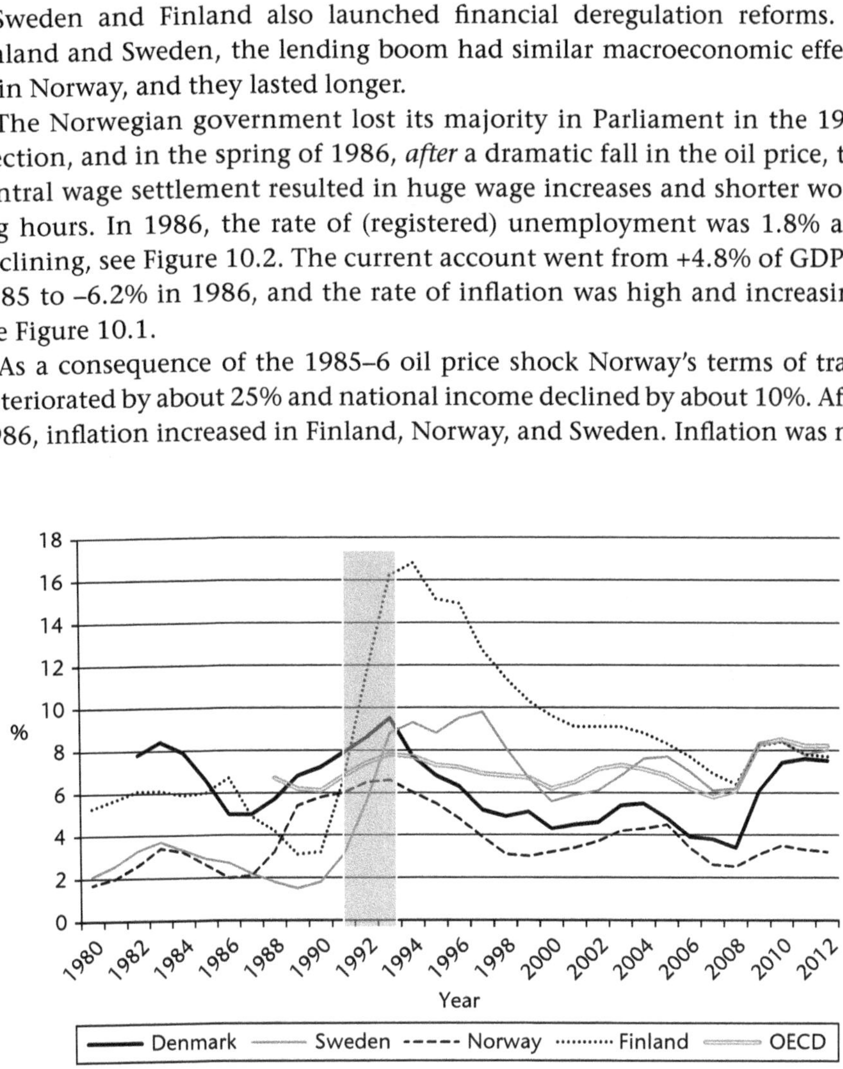

Figure 10.2. Harmonized unemployment rates in Denmark, Sweden, Norway, and Finland, 1980–2008 (per cent of labour force)

Source: OECD.

curbed until the effects of recessions were felt in 1990 and onwards. The three countries that later experienced systemic banking crises (Finland, Norway, and Sweden) were therefore facing an extra output cost of disinflation that Denmark had already suffered in the mid 1980s.

The new Labour government that took over in May 1986 immediately devalued the krone, followed by an increase in the money market interest rate and a fiscal restraint programme. The new government justified the need for a fiscal austerity with the following strong words:

> Norway is now in the most serious situation of crisis. The country faces profound problems involving a huge weakening of the balance of payments and a consumption level that we as a nation cannot afford. The problems have been increasing during the last year, and were enhanced by the dramatic drop in the oil prices.
>
> (National Budget 1987, published in October 1986)

Even without the benefit of hindsight, the statement that Norway could not 'afford' the consumption level was a substantial exaggeration. In 1986, Norway's share of private consumption in total GDP was 52.3%, and total saving was 9% (of GDP). Compared with most other industrialized countries, Norway's saving rate was respectable, even after the oil price shock.[2] The statement cited above suggests that the Norwegian government intended to use the crisis to improve the economic policy framework, a goal that appeared politically impossible to achieve before the oil price shock. For example, one very difficult question for the Labour party was to justify to its members why Norges Bank should be in charge of monetary policy, and not the government.

The macroeconomic story from 1986 to the end of the decade was the familiar one of disinflation through restrictive macroeconomic policies, and a recession. Although the extent of the cyclical downturn in 1988–9 came as a surprise, the idea of bringing down inflation quickly by establishing credibility of the fixed exchange rate received support from a majority of Norwegian economists.

In 1990, a peg to the ecu replaced the currency basket. Soon, Finland and Sweden made the same decision. Before 1989, the German money market interest rate had been significantly lower than the US money market rate, but in the beginning of the 1990s, after the German unification, the German rate climbed far above the US rate. Monetary policy was geared to the fixed exchange rate and could not be tailored to the Norwegian business cycle.

[2] The negative oil price shock itself called for a long-run fiscal restraint due to the fall in government wealth. In a dependent economy theoretical framework, Steigum and Thøgersen (2003) show that optimal fiscal policy involves temporary deficits and a low neutral real rate of interest if sectorial adjustment is costly and time-consuming. In the Nordic countries, the real rate of interest became very high as a consequence of the fixed exchange rates, however, triggering an intertemporal coordination failure.

Consequently, monetary policy became increasingly tight and pro-cyclical in the late 1980s and early 1990s due to German monetary policy.

Figure 10.3 illustrates the booms and busts in the four Nordic countries. The Norwegian boom was the most short-lived, ending in 1987 due to restrictive monetary and fiscal policies. The 1986 oil price shock had weakened the current account significantly and given the Ministry of Finance arguments to recommend a switch to a Danish-style economic policy involving fiscal austerity, no more devaluations, and disinflation. We see from Figure 10.3 that the Danish and Norwegian booms were quite similar, both ending in 1987. In Finland and Sweden, however, there was no perception of a crisis, and the lending boom continued for three more years. We also see from Figure 10.3 that the Finnish boom was both rapid and long-lasting. Also Sweden's boom lasted longer than Norway's, but its speed was slower than the Finland's.

During lending booms, overinvestment in housing and commercial property is common. Typically, easy access to credit stimulates speculation and bubbles in asset markets, (Allan and Gale 2000). Inflated asset prices will usually create excessive incentives to invest in housing and commercial property. After the burst of the asset bubble, lending and construction suddenly stop and unemployment soars. Recent extreme cases are Ireland and Spain. In Finland, Norway, and Sweden, asset prices increased rapidly during the boom in the 1980s, and building and construction activities were high before collapsing after the bust.

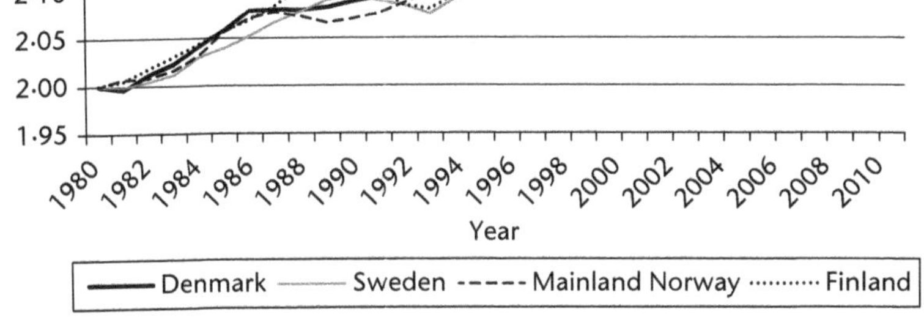

Figure 10.3. Log real GDP in Denmark, Sweden, Mainland Norway, and Finland, 1980–2012 (1980 = log100). Norway's business cycle is illustrated by Mainland Norway's GDP, excluding the petroleum sector and shipping overseas

Source: OECD.

Both Denmark and Norway experienced increasing banking distress from 1987, but as losses were larger and equity capital ratios were smaller in Norway, all the largest commercial banks (and a couple of large savings banks), had to be rescued by the Norwegian government in 1991 and 1992. Shortly afterwards, even more devastating banking crises shattered the economies of Finland and Sweden. As mentioned above, a common shock hitting the Nordic countries was the Bundesbank's shift to restrictive monetary policy and real appreciation after German unification in 1990, forcing the Nordic countries to increase real interest rates to keep the exchange rates fixed. This asymmetric shock was bad luck. On top of this, income tax rules in Norway and Finland were changed to reduce tax deductions for nominal interest payments. After-tax real rates of interest in Norway increased substantially. Both Sweden and in particular Finland were also affected by several negative external shocks that reduced export demand. These shocks as well as tighter monetary conditions also stimulated speculative attacks on a number of European currencies, including the four Nordic ones. Finland devaluated the markka in November 1991 and then floated it in September 1992. The speculative attacks improved competitiveness in Finland and Sweden and permitted lower real interest rates. Both countries shifted to inflation targeting and flexible exchange rates. In 1999 Finland joined the EMU and adopted the euro. The Norwegian krone was also attacked by speculators in December 1992, shortly after the attack on the Swedish krona. The effects on Norway's real exchange rate were small and temporary, however.

In all the three Nordic countries hit by banking crisis, the governments reacted very fast to rescue the large banks that had failed (Jonung et al., 2009 (chapter 2), and Steigum, 2009). Details differ, but the resolution policies were sufficient to restore bank lending and economic growth fairly quickly in all three countries. In Norway, the government immediately passed new legislation in Parliament in order to nationalize the three largest commercial banks without letting previous shareholders benefit from the rescue.

10.3 More Robust Banks and Better Financial Regulation

Norwegian commercial banks were poorly capitalized when loan markets were deregulated in 1984–5. During the period of financial deregulation and the lending boom, capital requirements in Norway were lax as the government had yielded to strong pressure from the banking industry.

The large commercial banks played a crucial role in the Norwegian banking crisis in 1991–2. Their vulnerability was related to low profitability in general. Average profits before tax of Norwegian commercial banks had already turned negative in 1987, and gradually deteriorated until the collapse in 1991–2 as a result of mounting losses that triggered the government rescue operations.

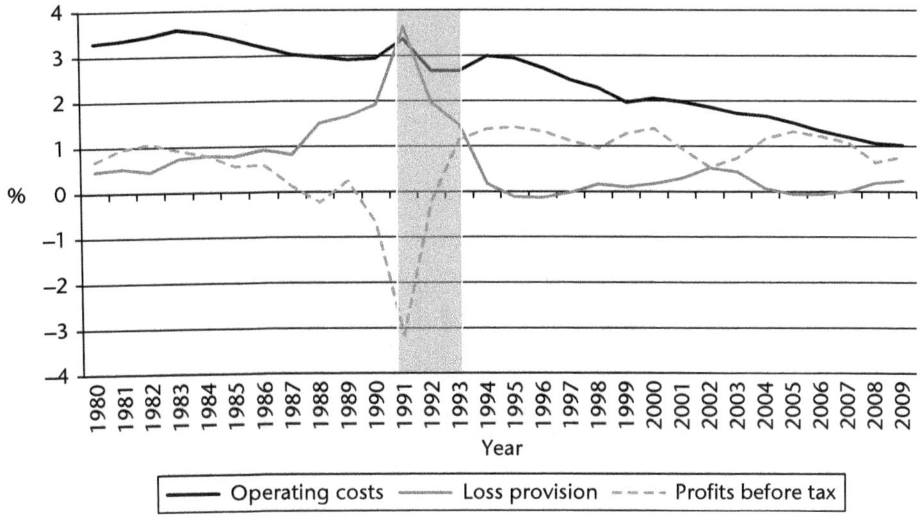

Figure 10.4. Operating costs, loss provision (net), and profits before tax in Norwegian banks, 1980–2009 (per cent of total assets)
Source: Statistics Norway.

Figure 10.4 shows that Norwegian banks (both commercial and savings banks) had much higher operating costs and losses in percent of total assets before the banking crisis than after the turn of the century. During the credit expansion period 1985–8, profits before tax deteriorated. Operating costs were 1% of total assets in 2009, down from 3.5% in 1984–5. According to figure 10.4, losses became slightly negative in 1995–7 as previous loss provisions had been higher than necessary ex post. This may partially be due to the fact that new managements of rescued banks had an incentive to exaggerate losses that were recognized as a possibility, in order to receive more equity capital from the government. On the other hand, the Norwegian economy did in fact recover faster than expected after 1993. Figure 10.4 shows that net losses were also negative in 2005–6. Looking at profitability before tax in 2008 and 2009, the effects of the recent international financial crisis have been minor.

Figure 10.5 shows that the Norwegian banking industry's loans and total assets have become much larger (relative to GDP) after the banking crisis. In 1989 the ratio was 66%, declining to 55% in 1993. It increased to 106% in 2007, before declining to 99% in 2009. This time, there was no banking crisis or even banking distress in Norway.

In the 1990s, the Norwegian government gradually sold part of its equity stakes in the commercial banks. The government has kept its minority share holdings in the largest bank, Den norske Bank, however, probably as a

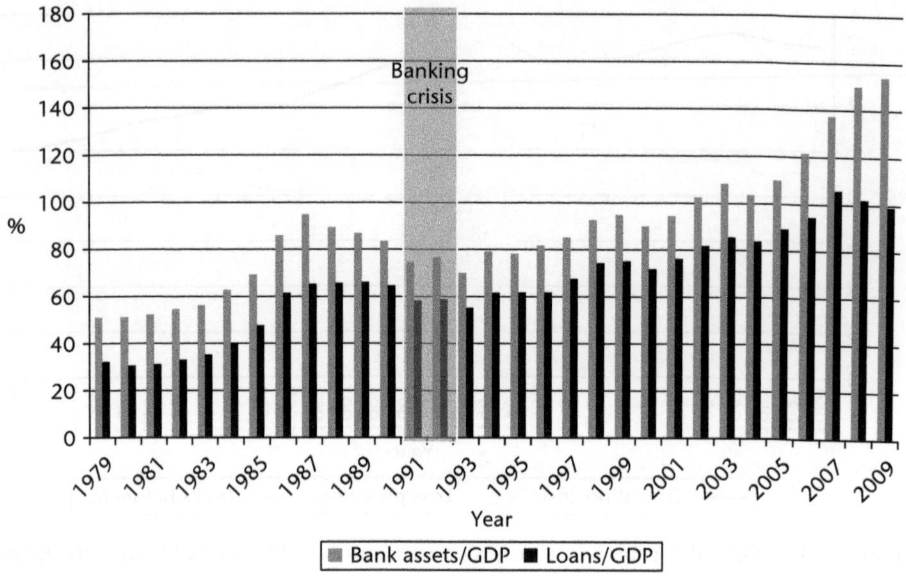

Figure 10.5. Bank assets and bank loans in Norway (per cent of GDP), 1979–2009
Source: Statistics Norway.

safeguard to prevent the bank from being sold to foreign banks and having its headquarters moved to another country. This is definitely a long-run effect of the banking crisis. Before the crisis, no Norwegian governments intended to become an owner of equity in commercial banks.

The government's involvement in the banking industry highlights the 'too-big-to-fail problem', which has become even more serious in all the Nordic countries, as bigger and more complex financial institutions have evolved over time. For example, the total assets of Den norske Bank amounted to about 90% of Mainland Norway's GDP in 2011. This ratio is higher than the corresponding number for the entire banking industry during the banking crisis.

Before the banking crisis, most Norwegian banks lacked competence or focus on risk management, resulting in excessive operational and credit risks. After the banking crisis, the focus of the new management groups switched to cost effectiveness and better risk management. New methods have been employed to calculate appropriate risk premiums in loan rates.

Also the Financial Supervisory Authority of Norway (FSA Norway) had insufficient competence in the critical years after financial deregulation. FSA Norway was established as an integrated supervisory institution in 1986 (*Kredittilsynet*, under the authority of the Ministry of Finance), after a merger of the two former supervisory authorities for banking and insurance. It employed only 71 staff members in 1986, and did not give priority to bank supervision during the lending boom. From the start it was responsible for prudential supervision of banks, insurance companies, and other financial institutions, as well as financial market surveillance and business and market conduct. Later the integrated supervisory model was adopted by Denmark (1988), Sweden (1991), and Finland (2009).

The banking crisis had a profound effect on FSA Norway. It won political support for allocation of more resources for expansion, and the banking crisis made it much easier to employ former bankers. In the three years after the banking crisis, its staff increased by 30% (from 99 full-time employees in 1992 to 129 in 1995). Another result of the banking crisis was the adoption of a new programme for macroeconomic surveillance in 1994. By 2010 the staff had further increased to 255 employees and the share of employees with a college degree had gone up significantly. The growth in staff numbers is also due to the fact that FSA Norway has been delegated additional responsibilities.[3]

An integrated financial supervision authority makes it easier to limit regulatory arbitrage and supervisory gaps. It gives FSA Norway more authority and makes it easier to hire highly qualified staff. It is also easier for an integrated supervisory authority to cooperate with the central bank and with financial supervisory authorities in other countries. After the banking crisis, the prudential supervision in Norway became different from the 'light touch' regulation by the FSA in London. It has defined its approach as 'active risk-based supervision' with regular on-site inspections and close contact (quarterly meetings) with managements of the most important financial institutions.

A close tripartite cooperation between FSA Norway, the Ministry of Finance, and Norges Bank has evolved after the banking crisis. The three of them share a common financial reporting database and have regular meetings to discuss financial stability issues. After the failure of Lehman Brothers in September 2008 and the freezing of the international money markets, there were frequent meetings between the three parties to discuss ways of securing medium-term bank funding. There is a particular close cooperation between FSA Norway and Norges Bank at top level and department head level, as well as at expert level.

10.4 Monetary Policy

What are the characteristics of successful monetary policy? Clearly, the consensus view has changed substantially over time. While for example the surprise element was seen as a prerequisite for successful exchange rate

[3] In addition to banks and insurance companies, the FSA Norway is now responsible for supervision of finance companies, pension funds, mortgage companies, investment firms, debt-collecting agencies, all markets for securities (including the stock market), auditors and auditing firms, external accountants, IFRS compliance, prospectuses, real estate agents, and IT supervision.

devaluations under the fixed-exchange-rate regime of the 1970s and early 1980s, the modern framework of flexible inflation targeting builds on the view that the reaction function of the central bank should be fully internalized by all agents in the economy.

The striking change in the monetary policy regime in Norway is not the result of any single comprehensive reform. It is rather the consequence of a gradual evolution in response to innovations in economic theory, experiences from actual policies, and changes in the domestic as well as global economic environment. Over time this has accumulated to significant changes in the monetary policy framework. Today, both Sweden and Norway have well-established and flexible inflation-targeting regimes. While Sweden adopted such a regime as early as 1993, the process towards inflation targeting was much more gradual and time-consuming in Norway. Inflation targeting was in effect adopted by Norges Bank in 1999 and formalized by a new regulation in 2001.

The inflation target was set to an annual 2.5% rate, and monetary policy was to be '. . . contributing to stable developments in output and employment', i.e. flexible inflation targeting. The new monetary regulation was introduced together with the announcement of new guidelines for fiscal policy (the 'Fiscal Rule'), highlighting a smooth and gradual spending path for the government's petroleum revenues, see Section 5 below. Giving fiscal policy a more long-run orientation implied that the role of monetary policy in macroeconomic stabilization was now becoming much more important.

Norway's inflation-targeting regime was to a great extent inspired by the monetary policy frameworks of the Bank of England and Swedish Riksbanken. Well-functioning inflation targeting requires that the target is credible and that the central bank's reaction function is understood and internalized by relevant agents in the economy. Maintaining credibility will rely on successful communication strategies and consistency in the actual policy decisions. Norges Bank had been publishing inflation reports regularly since 1995. In 1999 the Bank also began to present rather detailed press releases after the executive board's interest rate decisions. Moreover, from 2004, forward-looking strategy reports were included in the inflation reports (which later, in 2007, were renamed monetary policy reports). It is therefore fair to conclude that Norges Bank quickly caught up with best international communication practice.

The new inflation-targeting regime also had consequences for Norges Bank research and use of quantitative models in monetary policy analysis. The Bank needed a structural model for derivation of optimal interest rate paths, capturing theory-consistent, explicitly articulated assessments of the transmission mechanism. This paved the way for the development of a modern DSGE model nicknamed NEMO (Norwegian Economy MOdel). The use of the NEMO model seems to have been helpful in the interest-rate-setting decision process.

In the autumn of 2005, Norges Bank started to publish interest rate and exchange rate projection three years ahead in each monetary policy report. This was considered to be a natural step to improve credibility by being predictable. An explicit interest rate path including estimated probability distributions would be a much more precise tool for influencing agents' expectations than various verbal statements subject to all kinds of interpretations. The publishing of future interest rate and exchange rate paths is consistent with the importance of expectation formation for optimal policy in academic research. According to Woodford (2005): 'For not only do expectations matter, but (. . .) very little else matters'. Compared to the devaluation-biased monetary policy regime in use until the mid 1980s, today's framework built on publications of future interest rate paths and management of expectations à la Woodford, seems like the complete opposite!

Closely related to the publishing of the interest rate path is the publishing of a quantitative decomposition of the various sources for revisions of the path. This decomposition highlights that the interest rate path is a contingent forecast—that by definition will be revised in response to altered assumptions about various variables.

In every monetary policy report, the new interest rate path is discussed in the light of an explicit list of 'criteria for an appropriate interest rate path' and supported by a graphical analysis illustrating the impact of each criterion. The first of the criteria states that inflation over time should be brought back to its target level, while the second criterion states that it should be a reasonable balance between the path for inflation and the path for capacity utilization (the output gap). It follows that the first two criteria simply capture the two arguments in a standard loss function. The graphical illustration of how this trade-off is dealt with has earned recognition from Woodford (2007). The last criterion states that monetary policy should be robust in the sense that the risk of financial imbalances should be taken into account and, moreover, that an acceptable inflation–output gap development should be likely under alternative assumptions about the functioning of the economy (see the monetary policy report no. 2, 2013).

An interesting observation is how Norges Bank has changed the specified horizon for inflation to stabilize close to the inflation target. In 2001, the horizon was 2 years. Then, in 2004, the horizon was specified as normally 1–3 years. Later, the horizon was just specified as 'the medium term' with the additional explanation that the exact horizon will depend on which type of impulses the economy is exposed to and how they impact the prospects for inflation and the real economy. These changes in the specification of the

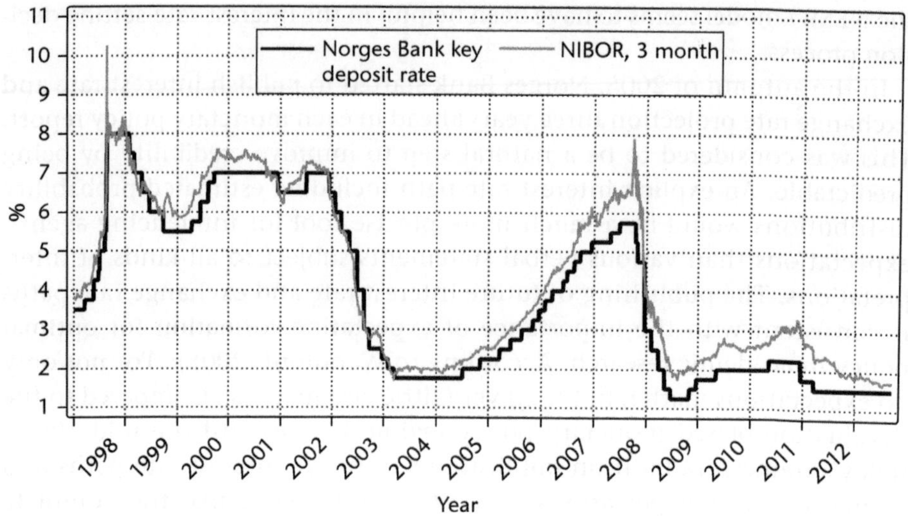

Figure 10.6. Norway—interest rates
Source: Macrobond Financial.

horizon can be rationalized by new insights after 2001 about the working of the Norwegian economy. In particular, a series of positive and persistent supply-side shocks (like increased import from China and other low-cost producers), a much larger inflow of immigrants to the Norwegian labour market, and, at least for some time, increased competition in several business sectors all contributed to below-target inflation. Allowing a flexible horizon, Norges Bank did not reduce its key rate below 1.75% in 2004 and 2005; see Figure 10.6.

10.5 Fiscal Policy—Adopting Sustainable Fiscal Strategies

While the huge government petroleum wealth is an obvious blessing for the Norwegian economy, it also makes fiscal policy much more challenging. More than 85% of the net cash flow from the petroleum sector is collected by the government by means of a special petroleum tax system and direct public ownership. This implies that public revenues have become severely exposed to oil price risk.

In Norway's early days as an oil exporter at the beginning of the 1970s, oil price risk did not receive much attention, at least not from a fiscal policy point of view. This partly reflected that the initial scale of the petroleum activities was not large. But, more importantly, the idea that oil prices would increase over time due to the non-renewable characteristics of oil and natural gas was widely accepted in the 1970s and early 1980s.[4] These perceptions changed completely during the 1980s due to considerable upward revisions of global resources. For Norway, the period of high oil prices and large and growing petroleum revenues abruptly came to an end when oil prices plunged in 1985–6. To illustrate the size of this adverse terms-of-trade shock, the estimated present value of the future government net petroleum revenues, as calculated by Statistics Norway, was reduced from 1388 billion kroner in 1986 (i.e. 275% of Mainland GDP at the time) to a low 413 billion kroner in 1988 (approximately 80% of GDP), (Thøgersen, 1994).[5]

The experience of the 1980s highlighted the need for mechanisms that could smooth the spending of petroleum revenues over time. Otherwise, erupting sectorial imbalances and increasing future net tax burdens would potentially create severe problems. Before 1986, the government made plans to regulate and limit the level of annual extraction of petroleum. The idea of using global financial markets to accumulate a financial petroleum fund in one way or another was dismissed in the 1970s, reflecting a lack of trust in the working of the financial markets.[6]

As it turned out, the early political ambitions to regulate the extraction level never materialized. Given the technological complexities and the long-run nature of oil and gas investment projects in the North Sea, this was hardly surprising. Consequently, the need to separate extraction and collection of resource revenues from a preferred smooth, long-run spending path called for strategies to accumulate foreign financial assets in a public petroleum fund in years of large petroleum revenues. This idea was discussed in two government White Papers during the 1980s.[7] The first was published in 1983 and discussed the design of a 'buffer fund' to smooth revenues over an intermediate time horizon. Scepticism about the ability and discipline of the political system to accumulate a large fund remained. The second report, published in 1988, emphasized that a petroleum fund could be an instrument for transferring resource wealth into foreign assets, limiting spending (including tax cuts) to the permanent income of the sum of the petroleum fund and the remaining resource wealth.

It took many years before the actual accumulation of financial assets into a Norwegian petroleum fund occurred. Formally, the legislation of

[4] The theoretical basis for these forecasts is the Hotelling rule. This rule predicts that in equilibrium the (net) price of an exhaustible resource like oil should increase exponentially over time due to resource scarcity, see for example Dasgupta and Heal (1979).

[5] The petroleum wealth estimate was even higher in the first part of the 1980s. In 1981, for example, the estimate was close to 500% of GDP.

[6] As described in more detail in Thøgersen (1994), leading politicians and bureaucrats at the time referred to the risks of revolutions and hyperinflation as the reason for avoiding accumulation of significant amounts of financial assets.

[7] See the government White Papers NOU 1983:27 and 1988:21 respectively.

such a fund, which initially was named the Norwegian State Petroleum Fund, was passed by the Storting (Norwegian Parliament) in January 1990, and according to its rules, the growth of the fund had to be linked to fiscal surpluses, to be invested in foreign assets. Fiscal deficits in the first years after 1990 prevented any accumulation in the fund. Gradually, however, the macroeconomic performance of the Norwegian economy improved during the 1990s, helped by steady increases in petroleum production. Accordingly, the oil price exposure remained high. In 1995, the fiscal budget posted a small surplus, and this led to the first allocation to the petroleum fund in 1996.

10.5.1 *The Government Pension Fund Global*

Norges Bank was given the responsibility of managing the foreign assets in the State Petroleum Fund—which later, in 2006, was renamed the Government Pension Fund Global. At the outset, the idea was to utilize Norges Bank's experience in managing foreign currency reserves, and the first allocations were invested in sovereign bonds only. Due to the substantial increase in the world oil price after the turn of the century, huge government cash flows from the petroleum sector have accelerated the growth of the fund; see Figure 10.7. In a relatively short time Norges Bank has built up a professionalized asset-management wing, called Norges Bank Investment Management (NBIM).

The fund started to invest in listed equity in 1998, and in 2011 made its first investment in real estate in London. The investments in stocks and fixed-income securities are based on a benchmark portfolio specified by the Ministry of Finance which captures the stock and bond markets of all developed and emerging markets. The benchmark portfolio is defined by general global indices. No attempts have been made to introduce a benchmark portfolio that could potentially serve as a hedge for the overall oil price exposure of the Norwegian economy, however.

In addition, the fund is given a small 'risk budget' for active management. The bulk of the investments, including the active positions, are taken in-house at the NBIM organization. However, several specialized investment mandates have also been allocated to external asset-management firms. The fund's assets now (January 2014) amount to more than 800 billion USD or 160% of one year's GDP. It is now one of the largest sovereign wealth funds in the world.[8]

[8] For more details about NBIM's organization and the fund's activities, see NBIM's homepage <http://www.nbim.no/en/>. A more general discussion of the role of sovereign wealth funds is given by Steigum (2013).

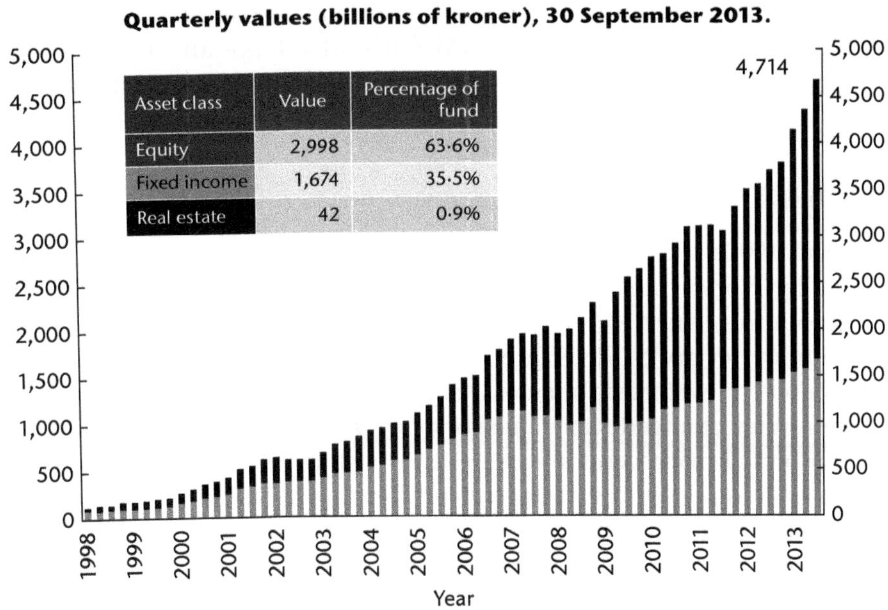

Figure 10.7. Market value of Government Pension Fund Global
Source: Norges Bank Investment Management.

As mentioned above, the fund's formal name changed to Government Pension Fund Global in 2006. This is in fact somewhat puzzling given that the fund is not a pension fund in the sense of having defined liabilities given by future pension outlays. The fund is rather an endowment fund without any underlying earmarking to specific purposes other than an instrument for supporting the welfare state and smoothing tax burdens over time and across generations.

Having large amounts of capital invested in a global fund involves considerable risks. During the recent financial crises in 2008–9 the value of the fund declined temporarily by almost 25%. This acted as a political stress test of the ability of the public and the media to cope with financial risks on a large scale. During the crisis and afterwards, there was no serious opposition to the chosen investment strategy, and the political parties appear to have accepted the risks to the value of the fund. The annualized real return of the fund is now slightly below the 4% real return which has been set as the long-run objective.

Clearly, the institutional framework of the fund is also exposed to domestic political risks. This includes the risks of political biases in the fund's allocations, both with respect to the design of the fund's benchmark and with respect to active management. Another is the risk of myopic overspending of the fund as a part of the annual decisions on the fiscal budget. Yet another risk is that the existence of a large and liquid fund will reduce the political system's ability to implement important structural reforms.

10.5.2 *The Fiscal Rule*

During the 1990s, the long-run effects of fiscal policy received increased attention by Norwegian governments. From the mid1990s, the 'generational accounting' method was employed to evaluate the intergenerational distribution of net tax burdens implied by current fiscal policies. When the petroleum revenues started to increase sharply after the turn of the century, the government changed the framework of monetary and fiscal policy in order to promote macroeconomic stability as well as to smooth the path of spending (including tax cuts) of petroleum revenues. The new 'Fiscal Rule' was announced, together with the new inflation-targeting framework of monetary policy in 2001. According to this rule, the non-oil fiscal deficit (i.e. the deficit before the net cash flow from the petroleum sector) should—in a normal year—be given by an upfront calculated 4% real return on the Government Pension Fund Global.

The rule has a 'bird-in-hand' property in the sense that only wealth accumulated in the fund matters, not the remaining petroleum wealth on the continental shelf. Therefore, the Fiscal Rule is not an optimal rule derived from economic theory, but rather a rule based on pragmatic considerations.[9]

Since population ageing will increase pension and health spending significantly in the future, the Fiscal Rule contributes to intertemporal smoothing of tax burdens. In addition, the rule is transparent and not difficult to explain and communicate to a broader audience.

The Fiscal Rule allows for some flexibility. First of all, the automatic fiscal stabilizers are allowed to work freely. Second, the Fiscal Rule refers to a 'normal year' and it allows for deviations caused by, for example, unexpected fluctuations in the magnitude of the fund or even active fiscal stimulus policy to assist monetary policy for stabilization purposes. An example of the latter is the active fiscal policy measures taken after the international financial crisis in 2009.

Figure 10.8 illustrates the extent to which the Fiscal Rule has been followed since 2001. We see that spending, measured by the structural non-oil deficit, has been close to the '4% path'. Years with some 'overspending' (like the period 2002–5) have been followed by fiscal discipline and 'underspending'.

[9] An optimal rule should be derived from a stochastic tax-smoothing model that captures precautionary saving, see van der Ploeg (2010a, 2010b) and Steigum (2002).

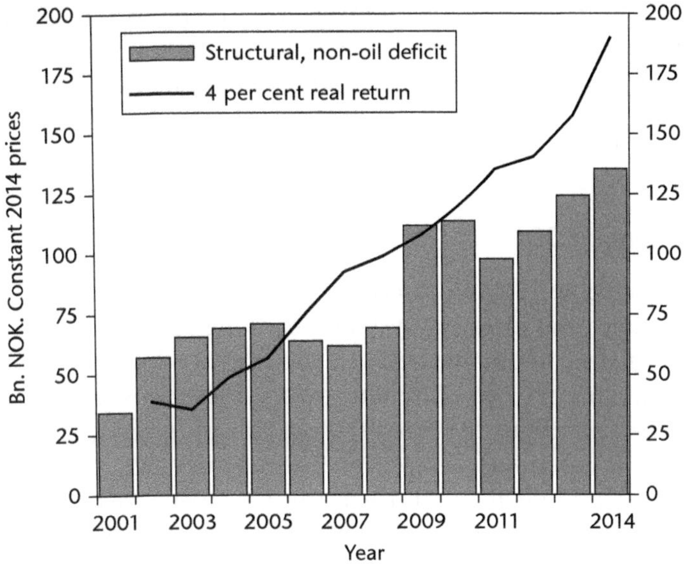

Figure 10.8. The fiscal rule in practice—the 4% rule versus the actual structural, non-oil fiscal deficit
Source: Ministry of Finance.

Compared with the familiar debt bias in most democracies as well as predictions from the political economy literature, the Fiscal Rule has served its purpose well. The Fiscal Rule has in fact been followed by both left- and right-wing governments so far. Among the possible explanations is a low degree of polarization among the political parties in Norway when it comes to economic policy. Another potentially important factor is the determination and professionalism of the non-elected civil service staff within the Ministry of Finance.

10.6 Benefitting from Reforms—Norway's Post-Crisis Macroeconomic Performance

Norway's growth and employment performance after the banking crisis have been very strong. We suggest that the banking crisis of the early 1990s had a favourable, albeit indirect, effect through structural and economic policy reforms. After the banking crisis, Norway's financial supervisory authority was strengthened considerably and the powers of the Ministry of Finance increased as a result of the perception of a national crisis after the oil price shock in 1985–6. Other structural reforms include a tax reform in 1992, closer income policy cooperation between the government and the central labour-market organizations to increase cost competitiveness and reduce unemployment, as well as a series of product-market reforms designed to increase competition and economic efficiency, including in energy markets, telecommunications, and markets for other non-traded services. More recently, in 2009, a reform of the old-age pension was introduced.

10.6.1 *Comparing GDP and Productivity*

Going back to Figure 10.3, we can compare the volume growth of GDP in the four Nordic countries after the systemic banking crises in the beginning of the 1990s. Finland's boom–bust cycle is the largest, while the Norwegian and Swedish cycles are not very different, except that the Norwegian bust happened much earlier than the Swedish and Finnish ones. The Danish boom and bust was much milder. Figure 10.3 also shows that since 1993 output growth in Finland and mainland Norway have been faster than real GDP growth in Denmark and Sweden. It is surprising that the performance of Denmark is inferior to the three other Nordic countries that experienced a banking sector meltdown in 1991–3. This fact makes it difficult to argue that Finland, Sweden, and Norway suffered from significant medium- or long-term economic costs due to their systemic banking crises.

Table 10.1 looks at what happened in the first seven years after the banking crisis. Finland, which had the largest decline in real GDP under the banking crisis, also had the best growth performance in the period 1993–2000, with an impressive average growth rate of 4.5 per year. The corresponding growth rate of mainland Norway was 3.68%, marginally higher the Sweden's average (GDP) growth rate of 3.52% over the same period. Denmark's growth rate was significantly smaller, only 2.37% on average. In the next eight years, the average growth rates became smaller for all countries. Now mainland Norway had the best growth performance (3.23%), followed by Finland (2.95%), Sweden (2.58%), and Denmark (1.3%).

Table 10.1. Average post-crisis real GDP growth rates in Denmark, Sweden, mainland Norway, and Finland, 1993–2008 (per cent per year)

	1993–2000	2000–8
Finland	4.51	2.95
Mainland Norway	3.68	3.23
Sweden	3.52	2.58
Denmark	2.37	1.30

Source: OECD.

Growth accounting suggests that multi-factor productivity growth is considerably lower in Denmark than in the other three countries. OECD finds that in the period 1993–2006, average multi-factor productivity growth in real GDP was 2.5% per year in Finland, 1.9% in Sweden, and only 0.8% in Denmark.

Andersen et al. (1999) emphasize that excessive real wage growth and reduced international competiveness are important factors behind the relatively modest economic growth in Denmark. Another explanatory factor is a low share of R&D expenditure relative to GDP. Whatever the causes, they are unlikely to have much to do with the fact that Denmark avoided a systemic banking crisis around 1990.

Previous papers on the real economic costs in terms of output loss of the Nordic crises are IMF (1998), Hoggarth and Saporta (2002), Schwierz (2004), and Hagberg and Jonung (2009) (the latter only analysing Finland and Sweden).[10] The results are sensitive to the measurement of output trends and to how the start of a banking crisis is identified. Some of these studies also pick up the effects of shocks that are not directly related to the banking crises, such as the shock hitting Finnish industry after the collapse of the Soviet Union in 1991. A surprising finding of the three first papers referred to above is a larger 'economic cost' in Norway than in Sweden and Finland, but this is probably an artefact of the particular methods used to measure trends and output gaps.

10.6.2 *Unemployment and Employment Rates*

Figure 10.2 reveals that the post-crisis unemployment rates differ a lot in the four countries. The unemployment crisis was worst in Finland, where the collapse of textile exports to the former Soviet Union had a devastating effect. The unemployment rate in Finland increased to nearly 17% in 1994. In 2000, seven years after the end of the banking crisis, the Finnish unemployment rate was still above 9%. It took another eight years to bring the unemployment rate in Finland back to the 1986 level. The Swedish unemployment rate also increased rapidly during the banking crisis, and reached almost 10% in 1997. So far it has not returned to the low levels of less than 4% observed in the mid1980s, however. The unemployment records of Finland and Sweden are therefore consistent with a negative persistent effect of the banking crisis.

In the cases of Norway and Denmark, the Danish unemployment rate has been systematically higher than the Norwegian one throughout the period covered by Figure 10.2. The Norwegian unemployment rate peaked at about 6.5% in 1993,

[10] These methods have been improved by Bordo et al. (2001).

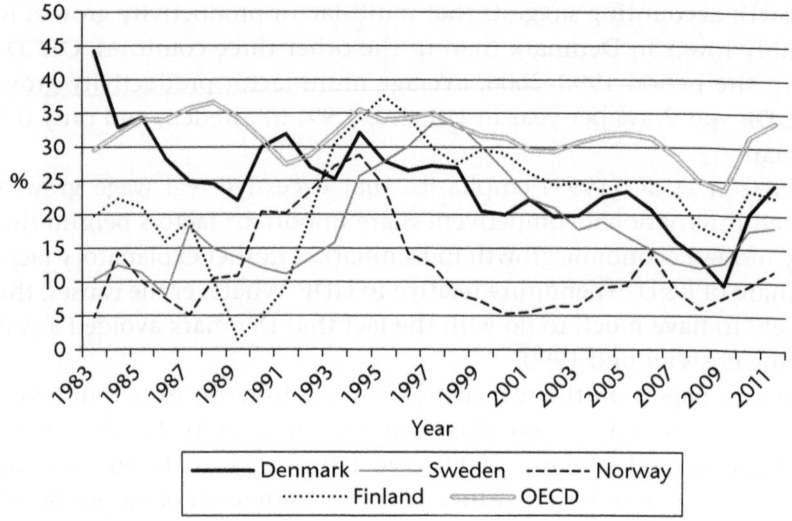

Figure 10.9. Long-term unemployment as a share of total unemployment in Denmark, Sweden, Norway, and Finland, 1993–2011
Source: OECD.

the first year after the end of the banking crisis.[11] Despite the fact that Denmark did not experience a systemic banking crisis, unemployment was much higher than in Norway during and after the Nordic banking crisis of 1991–3. In both countries the rates of unemployment have come down to mid-1980s levels.

Unemployment persistence is a mechanism through which banking crises may have negative medium- and long-term effects. Such effects are usually closely related to long-term unemployment, and in this regard Norway's performance has been much stronger than the three other countries. In addition to low unemployment, the share of long-term unemployed in total unemployment has been low and declining since 1994 (from 28.5%), see Figure 10.9. In the boom year 2000, long-term unemployment in Norway was only 5%. In Finland, the share of long-term unemployment declined from 37% in 1995 to 25% in 2001. Sweden's share of long-term unemployment increased for four years after the banking crisis, and declined from 33.5% in 1997–8 to 14% in 2005–6. Denmark also had its long-term unemployment share above 30% in 1994, and the decline afterwards has been more modest than in the three countries that experienced a systemic banking crisis.

[11] Both Norway and Sweden put in place labour-market programmes to increase the human capital of unemployed workers. Participants in such programmes are not counted as unemployed. If workers in such programmes are added to the unemployed, the gross rate of unemployment in Norway would have been about 8 percent in 1993. Still, this is significantly lower than the unemployment rate in Denmark.

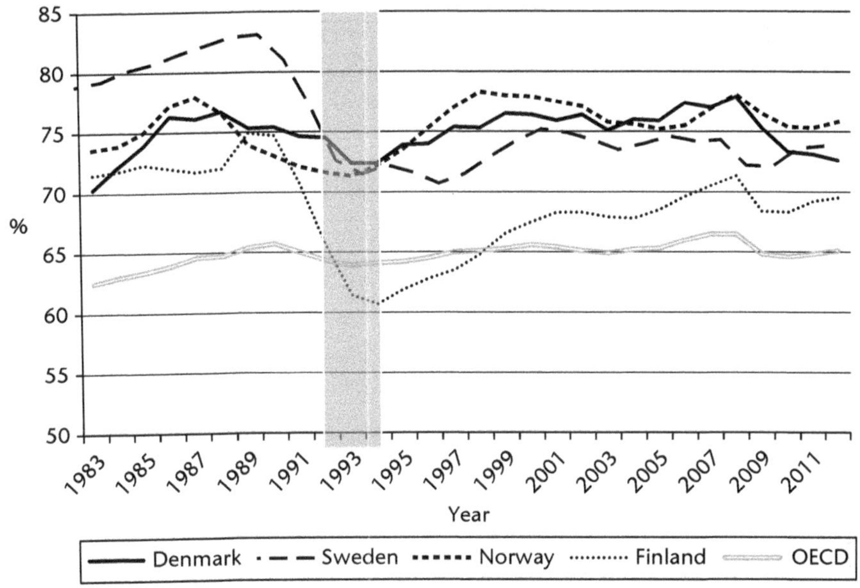

Figure 10.10. Employment rates in the Nordic countries and OECD average, 1983–2012. Share (percentage) of persons of working age (15 to 64 years) in employment
Source: OECD.

Finally, we look at employment rates (share of persons of working age 15 to 64 years) in employment—see Figure 10.10. Employment rates have traditionally been significantly higher in the Nordic countries than in the rest of OECD. The banking crises did not change this fact. However, there has been a considerable persistence in the decline in employment rates in Finland and Sweden. The Swedish case strongly suggests that the crisis in the early 1990s had a persistent effect on both unemployment and employment rates. In 1985–6, the Swedish employment rate was above 80% and increasing (the highest rate among the four Nordic countries), and in 2008 it was 76%. Again, Denmark and Norway experienced much smaller declines in employment rates during and after the Nordic banking crisis, and the employment rates more than recovered in the period. In 2008, the employment rates in Denmark and Norway were higher than Sweden's.

10.6.3 *Fiscal Deficits and Government Debt*

Government debt is another mechanism for persistent effects of banking crises. Figure 10.11 shows that the government deficits in Sweden and Finland increased substantially during the banking crisis. This was mostly due to automatic fiscal stabilizers, however. The fiscal costs of the banking crises in

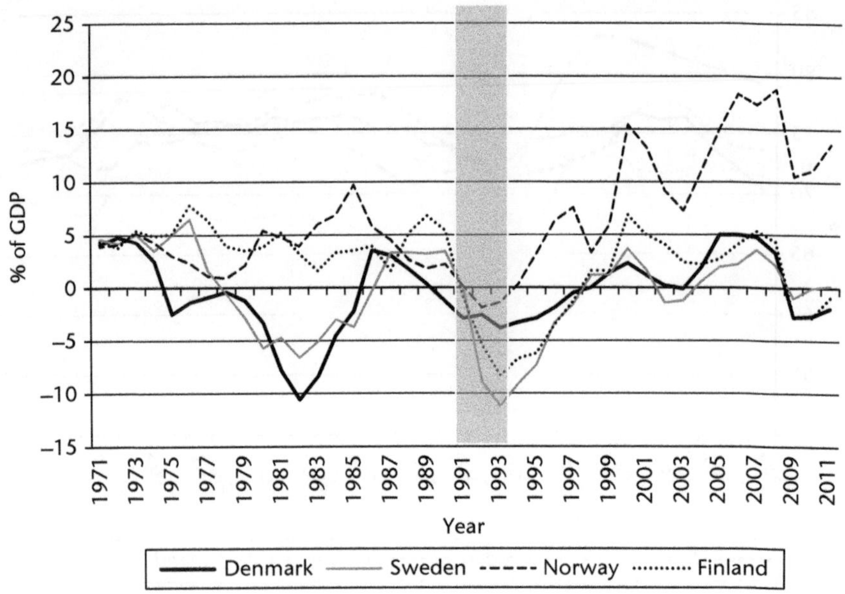

Figure 10.11. General government net lending in Denmark, Sweden, Norway, and Finland, 1971–2009
Source: OECD.

Finland and Sweden were modest (see Sandal 2004). In the last banking crisis year (1993), the fiscal deficits of Sweden and Finland were 11.2% and 8.3% of GDP, respectively. The Norwegian government also ran fiscal deficits in the early 1990s.

Table 10.2 reports gross public debts (per cent of GDP) for Sweden, Finland, and Denmark. Unfortunately, net debt numbers are not available. The increase in the debt from 1990 to 1995 was almost 50 percentage points in Finland and only a little smaller in Sweden. Denmark had more favourable macroeconomic developments, but still increased its public debt (as percentage of GDP) by about 13 percentage points from 1990 to 1995. In the period 1995–2008, Denmark reduced its gross public debt to a much lower level than in 1990. By 2008, the gross debt in Sweden was back to the 1990 level. In Finland, however, the gross public debt in 2008 has not recovered from the crisis in the 1990s. Again, it is worth emphasizing that the data from Finland is influenced by the collapse of the exports to the Soviet Union.

10.6.4 *Norway's Performance During the Great Recession*

The recession in Norway turned out to be much milder and more short-lived than in most other OECD countries (see Bjørnland et al., 2010). The rate of

Table 10.2. General government gross financial liabilities for Sweden, Finland, and Denmark, 1990–2008 (as percentage of GDP)

Year	Sweden	Finland	Denmark
1990	46.3	16.3	66.4
1995*	81	65.2	79.3
2000	64.7	52.3	57.1
2008	47.1	40.7	39.8

* Maximum gross debt share, except in Sweden where the share increased to 84.4% in 1996.

Source: OECD.

unemployment (according to the labour market survey) only increased from 2.5% in 2007 to 3.6% in 2010 (and down to 3.3% in 2011). The growth rate of mainland GDP declined from 5.3% in 2007 to 1.5% in 2008 and -1.6% in 2009. Thereafter, the percentage growth rate increased to 1.7 in 2010, 2.5 in 2011, and 3.5 in 2012. Despite a deep, temporary decline in the oil price in 2008, Norway has been running huge current account surpluses of more than 11% of GDP before, during, and after the Great Recession.

The relatively good macroeconomic performance during the Great Recession and afterwards is probably a result of the combination of good macroeconomic policies and good financial regulation—as well as good luck. Monetary policy in Norway was very expansionary since December 2008, when Norges Bank (following Riksbanken) cut the policy rate by 175 basis points. From August 2008 to June 2009 the policy rate declined from 5.75 to 1.25% (see Figure 10.6). Moreover, after the Lehman Brothers failure in mid September 2008, Norges Bank supplied more and longer krone funding as well as lending USD to domestic banks. In late October, a facility was passed in the Parliament to help Norwegian banks to exchange Norwegian covered bonds (OMFs) with government securities for a period of three to five years, (Bergman et al., 2009). In February 2009 the government established two new funds in order to strengthen Norwegian banks' tier-1 capital as well as providing a source of funds for industrial companies issuing bonds (Bjørnland et al., 2010). Although the international financial crisis temporarily interrupted international funding to many Norwegian banks, this problem was cleverly managed without any sizeable credit crunch.

The effects of monetary policy on aggregate demand appear to be greater in Norway than in most other European countries due to a combination of high household indebtedness and floating mortgage rates. Fiscal policy also became much more expansionary in 2009, adding to the effects of strong automatic stabilizers. The expansionary monetary and fiscal policy measures bolstered consumer confidence and stopped the decline in house prices; Norwegian house prices had been falling through 2008, but have been increasing in the period 2009–14.

Good policies and financial regulation are other factors that could explain the absence of a banking crisis, or of severe problems in any of the Norwegian banks in 2009. It was also fortunate that the oil price (in USD) doubled in the course of 2009 and that the Norwegian manufacturing sector is relatively small, has high capital intensity, and does not engage in producing consumer durables to any large extent.

10.7 Final Remarks

Apparently, the systemic Nordic banking crisis did not have sizeable negative medium-term macroeconomic effects in Finland, Norway, or Sweden. There were no signs of a lost decade for the three countries hit by systemic banking crises in the beginning of the 1990s. On the contrary, the country that had the least-impressive growth performance after 1993 was Denmark, the only Nordic country (together with Iceland) avoiding a systemic banking crisis in the beginning of the 1990s. In the labour markets, however, there are signs of persistent and negative employment effects in Finland and Sweden. The labour-market performance was much better in Norway and Denmark.

The main reason why the banking crises did not have strong negative effects is probably the fast and efficient banking crisis resolution by the Nordic governments. The failing banks were quickly re-capitalized (and re-managed) and were able to support new economic growth without any credit crunch.

The increase in government debt from 1990 to 1995 was almost 50 percentage points in Finland and not a great deal less in Sweden. By 2008, the gross public debt in Sweden (relative to GDP) was back to the 1990 level. In Finland, however, the gross debt share in 2008 has not recovered from the crisis in the 1990s.

It is likely that the Norwegian banking crisis indirectly had favourable economic effects due to structural policy reforms that became possible to implement as a result of the perception of a national crisis by politicians and voters. Probably, the crises also had a positive learning effect in the banking industries of Finland, Norway, and Sweden, preventing their banks from excessive risk-taking of the style prevalent in many US and European banks.

We have presented evidence that strongly suggest that the cost-efficiency and risk management of the Norwegian banking industry have improved substantially after the banking crisis. At the same time, Norway's supervisory authority has become much stronger and more competent as a result of the crisis. There are also reasons to believe that the performance and effectiveness of the banking industries and prudential regulation in Finland and Sweden have improved in a similar manner as a result of the banking crises.

The Nordic experience shows that a quick and efficient government resolution of the banking crisis could restore economic growth quite quickly despite previous economic policy and financial regulation failures before the crisis. Instead of a lost decade after the banking crisis, the economic growth of Finland, Norway, and Sweden outperformed that of neighbouring Denmark.

The system of pegged or fixed exchange rates did not serve the Nordic countries well after financial deregulation. Monetary policy became increasingly procyclical during the boom and bust, and changes in income taxation rules contributed to high real after-tax interest rates before and during the banking crises. Flexible exchange rates and inflation targeting have worked well in Sweden and Norway, making it easier to move the real rate of interest countercyclically. An important lesson for small open economies that intend to open up their capital accounts to learn is that they should permit exchange rate flexibility. When Finland and Sweden finally stopped defending their pegs, real depreciations and lower interest rates laid the ground for aggregate demand stimuli and economic growth.

Norway's impressive macroeconomic performance is both a result of favourable terms-of-trade developments and of a series of institutional and structural reforms that increased productivity and improved the framework of monetary and fiscal policy. The most important reform was the introduction of flexible inflation targeting and the new Fiscal Rule that permitted a smooth path of spending of petroleum revenues and the accumulation of a sovereign wealth fund.

A final lesson concerns the importance of the financial supervisory authorities. These institutions were weak and lacked competence during the credit-expansion period leading up to the Nordic banking crises. Capital requirements were too lax (except in Denmark). After the crises, these institutions have been strengthened considerably. The integrated supervision model in Norway has been a success, and many countries adopted this model in the 1990s and 2000s. After the banking crisis, Norway's Financial Supervisory Authority adopted an 'active risk-based supervision' approach, and a close tripartite cooperation with the Ministry of Finance and Norges Bank has evolved to deal with financial and macro-prudential stability issues. Strengthened financial supervision and regulation, as well as the learning effect of the banking crisis in the early 1990s, seem to have prevented Norwegian banks from excessive risk-taking before the recent international financial crisis.

The Nordic governments' crisis-resolution policies did not address the too-big-to-fail distortion. On the contrary, the implicit subsidies given to holders of bank debt as a result of the government rescue policies have probably reduced risk premiums and given the large Nordic banks a competitive advantage in funding relative to smaller banks. If this problem is not dealt with, the implicit subsidies to large banks may trigger industry dynamics that make the too-big-to-fail problem even more dangerous over time.

References

Allan, F. and D. Gale (2000), 'Bubbles and Crises', *Economic Journal*, 110, 236–55.

Andersen, T. M., S. E. Hougaard Jensen, and O. Risager (1999), 'Macroeconomic Perspectives on the Danish Economy: Problems, Policies and Prospects,' in Andersen, T. M. and S. E. Hougaard Jensen (eds): *Macroeconomic Perspectives on the Danish Economy*, London: Macmillan.

Bergman, M., S. Juel, and E. Steigum (2009), 'Monetary Policy and the Financial Turmoil', *Norges Bank Watch Report Series* No. 10, Oslo: Centre for Monetary Economics, BI Norwegian School of Management.

Bjørnland, H. C., R. Clarida, E. Holvik, and E. Steigum (2010), 'An Independent Evaluation of Monetary Policy in Norway'. Norges Bank Watch Report Series No. 11, Oslo: Centre for Monetary Economics, BI Norwegian School of Management.

Bordo, M., B. Eichengreen, D. Klingebiel, and M. S. Martinez-Peria (2001), 'Is the Crisis Problem Growing More Severe?' *Economic Policy*, 32, 51–82.

Dasgupta, P. S. and G. M. Heal (1979), *Economic Theory and Exhaustible Resources*, Cambridge: Cambridge University Press.

Hagberg, T. and L. Jonung (2009), 'How Costly was the Crisis in Finland and Sweden?' in Jonung, L., J. Kiander, and P. Vartia (eds), *The Great Financial Crisis in Finland and Sweden: The Nordic Experience of Financial Liberalization*, Cheltenham: Edward Elgar, chapter 5, pp. 158–80.

Hoggarth, G. R. and V. Saporta (2002), 'Costs of Banking Instability: Some Empirical Evidence', *Journal of Banking and Finance*, 26, 825–55.

IMF (1998), World Economic Outlook, May, Washington DC: IMF.

Jonung, L., J. Kiander, and P. Vartia (eds) (2009), *The Great Financial Crisis in Finland and Sweden: The Nordic Experience of Financial Liberalization*, Cheltenham: Edward Elgar.

van der Ploeg, F. (2010a), 'Political Economy of Prudent Budgetary Policy', *International Tax and Public Finance*, 17, 295–314.

van der Ploeg, F. (2010b), 'Aggressive Oil Extraction and Precautionary Saving: Coping with Volatility', *Journal of Public Economics*, 94, 421–33.

Reinhart, C. M. and K. Rogoff (2009), *This Time is Different. Eight Centuries of Financial Folly*, Princeton: Princeton University Press.

Sandal, K. (2004), 'The Nordic Banking Crises in the Early 1990s—Resolution Methods and Fiscal Costs', in T. Moe, J.A. Solheim, and B. Vale (eds.): *The Norwegian Banking Crisis*. Oslo: Norges Bank's Occasional Papers, no. 33, chapter 3, pp. 77–115.

Schwierz, C. (2004), 'Economic Costs Associated with the Nordic Banking Crisis', in T. Moe, J.A. Solheim, and B. Vale (eds): *The Norwegian Banking Crisis*. Oslo: Norges Bank's Occasional Papers, no. 33, chapter 4, pp. 117–44.

Steigum, E. (1992), 'Financial Deregulation, Credit Boom and Banking Crisis: The Case of Norway', Discussion Paper, 15/92, Norwegian School of Economics and Business Administration, Bergen. Translated to Finnish and published in *PTT Katsaus*, 4, 10–31 (1992).

Steigum, E. (2002), 'Oil Price risk, Prudent Fiscal Policy, and Generational Accounting', Report No. 22/02, Institute for Research in Economics and Business Administration (SNF), Bergen.

Steigum, E. (2009), 'The Boom and Bust Cycle in Norway', in Jonung, L., J. Kiander and P. Vartia, *The Great Financial Crisis in Finland and Sweden: The Nordic Experience of Financial Liberalization,* Cheltenham: Edward Elgar, chapter 7, 202–44.

Steigum, E. (2013), 'Sovereign Wealth Funds for Macroeconomic Purposes', Report to the Swedish Fiscal Policy Council (Finanspolitiska Rådet) 2013/4.

Steigum, E. and Ø. Thøgersen (2003), 'Borrow and Adjust: Fiscal Policy and Sectoral Adjustment in an Open Economy', *International Economic Review*, 44, 699–724.

Thøgersen, Ø. (1994), 'Economic Policy, Macroeconomic Performance and Norwegian Petroleum Wealth—a Survey", NHH Discussion Paper 21/94, NHH Norwegian School of Economics.

Vastrup, C. (2009), 'How did Denmark Avoid a Banking Crisis?', in Jonung, L. J. Kiander, and P. Vartia (2009), *The Great Financial Crisis in Finland and Sweden: The Nordic Experience of Financial Liberalization,* Cheltenham: Edward Elgar chapter 8, 245–64.

Woodford, M. (2005), 'Central Bank Communication and Policy Effectiveness', in *The Greenspan Era: Lessons for the Future*, Kansas City: Federal Reserve Bank of Kansas.

Woodford, M. (2007), 'The Case for Forecast Targeting as a Monetary Policy Strategy', *Journal of Economic Perspectives*, 21, 3–24.

Comments on 'A Crisis Not Wasted: Institutional and Structural Reforms Behind Norway's Strong Macroeconomic Performance' by Erling Steigum and Øystein Thøgersen

Hans Tson Söderström

We should be grateful to Steigum and Thøgersen for providing us with such a detailed, yet concise, overview of Norwegian macroeconomic developments and policies over the last few decades. It nicely complements a number of recent comparative studies of the Nordic economies where Norway has often been left out for being a 'special case'.

The Nordic countries can indeed serve as a useful research laboratory for macroeconomic and structural policies over the last few decades. Our economies share a number of traits with respect to demographics, educational levels, labour market structure, degree of openness, size of the public sector, etc. In joint work with a group of Nordic economists (Andersen et al., 2007) we tried to capture the essence of the Nordic model in two key ingredients: 'embracing globalization' and 'sharing risks'. By 'embracing globalization' we mean that the long-term economic success of the Nordic countries is solidly founded in deep-rooted participation in the global division of labour, reaping the fruits of gains from trade and factor mobility. By 'sharing risks' we mean that popular support for a high degree of openness—with the adjustment burden it constantly puts on labour and capital—can only be secured in a democracy if the costs and benefits are perceived as fairly distributed, with a reasonable degree of protection for the weaker groups in society. Our analysis pointed to some reforms of the model made necessary by the increasing pace of globalization and the demographic pressure of ageing populations.

The laboratory is particularly useful as—in spite of all the structural similarities and in spite of continuous political efforts at Nordic collaboration in all areas of economic policy—the Nordic countries have over a longer time period chosen different macroeconomic policy strategies with respect to both fiscal and monetary policy. All countries have demonstrated a relatively high degree of policy activism, but with varying emphasis on fiscal and monetary policy. Finland was more prone to take recourse to exchange rate adjustments in order to maintain international competitiveness and protect employment in the tradables sector of the economy, whereas Sweden demonstrated a higher degree of fiscal activism until uncontrollable fiscal deficits forced the country into a series of devaluations from 1977 to 1982. A reader of the Steigum–Thøgersen chapter is left with the impression that Norway may have been the most active of the Nordic countries with respect to discretionary stabilization policy: active exchange rate policy, repeated recourse to price and wage controls, and relatively high amplitude in the time series for government net lending. Norway also seems to be a latecomer to the group of countries who believe that rules can be better than discretion in stabilizing macroeconomic activity. A final verdict on these points will have to await, however, a more systematic comparison of stabilization policies in the Nordics.

When it comes to relations with the European Union the different policy choices become even more striking. One might have expected a joint Nordic strategy with respect to European affairs in order to gain influence for common interests and Nordic points of view. In contrast, four distinctly different approaches to EU collaboration have materialized: Norway (and Iceland) have—so far—remained entirely outside the union. Denmark, Finland, and Sweden are union members, but with different approaches to monetary collaboration. Only Finland has adopted the euro. Denmark has maintained the krone, but with a fixed exchange rate to the euro, and the Swedish krona has been floating since the krona peg had to be given up in November 1992. The outcomes of these different policy choices provide interesting—and continuously developing—material for comparative macroeconomic studies. A study in which I participated (Gylfason et al., 2010) led to a provisional conclusion that the floating exchange rate did not help Sweden noticeably relative to Finland through the global financial crisis of 2008–9. However, more recent data seem to indicate that Finland has been punished by a loss of competitiveness due to its adherence to the euro group.

A key proposition of the Steigum–Thøgersen chapter is that the systemic banking crises of the early 1990s did not have a lasting negative effect on macroeconomic developments in the Nordic countries. Quite to the contrary, they seem to argue that Finland, Norway, and Sweden had a stronger macroeconomic development than would otherwise have been the case, due not only to efficient crisis resolution but also because the crisis itself led to a number of beneficial institutional reforms. This is a provocative position as is can lead to the conclusion that financial crises are desirable, as they tend to speed up the reform agenda and thereby lead to higher long-term growth. Before we are lead to adopt such a controversial proposition (not openly advanced by the authors) we should ask ourselves a number of questions raised by the chapter:

- Did Norway have an exceptionally good growth performance after the systemic banking crisis of the early 1990s (in terms of GDP, GNI, output per man-hour, and total factor productivity)?
- If so, to what extent must the superior performance be explained by institutional and structural reforms in contrast to other factors—temporary or permanent, domestic or international?
- Was a systemic banking crisis necessary in order to provoke—or speed up—these reforms? Can one conceive of other factors—economic and/or political—that could have resulted in a similar (or even better) reform agenda?

The Steigum–Thøgersen chapter: leads us to constructive thinking about these important points, and their provisional answers add to our knowledge in the field of Nordic stabilization policies. Whatever conclusions are reached as economic developments evolve and our understanding increases this chapter provides an excellent starting point for any student of macroeconomic developments in Norway.

A final point worth making: Norwegian economic policy will definitely stand out as a leading example of how to handle the potentially disastrous effects on the Norwegian economy of the 'resource curse' connected to the discovery and exploitation of North Sea oil. Norwegian economists and politicians had the advantage of having at hand previous bad examples of how the—by now well-known—'Dutch disease' could threaten to strangle domestic economic activity as factor price increases related to resource extraction crowd out other productive activities. I found the chapter's section on sustainable fiscal strategies particularly instructive in this respect. The channeling of all net oil revenues into the so-called Government Pension Fund Global—by now the world's largest sovereign wealth fund—and the strategy of investing 100 per cent of the fund's resources in assets outside the Norwegian economy have so far proved a successful prevention of Dutch disease symptoms.

Today, the fund's net wealth amounts to an amazing one-million NOK (163 000 USD) per capita. Any student of modern macroeconomics would expect this enormous accumulation of wealth in the public sector to be reflected in declining and increasingly negative savings rates in the private sector. From the data provided by Steigum and Thøgersen this has not happened in Norway. With the exception of the years 2006–7 household savings rates have remained safely on the positive side since before the financial crisis of the early 1990s, and there is no discernable long-term negative trend. Hence the Norwegian experience seems to be a kiss of death to Ricardian equivalence as we know it. Steigum and Thøgersen do not comment on possible explanations of what seems to be a complete household insensitivity to sovereign wealth accumulation.

It is also impressive to note how Norwegian monetary policy has managed to prevent the krone from appreciating in spite of many years of cumulative current account surpluses. Consequently, Norway has—so far—proved immune to not only the Dutch but also the 'Swiss disease'. One cannot demand everything from a chapter with such broad ambitions, but for the future it would indeed be interesting to dig deeper into the mechanisms behind these intriguing puzzles.

References

Andersen, T.M., B. Holmström, S. Honkapohja, S. Korkman, H.T. Söderström, and J. Vartiainen (2007), *The Nordic Model—Embracing Globalization and Sharing Risks*, Helsinki: ETLA.

Gylfason, T., B. Holmström, S. Korkman, H.T. Söderström, and J. Vihriälä (2010), *Nordics in Global Crisis—Vulnerability and Resilience*, Helsinki: ETLA.

11

Finland and Sweden in a Cross-Country Comparison

What Are the Lessons?[1]

Sixten Korkman and Antti Suvanto

11.1 Introduction

Sweden and Finland are quite similar countries. They have a lot in common in terms of history and basic institutions of society. They have similar economic structures as well as aspirations for and ways of implementing economic policies. As will be seen, Finland and Sweden have performed in very similar ways in the past 20 years (as well as before that). Overall, the economic developments appear rather favourable in an international comparison.

Finland and Sweden experienced a banking crisis and a serious recession (or a depression) in the early 1990s. That experience had profound effects on economic policies. It triggered a process of structural reform and contributed to the emphasis being given to price stability and sound public finances in subsequent years. While the banking crisis and its effects were traumatic, later developments suggest that much was learnt from that experience.

Both Finland and Sweden joined the EU in 1995. In 1999 Finland also joined (Stage 3 of) EMU, while Sweden decided to stay outside. While far

[1] Earlier versions of the chapter were presented at the International Conference on 'Reform Capacity and Macroeconomic Performance in the Nordic countries' at Copenhagen Business School, Copenhagen, 20–21 September 2013; the tenth Euroframe Conference 'Towards a Better Governance in the EU', Warsaw, 24 May 2013; and at the seminar on 'Structural Reforms and Fiscal Policy Governance in Northern Europe', University of Edinburgh, 24 November 2012. We are grateful for comments by Fredrik Andersson, Seppo Honkapohja, Samu Kurri, and David Mayes as well as the participants of the above-mentioned seminars. The views expressed in this chapter are those of the authors, and do not necessarily reflect the views of the Bank of Finland.

from being identical twins, the economies and economic policies of these two countries are nevertheless exceptionally similar in most respects, except for the monetary regime. This chapter explores the similarity between Finland and Sweden in order to appreciate the significance of EMU membership. However, given the uncertain outcome of the current euro area debt crisis, any appreciation of the significance of the monetary union is associated with a number of caveats.[2]

11.2 Economic Performance

11.2.1 *Background*

Both Finland and Sweden went through a severe recession in the early 1990s.[3] GDP fell in Finland by 13 per cent from peak to trough between 1990 and 1993. The rate of unemployment increased five-fold from 3 to 16 per cent, and the government debt ratio increased four-fold from 14 to 58 per cent. Stock prices and house prices declined by one-half. Foreign indebtedness doubled, the currency lost one-third of its external value, the foreign exchange reserves of the central bank were depleted, and the banking sector was faltering.

In Sweden the fall of GDP was 5 per cent between 1990 and 1993. The decline was smaller than in Finland, but still dramatic in international as well as historical comparison. The unemployment rate rose from 2 to 9 per cent, and the government debt ratio rose from below 40 per cent to 75 per cent. Stock prices declined by 25 per cent, as did house prices. The currency weakened by about 20 per cent soon after the decision to float the currency in November 1992.

The recession was much more severe in Finland largely as a consequence of the fact that a significant export market was lost almost overnight following the collapse of the Soviet Union in 1991.

The build-up of the Finnish and Swedish crises in the early 1990s resembles the developments in Ireland and Spain 20 years later.[4] The recession was preceded by a boom associated with rapidly growing indebtedness and

[2] As far as we are aware there are three other studies comparing the relative performance of Finland and Sweden since the launch of the EMU: Mayes and Suvanto (2007), Gylfason et al. (2010, Ch.8), and Suni and Vihriälä (2013).

[3] For the crisis of the Nordic countries in the early 1990s, see Jonung et al. (2009). Bordes et al. (1993) present an early analysis of the crisis in Finland. A recent assessment is found in Honkapohja et al. (2009).

[4] Kindleberger and Aliber (2011, 11) include the booms in Sweden, Norway, and Finland in 1985–9 as well as the real estate bubbles in the US, Britain, Spain, Iceland, and Ireland in 2002–7 among the 'big ten financial bubbles' in history. Reinhard and Rogoff (2008) include the Finnish and Swedish episodes of the early 1990s among the 'big five' in the history of banking crises.

rising property prices. When the bust occurred in 1991–2 the balance sheets of banks weakened sharply. The very high interest rates resulting from the speculative attacks against the currency and the credit crunch resulting from the weakening balance sheets of banks depressed the economy even further. Also, competitiveness had been eroded by excessive wage inflation over a number of years in combination with weak productivity developments. Finland and Sweden were confronted with a banking crisis as well as a cost and currency crisis.

The export-led recovery started in both countries in 1993. Exports were boosted by exchange rate depreciation and the recovery in the rest of the world. In relation to the ECU the Swedish krona was some 25 per cent and the Finnish markka around 20 per cent weaker in 1995–9 as compared to the period 1985–9. In Finland the exchange rate overshot immediately after the decision to allow the currency to float in September 1992. The depreciation was widely considered as excessive and inconsistent with the new inflation target of the central bank announced in February 1993. The expected appreciation as a consequence of the overshooting facilitated the sharp decline in short-term interest rates in 1993.[5]

It took much longer in both countries for domestic demand to return to the pre-crisis level. This is consistent with the international experience from earlier banking crises (Reinhart and Rogoff 2009). It confirms the fact that it takes many years of painful adjustment for the balance sheets to adjust to excessive indebtedness.

11.2.2 *Economic Performance Since 1998*

By 1998 both Finland and Sweden had more or less fully recovered from the banking crisis and the recession. By that date both countries had joined the European Union. Finland had also decided to join the euro area, while Sweden decided to stay outside with a floating exchange rate.

Figure 11.1 depicts the output performance of Finland and Sweden compared to that of the euro area average. As is seen, until recently output growth in the two Nordic countries has been almost identical and it has outperformed the euro area average by a clear margin. The recovery from the great recession of 2008–9 was stronger and more sustained in Sweden. We will return to the recession experience below.

The same is true of inflation. As seen in Figure 11.2, between 1998 and 2008 the average rate of increase of the consumer price index (HICP) has on average been below 2 per cent (but close to it) in Sweden and Finland, while

[5] This is an example of the Dornbusch overshooting mechanism at work; Dornbusch (1976).

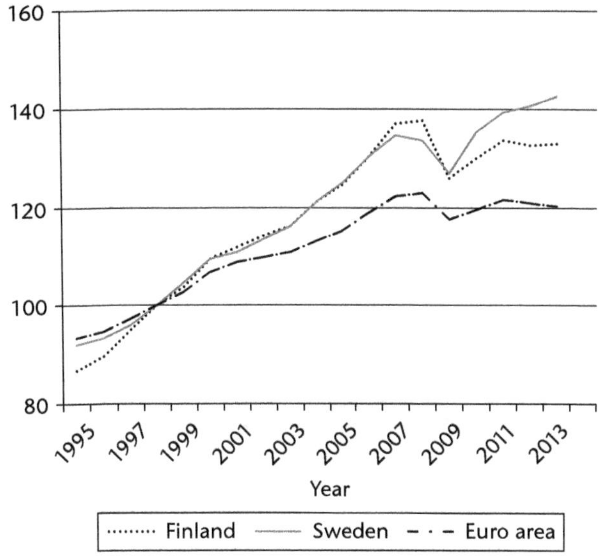

Growth, % p·a·	Finland	Sweden	Euro area
1998–2008	3,2	2,9	2,0
1998–2013	1,9	2,4	1,2

Figure 11.1. Economic performance: GDP level (1998=100)
Sources: Eurostat, European Commission (2013 Autumn Forecast).

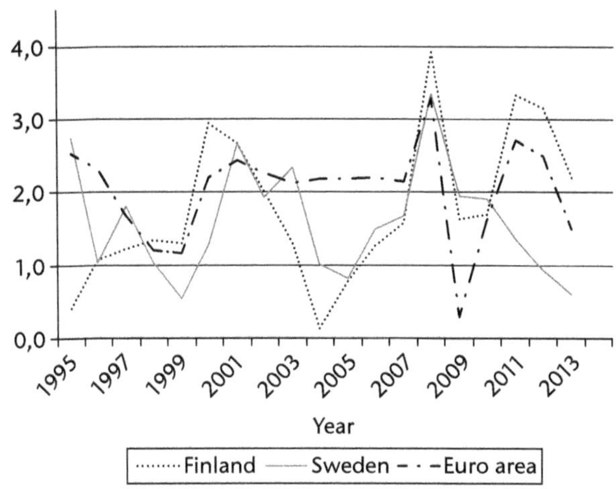

Average, % p·a·	Finland	Sweden	Euro area
1998–2008	1,8	1,7	2,1
1998–2013	2,0	1,6	2,0

Figure 11.2. Economic performance: Inflation, % p.a
Sources: Eurostat, European Commission (2013 Autumn Forecast).

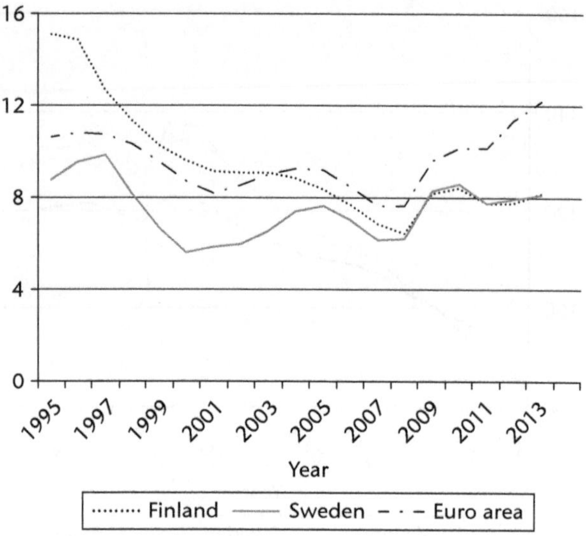

Figure 11.3. Unemployment rate, % of labour force
Source: Eurostat, European Commission (2013 Autumn Forecast).

in the euro area on average the rate of inflation has been slightly above 2 per cent.

There is practically no difference between the two countries as far as the broad macroeconomic performance indicators, such as growth and inflation, are concerned. Finland and Sweden have outperformed the euro area average on both accounts, despite the different choices regarding the EMU. This implies that membership in the EMU alone can hardly explain the performance or underperformance of countries. As we will argue below, what matters is the quality of institutions and the flexibility of the economy as well as the economic policies pursued.

While the overall performance of the two countries has been broadly similar in terms of growth and inflation, there are some differences regarding unemployment and current account developments. As depicted in Figure 11.3, unemployment was high in Finland in the mid 1990s. This was the legacy of the banking crisis and the deep recession. Unemployment was on a path of steady decline until recently, and it is now at the same level as in Sweden, and below the euro area average by a large margin.

The current account, which in the past used to be persistently in the deficit, has shown sizeable surpluses since the mid 1990s (Figure 11.4). In Sweden this has continued to be the case until now while Finland moved into a deficit in 2011. During the past ten years Finland has lost comparative advantage in two major sectors; the paper industry and the ICT

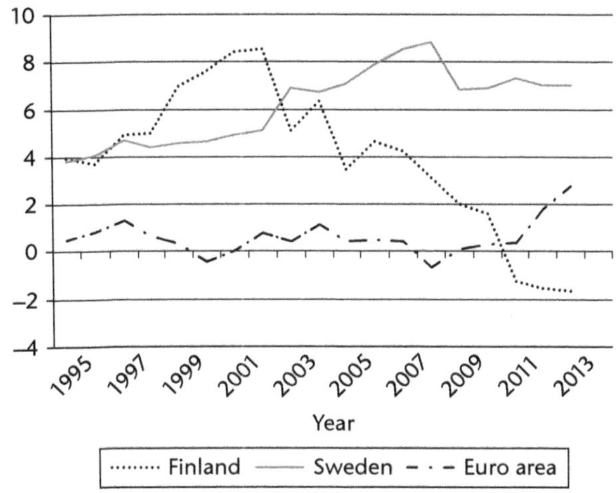

Figure 11.4. Current account, % of GDP
Source: Eurostat, European Commission (2013 Autumn Forecast).

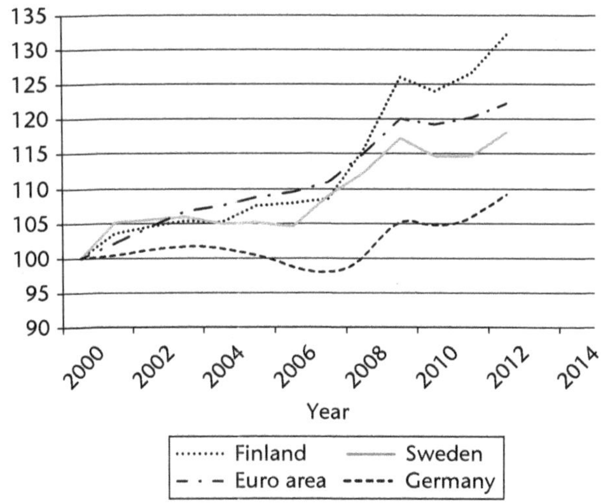

Figure 11.5. Unit labour cost (total economy) (2000=100)
Source: Eurostat.

industry. Sweden has been affected by the same developments, but because of its broader industrial base these industries are not as dominant as they have been in Finland. Also, Finland has lost cost competitiveness in recent years, not only in relation to Germany but also in relation to Sweden (Figure 11.5).

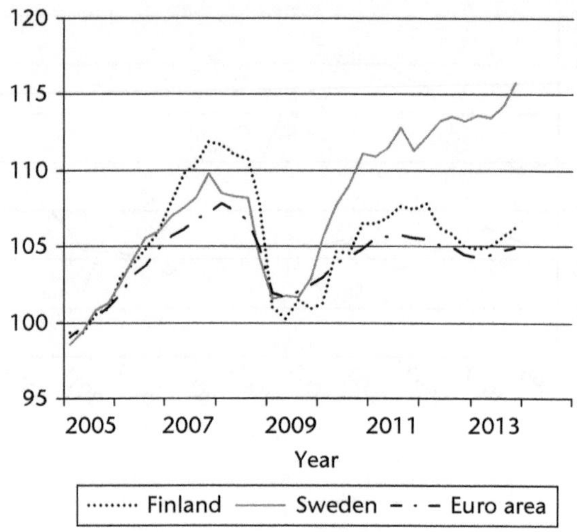

Figure 11.6. The recession experience: GDP (2005=100)
Source: Eurostat, European Commission (2013 Autumn Forecast).

11.2.3 *The Recession Experience*

Finland and Sweden were badly hit by the global financial crisis in the autumn of 2008. Both countries witnessed a sharp decline in GDP (Figure 11.6). In relative terms the fall in output was more pronounced in Finland than in Sweden. A noteworthy difference emerged in the recovery phase. The Swedish recovery was sharp, and total output reached the pre-recession level by 2011, while Finland's GDP still lies below the previous peak.

Both countries are highly dependent on international trade, and therefore they were hit hard by the sharp drop in world trade. As seen in Figure 11.7 the fall of exports in Finland was deeper than in Sweden, partly because the preceding growth had been largely based on exports of capital goods. These exports collapsed due to the sudden halt of investment activity globally. However, adjusted for the differences in the structure of exports (that of Sweden being more broadly based) the decline of export volumes was of the same order of magnitude in both countries. The sharp depreciation of the Swedish currency may have supported profitability of the export industry, but this weakness of the currency proved to be short-lived and hardly had time to affect export volumes significantly. The recovery of exports took place at the same time as the currency was appreciating. In mid 2012 Sweden's competitiveness started to deteriorate as a result of a sharp appreciation of the currency.

In both countries the effect of the global recession on private consumption was relatively mild and temporary. In both countries private consumption exceeds the previous peak by a clear margin, while in the euro area as a

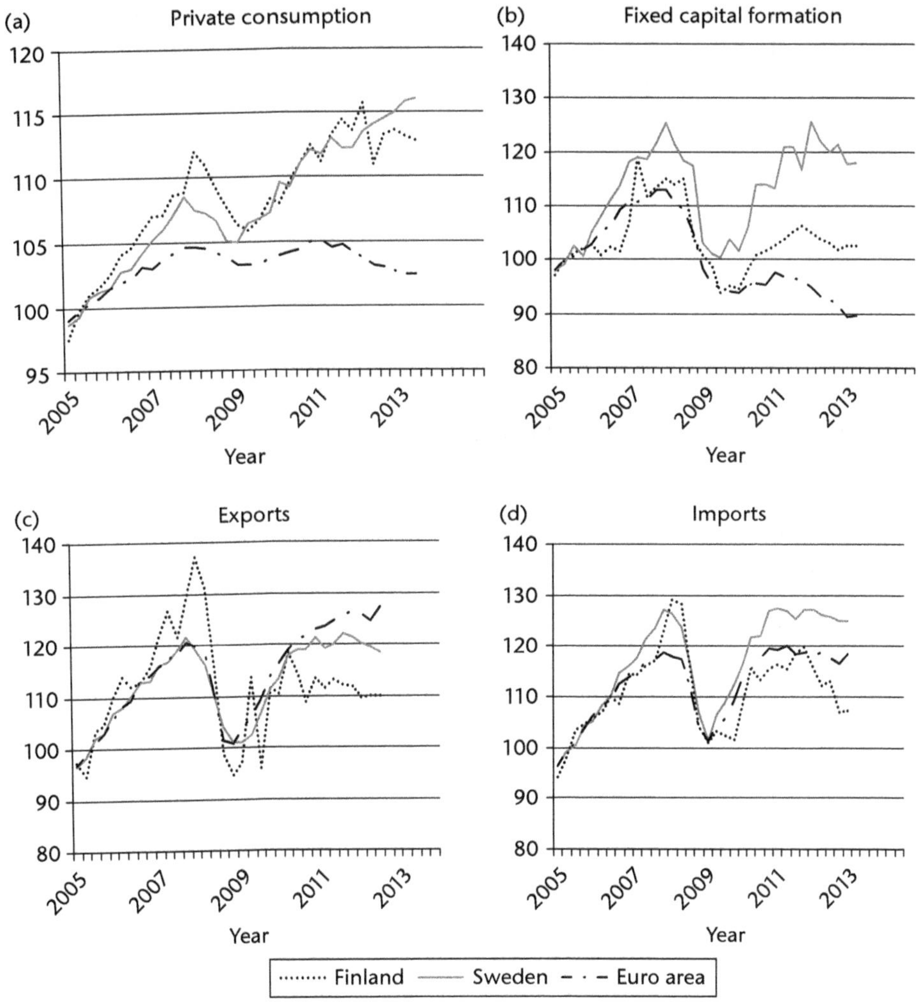

Figure 11.7. The recession experience, GDP components, 2005–13
Source: Eurostat.

whole it has remained stagnant for more than five years. In Sweden the recovery was broadly based, with consumption, investment, and exports all contributing to the it. The recovery of exports took place at the same time as the currency was appreciating. The decline in imports in 2009 was of the same magnitude in Finland and Sweden. In Sweden the imports have recovered above the pre-crisis level, while in Finland imports have stagnated.

Finland's relative underperformance vis à vis Sweden during the recovery phase can be accounted for mainly by weak export growth and anemic investment. The weak export performance of Finland reflects mainly the structural factors, such as the loss of comparative advantage in the paper and ICT industries, as well as deteriorated competitiveness since 2007. We have no good explanation for the recent weakness of investment except the excess capacity and weak demand.

The picture emerging from this descriptive analysis does not contradict the one painted by Suni and Vihriälä (2013). A novelty in their study is the use of an econometric multi-country model (NIGEM) to simulate a counterfactual assuming that Sweden would have participated in the EMU from the beginning. Under this assumption the Riksbank would have pursued exactly the same monetary policy as the ECB, and that the krona exchange rate would have been in a stable relation to the euro. The simulation exercise does not point out any significant effects. The GDP is slightly lower in 2009–11, mainly due to lower domestic demand (higher interest rate) and stronger imports. Interestingly, exports in the counterfactual deviate very little from the factual development, despite a sharp depreciation in 2009 and sharp appreciation thereafter. The overall conclusion of their study is the same as ours, according to which the different choices with regard to the EMU have not affected macroeconomic performance very much (at least not so far).

11.3 Macroeconomic Policies

This section will compare the macroeconomic or fiscal and monetary policies of Finland and Sweden with each other as well as with the policies pursued in other EU15 countries. Obviously, Finland is not running a monetary policy of its own, as monetary policy is decided upon by the European Central Bank (ECB).

11.3.1 *Monetary Policy*

Repeated speculative attacks against the currency forced the Bank of Finland to abandon the pegged exchange rate regime in September 1992. The immediate effect of the decision to float was an effective (trade-weighted) depreciation of the Finnish markka by about 15 per cent. This came on top of the discrete devaluation by some 10 per cent in November 1991. Sweden followed suit two months later; the Riksbank abandoned the peg in November 1992. The immediate effect was a depreciation of the krona by about 10 per cent.[6]

[6] The early experience of floating exchange rates and inflation targeting in Finland and Sweden is described in Pikkarainen et al. (1997) and Berg and Gröttheim (1997), both published in BIS Policy Paper No. 2—Monetary Policy in the Nordic Countries: Experiences Since 1992.

The Finnish currency was in a free fall until February 1993, when the Bank of Finland announced an inflation target of 2 per cent to be achieved by 1995. In Sweden the central bank had made a similar move one month earlier. Thereafter the Finnish markka was on an appreciating trend until 1995. The Swedish krona continued to depreciate very gradually until 1995 when the trend turned.

In both countries the inflation target of 2 per cent was achieved well before the 1995 deadline. In Finland the rate of inflation was in fact below the target (close to zero) for many years in the mid 1990s. In both countries low inflation quickly became widely accepted as a societal goal and well anchored in expectations. Interest rates declined sharply in the course of 1993. In Finland this was helped by the expectation of an appreciation of the currency as the central bank was restoring its foreign exchange reserves.

Although the floating-exchange-rate regime with inflation targeting proved to be a success, Finland started to orientate itself towards EMU membership in the mid 1990s. In October 1996 the Finnish markka was linked to the European exchange rate mechanism ERM. In early 1997 there was some speculation about a realignment (revaluation) of the markka before the final fixing of the conversion rates expected to take place in May 1998. The Bank of Finland engaged in huge interventions to prevent appreciation of the currency. As of the beginning of 1999 national monetary policy was history in Finland.

The Swedish central bank has successfully continued to maintain inflation targeting with a numerical target of 2 per cent and a ±1 per cent tolerance interval. The implementation of the inflation-targeting strategy has been fine-tuned over the years. Based on the ideas of Svensson (1997) the Riksbank has adopted a version of inflation forecast targeting, where the central bank forecasts the future interest rate path consistent with the achievement of the inflation target. Since 2007, the Riksbank has published its interest rate path (with uncertainty bands) together with its inflation forecast.[7]

The ECB's primary objective is price stability. The Governing Council has given an operational definition for price stability. According to this definition the rate of increase of the harmonized index of consumer prices (HICP) in the euro area should stay below two per cent but close to it in the medium term. This is an asymmetric inflation target compared to the Riksbank's two per cent target with a ±1 per cent tolerance interval.

While the Riksbank publishes the interest rate path consistent with the inflation forecast, the ECB has so far been much more restrictive regarding the details of its inflation outlook, not to mention the likely interest rate

[7] This kind of approach was first adopted by the central bank of Norway. By its proponents it is called 'the best-practice monetary policy' (Svensson, 2006).

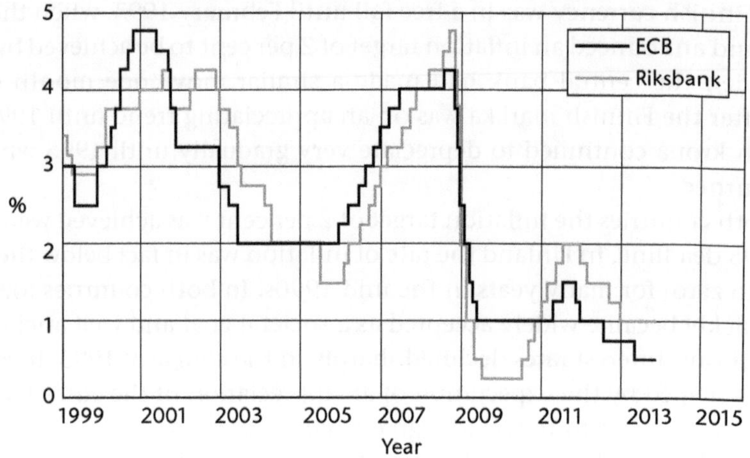

Figure 11.8. Central bank policy rates
Source: Bloomberg.

path in the future. Quantitatively the difference between the price stability objective of the ECB and the Riksbank is not large. It follows that if the cyclical development in Sweden is closely correlated with that in the euro area the interest rate policies are likely to exhibit a rather synchronous pattern.

This is what we see in the data (Figure 11.8). The interest rate cycle in Sweden has been broadly similar to that in the euro area. In 2000 the ECB's monetary policy was slightly more aggressive than in Sweden, which is consistent with the inflation outlook at the time. The ECB started the easing cycle in 2001 with the Riksbank following one year later. More recently Riksbank's monetary policy has been slightly more aggressive. During the tightening cycle in 2006–8, the Riksbank followed the ECB with a lag of one to two months. Both central banks quickly reversed the stance once the global financial crisis erupted in October 2008. The Riksbank went all the way close to the zero lower bound, while the ECB then stopped at the one per cent level. In practice the shortest money market rates in the euro area were equally low as in Sweden due to the unconventional monetary policy of the ECB (longer maturities and fixed-rate full-allocation provision of liquidity). The recent relative tightening in Sweden is consistent with differences in the cyclical situation. Sweden is recovering from the recession while the euro area is suffering from recessionary tendencies fed by the sovereign debt crisis.

Despite the fact that the euro and the krona are both floating currencies, the exchange rate between them has remained fairly stable since the introduction of the euro in 1999 (Figure 11.9). Between 2001 and early 2008 the

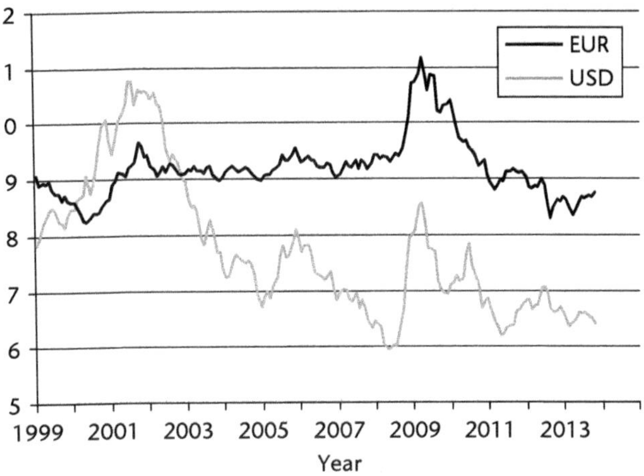

Figure 11.9. SEK exchange rates
Source: Riksbank.

euro traded in the krona 9 to 9.50 range. At the same time both currencies appreciated trend-wise vis à vis the US dollar.

There are, however, three interesting episodes in the euro/krona exchange rate path since 1999. The first is in 1999 and 2000 when the krona appreciated quite strongly against the euro. This reflects the unexpected weakness of the euro in the beginning of its life as a currency. At the same time, the Swedish economy was buoyant due to the global boom in the ICT sector. If Finland had maintained its own currency it is likely that the markka would have appreciated strongly in 1999–2000, that is in the period when foreigners started to buy the stocks of Finnish companies, especially Nokia.

The second interesting period is late 2008 when the krona depreciated sharply against the euro. This hurt some Finnish industries (e.g. the paper and wood industry) for a while. Depreciation did not prevent the Swedish exports from falling significantly; in fact the collapse of exports was of the same magnitude as in Finland if one takes differences in the export structure into account. More recently the krona has appreciated strongly, reflecting in part the fact that Sweden is perceived as one of the few safe havens in Europe.

The Lehman Brothers episode in September 2008 marked an abrupt stop to the normal functioning of the global financial markets. The effects were felt everywhere, including in the Nordic countries. The main effect in Europe was that the banks faced increasing difficulties to refinance their assets in the market.

In order to ensure the liquidity of the banking system, the central banks had to intervene. The ECB started to offer longer-term refinancing for banks (against collateral) on the fixed-rate full-allocation basis. This led to a sharp

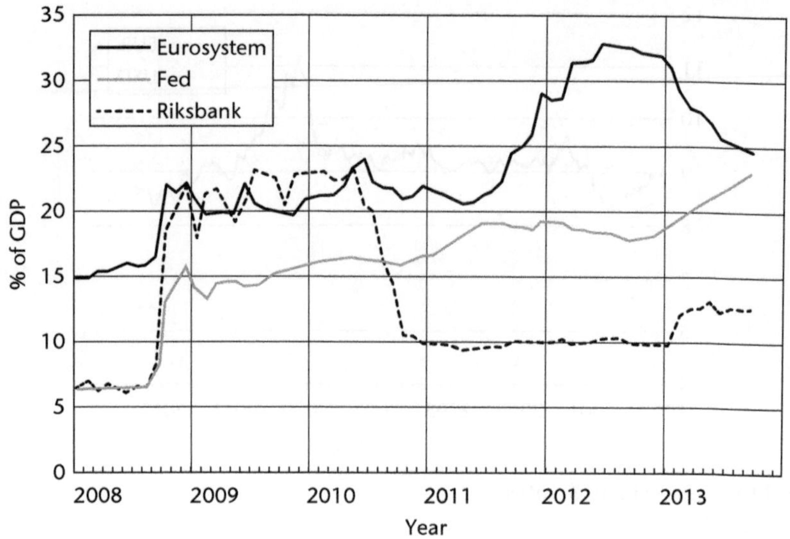

Figure 11.10. Central bank balance sheets, % of GDP
Sources: Eurostat and Bloomberg.

expansion of the Eurosystem balance sheet in October 2008. Later the Eurosystem introduced the covered bond purchasing programme and the securities market purchasing programme in order to improve the transmission of monetary policy. In the end of 2011 and the beginning of 2012 the Eurosystem balance sheet expanded further as a result of two three-year operations. As a result the Eurosystem balance sheet expanded first by 5 per cent in relation to GDP and later by a further 15 per cent in the autumn of 2011.

The situation was no different in Sweden in the autumn of 2008 as regards the funding situation of banks. As longer-term refinancing in the market became impossible, the Riksbank increased its lending to banks both in Swedish krona and US dollars (facilitated by the swap arrangement with the Fed). The collateral rules were relaxed for the banks' central bank financing and the number of counterparties was increased. Finally the Riksbank extended one-year lending to banks at fixed interest rates in three tranches (SEK 100 billion each). As a result the Riksbank's balance sheet expanded by 20 per cent in relation to GDP (Figure 11.10).

The Swedish central bank succeeded to make a smooth exit from the unconventional monetary policy measures in the latter half of 2010, as the banks' funding situation improved and the three one-year operations expired. This is not the case in the euro area, where the interbank market does not function properly across borders and a large number of banks have continued to face funding difficulties. The situation started to improve in the letter half of 2012. Between mid 2012 and autumn 2013 the size of the Eurosystem

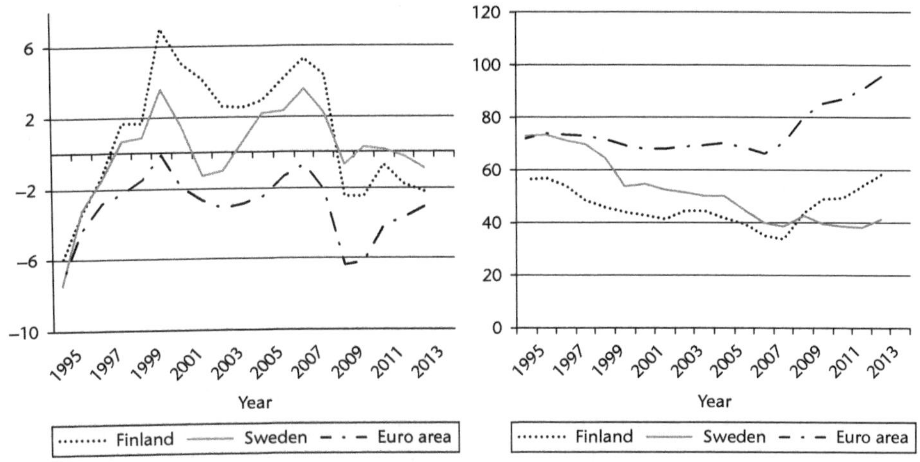

Average, %	Finland	Sweden	Euro area
1998–2008	3,8	1,4	−1,9
1998–2013	2,0	0,9	−2,8

Average, %	Finland	Sweden	Euro area
1998–2008	41,9	52,0	69,4
1998–2013	44,7	48,2	75,1

Figure 11.11. Public deficit and debt, % of GDP

balance sheet diminished by 8 per cent of GDP reflecting the diminution of the banks' excess reserves which had risen to record levels as a result of the two allocations of the long-term (36-month) refinancing operations (LTRO) in December 2011 and February 2012.

The Bank of Finland's balance sheet expanded markedly in late 2011 and early 2012. The reason, however, was not the funding difficulties of the banks operating in Finland (many of which are Nordic-owned). In fact, the banks were holding huge amounts of excess liquidity in the form of overnight and term-deposits with the Bank of Finland. The main counterpart of these deposits on the asset side of the balance sheet is the Target2 balances which are claims of the Bank of Finland on the ECB.[8] Most of these excess reserves disappeared in the course of 2013.

11.3.2 *Fiscal Policy*

From late 1990s until the recession in 2009, both countries were running sizeable surpluses (Figure 11.11). As a result the public debt ratio was on a declining trend. In Finland the fiscal balance turned into deficit during the

[8] Target2 is the payments systems of the Eurosystem. In October 2012 The Bank of Finland had in this system a receivable of EUR 61 billion, which is formally a claim of the Bank of Finland on the ECB. On the liability side were the banks' balances on their current accounts (EUR 31 billion, including minimum reserves), banks' overnight deposits (EUR 16 billion), and term deposits (EUR 18 billion). One year later, in October 2013, the Bank of Finland's claim on the ECB in the form of Target2 balances had diminished to EUR 16 billion.

recession, while in Sweden it has remained more or less in balance and the debt ratio has continued to fall.

The problems faced in decision-making on fiscal policies have changed significantly during the past 25 years. As already noted, in the late 1980s and early 1990s Finland and Sweden experienced a period of boom and bust associated with a banking and currency crisis. Fiscal policies were tightened somewhat in the last years of the 1980s in both Finland and Sweden, but the degree of tightening was insufficient to offset the effects of rapid credit expansion. The subsequent decline of the GDP gave rise to large output gaps (Figure 11.12).

According to the OECD's measure of the fiscal impulse (the change in the cyclically adjusted general government balance), there was some discretionary easing of fiscal policy in the same years, significantly more so in Sweden than in Finland. One of the reasons for the cautious fiscal policy stance in Finland was the lack of confidence in the international financial markets in Finnish banks and also in the credit worthiness of the Finnish government in the light of the big current account deficit, rapidly increasing budget deficit, and weak competitiveness. Emphasis on fiscal consolidation was felt to be necessary to contain further rises in interest rates and an even sharper process of deflation (declines in prices of real estate).

Starting in 1994, both countries initiated comprehensive programs of fiscal consolidation. This was made easier by the large currency depreciations and the favourable growth in world markets. By 1998 Sweden had improved it cyclically adjusted balance by close to 10 per cent of GDP and Finland by slightly above 5 per cent. In Finland the cyclically adjusted balance continued to strengthen, reflecting in part the unexpected and extraordinary revenue growth related to the ICT boom.

The first decade of the monetary union was in many of its member states characterized by lax and pro-cyclical fiscal policies. Finland and Sweden stand out, however, as countries which have pursued mainly counter-cyclical policies and which have also maintained significant general government financial surpluses over that period (Figure 11.13) (Gylfason et al., 2010, p. 43).

Consequently, the level of public indebtedness declined markedly and to relatively favourable levels in these two countries. Table 11.1 reports the change in the level of public debt from 1996 to 2011 in terms of both the net and the gross debt, as these in some cases give quite different results.[9] The

[9] Finland is a case in point, as the decline in the net debt ratio is much larger than in the gross debt. This partly reflects the growth of social security (pension) funds and a reallocation of pension funds from holdings of government bonds into holdings of equity. As government gross debt is reported on a consolidated basis, government debt held by social security funds is netted out. Obviously, gross debt does not consider government assets, which notably in the Nordic countries are of significant size. Valuation effects are another important factor affecting notably the net debt position; see Flodén (2012).

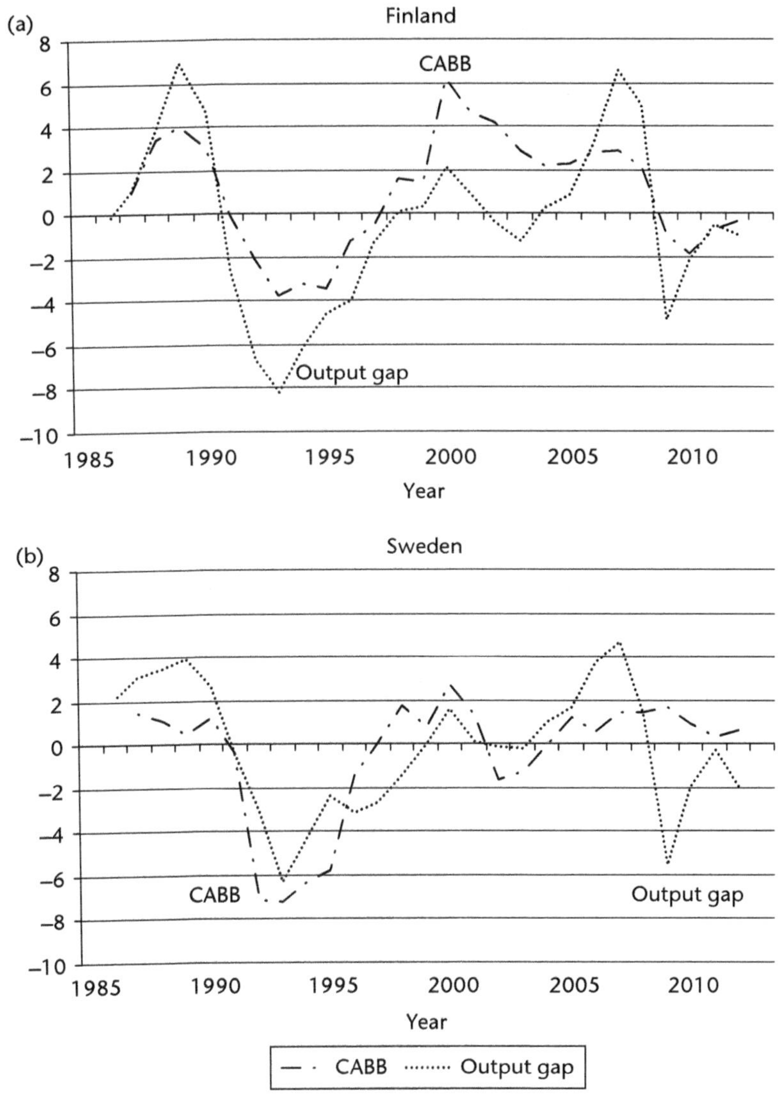

Figure 11.12. Output gap and the general government cyclically adjusted budget balance (CABB), % of GDP

decline in the debt ratio was large in the Nordic countries and notably so for the net debt ratio.

Also, the overall tax rate declined in the last decade, though it remains higher in Sweden than in other countries (except Denmark). Notably, the tax wedge on labour was reduced more than in other countries, which most likely helped to raise employment rates, as seen in the right-hand column of Table 11.1.

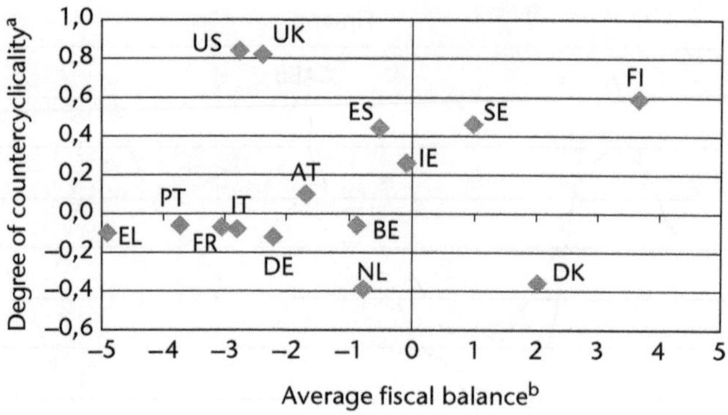

Figure 11.13. Fiscal policy and consolidation 1999–2008

[a] Correlation coefficient of output gap and fiscal impulse measured by change in cyclically adjusted budget balance, % of GDP.

[b] General government financial balance on average in 1999–2008, % of GDP.

Source: OECD Economic Outlook No 86, November.

Fiscal policy has recently been confronted with the consequences of the global financial crisis and the euro area debt crisis. Almost all governments initiated fiscal expansion in 2008–9 in response to the sharp decline in the economy. The amount of fiscal expansion in Finland in 2008–10 amounted to some 5 per cent of GDP. In Sweden, however, the amount of fiscal expansion was barely one per cent of GDP. This contrasts with Swedish history and may be seen as remarkable as Sweden had (and still has) a strong competitive position, is running large current account surpluses, and has no inflationary pressure and a comfortable budgetary position. A natural interpretation is that Sweden, given the flexible exchange rate, now prefers to meet a slump by monetary easing rather than fiscal expansion.

As will be explained below, fiscal consolidation in the 1990s was associated with significant structural reform, including reforms of the fiscal framework. These reforms reinforced the process of fiscal consolidation and helped to put it on a sustainable basis. It would be tempting to conclude from the experiences of Finland and Sweden that other countries in crisis, notably today in Southern Europe, could follow the same strategy and thereby succeed in getting their economies on a path of reform and growth. As has been pointed out by, e.g., Flodén (2012), however, the situation is far from comparable and the current problems of Southern Europe look much more severe. Not only is the current level of public debt much higher in the crisis countries today than was the case in Finland and Sweden in the 1990s, but also the demographic challenge is now much more demanding. Furthermore, the international environment is unhelpful in that external demand growth is weak. And above all, the crisis countries cannot depreciate and thereby

Table 11.1. Debt ratio and tax wedge on labour

	General government debt. % of GDP						Tax wedge on wage income		
	Gross			Net					
	1996	2011	Δ	2000	2011	Δ	2000	2011	Δ
	68.1	72.4	+4.3	40.2	45.2	+5.0	47.3	48.4	+1.1
Belgium	127.2	97.8	−30.5	115.3	80.4	−34.9	57.1	55.6	−1.5
Denmark	69.4	46.6	−22.8	33.3	2.4	−30.9	44.1	38.4	−5.7
Finland	**57.0**	**49.0**	**−8.0**	**−6.7**	**−60.9**	**−53.8**	**47.8**	**42.7**	**−5.1**
France	58.0	86.0	+28.0	41.9	62.7	+20.8	49.6	49.4	−0.2
Germany	58.5	80.5	+22.0	32.7	51.5	+18.8	52.9	49.8	−3.1
Greece	99.4	170.6	+71.0	82.2	133.1	+50.9	35.2	38.2	+3.0
Ireland	71.7	106.4	+34.7	42.2	65.0	+22.8	28.9	26.8	−2.1
Italy	120.2	120.7	+0.5	103.9	100.2	−3.7	47.1	47.6	+0.5
Netherlands	74.1	65.5	−8.6	52.7	37.7	−15.0	40.0	37.8	−2.2
Portugal	58.2	108.1	+49.9	26.5	75.8	+49.3	37.3	39.0	+1.7
Spain	67.4	69.3	+1.9	55.5	45.5	−10.0	38.6	39.9	+1.3
Sweden	**73.3**	**38.4**	**−34.9**	**26.6**	**−24.9**	**−51.5**	**50.1**	**42.8**	**−7.3**
UK	51.3	85.0	+33.7	27.9	61.7	+44.0	32.6	32.5	−0.1

Sources: Floden (2012) and OECD.

engineer a process of export-led growth as was done by Finland and Sweden in the late 1990s.

11.4 Institutions and Structural Policies

As set out by Esping-Andersen (1990), the Nordic model (or the social democratic model) differs in certain respects from the other members of the family of European socio-economic models. In our view the Nordic model is characterized by three broad features (Andersen et al., 2007 and Gylfason et al., 2010). One of these is a set of labour market institutions that include a high unionization rate, a strong role for labour market organizations in negotiations, significant elements of wage coordination, relatively generous unemployment benefits, and a prominent role for active labour market policies. A second feature is the high level of public and/or private spending on investment in human capital, including childcare and education as well as R&D. Third, the Nordics maintain a comprehensive and inclusive welfare state, based (largely) on universalist principles, with emphasis on transfers to households and publicly provided social services financed by high taxes. While classifications are always open to objections (as all countries are unique), it is a fact that the Nordics in international comparisons tend to form a cluster of their own, though some other small and open countries (notably the Netherlands) also share many of their characteristics.

As noted above, Finland and Sweden both experienced a banking crisis and a depression in the early 1990s. The crisis management in the early 1990s has been the focus of much attention, notably so for the handling of the banking crisis. Both countries undertook a number of important measures to safeguard the functioning of their banking systems, and this was surely instrumental in facilitating the subsequent recovery (see, e.g. Honkapohja 2009 and Gylfason et al. 2010). By contrast, one of the most regrettable aspects of the handling of the current euro-area debt crisis is that action with regard to the banking system has in many countries been lacking or insufficient. (This is also a striking difference when comparing crisis management in the US and the EU.)

One key factor in the recovery process was undoubtedly the large depreciation of the currencies which followed upon the abolition of the pegged exchange rate regime. As noted above, the large improvement in competitiveness, in combination with growth in international markets, was instrumental in creating a strong process of export-led growth in the latter part of the 1990s.

A long-lasting consequence of the crisis was that it paved the way for a number of structural reforms. Most of these were undertaken more or less in parallel and they were often rather similar, partly because they were stimulated by international developments (such as the US tax reform in the 1980s) or because authorities in Finland were encouraged by initiatives in Sweden. The most important structural reforms were probably those concerning the tax system and the pension system as well as the frameworks of monetary and fiscal policies. Many of these reforms were proposed and discussed in the report of the so called Lindbeck Commission (Lindbeck et al., 1994).

Both countries undertook *tax reforms* with the aim of broadening the tax bases and reducing marginal rates. Most importantly, the dual tax system was introduced, meaning that capital income was taxed at a proportional tax rate (of 30 per cent in Sweden and 25 per cent initially in Finland). Finland also introduced the *avoir fiscal system* such that the double taxation of corporate income was eliminated. (Subsequently the *avoir fiscal system* has been abolished but the dual tax system retained.) This constituted a big change as compared to the earlier system with generous depreciation allowances and double taxation of dividends in combination with no tax on capital gains on holdings exceeding ten years. The new tax system made it possible to reallocate resources arising out of profits across companies and sectors, thus facilitating a process of 'creative destruction' and the transformation towards an economy relying on high-tech exports.

Work was started on reforms of the compulsory *pension system*. In Sweden this led to a changeover from a defined benefit to a defined contribution system that was adopted in 1999. This pension reform is a benchmark case and has attracted a lot of international interest; cf. Holzman and Palmer (2003). It is believed to have put the Swedish pension system on a sustainable footing, avoiding the need for increases in the contribution rate in coming decades in spite of ageing populations. The reform of the Finnish pension system was less radical and was implemented as late as in 2005, but notably the introduction of a life expectancy parameter cutting monthly pensions as life expectancy increases (an idea borrowed from the Swedish reform) will help to reduce pressure on contribution rates.

The *fiscal framework* was modernized in both countries, notably by introducing multiannual expenditure ceilings. Sweden also introduced a surplus target for public finances and balanced-budget requirements for municipalities. Most importantly, a tradition has emerged in which the prime minister and the minister of finance generally cooperate to ensure that the budget ceiling is respected. This practice has been strongly established in both countries.

More recently, in 2007, Sweden introduced a fiscal policy council. In accordance with the requirements of the so called Fiscal Compact, Finland has recently established such a council. It is an open issue whether the fiscal policy council is essential for enhancing budget discipline. However, the fiscal council should be helpful in improving transparency of policies and the quality of public debate.

Both countries reformed the *monetary framework* by setting up independent central banks with inflation targets and operating in a regime of floating exchange rates. This may partly be seen as a consequence of the decision to join the EU (in 1995) but it also reflects the traumatic experiences of the preceding pegged exchange rate regime.

Other actions undertaken aimed at improving competition on markets for goods and services and to improve the functioning of labour markets. Sweden also prolonged election periods of the Parliament from three to four years. A specific feature of Finnish policies was the relatively strong increase in government spending on R&D in the midst of the crisis and in spite of cuts in most government spending and rises in tax rates. This contributed to a rapid structural change, as a result of which the export structure became more broadly based, reducing the country's dependence on the forest-based industries.

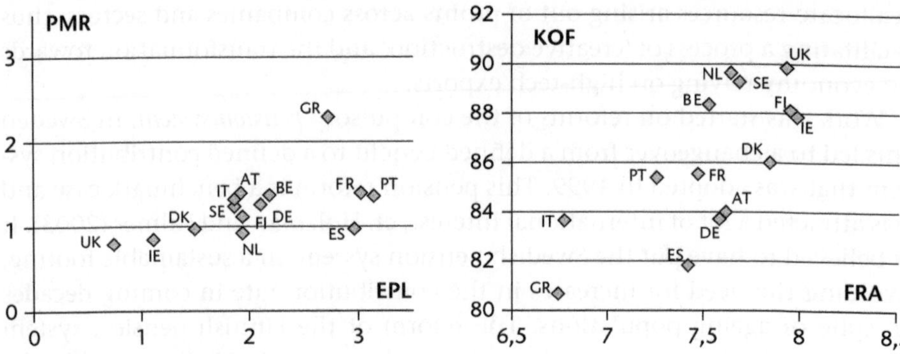

Figure 11.14. Structural indicators (2008)
Source: OECD Konjunkturforschungsstelle (EHT Zurich) and Fraser Institute.

In all, these structural reforms helped to transform the economy in a liberal or market-friendly direction—something which had not been a trade mark of these countries in earlier decades. It should be stressed that the process had already begun with the financial deregulation in the 1980s and was then followed by the reforms initiated during the depression in the 1990s. While the pace may have slowed, the Nordics have now established themselves as countries that combine a comprehensive welfare state with a low level of regulation of markets. The latter point is illustrated in Figure 11.14, which shows the degree of regulation in the 'old' EU member states (except for Luxemburg), which constitute a reasonable reference point when making cross-country comparisons.

The first indicator is the OECD indicator of product market regulation (PMR) and the second is the OECD indicator on employment protection legislation (EPL). As is seen, the regulatory policies of the Nordic member states of the EU are in general more liberal than in other countries, except for the UK and Ireland.

The general impression is that the Nordics are running structural policies geared towards allowing markets to function effectively. The continental countries and notably the countries in Southern Europe impose more heavy regulation, although this has started to change as a consequence of the crisis experience in recent years.

The Fraser index of economic freedom and the KOF index of globalization have been widely used in economic research (Bergh and Henrekson, 2012). In particular, an increase in one or both of these factors should be conducive to a favourable growth performance (Dreher, 2006). The right-hand part of Figure 11.14 depicts the changes in economic freedom from the year 1980 to 2000 and in globalization from 1978 to 1998 (a slightly different time period because of data availability). We choose this time period because financial liberalization in Finland and notably in Sweden started in the early 1980s, and as the structural reforms triggered by the depression in the early 1990s were by and large implemented by the end of the decade.

The KOF index used here measures the regulatory aspect of globalization in terms of restrictions on trade and capital. The Fraser index is a summary index measuring economic freedom in terms of the size of government, the legal system and property rights, sound money, freedom of trade, and regulation. Following Bergh (2006), we exclude the first component in our index of economic freedom. After all, the impact on growth of the size of the public sector will depend crucially on how revenues are spent. For instance, during the depression Finland increased spending on R&D while making cuts to social spending. In addition, a significant proportion of public spending in the Nordic countries is spent in a manner which directly raises the labour supply (e.g. day care of children).[10]

As can be seen, Sweden was for two decades the country experiencing the fastest rate of globalization and Finland was number two. Economic freedom increased most in Ireland and Denmark, but Sweden was number three and Finland number five (with the UK in between as number four). Taken together, it might be argued that Sweden and Finland had a particularly impressive combination of deepening globalization and increasing economic freedom.[11]

While we make no attempt at explaining relative growth performance, we think it is likely that these developments contributed to the generally favourable economic performance that Finland and Sweden experienced in the period up to 2008 (when financial turmoil erupted).

11.5 EMU: Better to be In or Out?

The setting up of an economic and monetary union in its current form, a currency without a state, is a historically unique experiment. After its first decade in existence EMU was widely considered a success. Yet, only a few years later the euro area was risking financial collapse. Most of its member

[10] The relative performance of Finland would be slightly weaker without this adjustment. Also, the performance of Sweden and notably of Finland is less impressive if comparisons are made using more recent observations. This is compatible with the hypothesis that the depression of the 1990s was of particular importance for structural policies and developments.

[11] This statement is consistent with a similar chart by Bergh and Henreksson (2012, p. 120), though they cover a somewhat different set of countries and a longer time period.

states are in a recession, and some in a depression with unemployment of more than 25 per cent. Political tensions between and within member states are increasing, and there is disagreement concerning the proper mission and mandate of the ECB.

Much time and effort will be needed to disentangle the experiences with a view to drawing conclusions about the causes of the problems and the best remedies. The lack of the counterfactual makes it very hard to assess these issues and to evaluate the degree of success or failure of the whole project.

Finland and Sweden joined the EU too late to be in a position to influence the Maastricht treaty or the main architecture of the EMU. Given that it was being set up, they nevertheless had to decide on their own attitude to EMU. The governments of both countries set up expert committees to evaluate the likely consequences of going in or staying out of EMU. The Swedish Calmfors Commission acknowledged the efficiency advantages of a common currency but argued that the risk of mistakes in wage-setting and/or in fiscal policy in Sweden spoke against joining at the time (Calmfors et al. 1997). (With the benefit of hindsight one might argue that the Commission may have come to the right conclusion, but not for the right reasons.) The Finnish Pekkarinen commission did not directly take a stand on whether Finland should join but rather discussed measures to improve fiscal consolidation and resilience of the economy in the face of shocks (Prime Minister's Office 1997).

The experiences of Finland and Sweden of the pegged exchange rate regime were a source of frustration. In retrospect it seems almost inevitable that the regime had to be abandoned. As is well known from the 'impossible trinity', a fixed exchange rate is incompatible with free capital movements and the ambition to run an autonomous monetary policy. Interestingly, Finland and Sweden would seem to have drawn different conclusions from this: Finland gave up its monetary policy, while Sweden abandoned the fixed exchange rate.

However, economic considerations or the views of these expert committees were not decisive regarding the membership in the EMU. Both countries made their decisions primarily on the basis of political factors. Finland joined the EU in order to clarify its geopolitical identity, having lived for many decades in the problematic shadow of the Soviet Union. Given the possibility, the Finnish political and economic establishment wanted to join not only the EU but also its 'hard core', the EMU. In Sweden there were no similar considerations to support membership in the EMU, and after a referendum with a negative outcome the Swedish government decided to stay outside for the time being. It is our contention that the decisions on EMU membership were not due to differences in economic structure; they rather reflect differences in political appreciations of EMU.

Which country made the better choice? As seen in Section 2 above, economic developments in Finland and Sweden have been quite similar. Also, where differences emerge, these can mostly be better explained by other factors than the difference in the monetary regime. The main impression is that differences in the monetary regime have not been associated with great differences in economic performance in Finland as compared to Sweden. This is compatible with a broad interpretation of the traditional view that money is 'neutral' in the long run. However, this observation contradicts claims, made in the heated debates on EMU in the years before the single currency came into operation, that EMU would be either a curse (opponents) or a salvation (protagonists). Our conclusion, with a number of caveats, is that the institutions of the socio-economic model at large and the economic policies pursued are more important than the monetary regime as such.

One caveat is that the conclusion may hold only for countries pursuing relatively 'sound' economic policies; for countries unable to 'keep their house in order', being outside the euro area may be a less risky alternative than joining the euro. Given the experiences and prospects of countries like Greece and Spain it is hard to foresee a turnaround sufficiently robust to avoid thinking that the cumulative amount of problems might have been less if these countries had experienced neither the low interest rates following upon entry into the euro area nor the subsequent difficulties of restoring competitiveness and the high interest rates associated with their debt problems.

A related caveat is that a credible national central bank may help support wage moderation. Swedish labour market organizations are aware of the risk that excessive wage inflation will trigger a tightening of monetary policy of the Riksbank. In Finland there is no similar feedback from wage behaviour to interest rates. This is conceivably a factor weakening wage discipline in Finland as compared to Sweden (in otherwise comparable labour market situations). Recent developments suggest this concern may not be unfounded.[12]

A further caveat is that membership may also conceivably turn into a real liability for Finland if the debt crisis of the euro area is seriously mismanaged and the monetary union is in one way or another transformed into a 'transfer union'. This could happen through OSI (official sector involvement) in debt restructurings (or through inflation). As part of the various rescue packages the Finnish government has given guarantees and loans amounting by now

[12] This argument has been elaborated upon by Holden (2002) and Vartiainen (2002). Interestingly, Denmark also maintains the fixed exchange rate, but has been successful in

to some 10 per cent of GDP—even if the TARGET balance of the Bank of Finland were to be disregarded.[13] While the sums are large, however, they would even in a bad scenario amount to only a fraction of a per cent in terms of the sustainability gap of public finances. The main risk, for Finland as well as for Sweden, is a collapse of the EMU, which would trigger a Europe-wide banking crisis and depression.

Another path to a transfer union would be to introduce Eurobonds as an instrument of government borrowing for the euro area as a whole. However, this would require a change of the treaty and could hardly win acceptance in parliaments in Germany, the Netherlands, or (perhaps particularly) Finland. Overall the conclusion remains: although EMU may or may not have been a bad idea, its design was certainly flawed[14] and its implementation suffered from many errors; but it is not clear on the basis of experience so far that the decisions on membership of EMU have created significant differences in the performance or prospects of Finland and Sweden.

11.6 Concluding Remarks

A comparison of the economic performance of Sweden and Finland supports three conclusions that amount to rather sweeping generalizations. First, it is tempting to see a causal link from crisis to reform illustrated by the developments and economic policies in Finland and Sweden following the crisis in the early 1990s. With the benefit of hindsight, that crisis may be seen as something of a blessing in disguise. It created a political situation that allowed significant structural reforms to be undertaken, and economic policies have, since the crisis, been more successful and 'responsible' than in earlier periods.[15] Policies have been geared towards,

maintaining wage moderation, presumably because wage formation in the traded goods sector is generally accepted as a benchmark for overall wage formation.

[13] It may be noted that the current Finnish government has insisted that any guarantees or loans given by Finland must be backed up by collateral covering 40 per cent of the commitment. In effect, the collaterals have reduced the net contribution of Finland to the financial packages. On the significance of TARGET balances see de Grauwe (2012).

[14] There is no reason to enter into the debate about the proper design of EMU in this context. However, most economists would by now acknowledge that a single currency needs to be supported by some form of a banking union.

[15] One may add that the reorientation of economic policies in Finland and Sweden started before the crisis in the 1990s. After all, the crisis itself was triggered by the consequences of the deregulation of capital flows and financial markets in the 1980s. Also, the Swedish tax reform was prepared and even implemented before the crisis. These developments were inspired partly by the change in economic policy thinking, emphasizing deregulation and market efficiency. Another factor was the failure of the policy of recurrent devaluations and public-sector expansion to generate sustainable growth, which led to the adoption of the fixed exchange rate as a

inter alia, allowing or fostering structural change and maintaining sound public finances.

One would like to think that the current crisis in the southern part of the euro area will in a similar way trigger steps towards a reform path with large payoffs in future years. As pointed out above and discussed in some detail by Floden (2012), however, the crisis countries in the euro area are presently facing a more difficult situation than Finland and Sweden did in the 1990s, when the Nordics were able to benefit from large currency depreciations and favourable external conditions.

A second sweeping generalization, supported by the observations above, as well as other observations, is that the (current version of the) 'Nordic model' is relatively successful in combining equity and efficiency. While caveats and qualifications are necessary, it remains a pertinent observation that the Nordic countries seem to outperform many others in terms of a number of social and economic indicators.

A third conclusion, with certain caveats, is that the monetary regime may matter less for economic performance than often argued in the heated debate on the pros and cons of a single currency. While not constituting a laboratory experiment, a comparison of the performance of Finland and Sweden supports this contention. Admittedly, the jury is still out in the sense that Finland is now facing a structural weakness of its export base, and it remains to be seen whether domestic wage adjustment will allow this difficulty to be overcome within a reasonable time span.

References

Andersen, T., B. Holmström, S. Honkapohja, S. Korkman, H. Tson Söderström, and J. Vartiainen (2007), *The Nordic Model—Embracing Globalization and Sharing Risks,* The Research Institute of the Finnish Economy (ETLA).

Bordes, C., D. Currie, and H. Tson Söderström (1993), *Three Assessments of Finland's Economic Crisis and Economic Policy,* Helsinki: Bank of Finland Publications C:9.

Berg, C. and R. Gröttheim (1997), 'Monetary Policy in Sweden since 1992', in *Monetary policy in the Nordic countries: Experiences since 1992,* BIS Policy Papers No 2.

Bergh, A. (2006), 'Explaining Welfare State Survival: The Role of Economic Freedom and Globalization', Available at SSRN: <http://ssrn.com/abstract=897746>.

Bergh, A. and M. Henreksson (2012), *Varför går det bra för Sverige,* Stockholm: Fores+Ivrig.

key policy objective or constraint. One might also argue that the banking crisis was due mainly to the deregulation and the hard currency policy and had little to do with the problems that the structural reforms in the 1990s were meant to tackle. However, it remains the case that the crisis created the mental or political preconditions for reforms to be undertaken.

Calmfors, L., H. Flam, N. Gottfries, J. H. Matlary, M. Jerneck, R. Lindahl, C. N. Berntsson, E. Rabinowicz, and A. Vredin (1997), *EMU—A Swedish Perspective*, Dordrecht: Kluwer.

Dornbusch, R. (1976). 'Expectations and Exchange Rate Dynamics', *Journal of Political Economy* 84, pp. 1161–76.

Dreher, A. (2006), 'Does Globalization Affect Growth? Empirical Evidence from a New Index', *Applied Economics* 38, pp. 1091–110.

Esping-Andersen, G. (1990), *The Three Worlds of Welfare Capitalism*. Cambridge: Polity Press, and Princeton: Princeton University Press.

Flodén, M. (2012), 'A Role Model for the Conduct of Fiscal Policy? Experiences for Sweden', CEPR Discussion Paper 095.

Gylfason, T., B. Holmström, S. Korkman, H. Tson Söderström, and V. Vihriälä (2010), *Nordics in Global Crisis—Vulnerability and Resilience,* Helsinki: The Research Institute of the Finnish Economy (ETLA).

Holden, S. (2002), 'Wage Setting under Different Monetary Regimes', *Economica* 70, 251–66.

Holzman, R. and E. Palmer, eds (2003), *Pension Reform: Issues and Prospects for Non-Financial Defined Contribution (NDC) Schemes*, Washington D.C.: The World Bank.

Honkapohja, S. (2009), 'The 1990s Financial Crisis in Nordic Countries', Bank of Finland Discussion Papers No. 5.

Honkapohja, S., E. Koskela, W. Leibfritz, and R. Uusitalo (2009), *Economic Prosperity Recaptured: The Finnish Path from Crisis to Rapid Growth*, Cambridge Mass.: MIT Press.

Jonung, L., J. Kiander, and P. Vartia (eds) (2009), *The Great Financial Crisis in Finland and Sweden: The Nordic Experience of Financial Liberalization*, Cheltenham: Edward Elgar.

Kindleberger, C. and R. Aliber (2011), *Manias, Panics, and Crashes* (sixth edn), New York: Palgrave MacMillan.

Lindbeck. A., P. Molander, T. Persson, O. Peterson, A. Sandmo, B. Swdenborg, and N. Thygesen (1994), *Turning Sweden Around,* Cambridge, Mass.: MIT Press (In Swedish SOU 1993:16, 1993).

Pikkarainen, P., A. Suvanto, J. Hukkinen, and I. Pyyhtiä (1997), 'Monetary Policy in Finland: Experiences Since 1992', in *Monetary Policy in the Nordic Countries: Experiences Since 1992*, BIS Policy Papers No 2.

Prime Minister's Office (1997), *Finland and EMU*, Publication 1997/26, Helsinki.

Mayes, D. and A. Suvanto (2007), 'Meeting the Challenge of Monetary Union: Lessons from the Finnish Experience', *Bank i Kredyt* 38(10): 3–14.

Reinhart, C. and K. Rogoff (2008), 'Is the 2007 US Sub-Prime Financial Crisis So Different? An International Historical Comparison', *American Economic Review* 98, pp. 339–44.

Reinhart, C. and K. Rogoff (2009), *This Time Is Different: Eight Centuries of Financial Folly,* Princeton, NJ: Princeton University Press.

Suni, P. and V. Vihriälä (2013), 'Euro—How Big a Difference: Finland and Sweden in Search of Macro Stability', ETLA Reports No 7, 4 March.

Svensson, L. E. O., (1997), 'Inflation Forecast Targeting: Implementing and Monitoring Inflation Targets', *European Economic Review* 41, 1111–46.

Svensson, L.E.O. (2006), 'The Role of Science in Best-Practice Monetary Policy: In Honor of Otmar Issing', paper presented at the ECB Colloqium held in honour of Otmar Issing in Frankfurt, 16–17 March 2006.

Vartiainen, J. (2002), 'Relative Prices in Monetary Union and Floating', *Scandinavian Journal of Economics* 104, 277–87.

Comments on 'Finland and Sweden in Cross-Country Comparison: What are the Lessons?' by Sixten Korkman and Antti Suvanto

Fredrik Andersson

Both the Finnish and the Swedish economies have performed quite well compared to other European economies over the last twenty years. In many ways Finland and Sweden are similar countries with common political goals, but there are also differences. One major difference is Finland's decision to join the euro area while Sweden decided to keep the krona. Because the countries are similar in most other respects, Korkman and Suvanto explore the similarities to analyze whether there are any economic effects of being a member of the euro area. They reach three main conclusions: (i) that the great Nordic crisis during the early nineties was a 'blessing in disguise' that paved the way for necessary structural reforms in both countries; (ii) that the present Nordic model successfully combines equity and efficiency; and (iii) that the exchange rate regime does not matter for the economic outcome.

The nineties was a period of reform in the Nordic countries. The fiscal and monetary frameworks were changed and policies were implemented to improve the economies' flexibility and competitiveness. It is tempting to link these reforms to the economic upswing that took place at the end of the decade. However, it is also possible to question to what extent the reforms caused the upswing. Finland and Sweden were not alone in pursuing a reform agenda during this period. The creation of the European single market increased competition and reduced trade barriers throughout the then European Economic Community. Most European countries that later joined the single currency also reformed their monetary and fiscal frameworks. Growth, however, did

Table C11.1. Indices of market regulation and ICT growth

		KOF Index Restrictions		Fraser Index Economic Freedom		
	Change 1980–90	Change 1990–2000	Level 2000	Change 1980–90	Change 1990–2000	Level 2000
	(1)	(2)	(3)	(4)	(5)	(6)
Finland	+5%	+35%	97.6	+11%	+16%	8.9
Sweden	+27%	−2%	94.6	+22%	+7%	8.7
France	+15%	+19%	93.3	+20%	+8%	8.5
Italy	+2%	+20%	94.2	+28%	+6%	8.1
United Kingdom	+2%	+10%	97.8	+19%	+3%	9.1
United States	+2%	+6%	88.9	+1%	+2%	9.1

Sources: KOF index: http://globalization.kof.ethz.ch; Fraser index: <http://www.freetheworld.com/>.

not generally increase throughout Western Europe, despite these reforms. Therefore, even though reforms were necessary to improve the economic performance Finnish and Swedish economies, they alone cannot explain the acceleration of growth that took place afterwards.

Korkman and Suvanto use several indices to illustrate the effect of the Finnish and Swedish structural reforms on the countries' economic institutions. Two of those indices, the KOF index and the Fraser index, are illustrated in Table C11.1 for six countries: Finland, Sweden, France, Italy, the UK, and the US.[1] The KOF index measures globalization in terms of restrictions on trade and capital and the Fraser index measures the degree of economic freedom. Columns 1 and 2 of Table C11.1 show the percentage change in the KOF index during the eighties and nineties respectively and column 3 the index level in the year 2000.[2] Columns 4, 5, and 6 show the corresponding developments for the Fraser index. As can be observed in the table, there was a reduction of trade barriers and an expansion of economic freedom in all countries. Furthermore, at the end of the reform period (the year 2000) all countries are almost equally open and equally free according to these indices.

The average annual GDP growth rate is shown in Table C11.2 for two time periods: a pre-reform period in column 1 (1978 to 1990) and a post-reform period in column 2 (1995 to 2007).[3] For the US growth is about the same

[1] We only include two of the indices used by Korkman and Suvanto, but the other indices show similar developments.

[2] We report the level for the year 2000 since this is the year reported by Korkman and Suvanto. Most changes in the indices took place during the eighties and nineties and there have only been small changes in the index numbers during the last decade.

[3] To exclude the effect of the financial crisis and the debt crisis the post-reform period ends in 2007.

Table C11.2. Average annual GDP growth rates and average annual ICT contribution to GDP growth

	Average GDP growth		ICT contribution to GDP growth
	1978–90	1995–2007	1995–2007
	(1)	(2)	(3)
Finland	3.5%	3.9%	+0.8%
Sweden	2.1%	3.3%	+0.6%
France	2.3%	2.1%	+0.3%
Italy	2.7%	1.6%	+0.3%
United Kingdom	2.4%	3.2%	+0.8%
United States	3.2%	3.1%	+0.8%

Source: GDP growth rate <http://www.conference-board.org/>; information and communication technology statistics <http://www.conference-board.org/>.

in both periods. For Finland, Sweden, and the UK growth increases in the post-reform period compared to the pre-reform period. For France and Italy growth declines in the post-reform period compared to the pre-reform period despite similar improvements in the institutional indices.

The decline in growth despite structural improvements raises the question why France and Italy did not benefit from the structural reforms when other countries did. A potential answer to that question is lower investments in information and communications technologies (ICT). ICT has been a main contributor to economic growth since the nineties (see e.g. Oliner and Sichel 2000; von Ark et al. 2008). The importance of ICT is illustrated in column 3 in Table C11.2, which shows the average annual contribution of ICT capital services to GDP growth for the post reform period. Countries with a high GDP growth rate in the post-reform period also have a high growth rate of ICT capital services and vice versa.

Several studies have shown that there is a clear link between deregulation of the telecom markets and ICT growth. Less regulation and early deregulation are associated with higher economic growth (OECD, 2003; 2006). Finland, Sweden, the UK, and the US were among the early deregulators of the telecom markets and therefore well placed to greatly benefit from the ICT revolution while countries such as France and Italy with regulated telecom markets were not.

Structural reforms can lay the foundation for higher growth but it doesn't automatically follow that the private sector to respond positively to such changes. Growth continued to decline in France and Italy despite their structural reforms and eventual deregulation of the telecom markets. Why the structural reforms in Finland and Sweden were more successful than similar reforms in France and Italy is debatable. According to Brandal, Bratberg, and Thorsen (2013) one of the Nordic model's key strengths is that it encourages people and businesses to respond positively to change and quickly adapt new technologies. Korkman and Suvanto, on the other hand, argue that it was the great Nordic crisis that accidentally caused a wave of reforms and a greater awareness among the public that change was necessary. Regardless of who is right, the Nordic example illustrates that the economic outcome depends not just on structural reforms but also the private-sector response to those reforms.

References

von Ark, Bart, Mary O'Mahony, and Marcel P. Timmer (2008), 'The Productivity Gap between Europe and the United States: Trends and Causes'. *Journal of Economic Perspectives*, 22 (1), 25–44.

Brandal, Nik, Öivind Bratberg, and Dag Einer Thorsen (2013), *The Nordic Model of Social Democracy*. New York: Palgrave and Macmillan.

OECD, (2003), *ICT and Economic Growth. Evidence from OECD Countries, Industries and Firms*. Paris: OECD.

OECD, (2006), 'Product Market Regulation and Productivity Convergence'. *OECD Economic Studies* No. 43, 39–76.

Oliner, Stephen and Daniel Sichel (2000), 'The Resurgence of Growth in the Late 1990s: Is Information Technology the Story?' *Journal of Economic Perspectives*, 14 (4), 3–22.

12

Iceland

How Could This Happen?

Thorvaldur Gylfason

> *The Chamber of Commerce recommends that Iceland stop comparing itself with other Nordic countries because we are superior to them in most respects.*
>
> Iceland Chamber of Commerce, February 2008[1]

12.1 Introduction

This chapter reviews recent economic developments in Iceland following its financial collapse in 2008, focusing on causes and consequences of the crash.[2] The review is presented in the context of the Nordic region, with broad comparisons also with developments elsewhere on the periphery of Europe; in Greece, Ireland, and Portugal—all small countries. In telling my story, I will need to look beyond economics in a narrow sense of the term because Iceland's troubles are as much political as economic. Think of it this way: you would not undertake to analyse, for example, Ukrainian events by econometrics alone, or by IS-LM curves, because you need a bit

[1] Undeterred by events, the Iceland Chamber of Commerce continues to dispense its advice. In mid 2013, the Icelandic government proposed a new law that would make it illegal not to consult the Iceland Chamber of Commerce, the Confederation of Icelandic Employers, the Icelandic Confederation of Labour, and the Association of Local Authorities concerning legislation and administrative decisions of interest to them.

[2] This chapter is a revised, written version of my presentation at the conference on 'Reform Capacity and Macroeconomic Performance in the Nordic Countries' held at the Copenhagen Business School in Copenhagen, Denmark, 20–21 September 2013. I am grateful to my discussant, Søren Bo Nielsen, as well as to other conference participants and several other readers at home and abroad for their reactions to my earlier version of the story.

more: you need historical and political context, among other things. In some ways, as you will see, Iceland resembles Italy, Japan, and Russia more than it resembles its Nordic neighbours or even Ireland.[3] Iceland has taken a path in economic, political, and social affairs that is in some ways quite different from that of its Nordic neighbours, with results that have proved correspondingly different.

This chapter surveys Iceland's economic landscape five years after the crash of 2008 by providing broad historical cross-country macroeconomic comparisons with an emphasis on failed banks and broken trust. It also considers the uncertain prospects for reforms and restoration. As a brief bonus toward the end I stress the striking resemblance between developments in Iceland and those in its closest neighbour, the Faroe Islands—a self-governing country of 50,000 people, within the Danish Realm since 1948. I also suggest directions for further research on the possible effects of Iceland's financial crash in 2008 on social, human, and real capital and thereby ultimately on long-run economic growth.

12.2 Background

In 1904 when Iceland was granted long-wished-for home rule by Denmark, the opportunity emerged from a new liberal government in Denmark (*systemskiftet* 1901). For 30 years, or 55 years, depending on how you count,[4] Icelandic politicians had sought increased sovereignty. This was in vain, due to divisive internal squabbling as well as to firm opposition by the Danish king. At the time, around 1900, Iceland's per capita gross national income was about half that of Denmark's. In today's money, that was roughly equivalent to Ghana's current per capita GNI at purchasing power parity. Over the next few decades, Iceland caught up with Denmark, reaching parity with today's India in 1930, China in 1960, and Korea in 2008.[5] The approximate parity with Denmark and the rest of the Nordic countries in terms of per capita GNI from at least 1980 onward (PPP-adjusted estimates

[3] Anthropological research suggests that about two-thirds of the Viking settlers of Iceland from the ninth century onward came from Norway while the remaining third arrived from Ireland.

[4] One may start counting in 1874 when the Icelanders celebrated the 1000th anniversary of the country's settlement and Christian IX King of Denmark handed the Icelanders their first constitution, essentially a copy of the Danish one; or in 1851 when, in the wake of Denmark's National Assembly of 1849, Iceland's National Assembly was, in the spirit of the times, unilaterally dissolved by the local representative of the Danish king. The National Assembly of 1851 was not a complete fiasco, however, because it laid the basis for the elimination of the last vestiges of the Danish trade monopoly in Iceland in 1855.

[5] These comparisons are updated versions of those presented in Gylfason (2008).

of national income do not reach farther back) was abruptly severed by the crash of 2008 (Figure 12.1).

Figure 12.1 highlights several points. First, Norway parted company with the rest of the Nordics in terms of per capita GNI before 2000, aided by its judiciously managed oil wealth, and remains in a class its own. The figure actually understates Norway's surge ahead of the rest of the pack because the Norwegians have cashed out on their economic success through fewer hours of work as well as higher incomes (Figure 12.2). By showing hours of work per employee rather than per capita, Figure 12.2 makes too little of the difference between Iceland and the rest because Iceland's labour force participation rate of about 75% since 1990 is far higher than in the rest of the Nordics (61 to 66% on average) as well as in the periphery (52 to 61%). Figure 12.3 shows hours of work per capita obtained by multiplying hours of work per employee by the participation rate. Figure 12.4 shows that, in terms of GNI per hour worked, Iceland started long before the crash to lag behind its neighbours for various well-known reasons of inefficiency to be addressed below.

Second, Ireland parted company with Greece and Portugal after 1990 and bypassed Iceland some ten years later. One difference between the economic surges of Norway and Ireland is that Norway only experienced relatively minor effects of the Great Recession triggered by the collapse of Lehman Brothers in 2008,[6] while Ireland, like Iceland, suffered grave consequences, mostly of its own making (O'Toole, 2009). Figure 12.1 shows that Iceland's pre-crash boom does not stand out from trend in the way that Ireland's does. This suggests that the crash may have brought Iceland down to a lower but not necessarily flatter growth trajectory while Ireland may return to its pre-1995 trajectory. As in Iceland, per capita GNI in Ireland fell by 10% after 2008, compared with 20% in Latvia, an extreme case (not shown). Even so, joblessness rose far higher in Ireland than in Iceland and higher still in Greece (Figure 12.5).

Third, in terms of the purchasing power of per capita GNI, Iceland parted company with the rest of the Nordics with the crash of 2008. The prospects for a return to the rest of the Nordic group are uncertain for reasons to be discussed in what follows. Figure 12.1 contradicts claims that Iceland as well as Ireland and Greece were innocent victims of a worldwide downswing. If they were innocent bystanders, the rest of the Nordics would have been similarly afflicted, but they were not.

In terms of income distribution, Iceland parted company with the Nordics as witnessed by the steady and unprecedented increase in economic inequality in Iceland during the 15 years preceding the crash (Gylfason et al., 2010, 155–6; Ólafsson and Kristjánsson, 2013). Iceland's experience echoes that of the Roaring Twenties in the United States where widening disparities

[6] For an excellent account of the US financial crisis, see Blinder (2013).

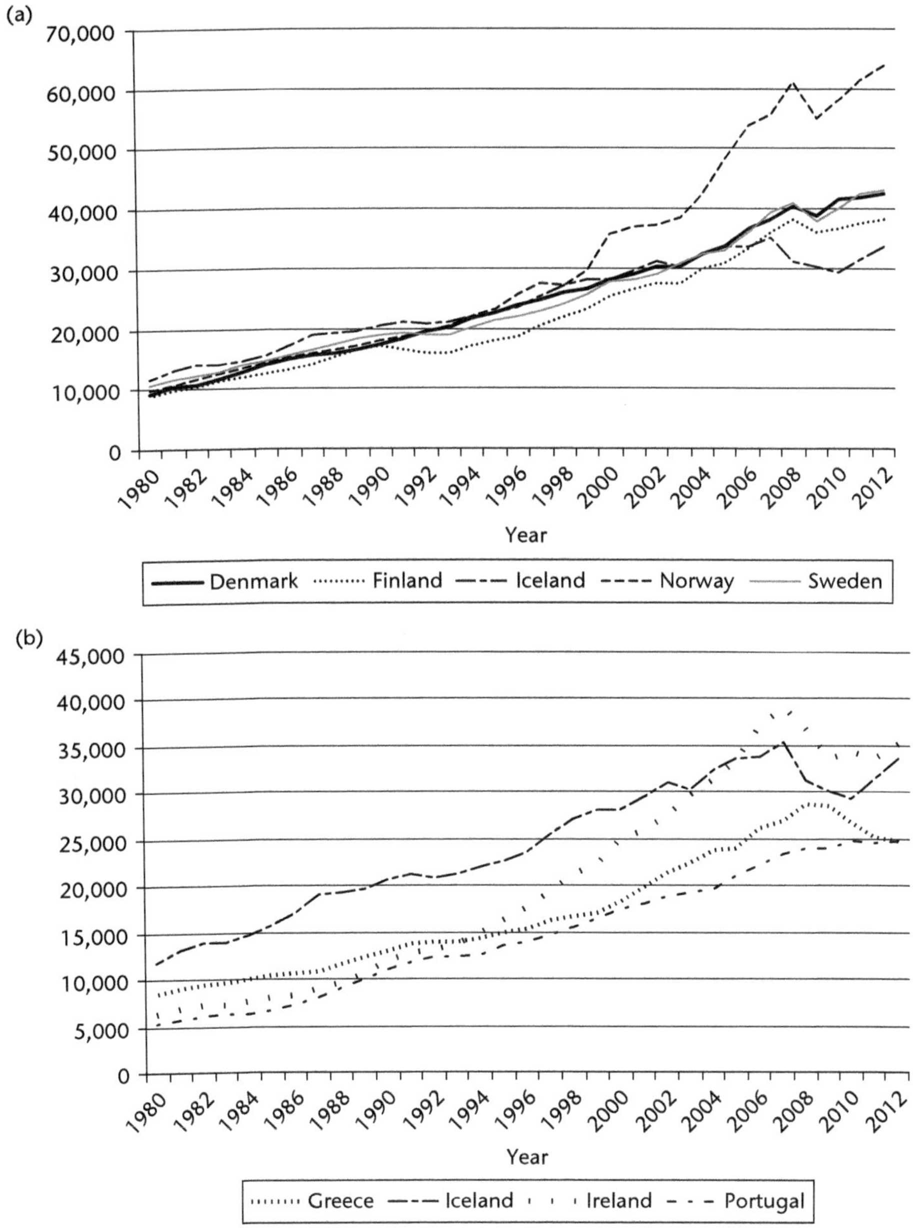

Figure 12.1. GNI per capita 1980–2012 (Current international $, PPP)*

* The source behind the figures throughout the chapter is the World Bank's *World Development Indicators* unless otherwise indicated.

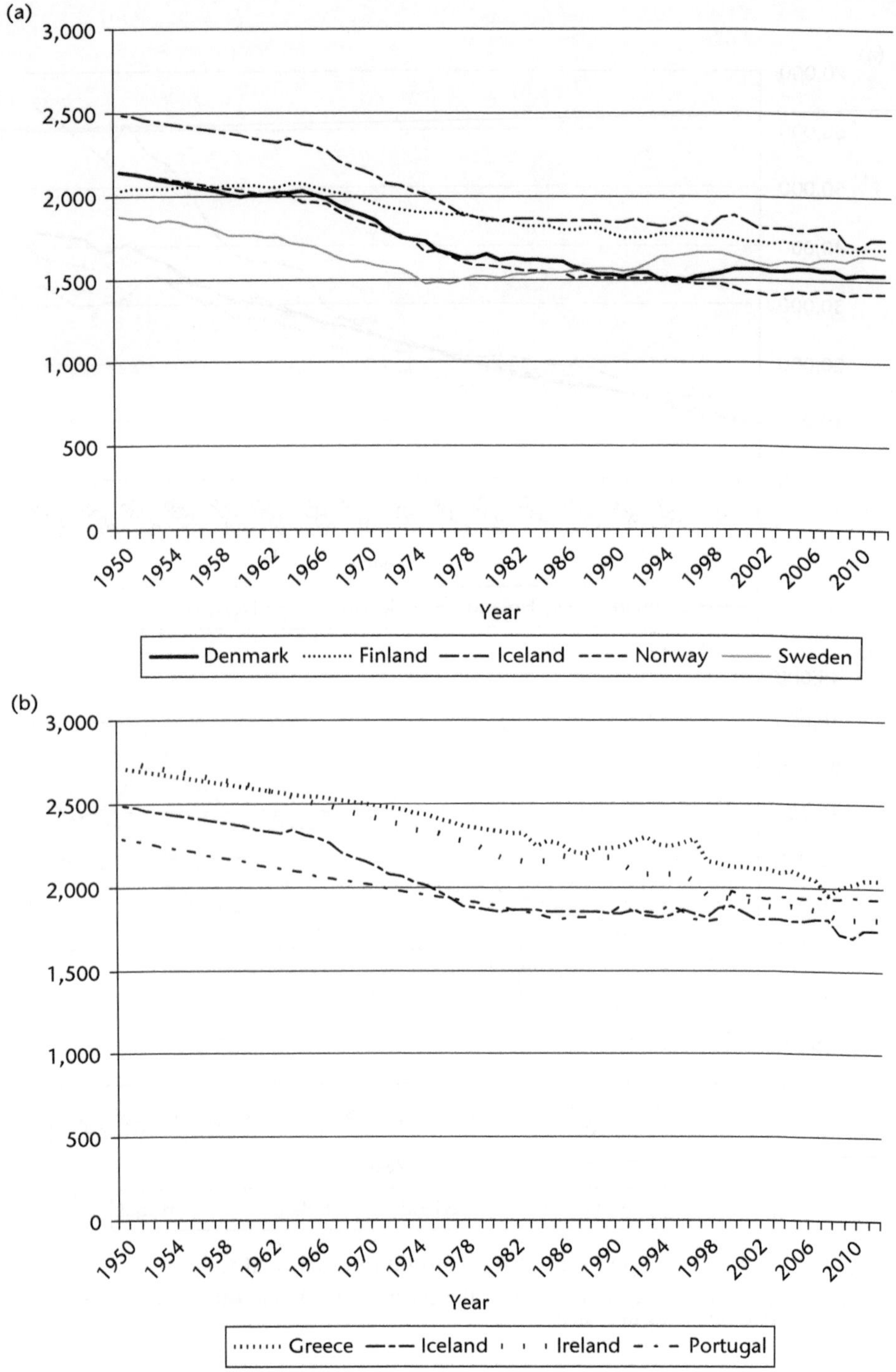

Figure 12.2. Hours of work per employee 1950–2012

Source: The Conference Board Total Economy Database™, January 2013, <http://www.conference-board.org/data/economydatabase/>.

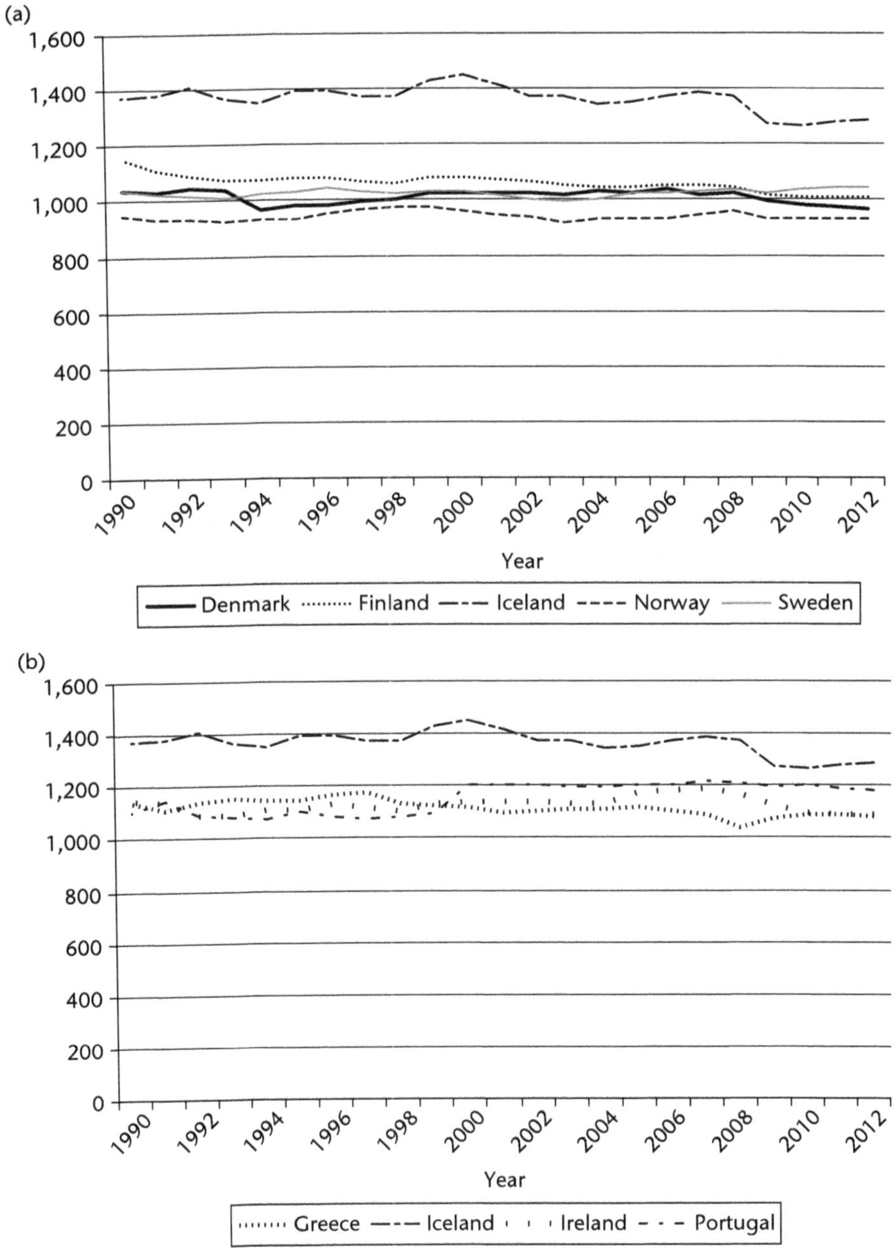

Figure 12.3. Hours of work per capita 1950–2012

Source: Author's computations based on Total Economy Database™, as well as the World Bank's *World Development Indicators*.

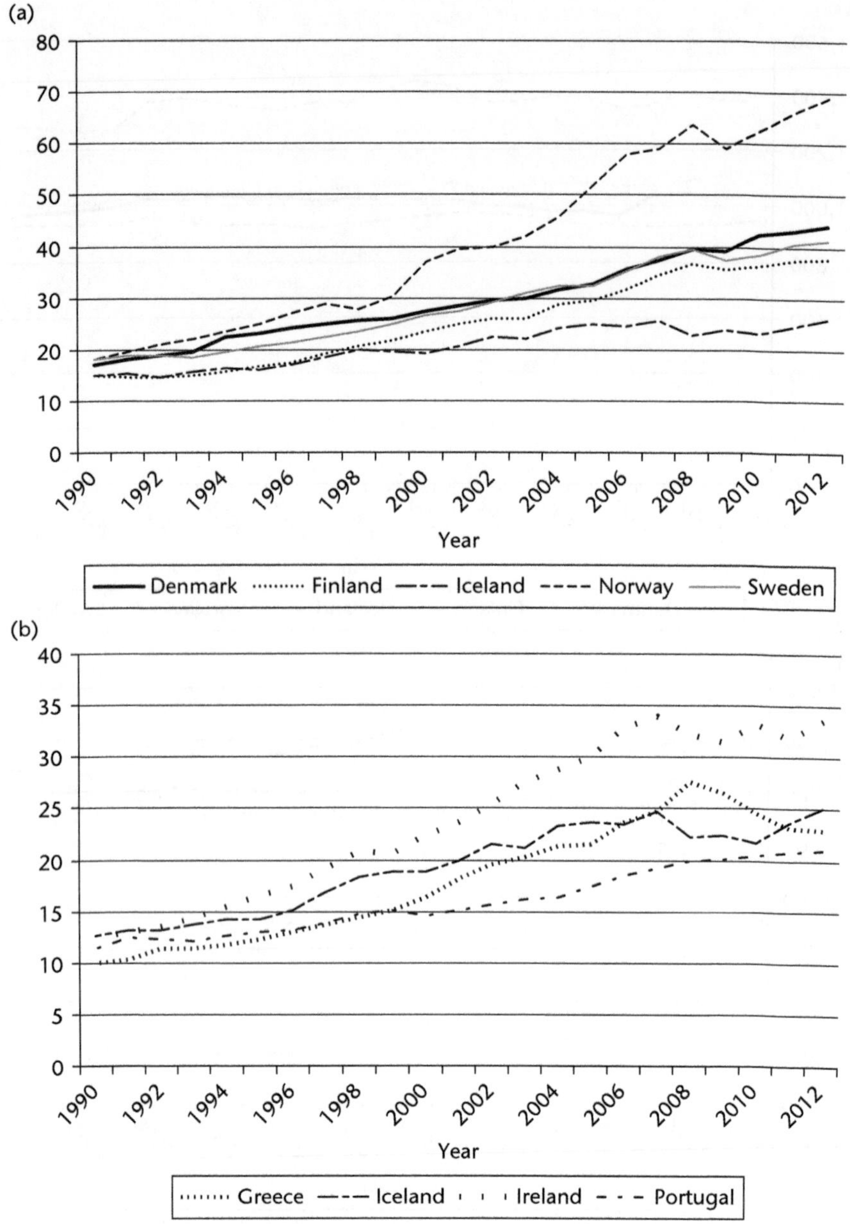

Figure 12.4. GNI per hour worked 1990–2012 (Current international $, PPP)*

* *Source*: Author's computations based on data presented in Figs. 12.1 and 12.3.

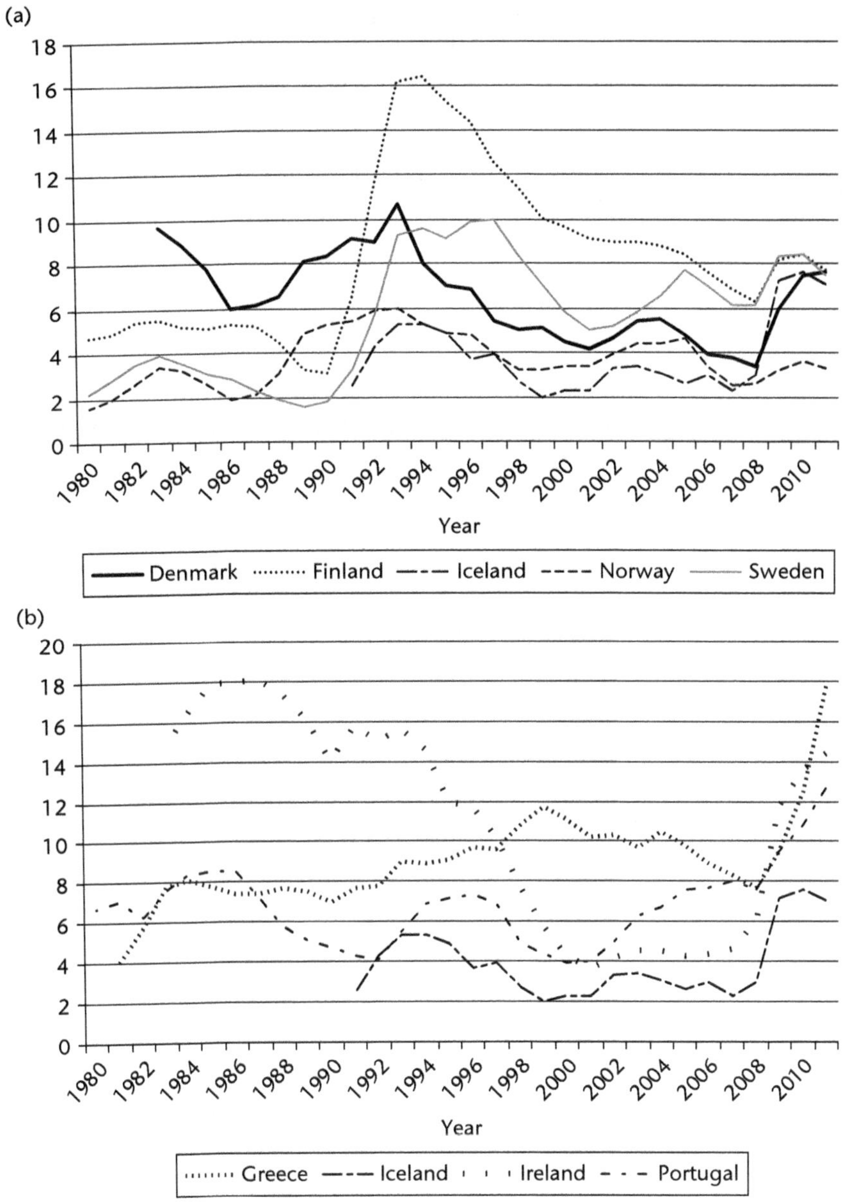

Figure 12.5. Unemployment 1980–2011 (% of labour force)

in the distribution of income and wealth preceded—some would say, paved the way for—the Great Crash of 1929 (Galbraith, 1988, pp. 177–8; see also Galbraith, 2012). Equality increased again after the crash under the rescue package supported by the IMF.

In terms of inflation, Iceland long ago parted company with the rest of the Nordics (Figure 12.6). Since 1939, the Icelandic króna has lost 95.95% of its value against the Danish krone. Iceland's inflation record is a long story of mismanagement, consistently evidenced by the OECD region's second-highest inflation rate after Turkey. The problem persists: from 2005 to 2012, prices in Iceland rose by 58%, compared with 17% in Denmark. Since 2005 the Central Bank has only once—briefly, in 2011—met its inflation target of 2.5%. To assess the effectiveness of Iceland's monetary policy it is not enough, however, to know the Central Bank's Taylor rule and such; you also need to know that (a) in 2008 the Central Bank, having accepted worthless collateral, became technically bankrupt and needed to be bailed out at a cost equivalent to 18% of GDP[7] and (b) the (post-crash) governor sued the bank in a salary dispute,[8] thus undermining the bank's pleas for general wage restraint.

The next section briefly discusses the collapse of 2008, then looks at some key determinants of long-run economic performance, spelling out Iceland's weak economic position vis-à-vis the rest of the Nordics (recall Figures 12.1 and 12.4). The crash and Iceland's less than stellar fundamentals may have a common origin in Iceland's political culture. Up against the wall, Parliament resolved unanimously in 2010 that (you may have to read this twice): 'criticism of Iceland's political culture must be taken seriously and [Parliament] stresses the need for lessons to be learned from it. Parliament resolves that the report of the Special Investigation Commission of the Parliament constitutes a condemnation of the government, politicians, and public administration.' [My translation.]

12.3 The Banks

One reason why Finland, Norway, and Sweden avoided major fallout from the Great Recession starting in 2008 is that they had learned their lesson from their own financial crises of 1988–93 (Denmark escaped unscathed). At

[7] In 2012, senior Central Bank officials testified in the Court of Impeachment hearing of the criminal case brought by Parliament against Iceland's pre-crash Prime Minister, Geir Haarde, that the writing was on the wall already in 2006. On the stand, one senior Central Bank official likened the operations of the Icelandic banks before the crash to the Ponzi scheme operated by Bernard Madoff in the US. Even so, the Central Bank continued to lend money to the banks without adequate collateral, bankrupting itself in the process. The fiscal cost of recapitalizing the three commercial banks amounted to another 18% of GDP (source: IMF).

[8] The governor lost his case in a lower court as well as in the Supreme Court.

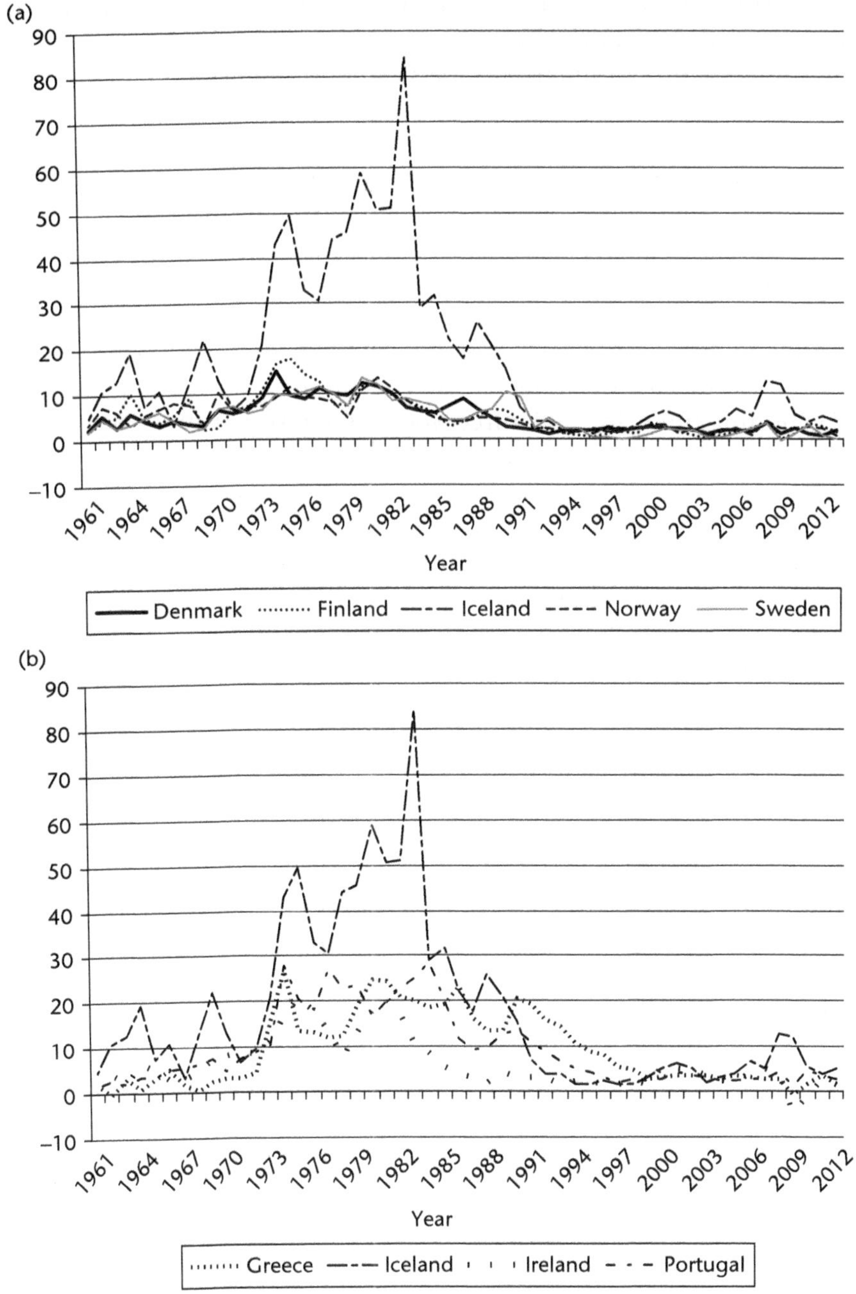

Figure 12.6. Inflation 1961–2012 (Consumer prices, % per year)

that time Finland, Norway, and Sweden were hit by serious bank failures following significant liberalization of the financial system without a commensurate strengthening of financial supervision (Jonung, Kiander, and Vartia, 2009). After that crash when unemployment in Finland, exacerbated by the collapse of trade with the former Soviet Union, increased to 16% of the labour force in 1993–4, Finland, Norway, and Sweden beefed up their banking systems through private as well as public recapitalization and reorganization in a bipartisan spirit of transparency and openness (Honkapohja, 2009).

At the time of the Nordic banking crisis of 1988–93 Iceland's state banks wrote off loans on an even larger scale relative to GDP than did the banks in the crisis-struck neighbouring countries whose write-offs, in turn, exceeded those triggered by the Savings and Loans scandal of the 1980s and 1990s in the United States (Gylfason, 1995, Ch. 9).[9] Even so, the Icelandic authorities did not acknowledge that there was a local financial crisis in the early 1990s. They did not have to do so because the banks faced no foreign competition, so they could get back on an even keel simply by increasing the interest rate spread far beyond Nordic norms (more on this below).

Having thus got away with a cover-up, the Icelandic government was in no hurry to privatize its dysfunctional banking system, even as the banks in East and Central Europe were being privatized in rapid succession after the collapse of communism in 1989–91, many quite successfully. Estonia, for example, sold virtually all its bank assets to foreign owners.

With their ability to ration loans and foreign exchange, the state banks in Iceland were an essential part of the political power structure. The Icelandic crash of 2008, when in a matter of days the entire banking system collapsed, followed a similar pattern to the Nordic crises twenty years before. The pattern was liberalization without appropriate supervision but, in Iceland, preceded by Russian-style privatization. Two of the three state banks were sold at once at modest prices to well-connected locals rather than to experienced foreign bank owners as was done, for instance, in the Baltic countries lacking local financial expertise. Plans to sell the largest bank (Landsbanki) to Skandinaviska Enskilda Banken were suddenly shelved in favour of an Icelandic father-and-son team with business experience from St. Petersburg, Russia.

Under new private owners that found Iceland too small and unexciting, the three large Icelandic banks (Glitnir, Landsbanki, and Kaupthing) decided to become international banks. Within a few years, they outgrew

[9] From 1987 to 1993, the Icelandic banks and other financial institutions wrote off loans equivalent to 11% of GDP in 1993. Original sources (in Icelandic) are given in Gylfason (1995, Ch. 9).

by far the ability of the government to stand behind them as lenders, or rather borrowers, of last resort.[10] What were the new owners thinking? By their own account, they grew to grow (Figure 12.7). The result was the abrupt bankruptcy of all three banks, surpassed in dollar terms only by the bankruptcy of Lehman Brothers and Washington Mutual in the United States (Gylfason, 2012, Fig. 1), including the personal bankruptcy of the main owner of Landsbanki ($750 million, two-thirds of which was owed to Landsbanki). This was apparently the biggest personal bankruptcy on record anywhere, including Texas.

How did the Icelandic banks manage to sink so fast and so deep? The answer lies not least in the corrupt manner of their privatization—which at long last, under pressure from the public, Parliament in 2013 decided to have investigated, without, however, appointing an investigation committee.[11] As a result, there is as yet no sign of a pending investigation. Another contributing factor was the ineffectiveness of financial supervision which is best described as having been designed to fail. The 2,400-page report of the Special Investigation Commission (2010, vol. 2, p. 313) appointed by Parliament states clearly that the banks violated the law. Further, the SIC concluded that three Central Bank governors as well as the director of the Financial Supervision Authority plus three former ministers 'showed neglect' in the exercise of their duties. Among all the bankers and politicians interviewed by the SIC, none expressed regret or accepted any responsibility for what happened. General amnesty appears unlikely. Forgiveness presupposes remorse, or at least an apology. Reconciliation requires truth. To heal, wounds must first be cleaned, as every doctor knows.

Under a new, apolitical, competent, and, as it turned out, temporary post-crash management, the FSA referred some 80 cases of suspected violations of the law to the Special Prosecutor, involving over 200 individuals suspected of insider trading, market manipulation, breach of fiduciary trust, and false accounting. At the end of 2012, the CEO of Glitnir was sentenced to nine months in prison. A year later, the CEO and Chairman of Kaupthing were sentenced to five-and-a-half years and five years in prison, respectively. In 2013, the CEOs of two smaller banks, Byr and MP banki, and

[10] See Matthíasson (2008), Wade (2009), Gylfason et al. (2010), Benediktsdóttir, Daníelsson, and Zoega (2011), Wade and Sigurgeirsdóttir (2012), and Níelsson and Torfason (2012). For a collection of writings on events in Iceland before the crash, including a couple of pieces claiming all was well, see Aliber and Zoega (2011). For more on the two pieces in question, see Ferguson (2012, Ch. 8).

[11] Iceland's apparently tailor-made Law on financial institutions from 2002, article 52, states: 'Directors and managers must . . . have an unblemished reputation, and must not *in the last five years* have been declared bankrupt. They must not . . . have been convicted *over the past 10 years* of a criminal offence under the Penal Code, . . .' [My translation, italics added]. This piece of legislation set the tone for things to come. The National Audit Office (2013) highlights various features of the banks' privatization that lowered their purchase price.

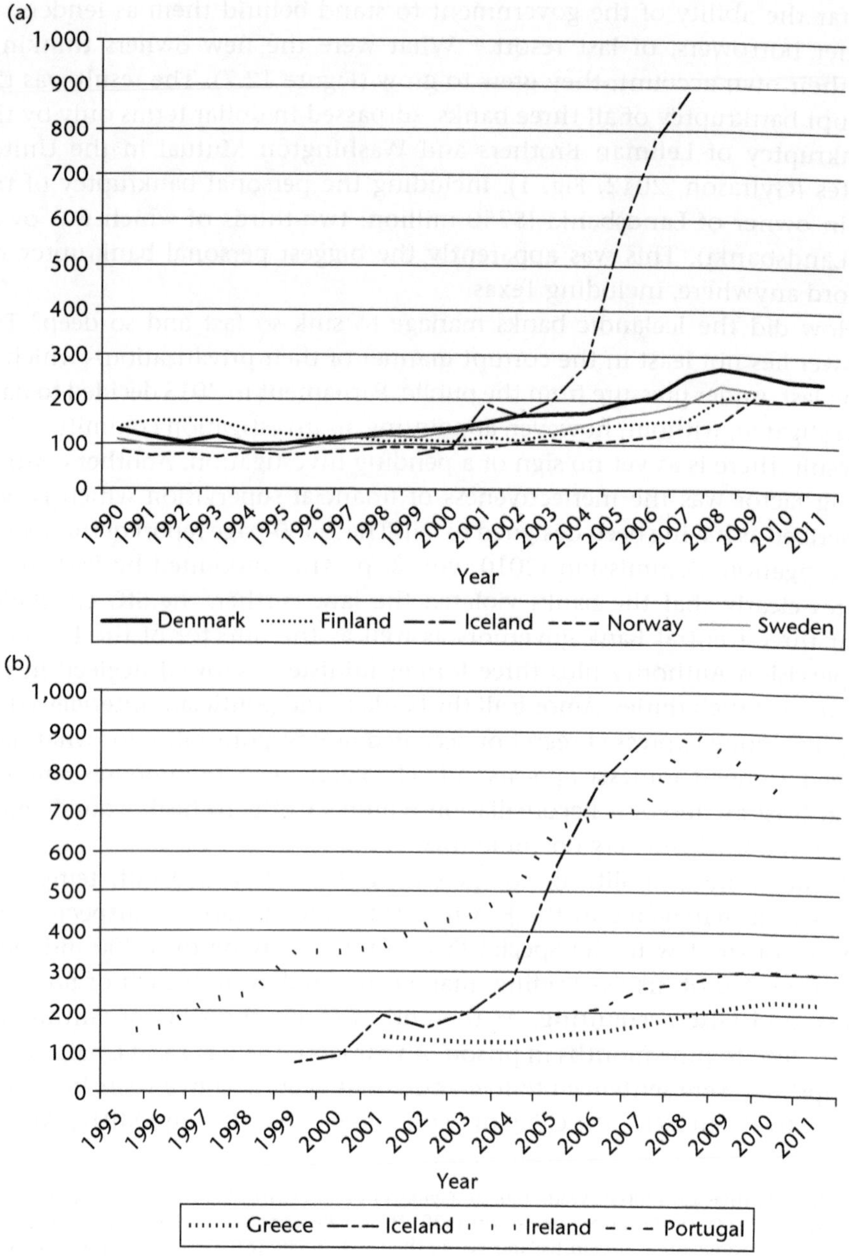

Figure 12.7. Bank assets 1990–2011 (% of GDP)

the Chairman of the latter got from one to four-and-a-half years for breach of trust. Several mid-level managers and accomplices have also been handed prison sentences. During 2014, further cases involving Landsbanki among others are scheduled to be heard in court.

In all this, Iceland is by no means unique. The Savings and Loans crisis in California and Texas twenty years ago landed more than a thousand senior bankers in jail. Mel Brooks, the film director, may be said to have provided the script, adapted from his Oscar-winning 1968 movie *The Producers* in which an over-the-hill Hollywood producer is convinced by his hapless accountant that a flop pays better than a hit (Gylfason, 2010). Following Brooks, Black (2005) enumerates the four main ingredients of bank fraud: extreme growth, making bad loans at a premium yield, extreme leverage, and grossly inadequate loss reserves.[12]

Unsurprisingly, Iceland's FSA had a bumpy ride. After repeated attempts by forces close to some of those under investigation to unseat the crime-busting post-crash director of the FSA, Mr Gunnar Andersen, they succeeded in 2012, but by that time the most important cases were already in the hands of the Special Prosecutor, who remains in office but whose budget allocation for 2014 was cut in half by a new government comprising the parties that privatized the banks in 1998–2003, paving the way to the cliff in 2008. In government circles, there are those who refer to the crash as the 'so-called crash', as if nothing had happened.[13]

But things did happen. For one thing, Iceland's gross government debt rose by two-thirds of GDP (Figure 12.8), making interest payments a huge public expenditure item absorbing five percent of GDP each year at least until 2018, crowding out essential expenditures to the point where Iceland's main hospital faces a life-threatening financial emergency. Of 147 banking crises since 1970, Iceland's crisis was the seventh-costliest in terms of increased public debt and the third-costliest in fiscal terms (Laeven and Valencia, 2012).[14] Local residents lost savings equivalent to two times GDP. Foreign creditors, shareholders, and depositors incurred losses equivalent to five times Iceland's annual GDP. Prices shot up as the króna lost half its value in nominal terms and a third of its value in real terms.

Unable to service their suddenly much larger mortgages, an average of three families a day saw their homes repossessed from 2009 to early 2013,

12 Are these isolated cases? No, says Black, quoting, among other sources, the US Treasury's Office of Comptroller of the Currency as saying: 'The FBI estimates that 80% of all mortgage fraud involves collaboration or collusion by industry insiders.' See also Akerlof and Romer (1993) and Stiglitz (2010, Ch. 5).

13 'There were older people who didn't even realize there had been a crisis', former Prime Minister Geir Haarde told *The Guardian*, 6 October 2013.

14 For comparison, Ireland's crisis was the sixth-costliest in terms of increased public debt and the seventh-costliest in fiscal terms.

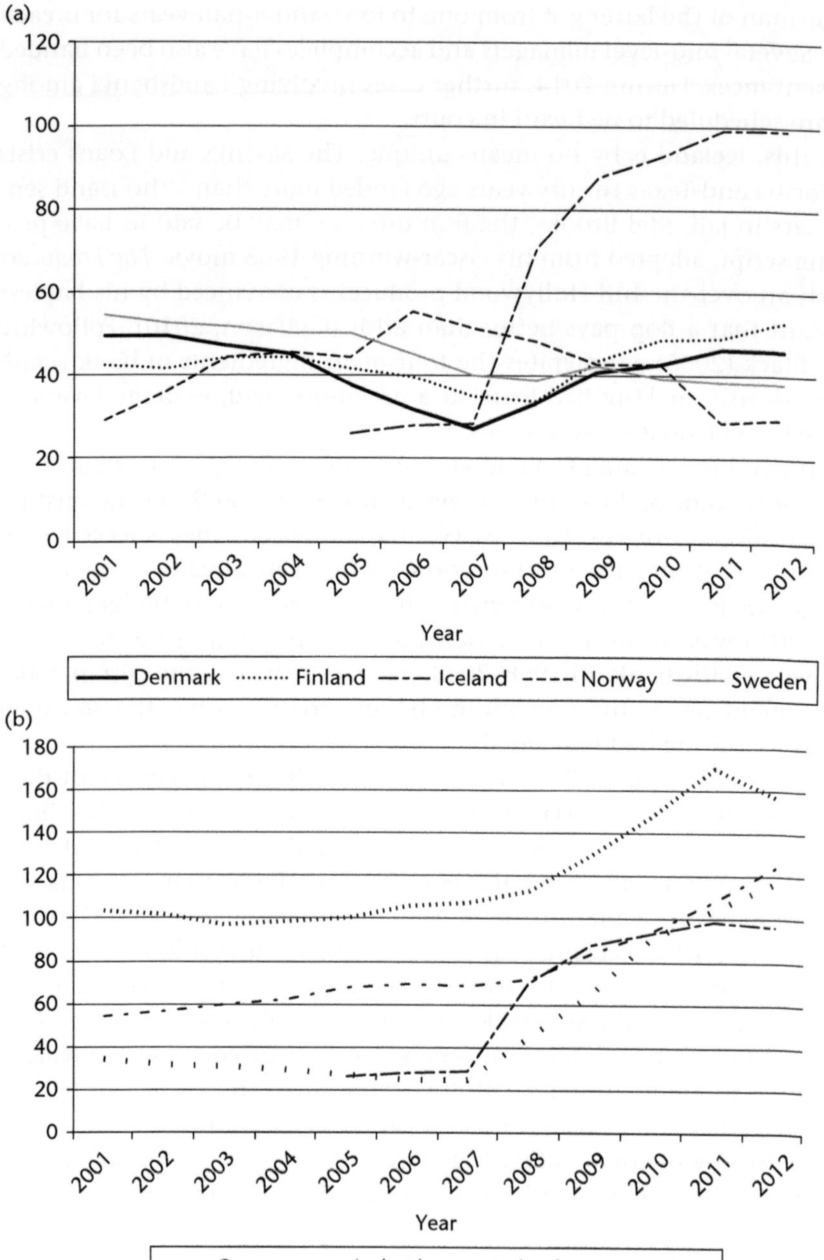

Figure 12.8. General government gross debt 2001–12 (% of GDP)

Source: Eurostat. Government debt is defined as consolidated general government gross debt of the whole general government sector.

by banks that continue in some ways to behave like a state within the state despite having been found guilty in court of legal violations, including the extension of foreign-currency-denominated loans ruled illegal by the Supreme Court.[15] A few years before the crash (2001), a Central Bank governor sat on the committee that drafted the legislation outlawing indexation to foreign currencies explicitly to protect unsuspecting domestic borrowers against predatory bank practices, but even so the Central Bank sat by idly as the banks extended such loans in large numbers. Thousands of gullible bank customers converted their high-interest local-currency loans indexed to domestic prices to low-interest loans indexed to foreign currencies only to see their loan principals double in local currency as the króna collapsed. Further, by its own admission, the Central Bank reduced reserve requirements to comply with the banks' wishes rather than trying to restrain their growth to safeguard financial stability.[16]

Five years after the crash, many borrowers remain unsure of the real value of their outstanding debts to the banks because the banks have been in no hurry to compensate their customers by writing down their loans, even after the Supreme Court has ruled the loans illegal. Individual borrowers have had to sue the banks in an attempt to induce them to comply with Supreme Court rulings. Further court cases involving controversial bank practices before and after the crash are pending.

In retrospect, the Icelandic banking sector was poorly prepared for liberalization, having been privatized as late as 1998–2003. For more than a hundred years the banking system had comprised inept state bank institutions run by political operatives allocating subsidized credits and scarce foreign exchange to favoured customers, paying scant attention to commercial profitability, risk, and economic health. In the 1990s, while dysfunctional banks in East and Central Europe were being transferred to new, often foreign, owners, Icelandic politicians could no longer resist demands for privatization, so they sold the banks—not to experienced foreign bank owners as initially envisaged but rather, at modest prices, to well-connected local parties entrusted to preserve the age-old umbilical cord binding politicians to the banks.

The new bank owners reciprocated the politicians' generosity. According to the Special Investigation Commission (2010, vol. 2, pp. 200–1, and vol. 8, pp. 164–70), the banks and related firms gave huge sums to political parties and politicians, equivalent to $8 per person in Iceland in 2006. Further, the SIC reports that ten Members of Parliament out of 63 each owed the

15 Source: <http://www.visir.is>, 4 April 2013. Comparable figures on repossessions before the crash are not available.

16 The Vice Governor of the Central Bank, still in office, made the admission at a public meeting at the University of Iceland in June 2008, three months before the crash.

banks one million euro or more when the banks collapsed. The personal debts of the ten MPs averaged €9 million. The ten MPs include the leader of the Independence Party (now Finance Minister), his former deputy (now Director of the Board of the Central Bank), and five other party comrades.[17] It is not known if these loans have been, or will be, settled. With many friends in political circles, the banks must have felt, and seemed to behave, like a state within the state, a sentiment seemingly exacerbated by unfettered cross-border banking and regulators and rating agencies looking the other way.

The three failed Icelandic banks, active in foreign markets, never faced foreign competition in the domestic market. Ireland's banking system, by comparison, despite seemingly lax supervision, was and remains competitive, engaging domestic and foreign banks in avid competition for local customers. The much larger domestic interest rate margin in Iceland than in Ireland reflects the oligopolistic inefficiency and excesses marring Icelandic banking before as well as after privatization (Figure 12.9).

Under normal conditions, the aim of privatization is to make banks more efficient for the benefit of their customers and the community by, for example, reducing the interest rate spread, a simple measure of bank efficiency. In Iceland, however, the interest rate spread did not decrease following the banks' privatization in 1998–2003. On the contrary, the spread increased and remained far above foreign levels. Without foreign competition, the Icelandic banks got away with continuing to squeeze their captive customers, borrowers as well as lenders. In Greece, Ireland, and Portugal, on the other hand, as well as in the rest of the Nordic region, local banks faced foreign competition from, among others, Icelandic banks.

Plainly, the Icelandic banks, like the Irish ones, borrowed too much. But there are two parties to every transaction. What were the creditors of the banks thinking? They had been led to believe that the government stood behind the banks. Rating agencies and accounting firms failed to warn of pending dangers. Unlike in Ireland where the government decided to bail out the banks at huge cost to Irish taxpayers and to the pace of economic recovery, the Icelandic government abandoned the banks (Gylfason, 2013a). There was no other way out because the hole that the banks had dug themselves into while the government looked the other way or even egged them on was too deep.[18] Had the scale of the problem been smaller, the Icelandic government might have done what the Irish government did, but that was not

[17] The Independence Party has been in government nearly 80% of the time since 1944.

[18] Shortly before the crash, Icelandic ministers and bank directors appeared side by side at meetings with creditors in London and New York to reassure them that everything was under control.

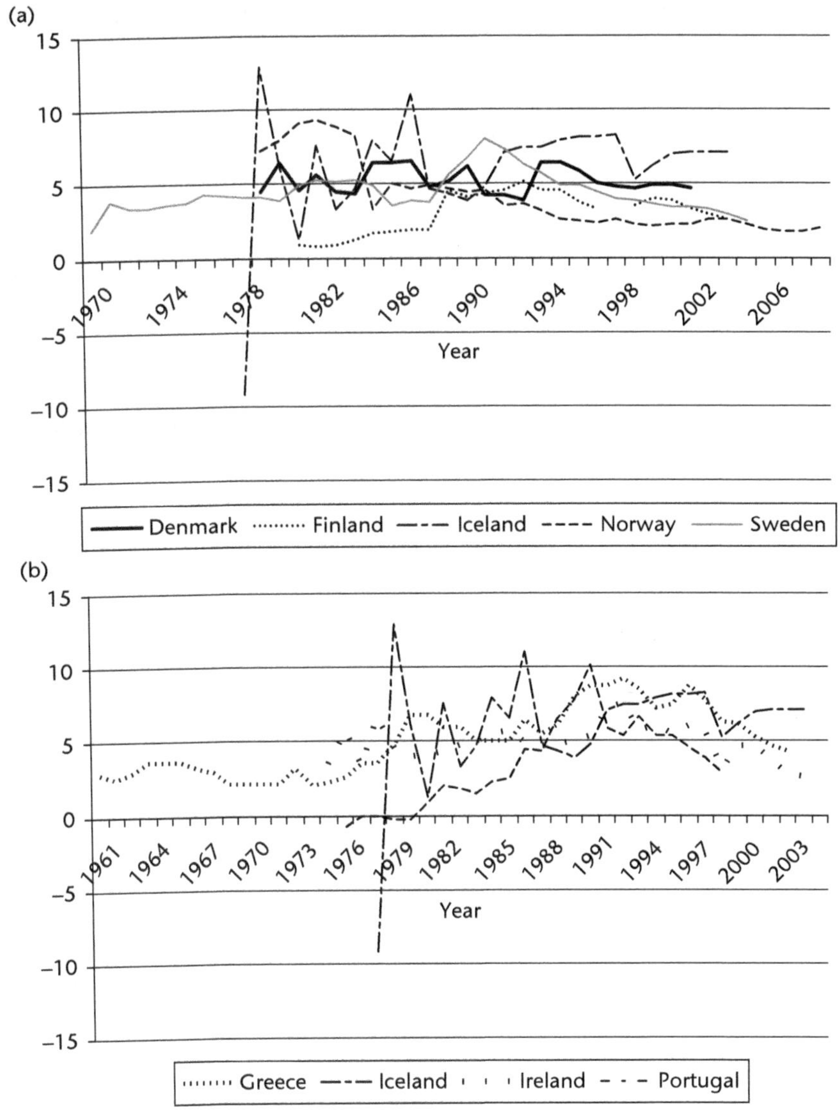

Figure 12.9. Interest rate spread 1970–2009 (lending rate minus deposit rate, %)

an option. So, there was nothing particularly courageous or virtuous about Iceland's 'standing up to' foreign banks. The road taken was necessary and inevitable.

In 2011, the Supreme Court upheld the emergency laws enacted during the 2008 crash to ensure that domestic depositors had priority over other claims on the assets of the failed banks. The ruling facilitated the settlement of Iceland's Icesave debt[19] to the governments of the United Kingdom and the Netherlands that had paid partial compensation to British and Dutch Icesave depositors, a settlement first approved by Parliament in two rounds, only to be rejected twice in national referenda, and ultimately dismissed on technical grounds by the EFTA court, the final arbiter of the case.

Five years after the crash, the Icelandic banks, still the only game in town, again make huge profits by local standards. They have resumed the payment of bonuses to their senior staff. They have written off huge amounts of loans, mostly to firms,[20] thus alleviating their need to lay off workers and in some cases enabling some of the major local players before the crash to stay in business. Even after huge write-offs, in 2011, the banks' nonperforming loans are equivalent to almost a quarter of their total assets (Figure 12.10).[21] The banks remain overstaffed. In 2012, the Icelandic banks employed 11.6 full-time staff per one thousand inhabitants compared with 8.1 in Denmark, 5.3 in Finland, 4.5 in Norway, and 3.6 in Sweden.[22] At the same time, the banks have become more vigilant. Loans without collateral—common before the crash—and other one-way bets against the banks are reportedly no longer made, or tolerated.

On the whole, the behaviour of the banks after the crash has not helped endear them to many of their customers. Public opinion research by MMR (Market and Media Research) and Capacent, an affiliate of Gallup, shows that the banking system enjoys less trust than any other public institution in Iceland (Figure 12.11). If any reputable foreign bank were to open offices in Iceland, it seems safe to assume that they would not face any shortage of local customers. Trust in Parliament declined from 40% in 2008 to 14% in 2013.

Readers of Transparency International's compilation of the corruption perceptions index may have noticed that Iceland does not lie far behind the rest of the Nordics (Figure 12.12). Transparency covers business corruption, bribes, and such; the higher the index, the less corrupt the country is perceived to be. Figure 12.12 also shows the results of a recent

[19] Icesave is the Landsbanki branch that, when liquidity began to dry up, went on to collect high-interest internet deposits in the UK and the Netherlands from some 400,000 depositors during 2006–8, and then collapsed.

[20] Through deleveraging and write-offs, household debt has fallen by 14%, in part because the Supreme Court ruled that the indexing of loans to foreign currencies was illegal, and corporate debt has fallen by 45% (IMF 2013), partly through concerted action by the government, financial institutions, and employers' associations. Following the Nordic financial crisis of 1988–93, household debt in Finland and Sweden fell by 30%.

[21] Nonperforming loans on a facility basis fell from a peak of 18% at the end of 2010 to 6% at the end of 2012. On a cross-default basis Fig. 12.8 classifies as nonperforming all loans to borrowers with at least one loan in default. Data for Iceland 2007–8 and 2012 (and Norway 2012) are not reported by the IMF, the source quoted by the Word Bank's *World Development Indicators*.

[22] Source: Finanssektorens Arbejdsgiverforening (2012).

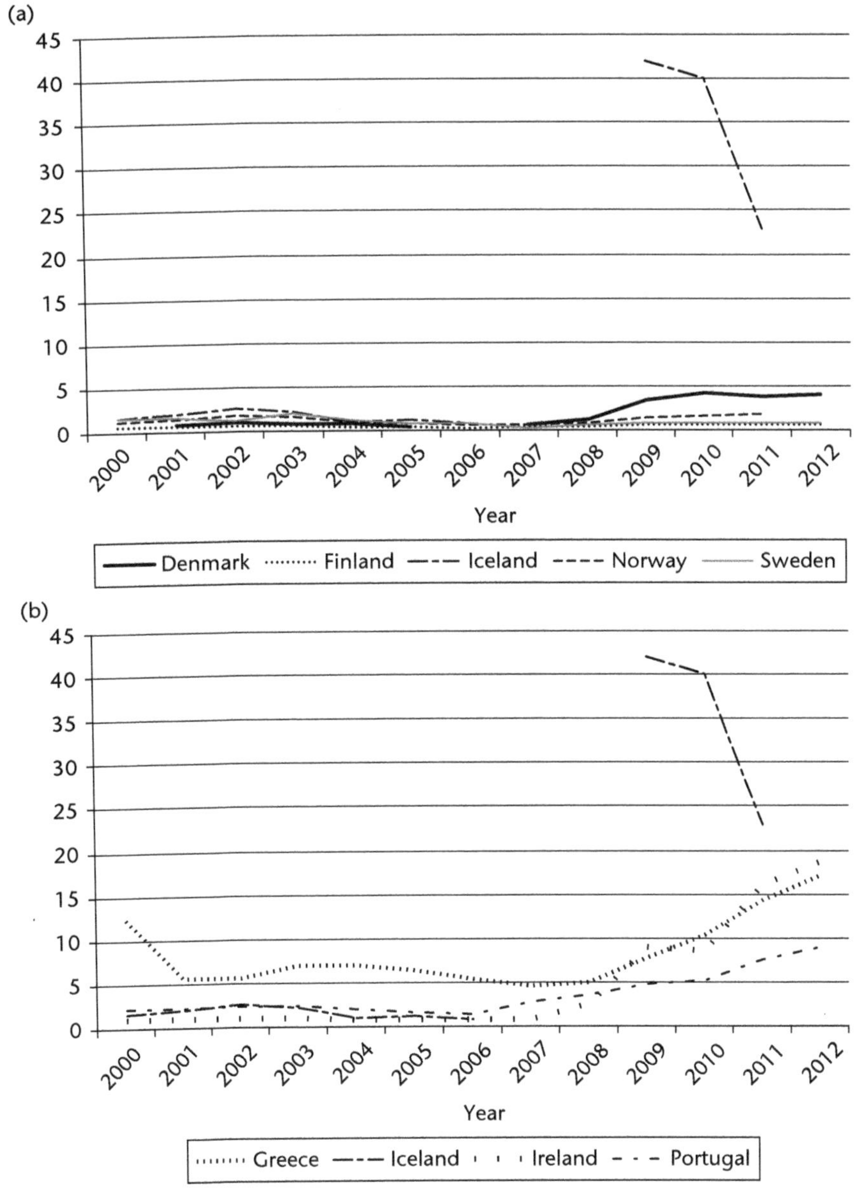

Figure 12.10. Bank nonperforming loans 2000–12 (% of gross loans)

Gallup poll where a large sample of voters in 129 countries was asked the following question: 'Is corruption widespread throughout the government in [country], or not?' Two-thirds of the Icelandic respondents consider their government corrupt compared with a fifth on average in the rest of the Nordics. Many people in government pretend not to have

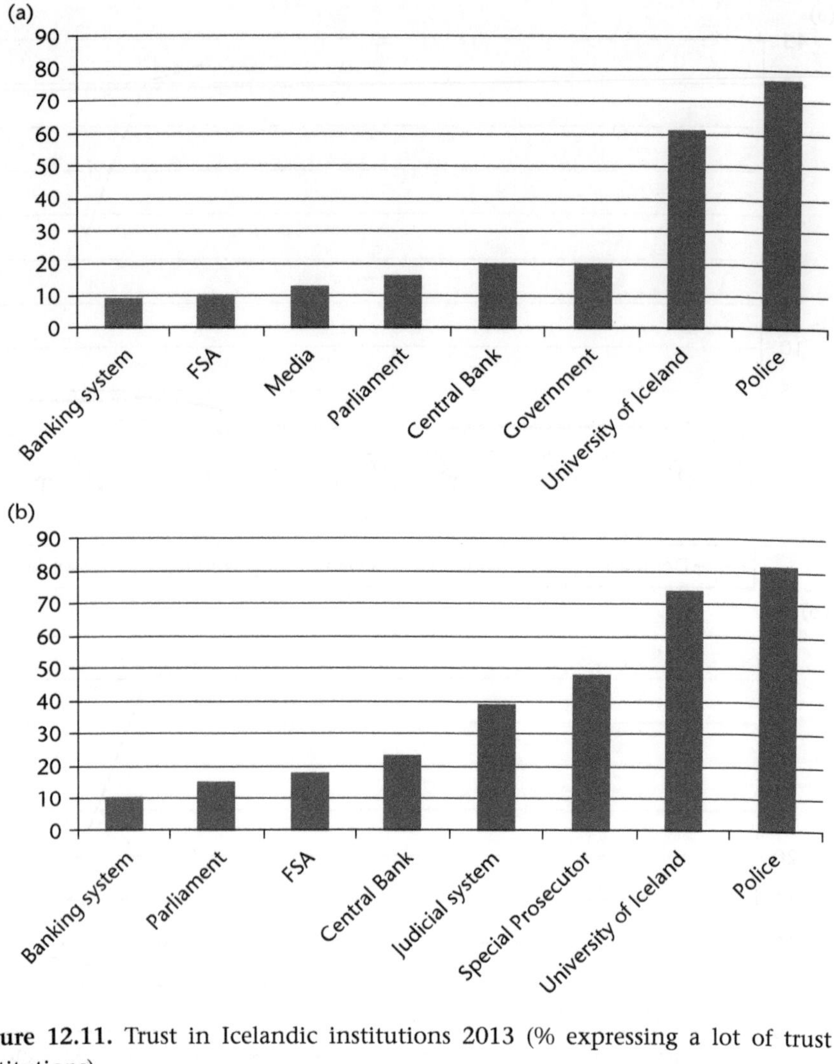

Figure 12.11. Trust in Icelandic institutions 2013 (% expressing a lot of trust in institutions)
Source: MMR and Capacent.

noticed, or, when presented with the evidence, react like French police captain Louis Renault in *Casablanca* who was '*shocked—shocked!*—to find that *gambling* is going on in here.'

There is nothing new in this. Before the crash, however, there was not much talk of corruption in public debate. A common if unspoken attitude was that if corruption was a problem it was affordable because, with living standards comparable to the rest of the Nordics, Iceland seemed to be doing quite well. The crash changed the rules of the game. With

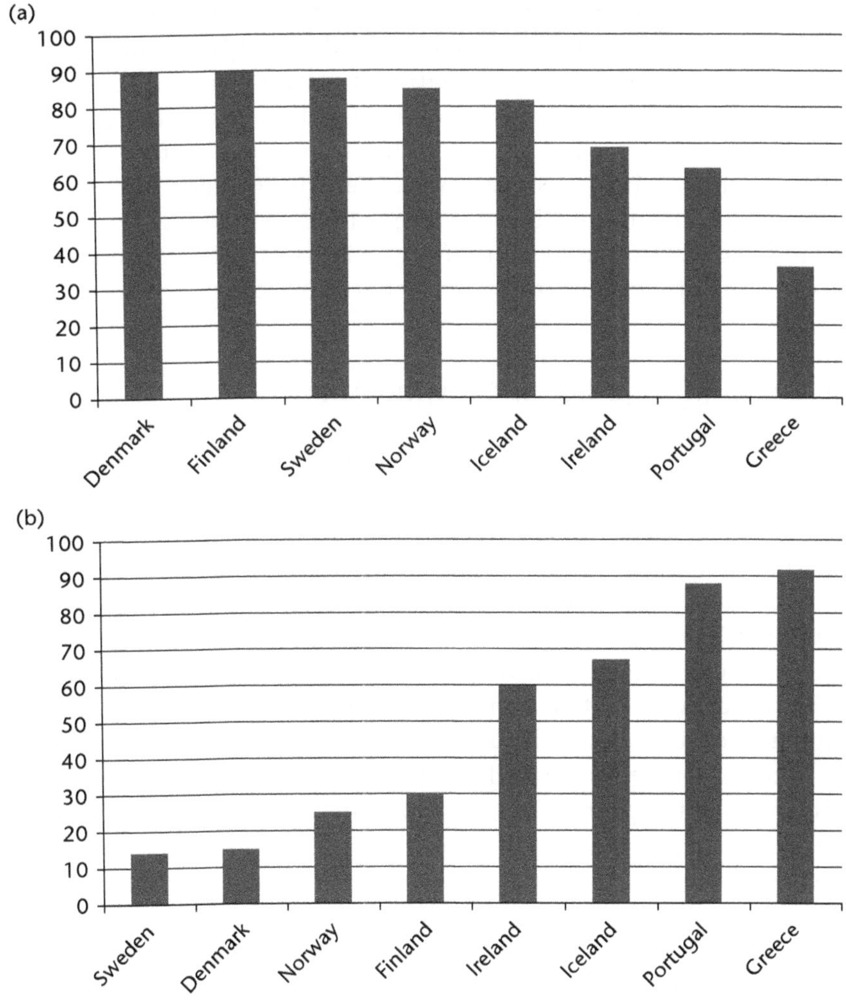

Figure 12.12. Corruption 2012 (a: Business corruption as measured by Transparency; b: political corruption as measured by Gallup)

Iceland's living standards now far behind the rest of the Nordics and with uncertain prospects for recovery, past and present corruption is on the table. Among the most glaring form of corruption in Iceland has been appointment corruption, including nepotism, by which incompetent people are appointed to public office—in ministries, public agencies, banks, courts, etc.[23] Five years after the crash, the problem persists.

[23] In 2011, the Supreme Court of Iceland awarded damages to an unsuccessful applicant for a district judgeship to which a close relative of a former Prime Minister, Foreign Minister, and Central Bank governor had been appointed.

This is why the constitutional bill drafted and unanimously approved by a directly elected Constitutional Council and subsequently accepted by two-thirds of the voters in a national referendum in 2012 features special provisions on the appointment of judges and other public officials.[24] Reykjavík elected as mayor in 2010, 18 months after the crash, a comedian whose winning slogan was: 'We will not keep our corruption from you!' All this matters because respect for democracy, trust, and the absence of corruption are essential ingredients of social capital (Paldam 2000) and thereby important sources of economic growth.

12.4 Growing Together or Growing Apart?

How did Iceland get into this remarkable mess? From the 1930s onwards Iceland, like the Republic of Ireland excluding Northern Ireland, was among the most conservative, regulated, and inward-looking societies in Western Europe. From the 1920s onwards, for example, to protect its farmers, Iceland prohibited the importation of dairy products and meat, a ban still essentially intact. In other respects as well, throughout the twentieth century, policies tended to favour farmers and other inhabitants of rural areas, a rather conservative social force. Rural areas were granted disproportionate political clout through an election system where it took far more votes to be elected to Parliament in the Reykjavík area, now home to two-thirds of the country's population, than it took in some rural areas. While the overrepresentation of rural areas in Parliament has been reduced over time, the problem persists: to be elected, some rural candidates still need only half as many votes as do candidates from the Reykjavík area. This is why one of the main provisions of the afore-mentioned constitutional bill stipulates 'one person, one vote', a provision supported by two-thirds of the voters in the 2012 referendum, casting doubt on the legitimacy of future parliamentary elections according to rules that the voters have rejected. Outward-looking, efficiency-oriented social democracy never took root in Iceland, or in Ireland, unlike in Scandinavia and the United Kingdom.

Let us take a quick look at exports, investment, and education—all important determinants of long-run growth. For a long time, Iceland has fared comparatively poorly by all three measures. Iceland was hampered by stagnant exports relative to GDP until the króna's perennial overvaluation ended with its collapse in 2008, enabling exports at long last to make some headway (Figure 12.13). At about a third of GDP since 1960 (in fact, since

[24] The bill has been put on ice by Parliament in a blatant attempt to thwart the will of the people.

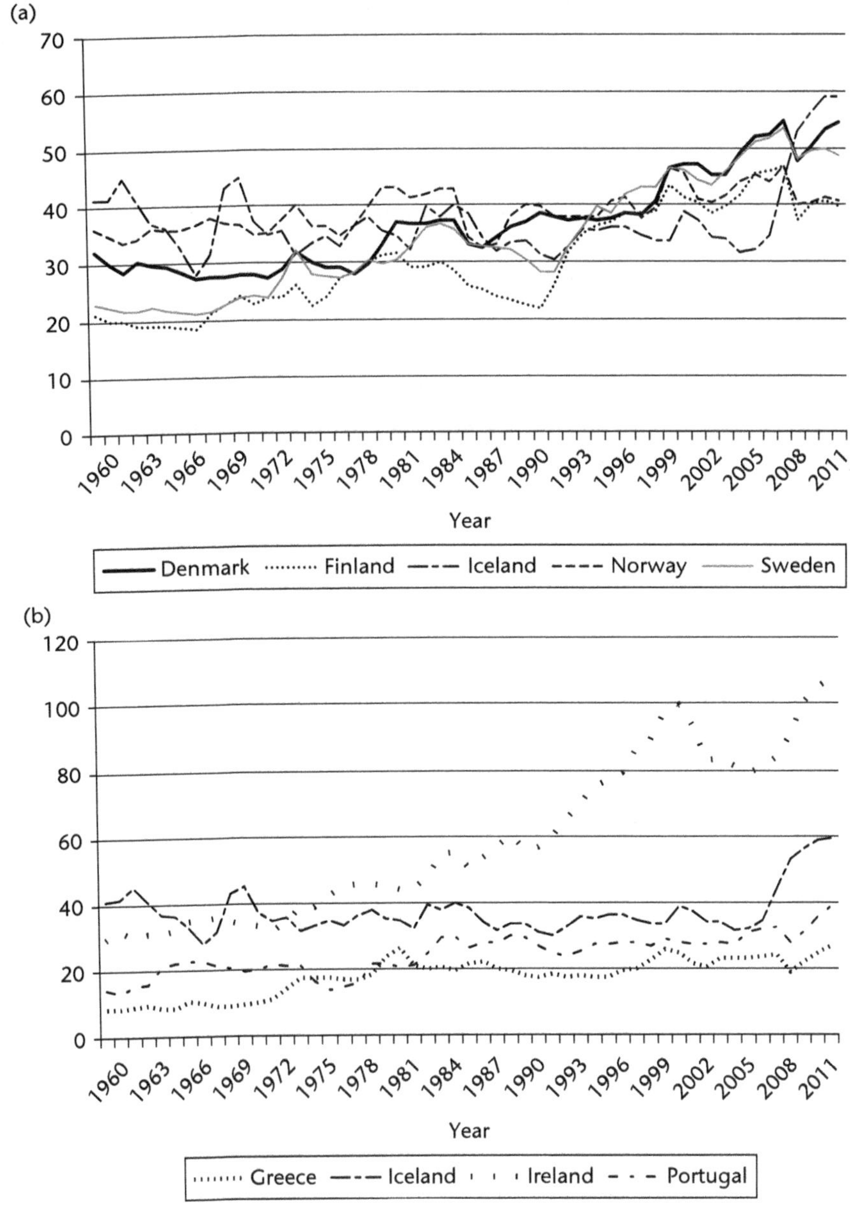

Figure 12.13. Exports of goods and services 1960–2012 (% of GDP)

1870, but leave that aside), Iceland's export ratio has been low in view of the small size of its economy. Figure 12.13 demonstrates the stimulating effect that a depreciation of the currency—in this case, by a third in real terms—can have on export earnings which have doubled relative to GDP. Notice also the sharp recovery of Irish exports despite the euro.

The behaviour of imports is also worth noting. In Iceland, the volume of imports rose by 80% from 2000 to 2008 after which it collapsed below its 2000 level, by far the most extreme pattern of import behaviour in the countries under comparison (Figure 12.14). The fact that import volume contracted by 44% after the crash while output fell by 10% suggests a strong effect of the depreciation of the currency on imports in Iceland. Greece, Ireland, and Portugal also experienced a sharp decline in imports.

The composition of Iceland's exports remains less growth-friendly than in Denmark, Finland, and Sweden as well as in Ireland and Portugal where manufactures comprise the bulk of merchandise exports (Figure 12.15). With a few exceptions (e.g., artificial limbs, computer games, fish processing equipment, and generic drugs), Iceland's exports are on the whole remarkably low-tech. In 2012, fish products accounted for 27% of total export earnings, aluminum for another 22%, and foreign tourism 24% (source: Statistics Iceland). Figure 12.15 also shows the sharp relative decline of Norway's manufacturing exports as a result of crowding out, a common symptom of the Dutch disease in natural-resource-rich countries.

Iceland's exports of fish and aluminum render its export structure highly concentrated (Figure 12.16); the Iceland figures compare with those of Saudi Arabia and Nigeria (not shown). Further, it is interesting to note that Norway used its oil wealth to build up a Pension Fund of more than $800 billion, invested overseas, the world's largest, equivalent to nearly $180,000 per person in Norway, while Iceland carries a crushing debt burden despite abundant fish and energy resources. Export concentration sometimes translates into concentration of political power, a problem that Norway judiciously avoided but Iceland did not (Gylfason, 2013a).

Investment in machinery and equipment as well as construction boomed before the crash of 2008 and then collapsed (Figure 12.17), so much so that net investment—that is, gross investment less depreciation—was negative from 2009 to 2012. This means that the physical capital stock declined four years in a row. Since the crash, foreign investment has been insignificant because potential investors lost confidence besides being discouraged by strict capital controls in effect since late 2008 with no end in sight.

Investment in human capital is described in Figures 12.18–12.20. Iceland has long had and still has a comparatively poorly educated labour force of which a relatively large proportion has at most acquired primary education (Figure 12.18), and of which a correspondingly small proportion has acquired secondary education (Figure 12.19) and tertiary education (Figure 12.20).

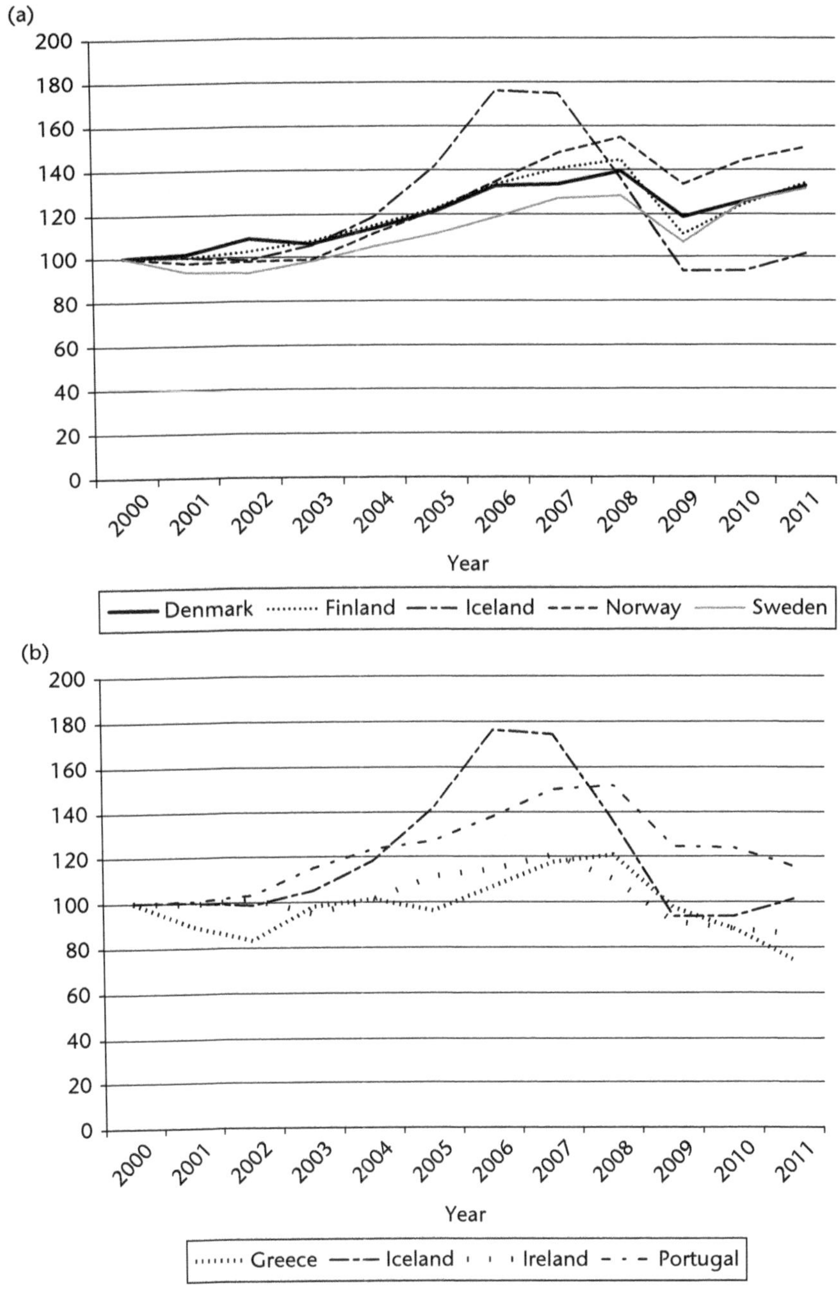

Figure 12.14. Import volume 2000–11 (2000 = 100)

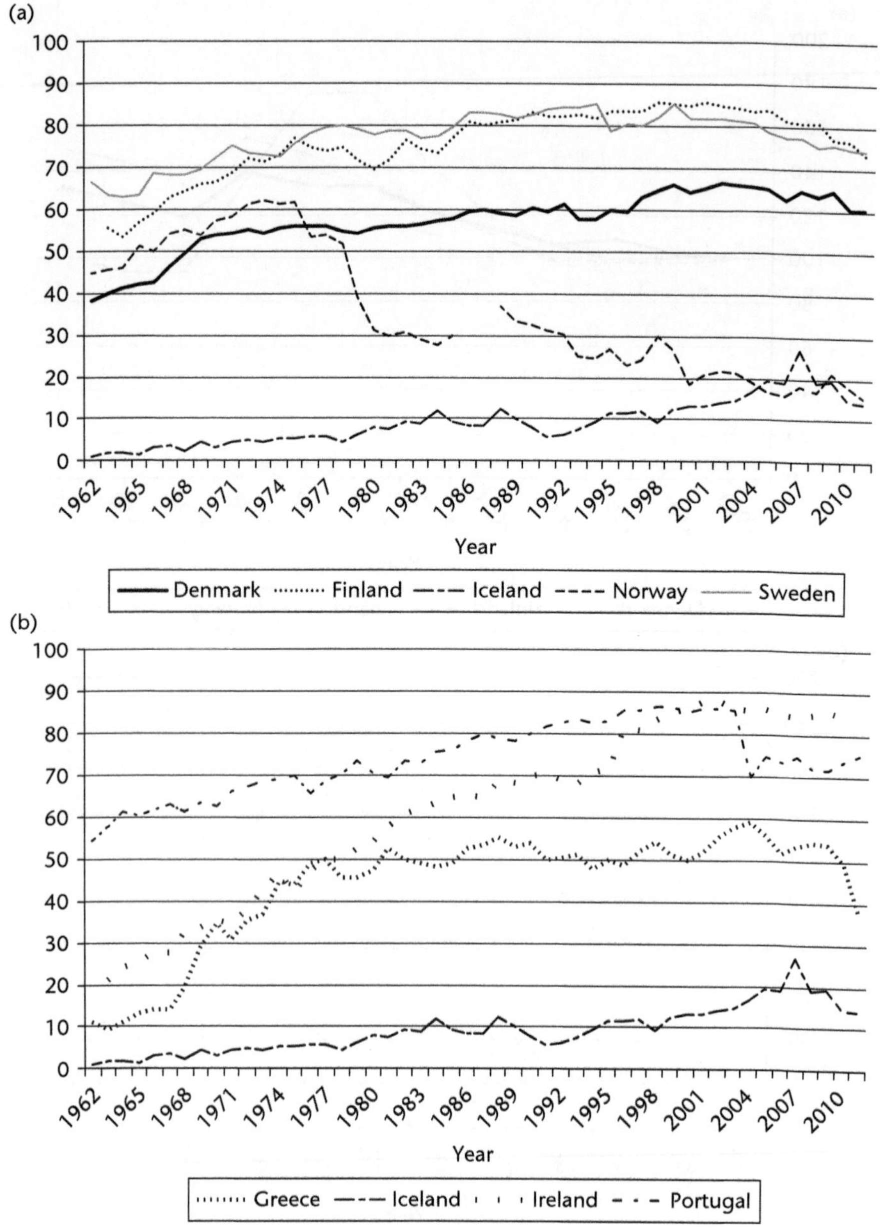

Figure 12.15. Manufactures exports 1962–2012 (% of total exports)

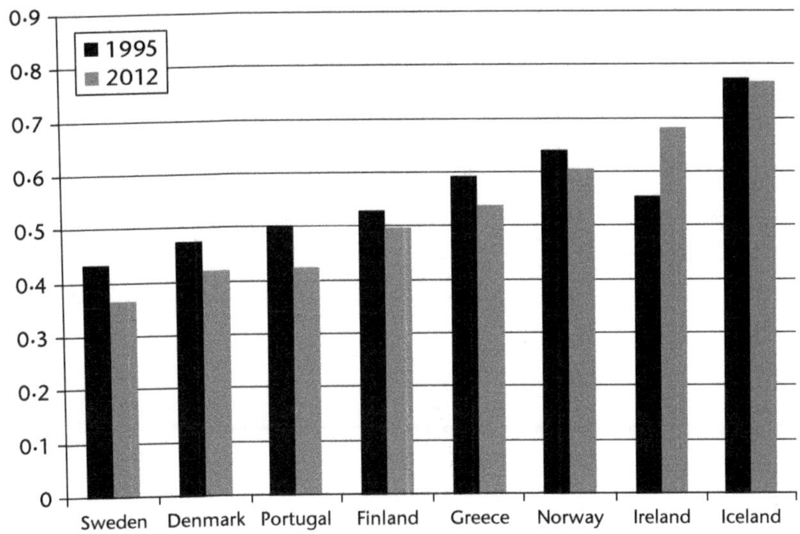

Figure 12.16. Herfindahl merchandise export diversification index 1995–2012

Note: The diversification index shows how the structure of exports by product of a given country differs from the world average. The index ranges from 0 to 1, with values closer to 1 indicating a bigger difference from the world average.

Source: UNCTAD.

In the group of countries under review, only Portugal has a less well-educated labour force than Iceland.[25] Other indicators point to the same conclusion. For example, in 2009, public expenditure per student at the tertiary level (college and university) amounted to 30% of per capita GDP in Iceland compared with 57% in Denmark, 39% in Finland, 49% in Norway, 45% in Sweden, 38% in Ireland, and 31% in Portugal.[26]

The curriculum also matters. Polishchuk and Natkhov (2012) argue that corruption tends to direct students from science to legal studies, reporting that, in the Ukraine, relatively many more students study law than in Poland where many more students study science than in the Ukraine. In Iceland, they also report, relatively many more study law than in Denmark, Finland, Norway, and Sweden while, in the latter group, many more study science than in Iceland.

In sum, Iceland's relatively weak performance for quite some time in terms of foreign trade (Figures 12.13–12.16) as well as in terms of the build-up of

[25] Based on a stochastic frontier model, the IMF (2013, Annex II) suggests that Iceland's labour productivity lags only slightly behind its Nordic neighbours (and exceeds that of European countries) while acknowledging that efficiency ratings have declined in recent years, 'underscoring the need to improve resource allocation and address legacy vulnerabilities, . . . including the imposition of capital controls and a weak banking system.'

[26] Source: UNESCO Institute for Statistics; figures on Greece are not available.

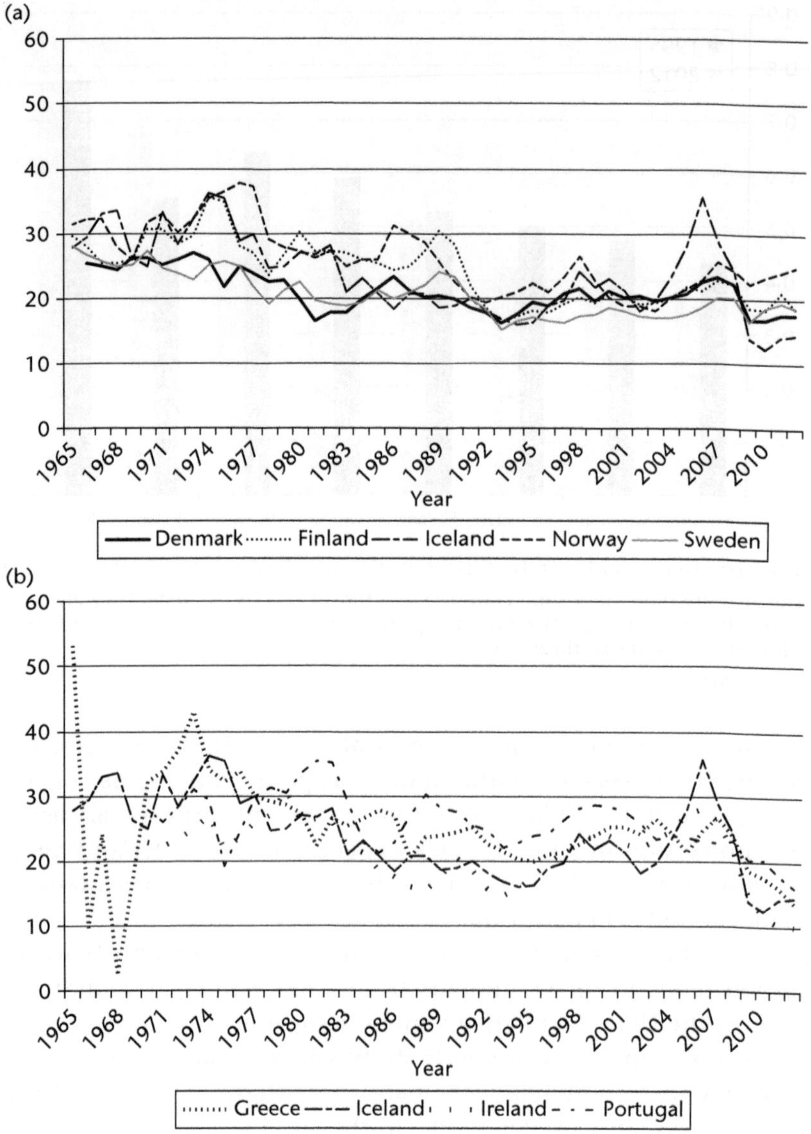

Figure 12.17. Gross investment 1965–2011 (% of GDP)

real capital (Figure 12.17), human capital (Figures 12.18–12.20), and social capital (Figures 12.11–12.12) may help explain the deterioration of its overall economic position within the Nordic group as well as the need for long hours of work (Figures 12.1–12.4). If so, the implications of these findings for long-run economic growth accord with the comparison of adjusted net

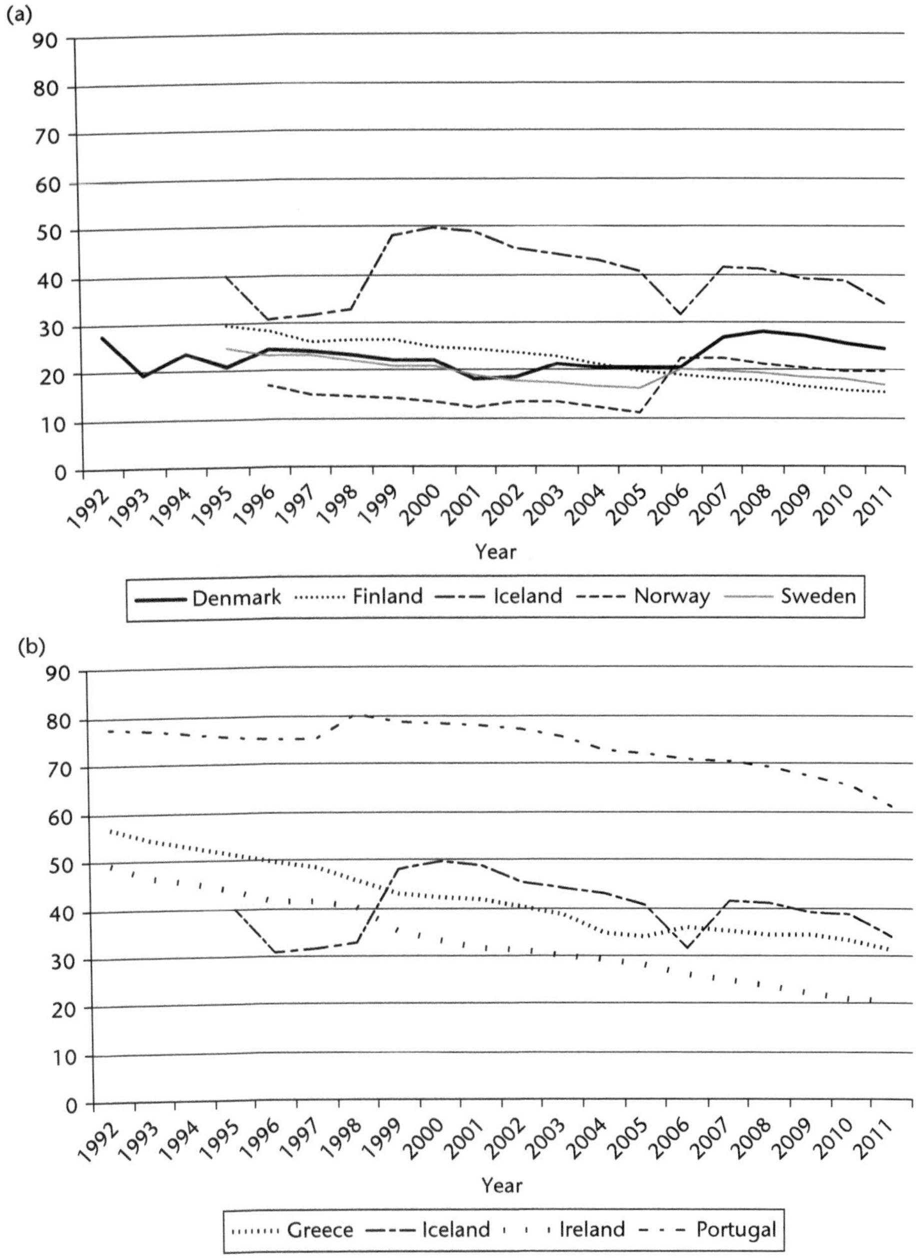

Figure 12.18. Labour force with at most primary education 1992–2011 (% of total)

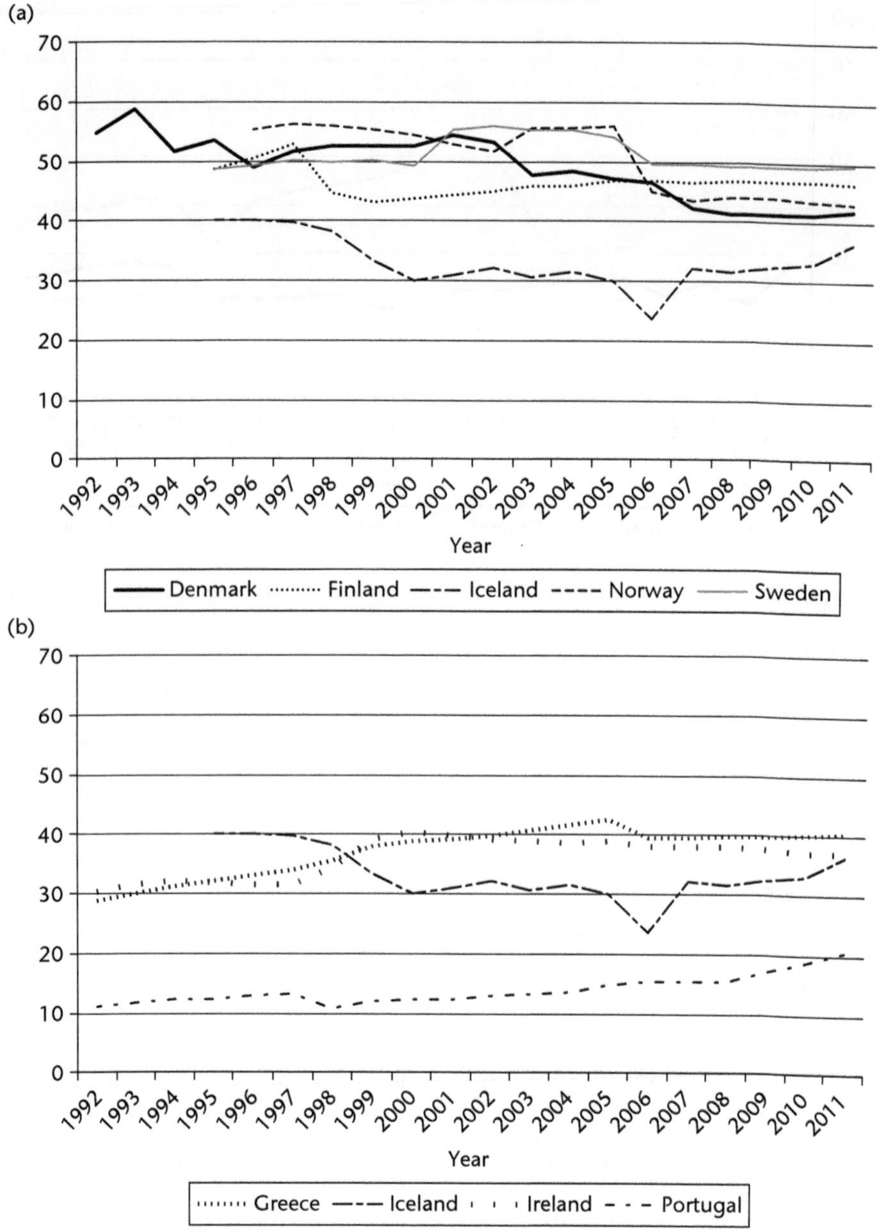

Figure 12.19. Labour force with at most secondary education 1992–2011 (% of total)

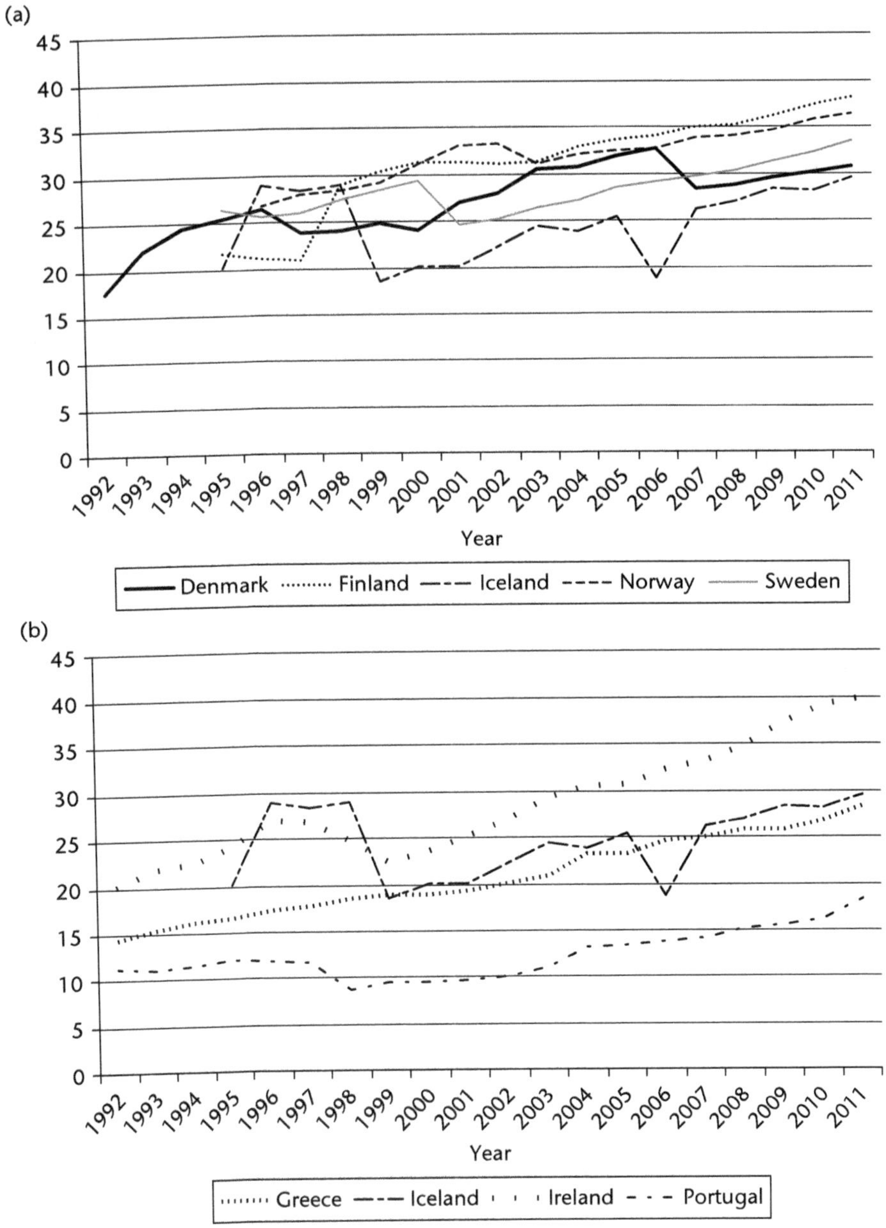

Figure 12.20. Labour force with tertiary education 1992–2011 (% of total)

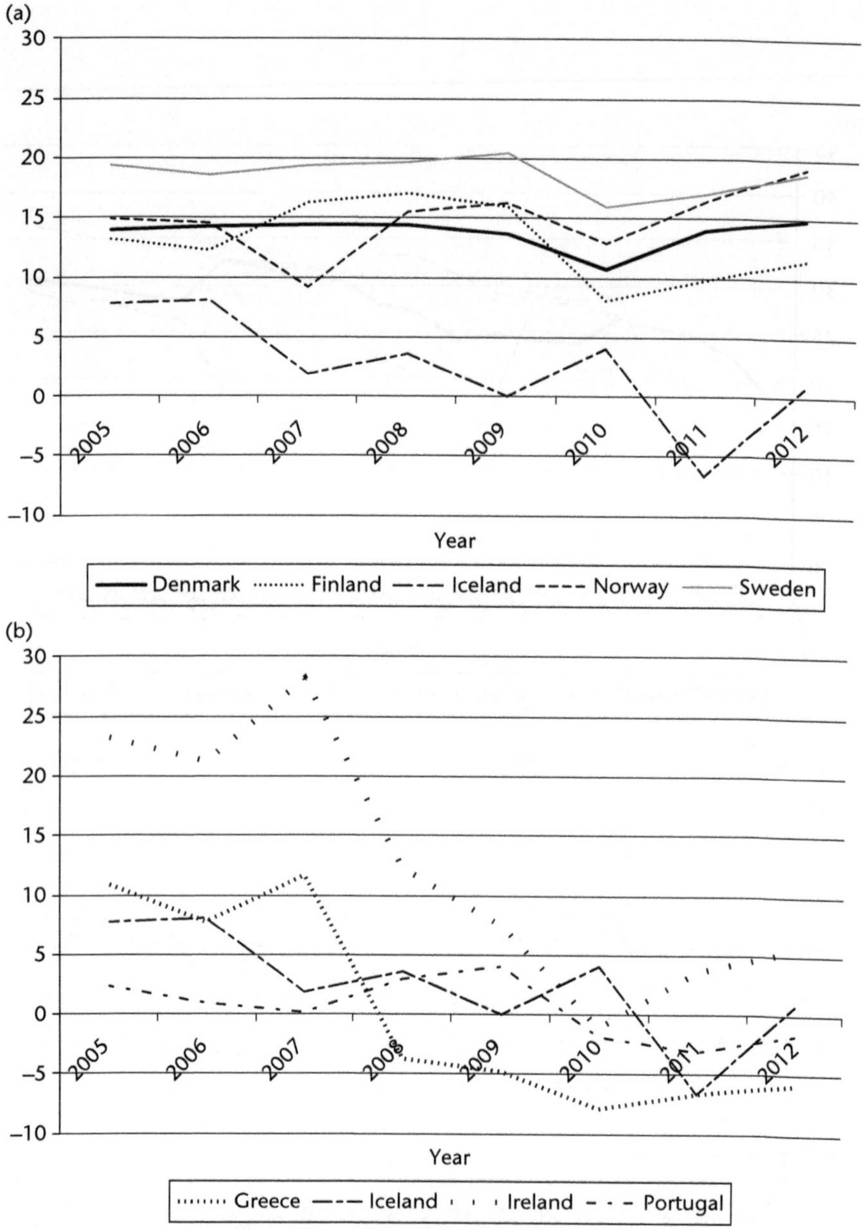

Figure 12.21. Adjusted net saving 2005–12 (% of GNI)

saving in Iceland with the rest of the Nordics (Figure 12.21).[27] Even during the boom before the crash of 2008, Iceland's adjusted net saving was far below that of all the countries under review except Greece and Portugal. Iceland's present predicament may not be just a consequence of the crash of 2008 and its aftermath, but also of neglectful policies with deep roots in a political culture that Parliament has unanimously resolved to do something about. It remains to be seen if the political class will keep its promise.

12.5 Miles to Go

How long will it take Iceland to regain economic and social parity with the rest of the Nordics? This is impossible to know. For one thing, no one knows how long the capital controls will remain in place—controls that were originally thought to be needed for two to three years but have become firmly entrenched as their abolition, especially if disorderly, would cause the króna to depreciate further, perhaps by 20% or 30% or more, something the government wants to avoid. Yet, the controls are incompatible with Iceland's membership in the European Economic Area except as a temporary emergency measure.

The government that took office in 2013 unilaterally withdrew from Iceland's accession negotiations with the EU in process since 2009. Further, no one knows if the political class will revert to its old habits now that the IMF has left the scene. The Central Bank repaid two-thirds of the IMF loan with borrowed money ahead of schedule, something that countries sometimes do to avoid unwelcome post-crisis attention from the Fund. The government promises significant household debt relief (on top of the write-downs already provided by the banks) without specifying clearly how this will be financed, ignoring the IMF's warnings that this may make inflation go up. Further, the regressive policy stance of the government—witnessed, for example, by its generosity to vessel owners who were, again in the face of IMF opposition, excused from paying higher fishing fees planned by the preceding government of 2009–13—may trigger compensating wage demands. The IMF (2013) warns in carefully coded language that 'legacy vulnerabilities are creating headwinds.' The Prime Minister refers to the IMF as a 'foreign acronym'.

27 Adjusted net saving aims to measure the real difference between production and consumption by adjusting net saving for changes in human capital (measured by spending on education and innovation) and depreciation or depletion of natural resources (e.g. through overfishing). See World Bank (2006).

Despite deleveraging through repayment, write-offs, and significant government help to distressed households, many households and firms remain in dire straits. For many wage earners the problem is that their indexed mortgages increased far more than their wages.[28] For many small and medium-sized firms the problem is that they are effectively bankrupt despite considerable debt restructuring.[29] For the government the problem is that allowing moderate inflation to deflate debts is a sensitive issue in a high-inflation country that introduced financial indexation some thirty years ago in reaction to the inequitable consequences of high inflation for borrowers and lenders. The government has not yet announced any plans for the future organization and ownership of banks in Iceland.

Clouds are gathering, yes, but amid this are rays of sunshine. With help from the IMF, Nordic governments, and Poland, Iceland avoided sovereign default after the crash and is growing again (recall Figure 12.1), but slowly, by about one percent per year or so per capita. The IMF (2013, Annex III) reckons that Iceland's foreign debt and public debt is on a sustainable path, even if 'risks remain elevated'. Many observers are encouraged by the Special Prosecutor's ability to let some of the culprits behind the crash face justice. Economics and law, efficiency and justice, must go hand in hand. Economic recovery is not enough. There is a need for accountability, responsibility, and transparency, and all three run like a red thread through the constitutional bill approved by the voters in 2012, only to be hijacked by a Parliament that openly flirts with, and even flaunts, the idea of contravening the popular will as expressed in the 2012 referendum as if no referendum had taken place (Gylfason, 2013a, 2013c).

Financial crises never destroy countries—firms, yes; people, sometimes; but not nations, for they always survive, even after they default on their debts, which Iceland did not. Financial wealth is such a small fraction of total national wealth that a financial crash, even the deepest plunge, rarely puts a big dent in national wealth because by far the most important part of a nation's total wealth is human resources and social capital. Financial wealth typically constitutes only about four to five percent of total national wealth (World Bank 2006). So, for a financial crash to do deep and lasting economic damage, it needs to destroy human capital or social capital by, for example, triggering a mass exodus of people or seriously undermining the country's institutions, including democracy.

[28] In 2012, about one in four Icelandic households had negative equity in their homes compared with roughly a half of Irish households.

[29] A little over a quarter of the 2,700 qualified SMEs accepted debt restructuring along the lines agreed by the government, financial institutions, and employers' associations.

The fear of mass migration has subsided. From 2009 to 2012, net emigration from Iceland amounted to less than three percent of the population compared with less than two percent in Ireland in 2008–12. 'Ireland does not exist in vain as long as she produces sons and daughters with sense enough to leave her', said George Bernard Shaw, the Irish playwright. That was then. For the most part, Iceland's social indicators were unaffected by the crisis. Suicides did not increase in number. Life expectancy shows no signs of going down, even if poverty has never been as visible as after the crash.

Both Iceland and Ireland have more than enough economic potential to be able to hold on to their human resources. A declaration of victory over the crash would be premature, however. O'Toole's (2009) description of Ireland as a First World country with a Third World political culture characterized by deep-seated cronyism and other forms of corruption also fits Iceland, even if details differ. For example, bank loans to building contractors played a larger role in Ireland than in Iceland. While in Ireland real estate prices rose by a factor of more than six from 1994 to 2006, or by over 16% per year on average, apparently a world record, in Iceland they rose by a factor of 2.5 from 2001 to 2008 or by 11% per year on average. Even so, the broad contours of the economic, political, and historical background are similar in both countries, including a legacy of foreign dominance that bred a lack of responsibility and accountability in the local elites that emerged in the twentieth century, a problem shared by many African countries and others, but not by Finland. Both Iceland and Ireland were bound to collapse regardless of the fate of Lehman Brothers (Gylfason, 2013b).

Another relevant comparison is that between Iceland and the Faroe Islands whose economic crash 1989–93 made GDP contract by a third, a unique event in Western Europe in peacetime that triggered the emigration of 15% of the population.[30] The root cause of both collapses was essentially the same, that is, a dire lack of checks and balances to protect the people against corruption in the form of cosy—some would say incestuous—relations among banks, business, and politics (Jónsson, 1994). In effect, both countries are client states, subordinate de facto to shifting states within the state—bank owners, boat owners, land owners, various interest organizations—with rampant rent capture, regulatory capture, media capture, academic capture,[31] and so on.

Remarkably, the Faroe Islands emerged from their deep plunge with an external debt to Denmark equivalent to 120% of GDP that they were able to repay with interest within six to eight years. The Faroe Islanders have

[30] A third of the emigrants returned within a few years, so net emigration amounted to 10% of the Faroese population, still a significant shock.

[31] For examples, see Ferguson (2012, Ch. 8).

taken significantly less financial support from Denmark after the crash than before. Apart from the net loss of ten percent of the population, the crisis in the Faroe Islands twenty years ago seems not to have seriously dented the country's social capital, with one qualification. The Parliament promised the people a constitution as well as a national referendum on that constitution, a fine bill prepared by a committee appointed by Parliament, but the referendum remains to be held. The politicians, including some of those who pushed the country off the cliff in 1989, have hijacked the constitutional bill, mainly, it seems, due to a provision guaranteeing nondiscriminatory natural resource management designed to honour the basic principle of human rights that the country's natural resources belong to the people (Wenar, 2008). Such a provision was deemed necessary to ensure equal access of all citizens to the nation's natural resources or to a fair share of the proceeds from the resources, as opposed to the selective allocation of valuable common-property fishing rights to a privileged few along Icelandic lines that were ruled unconstitutional by the Supreme Court of Iceland in 1998 as well as by the United Nations Committee on Human Rights in 2007 (Gylfason, 2012). The ongoing stalemate in the Faroe Islands between the rent seekers and the rest of the people remains unresolved.

In Iceland, after the crash of 2008, Parliament promised a new constitution and a national referendum on that constitution. A constitutional bill with a provision guaranteeing nondiscriminatory natural resource management was drafted and unanimously approved by a directly elected Constitutional Council.[32] The bill was subsequently accepted by two-thirds of the voters in a national referendum as was the provision stipulating 'one person, one vote'. Further, the nondiscriminatory natural resource management provision was approved by 83% of the voters. Even so, in a direct affront against democracy, Parliament hijacked the bill as if no referendum had taken place. It is one thing not to hold a promised referendum on a parliamentary bill as was done in the Faroe Islands. It is quite another to disrespect the overwhelming result of a constitutional referendum by putting democracy on ice as is now being attempted in Iceland by putting a new constitution already accepted by the voters into the hands of a parliamentary committee chaired by a sworn enemy of constitutional reform, as

[32] Three individuals with connections to the Independence Party filed technical complaints about the Constitutional Council election which led six Supreme Court justices to nullify the results of the election even if it was acknowledged that the alleged technical flaws could in no way have affected the results. Five of the six justices in question were Independence Party appointees. Parliament responded by appointing the elected representatives to the Council, including the author.

if no referendum had taken place (Gylfason, 2013c). Parliament is playing with fire. It risks the demotion of Iceland from the club of fully fledged democracies. A threat against democracy is a threat against social cohesion and peace and, by extension, against continued recovery and reform-based long-run growth. Rebuilding social capital is not easy if the preceding corrosion took the form of squandered trust. It is still too early to foretell the effects of Iceland's financial crash on its social capital.

References

Akerlof, George A. and Paul M. Romer (1993), 'Looting: The Economic Underworld of Bankruptcy for Profit', *Brookings Papers on Economic Activity*, Vol. 2, pp. 1–73.

Aliber, Robert Z. and Gylfi Zoega (eds) (2011), *Preludes to the Icelandic Financial Crisis*, New York: Palgrave Macmillan.

Benediktsdóttir, Sigríður, Jón Daníelsson, and Gylfi Zoega (2011), 'Lessons from a Collapse of a Financial System', *Economic Policy*, Vol. 26, No. 66, pp. 183–235, April.

Black, William K. (2005), *The Best Way to Rob a Bank Is to Own One: How Corporate Executives and Politicians Looted the S&L Industry*, Austin: University of Texas Press.

Blinder, Alan S. (2013), *After the Music Stopped: The Financial Crisis, the Response, and the Work Ahead*, New York: Penguin Press.

Ferguson, Charles H. (2012), *Predator Nation: Corporate Criminals, Political Corruption, and the Hijacking of America*, New York: Crown Business.

Finanssektorens Arbejdsgiverforening (2012), *Nordic Bank Statistics*, October.

Galbraith, John Kenneth (1988), *The Great Crash 1929*, Boston and New York: Houghton Mifflin Company.

Galbraith, James Kenneth (2012), *Inequality and Instability: A Study of the World Economy Just Before the Great Crisis*, Oxford and New York: Oxford University Press.

Gylfason, Thorvaldur (1995), *Síðustu forvöð (High Time)*, Reykjavík: Iceland University Press, Ch. 9. In Icelandic.

Gylfason, Thorvaldur (2008), 'When Iceland was Ghana', *VoxEU*, 28 January.

Gylfason, Thorvaldur (2009), 'Is Iceland too Small?' *VoxEU*, 19 August.

Gylfason, Thorvaldur (2010), 'Mel Brooks and the Bankers', *VoxEU*, 18 August.

Gylfason, Thorvaldur, Bengt Holmström, Sixten Korkman, Hans Tson Söderström, and Vesa Vihriala (2010), *Nordics in Global Crisis*, Taloustieto Oy: Research Institute of the Finnish Economy (ETLA).

Gylfason, Thorvaldur (2012), 'Constitutions: Financial Crisis Can Lead to Change', *Challenge*, September–October, pp. 106–22.

Gylfason, Thorvaldur (2013a), 'From Collapse to Constitution: The Case of Iceland', in Luigi Paganetto (ed.), *Public Debt, Global Governance and Economic Dynamism*, Milan: Springer Verlag, pp. 379–417.

Gylfason, Thorvaldur (2013b), 'A Tale of Two Debtors: Iceland, Ireland—and Their Banks', *Milken Institute Review*, April.

Gylfason, Thorvaldur (2013c), 'Democracy on Ice: A Post-mortem of the Icelandic Constitution', <http://www.opendemocracy.net>.

Honkapohja, Seppo (2009), 'The 1990s Financial Crises in Nordic Countries', Bank of Finland Research Discussion Papers No. 5.

International Monetary Fund (2013), 'Iceland Staff Report for the 2013 Article IV Consultation and Third Post-Program Monitoring Discussion', 16 July.

Jonung, Lars, Jaakko Kiander, and Pentti Vartia (2009), *The Great Financial Crisis in Finland and Sweden: The Nordic Experience of Financial Liberalization*, Cheltenham, Glos, and Northampton, Mass.: Edward Elgar.

Jónsson, Edvarð T. (1994), *Hlutskipti Færeyja* (The Fate of the Faroe Islands), Reykjavík: Mál og menning. In Icelandic.

Laeven, Luc and Fabián Valencia (2012), 'Systemic Banking Crises Data Base: An Update', IMF Working Paper WP/12/163.

Matthíasson, Thórólfur (2008), 'Spinning out of control, Iceland in crisis', *Nordic Journal of Political Economy*, Vol. 34, Article 3, pp. 1–19.

National Audit Office (2013), *Einkavæðing helstu ríkisfyrirtækja Árin 1998–2003* (Privatization of Main State Enterprises 1998–2003), December. In Icelandic.

Níelsson, Ulf and Bjarni K. Torfason (2012), 'Iceland's Economic Eruption and Meltdown', *Scandinavian Economic History Review*, Vol. 60, No. 1, pp. 3–30.

O'Toole, Fintan (2009), *Ship of Fools: How Stupidity and Corruption Killed the Celtic Tiger*, London: Faber and Faber Ltd.

Ólafsson, Stefán and Arnaldur Sölvi Kristjánsson (2013), 'Inequality in Boom and Bust: A Tale from Iceland's Bubble Economy', in Janet Gomick and Markus Jäntti (eds), *Income Inequality: Economic Disparities and the Middle Class in Affluent Countries*, Palo Alto: Stanford University Press, pp. 416–38.

Paldam, Martin (2000), 'Social Capital: One or Many? Definition and Measurement', *Journal of Economic Surveys*, Vol. 14, No. 5, December, pp. 629–53.

Polishchuk, Leonid and Timur Natkhov (2012), 'Institutions and the Allocation of Talent', Higher School of Economics Research Paper No. WP BRP 15/EC/2012.

Special Investigation Commission (2010), 'Report of the Special Investigation Commission (SIC)', report delivered to Parliament, 12 April.

Stiglitz, Joseph E. (2010), *Freefall: America, Free Markets, and the Sinking of the World Economy*, New York: W.W. Norton.

Wade, Robert H. (2009), 'Iceland as Icarus', *Challenge*, Vol. 52, No. 3, May–June, pp. 5–33.

Wade, Robert H. and Silla Sigurgeirsdóttir (2012), 'Iceland's Rise, Fall, Stabilisation and Beyond', *Cambridge Journal of Economics*, Vol. 36, No. 1, pp. 127–44.

Wenar, Leif (2008), 'Property Rights and the Resource Curse', *Philosophy and Public Affairs*, Vol. 36, No. 1, Winter, 1–32.

World Bank (2006), *Where Is the Wealth of Nations? Measuring Capital for the 21st Century*, Washington, DC.

Comments on 'Iceland: How Could This Happen?' by Thorvaldur Gylfason

Søren Bo Nielsen

Thorvaldur Gylfason has given us a very interesting overview of Iceland's road to the crash in 2008 and the factors precipitating the collapse in the first place. Adopting a comprehensive and not merely economic perspective, he gives us a thorough understanding of conditions for economic and financial policy in Iceland.

Gylfason goes through recent economic development in Iceland, the activities of its banks, and elements of its economic structure. He portrays an economy seemingly slowing down and troubled by an inflation problem before the crash. Further, this economy is ill-prepared for the future on account of the composition of foreign trade, and because it lags behind in build-up of real, human, and social capital. A combination of a questionable privatization process, incompetence and neglect on the part of the financial supervisory authority, and criminal behaviour of key players apparently caused the Icelandic banks to sink fast and deep. The bill, of course, had to be paid by the Icelandic society at large, resulting in many households still being technically insolvent and many firms effectively bankrupt. Gylfason claims that the crash and Iceland's less than stellar performance may have a common origin in Iceland's political culture, and the detailed evidence in the chapter convinces the reader.

The North Atlantic societies—Iceland, the Faroe Islands, and Greenland—are fascinating from an economic as well as a broader viewpoint. They are characterized by a rough, often hostile, nature and geographic isolation, not obviously conducive to economic affluence. Further, they feature relatively simple and relatively complex economies simultaneously. Simple, since they contain smaller populations and fewer sectors, so are easier to survey than, for instance, the continental Nordic countries ('Nordics' in Gylfason's terminology). But they are also more complex. The role of the public sector is more difficult to determine, as a number of markets likely would not function properly when left entirely to private firms; hence, the public sector has taken over. Moreover, small societies are bound to have greater problems with non-arm's-length relations; the distance between legislators and those affected by laws and regulations is simply shorter than in bigger societies. The political systems of all three societies are quite unstable, with large swings in voters' backing of parties and individual politicians.[1] And last, but certainly not least, the difficult management of renewable or exhaustible natural resources, and thus national wealth, features more prominently than in, say, the typical continental European country.

The Faroe Islands, for decades a self-governing part of the Danish Kingdom, remains heavily reliant on fishery and fish exports, and the associated management of species stocks has proved a great challenge over the years. The Faroes suffered a severe banking crisis in the late 1980s and early 1990s; as Gylfason notes, that banking crisis shared many features with the subsequent Icelandic crash. Interestingly, the financial crisis from 2008 onwards saw the loss of the second-largest bank in the Faroe Islands, Eik Banki, to the Danish banking regulator in October 2010.

Greenland now has self-rule—although this has only been the case since 2009—implying that most political decisions of importance to Greenland are now decided in Nuuk. But economic policy, save monetary and exchange rate policy which is determined in Copenhagen, has for decades been the responsibility of Greenland. Greenland has huge structural economic problems on many fronts, but people hope that an upcoming mining adventure will ease the adjustment to a difficult future (iron and rare earth element mines are due to open in some four years, if everything goes according to plan).

Iceland has had a remarkable development through the twentieth century. It is no longer as dependent on fishery and exports of fish products as are Greenland and the Faroe Islands. Aluminum and a select group of other products now constitute a sizeable fraction of exports. It exploits hydro power and hot springs, and tourism is important. The population is far better educated than that of Greenland (but not that of the Faroe Islands). Having earlier been admired for its rapid economic growth, the extensive collapse of Iceland's economy in 2008–9 came as a surprise to most observers. Another surprise, however, lies in the country's ability to somehow get back on track—although there are still considerable structural economic problems that need to be dealt with.

[1] Curiously, it is often seen that politicians who have previously fallen out of favour succeed in making a return to political power. Further, the partner of the head of government in Greenland was in December 2013 appointed special adviser to the minister of fishery there, triggering accusations of nepotism.

Gylfason provides us with a range of figures to explain the Icelandic crash and the demise of the largest banks. These figures, seen relative to Iceland's population, are truly dizzying. The costs of the crisis to Icelandic society at large can be measured in different ways, but they will always be far larger in per capita terms than similar measures for the rest of the Nordics. While Denmark has seen a series of court cases against key players in the financial and real estate sectors, the relative number of these, and relative amounts of money involved, are dwarfed by those for Iceland.

As Gylfason stresses, there are still many elements of economic policy in Iceland that need fixing. The process of restructuring of the banking sector must move forward, inflation needs to be controlled, and liberalization of capital accounts should take place, when circumstances permit. To this it is tempting to add the preparation of a model framework which will allow conducting quantitative analysis of long-term sustainability of public finances in Iceland.

The IMF has recently noted some slippage in fiscal policy in Iceland and urges reliance on more durable sources of fiscal consolidation over the medium term. Checking the sustainability of fiscal policy over the longer term has proved helpful elsewhere, and Iceland should similarly be able to benefit from examining public finance sustainability. Such investigations seem to discipline short-term fiscal policy, motivate needed economic reforms, and promote intergenerational balance in society. As an example, sustainability indicators for fiscal policy have been worked out in Denmark for more than a decade, and while fiscal policy for some years looked to be on an unsustainable path, a series of recent economic reforms implies that this is no longer the case, judging from the latest computations of the indicator.

Since 2010, an indicator for fiscal policy sustainability has also been computed by Greenland's Economic Council. While the public budget there currently is close to balance, over the next couple of decades projected public expenditures (at current standards) are bound to rise markedly without projected public income following suit. The main culprit here is the ageing of the Greenlandic population and the associated additional outlays to pensions, health, and care for the elderly, although the near-freezing of the massive block grant from Denmark to Greenland also plays a role. Two consequences follow: First, there is a considerable need for tightening fiscal policy and carrying out structural reforms. Second, there are severe limits as to the role which the public sector can take on in the planned future exploitation of Greenland's non-renewable resources.[2]

[2] See my article 'Exploitation of Natural Resources and the Public Sector in Greenland', working paper, Department of Economics, CBS, November 2013.

The computation of a fiscal sustainability indicator has helped shape discussions over fiscal policy in both Denmark and Greenland in healthy ways, and a similar gain would be harvested in Iceland. However, the combination of sustainability analysis, improved banking regulation, and liberalization of financial flows can only go so far. Repairs to the problems related to the workings of democracy and morale in Iceland are also required. An economist outsider is likely to come up short when deliberating how to overcome these problems.

13

Challenges to the Nordic Model

The Case of Finland

Seppo Honkapohja

13.1 Introduction

Finland is currently the only euro area country with a stable outlook and an AAA sovereign credit rating and from all major rating agencies.[1] Finland is known as a country with strong growth, strong competitiveness, strong fiscal balance, and strong banks. A common perception—until recently, at least—has been that the Finnish economy is a success story, though exports are currently suffering from the global financial crisis.

Among Finns, the humble attitudes following the deep depression of the early 1990s have long ago given way to a feeling that we are good in almost everything and that we can even teach others how to do things—even how to run an economy.

Is there a solid basis for such perceptions and attitudes? Perhaps you can already guess that the answer is negative. Unfortunately, in some important respects, the Finnish economy is not doing well. Developments during the past five years have revealed vulnerabilities in the economy.

Since the autumn of 2008, Finnish growth performance has been disappointing—weaker than the euro-area average. Finnish GDP is now 5% smaller than it was in mid 2008. Figure 13.1 shows the development of the level of GDP since 2007 for Finland, the average of other AAA euro

[1] Keynote dinner speech in the conference 'Reform Capacity and Macroeconomic Performance in the Nordic Countries', Copenhagen September, 2013. I am grateful for Dr Lauri Kajanoja for assistance and comments. Any views expressed are my own and do not necessarily represent those of the Bank of Finland.

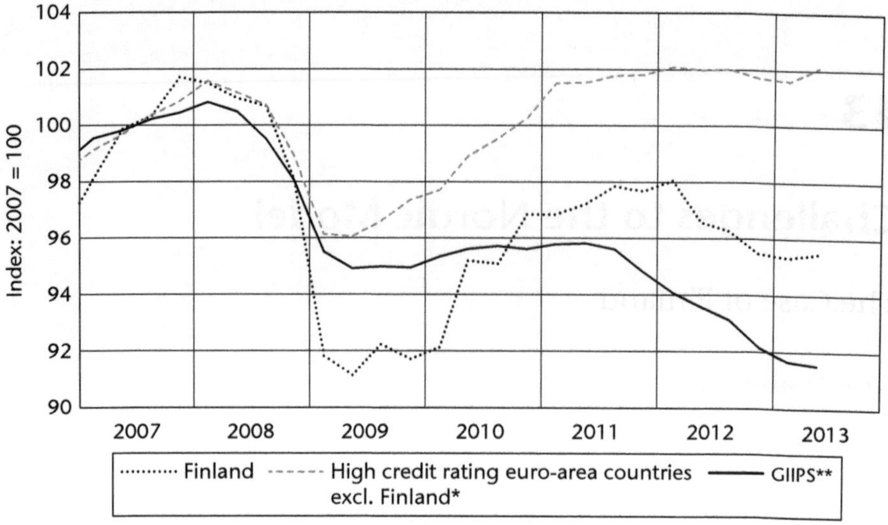

Figure 13.1. GDP

*Germany, France, Netherlands, Belgium, and Austria.

**Greece, Italy, Ireland, Portugal, and Spain.

Sources: Eurostat and Bank of Finland calculations.

countries, and the crisis countries. Developments in exports have been particularly poor, as exports are currently about 1/5 smaller than before the financial crisis.

The well-being of many Finns has, however, not been badly hurt by these developments. Unemployment has remained relatively low, and household real incomes have mostly been on an upward trend. Recently the future has become much more uncertain. There are big problems that need to be solved, and difficult political decisions that need to be made.

13.2 Current Difficulties

The economy is facing new challenges: exports have remained weak, and the current account has turned negative. Figure 13.2 shows the cumulative change in the world trade shares for EU countries in the period 2007–11. After 2007 the decline in exports has been the deepest among all euro area countries. In addition, there is one challenge which has not come as a surprise: the demographic change.

Three main reasons for the new challenges are (1) weakness in the international economy, (2) problems of electronics and paper industries, and (3) losses in cost competitiveness.

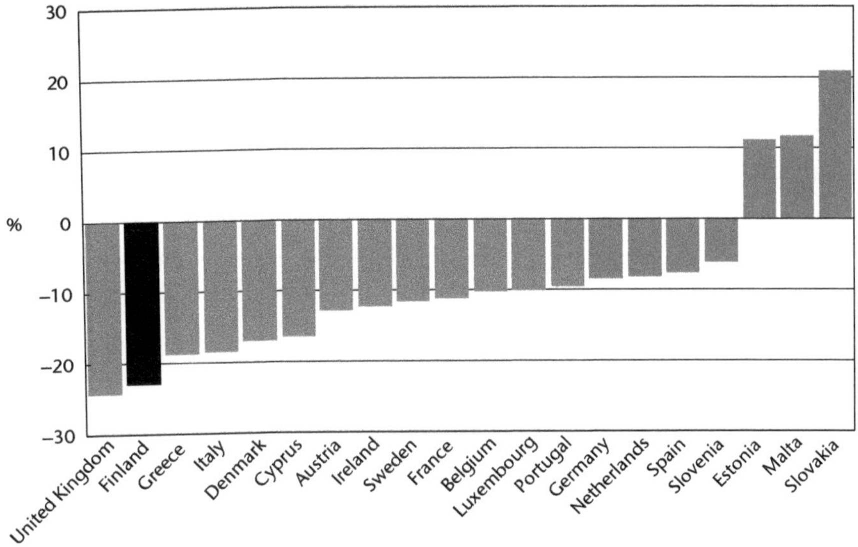

Figure 13.2. Share of world exports, cumulative change 2007–11
Source: Eurostat.

Weakness in the international economy has hurt Finnish exports, which are dominated by various investments goods. Investments have remained weak in developed economies for the past five years.

The problems in the electronics industry have been related to one large company, Nokia, which lost its technological advantage in mobile phones. The paper industry, in turn, suffers from the longer-term decline in demand for printing paper in Europe. Another major factor behind the decline in exports is the weakening of cost competitiveness. Wages and unit labour costs have increased by about 10% since 1999 compared to the average of all trading partners and compared to euro area. Figure 13.3 shows the development of unit labour costs for Finland, Sweden, Germany, and the euro area in the period 1999–2013.

How did cost competitiveness end up weakening so much? One part is misjudgement and bad luck regarding timing. Just before the global financial crises escalated, a round of union-level wage agreements took place. Amid rapid growth and with seemingly benign outlook, generous wage increases were agreed upon, and the contracts mostly extended for about two years. Then the financial crisis struck, leading to slowdown in wages in many countries while Finnish wages diverged.

Why was no correction made after the contracts had expired? The reason probably has a lot to do with the relatively muted increase in unemployment in Finland. Employment has been supported by growth in domestic demand,

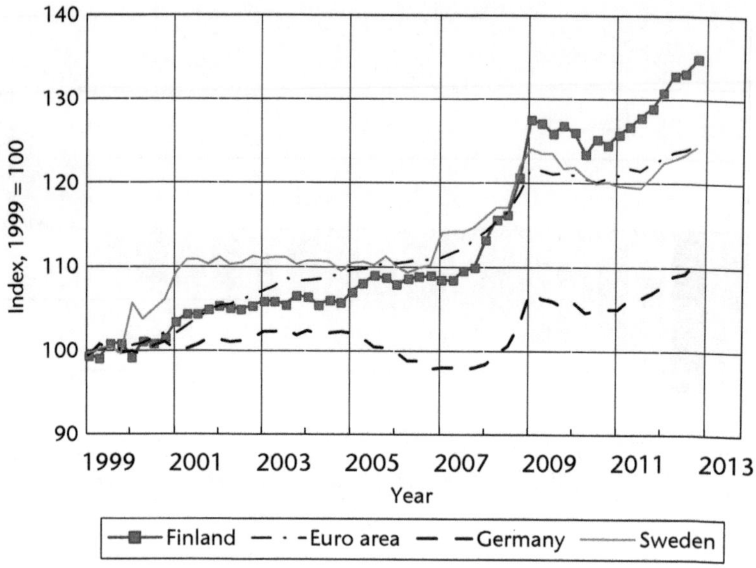

Figure 13.3. Unit labour costs, total economy

Note: Sweden in national currency.

Sources: Eurostat and OECD.

especially household consumption. Domestic demand has also been supported by loose fiscal policies and low ECB interest rates. The low interest rates were transmitted to loan costs of the public by the strong and stable banking system and the system of variable rate in most loans.

The growth in domestic demand in recent years has been financed to an increasing extent by debt, as households and the public sector have run financial deficits. This has been possible due to the strengths of the economy. Household and public-sector indebtedness remained relatively low in Finland in the years before the global financial crisis. However, the recent increases in debt are gradually adding to the vulnerabilities in the economy.

13.3 Competitiveness Issues

How much has Finnish cost competitiveness weakened? I already mentioned the increases in wages and unit labour costs for the whole economy. Developments in the open sector of the economy are obviously very significant, as manufactured goods account for much of foreign trade. Hence its cost competitiveness is important for the whole economy. Manufacturing unit labour costs in Finland are currently at about the same level as in 1999. However, manufacturing ULCs provide far too rosy a picture of cost competitiveness for Finnish manufacturing.

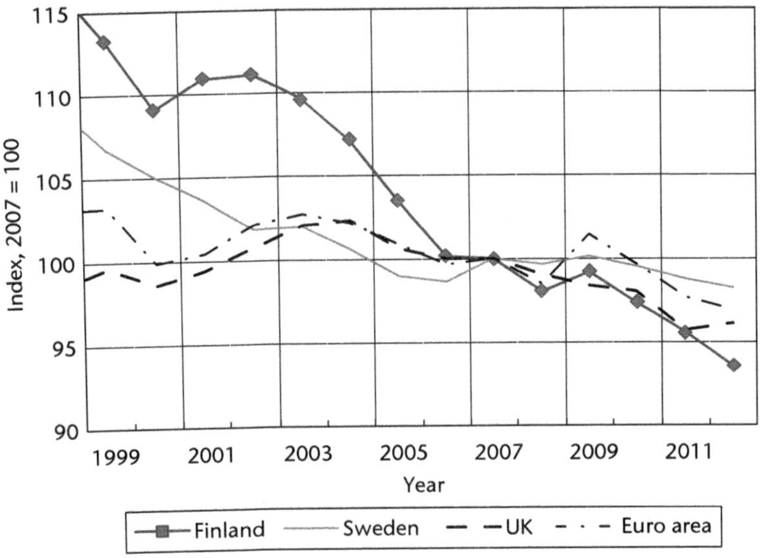

Figure 13.4. Terms of trade
Sources: Eurostat and European Commission (National Accounts).

This misperception arises because of price developments. The price component of value added has declined considerably in Finnish manufacturing since 1999. As prices have fallen, the value of production has increased a lot less than its volume. Figure 13.4 shows the development of the terms of trade for Finland, Sweden, the UK, and the euro area since 1999.The growth in labour productivity has not been accompanied by a corresponding increase in the ability of firms to pay higher wages.

The main reason for the exceptionally weak price developments is the large share that both paper and electronics industries have had in Finnish manufacturing. Price developments have been exceptional in these two industries. Decline in paper demand, together with overcapacity, has depressed paper prices. Prices in electronics, in turn, have declined due to the rapid technological advances leading to better and better products. As prices are measured in quality-adjusted terms, measured prices are declining, which means that measured production volumes increase significantly when compared to current-price production in electronics.

13.4 Asymmetric Shocks and Wage Divergence

The possibility of adverse developments like the current problems was foreseen in the Finnish discussion about the pros and cons of membership in a monetary union. For example, the Report of the Expert group commissioned by the Finnish Prime Minister in 1997[2] raised concerns about the risk of asymmetric negative shocks and about the risk of domestic wage developments diverging from those of other EMU countries.

Evidently, the two risks have been realized. The decline of Finland's electronics and paper industries is an example of a negative asymmetric shock. Wage developments since 2008 are a clear case of wage divergence between Finland and other EMU countries. To mitigate the impacts of these problems, the Finnish economy must try to create new areas of strength in industrial and service activities. Simultaneously there must be corrections to the wage divergences. The latter is not going to be easy for a monetary union country.

13.5 Public Finance Concerns

Even though the state of Finnish public finances is better than in many other European countries, there has been a clear deterioration. General government deficit has increased considerably. The debt level looks likely to exceed the 60% level soon, perhaps next year, unless new consolidation measures are imposed. Figure 13.5 shows the development of public deficits and debt for Finland and the euro area since 1999.

As the problems in the economy can be seen as being largely structural by nature and not only cyclical, the government deficit cannot be expected to be corrected by a recovery in the international economy.

At the same time, the effect of population ageing on the economy has begun to show. The size of the working-age population has started to diminish. Finnish public finances have a long-term sustainability gap of around 5 to 6%, by most estimates.

The Finnish economy is expected to suffer more from the effects of ageing than most other European countries. Old-age dependency ratio will be very high by 2030. This is because of the specific features of the intense post-war baby boom.

13.6 What Economic Policies are Needed in Finland?

One element should be low nominal wage growth in order to improve cost competitiveness. As wages have increased significantly compared to trading partners, they should increase less in the coming years. Wage increases in the

[2] *Finland and the EMU*, Publication 1997/26 of the Prime Minister's Office.

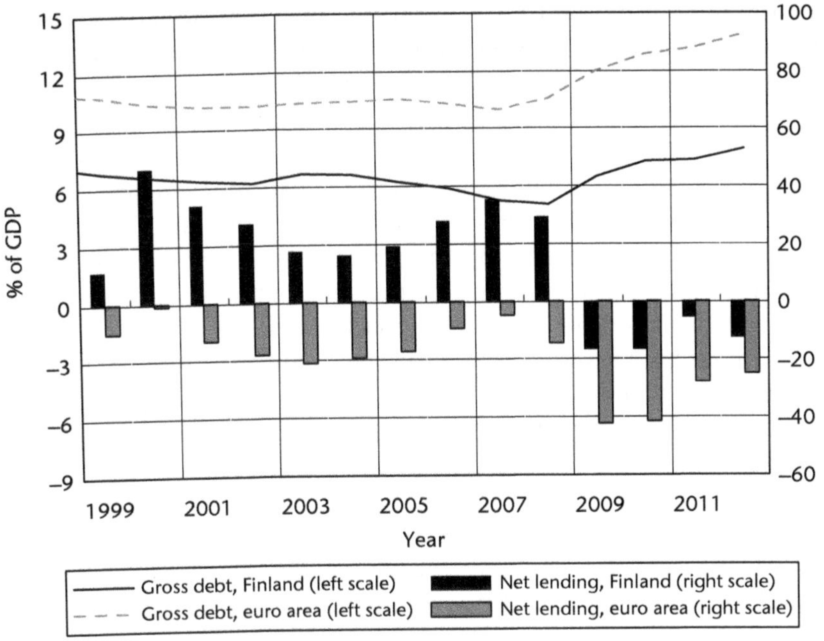

Figure 13.5. General government deficit and debt, Finland and euro area
Source: European Commission.

whole economy should be set according to the state of the economy's open sector.

The social partners recently signed a centralized wage agreement with relatively low wage increases.[3] Provided that the individual unions and employer organizations accept the centralized agreement, wage settlements are likely to lead to some improvement in Finnish cost competitiveness during the next two years.

Given that the problems of the Finnish economy are to a large extent structural by nature, structural reforms are needed in addition to improvements in cost competitiveness. The economy needs to make reforms to correct the structural problems.

It is important to emphasize that the economy has major strengths—education, infrastructure, effective government, reliable judicial system, etc. These must be preserved so that there is a solid basis for finding new areas of economic activity. However, one must not forget that structural reforms are needed; these reforms should lead to permanent increases in production potential.

[3] Pact for Employment and Growth. Agreement 30 August, 2013, <http://www.ek.fi/ek/en/pact_for_employment_and_growth_3082013-11222>.

Perhaps the most important area of reform concerns the labour supply. Working careers need to start earlier and end later. As the population ages, improving the production and productivity of publicly funded health and care services is a vital area for reform.

Let me mention a few other areas of reform. Competition could be increased in services and construction, with changes in regulations being one part of the possible reforms. Supply of housing and especially of land for housing development could be supported by the government policies. This would increase economic welfare by lowering the pace of growth in house prices and rents and facilitate efficiency of the labour market in bigger cities.

The government has recently laid out its programme for structural reforms with the purpose of improving the long-term sustainability of public finances.[4] The programme contains wide-ranging measures, and the goal of the government plans is ambitious. The purpose is to eliminate completely the fiscal sustainability gap.

At present the detailed contents of this government programme still remain mostly to be decided. However, the government plans to act relatively quickly and I certainly hope that the government will be able to agree on the important details of its programme. Success would be a very important step forward in solving the current problems of the Finnish economy.

13.7 Final Remarks

Rating agencies seem to have strong confidence in the Finnish political system's ability to make difficult decisions. At this point in time, such ability is badly needed. The difficult decisions can still be made with no external pressure. It is important to make the decisions early enough so that Finland can avoid the situation where market pressures force the government to make the decisions.

The coming months will be a major test for the reform capacity of the Finnish political system. Finland will thus be a case study for the subject matter of this conference. Progress in reforms is needed in order for the Finnish economy to be a success story again. What is certain is that things will change: the Finnish economy will not go back to what it was five years ago.

[4] Structural policy programme, adopted by the government 29 August 2018, <http://www.valtioneuvosto.fi/ajankohtaista/tiedotteet/tiedote/fi.jsp?oid=393064>.

Index

Index